Johann Strauss
The End of an Era

Johann Strauss. Lithograph by Kriehuber, 1848.

JOHANN STRAUSS

The End of an Era

Egon Gartenberg

A DA CAPO PAPERBACK

Library of Congress Cataloging in Publication Data

Gartenberg, Egon.
  Johann Strauss: the end of an era.

  (A Da Capo paperback)
  Reprint of the ed. published by Pennsylvania State
University Press, University Park.
  1. Strauss, Johann, 1825-1899. 2. Composers — Austria
— Biography.
[ML410.G91G3 1979]   785.4′1′0924 [B]   78-20841
ISBN 0-306-80098-5

ISBN 0-306-80098-5

First Paperback Edition 1979

This Da Capo Press paperback edition of *Johann Strauss:
The End of an Era* is an unabridged republication of the
first edition published by The Pennsylvania State University
Press in 1974. It is reprinted by arrangement with the
original publisher.

Published by Da Capo Press, Inc.
A Subsidiary of Plenum Publishing Corporation
227 West 17th Street, New York, N.Y. 10011

To Belle

who, patiently and passionately,
shares
my hopes and dreams
defeats and despairs
triumphs and elations.

Hast du vom Kahlenberg das Land dir rings besehn
*So wirst du, was ich schrieb und was ich bin, verstehn.**

Grillparzer

*If from the Kahlenberg your view has ringed the land
  Then what I wrote and what I am, you'll understand.

Contents

Preface

"Nero fiddled as Rome burned." Although musically inaccurate (Nero supposedly played the harp on that occasion), this statement concerning a tragically significant moment in history has a sequel in the recent past. Johann Strauss fiddled as the Habsburg empire sank into a quagmire, mostly of its own making. This study, originally intended as an expanded Strauss biography, expanded further with the vaster aspects and reviews of the times which formed Strauss and which, in turn, succumbed to his lure and influence.

Ironically and significantly, the legacy of the Habsburgs documented itself in the most felicitous as well as disastrous ways. Power initially amassed through shrewd diplomacy and intermarriage later dissipated in questionable political entanglements and ruinous wars. But the innate idealistic and artistic spirit of the Habsburgs gave its image to the city of Vienna. Thus it is that Habsburg spirit which, over a span of centuries, molded, encouraged, and mirrored the artistic, musical, philosophical, and even medical rise of the city, which continued unslackened at a time of political and diplomatic decline and demise.

That particular breed—the Viennese—is the product of a spirit and of a melting pot of basic German broth into which the spices of Italy in the south, of the Magyars in the east, and of the Slavs in the north were stirred. The result of the slow infusion of such diverse elements enabled Vienna to absorb and sublimate all of them in its own leisurely gait which is truly (and indescribably) Viennese.

The waltz is a natural outgrowth of such sublimation. The development of the heavy-footed alpine *Ländler* and the rapidly jumping *Langhaus* into the graceful rotation of the waltz was a century-long process which reached its culmination in the symphonic waltzes of Johann Strauss Son. However, the waltz form did not halt there nor did its proliferation. To Schubert it had remained a pleasant dance diversion, although his inspired waltz creations were more appropriate to the concert hall than the dance floor. Hummel accomplished that transformation just as Weber before him had raised the waltz into the rarified sphere of the symphonic poem. To Chopin it was a gossamer piano arabesque, to Tschaikovsky a terpsichorean spectacle, to Brahms a love song to the city, to Ravel the dance of a doomed era.

It was Strauss, more than Schubert, Mozart, Haydn, Beethoven, Brahms, Mahler, or Schoenberg, who made Vienna and the waltz household words throughout the world. On the dark side of the ledger, Strauss's music, the very spirit of his art, its joyous naivete, gave his time a false face, a mask of lighthearted well-being that was not consonant with the times. He carried the banner of dancing joy into hostile Hungary and Italy, thus soothing their Habsburg hostility, established rare Austrian victories on German soil, and brought "Viennese Joy" to the capital of Russia and the shores of the United States. Thus like honied syrup over spoiled sweets his waltzes and operettas glossed over repression and persecution, hunger, inefficiency, martial and diplomatic defeats, and political ineptness.

As the world's greatest composers assembled in three successive waves in Vienna, which inspired them in its artistic climate; as architecture, the arts, and the sciences reached their respective apexes and world renown, the Habsburgs and their empire, in inverse ratio, declined, diminished, deceased. This interrelationship is significant for it documents the persistent presence of the finest expressions of the Habsburg spirit, even in decline. Oblivious of the downward path, Strauss spread his glorious music like a mantle of gold, prompting historians to aver that Emperor Franz Joseph ceased to reign with the death of Johann Strauss although the monarch outlived the musician by seventeen years.

Donald James, in his review of my book *Vienna—Its Musical Heritage*, phrases the sense of the times and the music succinctly: "In the musical history of Vienna (and Austria) the Strausses are all-important to the pervading atmosphere of the nineteenth century." Thus the Straussian presence and contribution is significant far beyond its lilting melodious aspects, because Vienna, Austria, and Habsburg dined and danced, dallied and died to the beguiling strains of the waltz, oblivious of the fact that an era was drawing to a close.

E. G.

Acknowledgments

The author's thanks go to the following individuals and institutions for their generous assistance and cooperation.

Dr. Hilde Hellmann, Vienna, for historical and musicological material on the background and musical influence of the Habsburgs during the reigns of emperors Josef II, Franz II, and Franz Joseph.

Professor Rudolf Klein, musicologist of the *Gesellschaft für Musik* in Vienna, for material concerning Johann Strauss and the continuity of the late romantic idea in musical Austria.

Professor Rudolf Jettel, the Austrian State Academy of Music and the Vienna Philharmonic Orchestra, for background material on the Strauss family and Viennese folk song.

Professor Harry Zohn, department of Germanic languages at Brandeis University, for advice on Austrian literature and historic continuity, and for putting at my disposal rare material concerning literary Vienna of the nineteenth and twentieth centuries, as well as for a critical reading of the manuscript.

Dr. Günther Brosche, of the Music Collection of the Austrian National Library in Vienna, and Dr. Rosa Maria Steinbauer, for respective bibliographic research in Austrian musicology and history.

Dr. Beatrix Kempf, Ober-Redaktionsrat of the Austrian Chancellery, for political, diplomatic, and military background material concerning the Habsburg empire of the nineteenth and twentieth centuries.

Dr. Robert Kittler, Picture Archives and Portrait Gallery of the Austrian National Library in Vienna, for assistance in establishing pictorial continuity.

Mr. Karl Wackerlig, Secretary of the pictorial division of the *Bundespressedienst* of the Austrian Chancellory, for portraits of Austria's composers, musicians, poets, actors, statesmen, and artists.

Miss Elizabeth Thomas, librarian of The Pennsylvania State University, Mont Alto Commonwealth Campus, and her staff, for bibliographic research and the obtaining of rare and out-of-print material on the Austrian empire and the Strauss era.

Vorspiel

The Overture (Vorspiel) ought to apprise the spectators of the nature of the action that is to be represented and to form, so to speak, its argument.

Gluck

1725

Giocoso

Despite the early morning hour the Vienna inn *Zum Guten Hirten* (The Good Shepherd), near the Danube's edge, was wide awake with light, smoke, and noise which overflowed into the night and along the beaten earth path leading to the rickety landing. A boat coming down the Danube from upstate, from Linz, was expected; as a matter of fact its lights could already be seen in the distance through the river haze.

Its arrival an hour later was greeted with raucous laughter, coarse jokes and full beakers by the guests at the Shepherd and by the handlers waiting to unload the cargo. The first to get off the boat were not the captain, the crew, or an occasional passenger, but the eagerly awaited Linzer Fiddlers. The musicians, usually two violins, a guitar, and a bass, were known, awaited, and feted up and down the length of the Danube because, in the tradition of the medieval minstrels, they brought music and news from others parts of the realm.

That morning turned out to be something special; the musicians had brought with them a new melody, a rollicking dance, the *Langhaus*. When they led into it, those who had started to join them with their usual drunken crowing fell silent. As the four-man band walked across the gently swaying planks from the boat and up the path to the inn, the men began to sway with the music. This was something new, a melody easy to dance to, to sing to, to listen to. When the musicians had finished, a shout of gladness went up into the smoky night air and the players were plied with drinks by all present.

1775

Gracioso

Schönbrunn, the vast pleasure palace of the Habsburgs on the outskirts of Vienna, had fallen silent except for one wing from whose windows the flickering of many candles in crystal chandeliers threw bright patches onto the courtyard below. With the light traveled the graceful sounds of a minuet as the empress and her entourage, in wigs and satin raiments, went through the graceful dance steps, bowing and scraping in prescribed figures, with fingers barely touching.

Vorspiel

Suddenly the empress bade the musicians to halt the polite fiddling; the bowing and turning stopped. The sound heard next, upon a wave of her hand, took the court's breath away. Never had a folk dance entered the palace's hallowed halls. All had of course heard of that delightful, turning dance, the *Ländler*, many had even danced it in secret, but now the court's official approval pleasantly immobilized them in momentary disbelief. The next moment saw the younger set among Austria's nobility curve encircling arms around their partners' slender waists, and seconds later the Austrian court was wending its way in graceful circles over the mirror-polished floor of Schönbrunn, betraying secreted prior knowledge of the dance's pleasures.

The sound flooded into the night, into the vast gardens, up to the pleasure pavilion, the Gloriette, along the seemingly endless tall walls of artistically cut yew into whose dark recesses white marble figures had been set in exquisite contrast and artistry. As the white stone *amorettoes* silently played their stone flutes and harps, young people, ambling arm in arm along the paths of white crushed stone, stopped to listen. The young women lifted their faces under huge flat Florentine hats to lovers' kisses; their feet in dainty, silkband-tied shoes tapped gaily to the new rhythm from the palace. Their young companions in silk stockings and buckled shoes, tail coats of all hues, brocaded vests, flowing ties or *jabots*, tightened their holds on their partners' waists and repaid in like currency. As the intoxicating melody wafted through the dark gardens, gentle laughter, ardent whispers and avowals of love seemed gayer, and the white marble *amorettoes* in their dark niches seemed to weave and play in more animated silent rhythm.

1825

Con Brio

The ballroom of the *Sperl* was so long that one end was barely visible from the other despite the flickering of innumerable candles on walls and chandeliers. In the center of one long wall, on a platform five feet above the dance floor, an orchestra of eighteen musicians enthusiastically bowed, blew, and perspired profusely despite (or because of) the foaming glasses of beer always within reach. Their leader, a slender, blond young man encased in a tightly fitting waistcoat over white vest, high collar held by a huge black bow, either played his fiddle or conducted with the bow. The dancers looked up, nodded, smiled—"Pepi" Lanner sure knows how to play a waltz.

Beneath Lanner and his ensemble, in the flickering semidarkness innumerable couples either spun from one end of the hall to the other or gently turned, as the rhythm of the dance might command. Some of the girls wore basket hats secured by enormous satin bows; others, shedding their hats to better enjoy the nearness of their partners, exhibited artful structures of coiffure complete with bouncing ringlets. Soldiers, dandies, out for an evening of revelry, elegant in tight trousers, well-fitted vests, tailcoats, and stovepipe hats, tripped gaily; elderly burghers perspired profusely, their plump protuberances barely held in check by overly stylish vests with straining buttons. Their companions ranged from lightfooted creatures young enough to be their daughters to lusty matrons in corseted, barely adequate bodices. They all looked up to their partners with cheeks colored by strenuous pleasure.

All of them were bound up in the joy of Lanner's dances, which had long since lost early ease and comfortable speed to a more lusty expression of the people. Oblivious to the problems of their times, they immersed themselves in the most joyous of pursuits—dancing.

1850

Delirioso

Vienna, the capital of the empire, now a city of 400,000 souls, at heart had remained a provincial city. True, the nobles of the realm—of Hungary, Bohemia, Croatia, Galicia—had established their winter residences in Vienna, and their colorful uniforms, carriages, and servants enlivened the capital. But the feeling of splendor, of living in a world capital, was absent. The spirit of empire and of an imperial capital's central focus was to be absent for another quarter century.

This did not keep Vienna from indulging in musical and entertaining opulence perhaps unmatched since Roman times. Appreciation for its musical giants and their often probing music varied, of course. The musical philosophy of Beethoven was overshadowed by the sensuous and lighthearted flow of Italian melody from the pens of Bellini and Donizetti, and when Rossini arrived in Vienna with an Italian troupe handpicked by him to present his operas, the city developed "Rossini fever." Because of its wide-ranging, voracious appetite, Vienna became "the arbiter in matters operatic although most listeners did not sense it despite the flaming enthusiasm at the *Kärnthnerthor Theater*" (Decsey, 1922).

Vorspiel

The observer who wished to see Vienna at its most natural had to gain distance from the bustling city swarming with carriages, *chaises*, runners, Bohemian peddlers with pots and pans and mouse traps rattling on their backs, swarthy Venetians, mysterious Turks with curved daggers conspicuously displayed in their waistbands, and Jewish peddlers in high hats and kaftans, all milling in the narrow, cobblestone streets girded by the straightjacket of the walls. One had to pass through those mammoth medieval walls, through the fortified gates and portals, past the relaxed guards who casually checked the peasants' goods of geese and chicken, fruits and vegetables for the market, out into the suburbs.

While Vienna the city thrilled to the effervescent sparkle of Rossini's airs, Vienna of the suburbs resounded to the music of Schubert and the dances of Lanner and Strauss. In the suburbs, in its innumerable dance halls Vienna laughed, loved, and lingered. There in heedless ecstasy bourgeois and aristrocratic Vienna, each in its own way, gave themselves to the joy of joys, the waltz. In 1832 there were seven hundred seventy-two balls attended by two hundred thousand people or half of Vienna's populace, with the height of the merriment compressed into the *Fasching*, the pre-Lenten period. In 1842 the composer Peter Cornelius remarked on that highlight of Vienna's amusement opulence: "If life in Vienna is a red-letter day in the eternal calendar of time, then the *Fasching* is red on red, marked in doubly joyful letters. The entire year is gay but comes *Fasching* then it is the duty of every good Christian to do something extra ... The heart of Vienna's font are Schubert, Raimund, Strauss ... cheerfulness without vulgarity, humor without malice."

1875

Con Amore

Although Vienna's nobility was neither as avaricious nor as ruthless as, for instance, that of Paris, nonetheless the very sight of the heavy iron chains surrounding the palaces indicated the exclusion of the people from the world of the aristocracy and vice versa. Until the legal reforms instituted by Emperor Josef II, these chains also indicated that the aristocracy, subject only to the justice of its peers, was beyond the arm and justice of civil law. Despite that tacit law, the waltz formed a bridge secretly traveled in both directions.

In their limited way the people partook of aristocratic pleasures. At a princely ball commoners would jostle each other at the palace gates, held in check by swarthy unsmiling foreign mercenaries who were not beyond kicking an all-too-eager citizen with a shove of a halberd or a musket handle. But nothing could keep the burgher from gawking in wonder at the myriad lights in the chandeliers, the silhouettes of aristocracy, the lavish carriages disgorging the flower of the elegant Austrian elite. For the burgher longing for the realm of nobility and the aristocrat yearning for the people's simple pleasures, the waltz was the ideal intermediary. The burgher dreamt of attaining that courtly grace from which the nobleman wished to escape: *"Schönbrunn* and *Prater* eyed each other longingly" (Decsey, 1922).

Inevitably both aristocrat and burgher sought and gained entrance into each other's realm, often through backstairs and secret doors deviously opened. The duchess engaged as a valet the handsome young man she had espied while passing a dance hall in her carriage. The count traveled the Prater meadows or to a secluded Grinzing inn in his closed private *Fiaker* with his wife's chambermaid; or even more amusing, he would hie himself to one of the innumerable comfortable dance halls in the suburbs, insuring anonymity within the smoky intimacy of burgherdom's dancing waves. There they danced and whirled, aristocrat and burgher's daughter, in each other's arms without question or qualm. Forgotten was the fingertip touch of the minuet, "the model of taste and decorum." All abandoned themselves to the inescapable fever of the waltz; losing themselves in sensual desire evoked by speed, wine, embrace, they forgot—for an evening—war and want.

Thus the waltz provided an important link, a gust of fresh air which entered aristocratic chambers by the backstairs while the front remained barred by iron chains, mercenaries, and jealously guarded privileges. As the minuet, the gavotte and sarabande breathed their last gentle sighs, the mazurka and quadrille might briefly intrude, but it was the waltz that was to reign supreme, a peasant dance elevated to an art form by the grace of its rhythm and melody. While the birthplace of its forerunners may be located among the upper alpine reaches of Austria, it reached its zenith in the conducive air of Vienna. Nor did the waltz remain confined there. Although thoroughly Viennese in sentiment, its spirit proved equally exhilarating to the French, Italians, and Russians, all enjoying its *Schmiss* (verve) with equal vigor. Vienna changed, imperceptibly at first, violently later. The medieval walls were replaced with a vast expanse ready for future splendor and awaiting the flight of the crowded populace away from the city into the suburbs. The Viennese bemoaned the loss of the walls. Within them the Congress of Vienna had lit up the city ... students had marched, citizens had manned the barricades ... Vienna had revolted and lost ... but the dance had gone on, purposefully immersing its people in its whirling maelstrom—they forgot revolt, war, defeat, plague while harking for the jubilant cry: *"Heut' spielt der Strauss"* ("Today Strauss plays").

Vorspiel

1899

Grave

The messenger hurriedly approached the conductor and whispered in his ear. Eduard Kremser, who had concertized with his orchestra in the vast *Stadtpark* pavillion, listened, his face ashen, then motioned the orchestra to stop playing.

Total silence settled upon the vast crowd surrounding the pavillion. Slowly, mournfully the opening strains of the *Blue Danube* waltz resounded.

People rose from their seats and benches, men removed their hats, women quietly sobbed. They all knew.

Johann Strauss was dead.

Part I

The Father

1

The Forefathers

The stage was the same but the cast had changed. The calendar read 1780 and Empress Maria Theresia was dead. Her oldest son had finally, at age thirty-nine, ascended the throne as Joseph II of the Austrian empire. To be precise, after the death of his father in 1765 Joseph had become coregent with his mother, but that had been a "paper" appointment. Maria Theresia had long determined, forewarned by the digressions and indiscretions of her late charming husband Franz I, that neither husband nor son should interfere with her "absolute" control of affairs of state.

The new emperor's broom was as vigorous as it was relentless. His mother's court was reorganized almost overnight. Empress Maria Theresia had kept at court, in motherly protection from a cruel outside world unfamiliar to them after the isolation of court life, the widows of former employees, former governesses of her children, plus innumerable, mostly distant relatives. Now even close relatives whose presence impeded or did not contribute to the newly set standards and aims of the court were removed from the emperor's presence upon his orders. Oddly enough, such imperial decrees mostly affected female family and household members, possibly a subconscious reaction against the long female rule and supervision of Joseph's early life. His sister Maria Christine and her husband were shunted off to the Netherlands to be regents although they had not shown any particular talent at ruling anything or anybody; but this had been his mother's will and Joseph honored it. His sister Elizabeth was dispatched to Innsbruck in Tyrol, his sister Marianne to a convent in Klagenfurt in Carynthia to lord over a small coterie thoughtfully supplied by her imperial brother. All locations were purposefully selected to be far enough from the capital to prevent possible interference or intrigue.

Joseph lived mostly in a wing of the *Hofburg*. The only extravagance he permitted himself was a quiet retreat among the greenery of the small family palace in the *Augarten*, a walled park near the Danube. After the frenetic schedule of the court regimen—also soon to be drastically curtailed—he reveled in the quiet privacy

*Emperor Josef II. His enlightened liberal
absolutism attempted "too much too soon."
Oil portrait by an anonymous Austrian Court
painter, ca. 1770.*

of the place. "I dine alone in my garden with great pleasure ... tranquillity reigns," he related to his brother.

Not much quiet prevailed during Joseph's reign, however. Affairs and coffers of state were in equally deplorable condition after Maria Theresia's expensive and disastrous wars. Yet Joseph's many changes and reforms, promptly initiated and relentlessly executed, seemed "too much too soon" and thus were bound to encounter opposition from many quarters. This did not keep him from vigorously chopping away at mossy and musty ordinances and institutions maintained for the sake of "tradition." The elaborate wigs and costumes of Austrian nobles disappeared from court life and were replaced by simple tailored attire. The kneeling and hand-kissing gesture of "Spanish Reverence," a holdover from the rule of Charles VI was ended forever by one sentence, "Only before God shall men kneel." The galas, balls, and revelries for which the Austrian court had been famous for centuries became mostly a thing of the past. Gone were the twenty different dishes of meat and fowl, downed with twenty different wines, handled by eighteen stewards. The imperial coffers began to fill again when the monied aristocracy were given the opportunity to buy titles. Six thousand gulden would buy a sheepskin declaring that the recipient had become a baron; half a million would buy the title of prince.

Equally important, Joseph established contact with the people of the realm by personally receiving their petitions and complaints each morning and by opening the imperial hunting preserves in the *Prater* as public parks. Eventually he relinquished even his beloved *Augarten* for this purpose. The pomp of past generations of Habsburgs, even in the already relaxed routine of his mother's court, was anathema to Joseph. Literally hundreds of positions in the imperial household which had become fixtures as far back as the regime of Charles VI—butlers, cooks, furriers, priestly confessors, physicians, valets, barbers, wigmakers, chamberlains, lamp and candle lighters, food tasters and wine pourers, secretaries and pursers—were unceremoniously and drastically reduced in number or abolished outright.

Physically and psychologically the Habsburg household had been unwashed and undusted for nearly a hundred years. Emperor Joseph with undue haste attempted to open its windows on a new world. Hunting ceased to be a privilege of nobility and peasants were permitted to hunt for food and for animals which threatened or destroyed their crops. Nobles fumed in anguish at seeing serfdom summarily abolished from their estates and, to their horror, found themselves taxed for the first time in Austrian history. Joseph's concerned fervor reached into every phase of bureaucracy, administration, and ordinary life. Imperial decrees ordered the police to cease torture and imformed the nobility that dueling had been abolished. Education became compulsory, much to the dismay of the peasantry who could no longer use their young children for field labor. Fathers shook their heads in scorn and bewilderment; *Gott im Himmel*, what was the world coming to when even girls were required to get an education! Worst of all, the heavy chains before the palaces of Austrian nobility no longer symbolized aristocratic privilege—the nobility became subject to the same justice and law as all other citizens. No field of endeavor, no corner of the empire escaped Joseph's attention; lagging discipline in the army, potholes on the highways, highwaymen and robber barons, prostitution, the deaf, the blind, the crippled—all were noted, judged, attended to.

Thrifty to the point of frugality, Joseph shunned amusement except for an occasional visit to the theatre or opera. Musically his tastes were limited. After hearing Mozart's delightful opera *Die Entführung aus dem Serail (The Abduction from the Seraglio)* he was moved to comment to the composer: "Too fine for ours ears, my dear Mozart, and too many notes." Mozart, unfazed, replied: "Exactly as many as needed, your Majesty." After the death of *Kammerkompositeur* (court composer) Gluck the position of *Hofkapellmeister* (court conductor) became vacant. Joseph capitulated to the adamant urgings from his own Viennese nobility and appointed Mozart to the post—at two-fifths of Gluck's salary. Mozart's comment upon receiving the news: "Too much for what I do; too little for what I can do."

If the nobility watched Joseph's economic moves with a jaundiced eye, the clergy had even more cause to do so. The emperor's frugality struck at their vested interests, their vast land holdings, and their spheres of interest outside religion— mainly education. Joseph peremptorily shut abbeys, monasteries, and convents, confiscating in the name of the state vast clerical holdings and sources of income, which were used to build or upgrade schools and charities of the emperor's own choosing. Eventually the situation became so threatening that the Austrian clergy pressed Pope Pius VI into visiting Joseph in Vienna to attempt to alleviate their mounting plight. The pope was received by the emperor with all the pomp and ceremony due the first prince of the church; masses of Viennese knelt to be blessed by the pontiff wherever he appeared and countless officials and nobles kissed his ring and slipper. But after Pope Pius had left Vienna, Joseph single-mindedly continued his anticlerical moves. He was so convinced of the righteousness of his cause and his actions that he enforced them with a brusqueness which made few friends and alienated many. He reacted angrily when forced to relent, as in the case when the Viennese *en masse* protested his decree to have them buried in sacklike burial shrouds instead of coffins. "Since a great many [of my] subjects do not wish to understand the reasons for the regulations concerning burial sacks ... which were decreed out of regard for the health of the population; and since, moreover, they display so great an interest in their bodies even after their death, His Majesty no longer cares how they bury themselves in the future." But even such grudging retractions were rare. Dedicated, stubborn in his righteousness to the point of tactlessness, he proceeded with his reforms. Appalled by Vienna's horrible health conditions and death rate, particularly in times of the repeated epidemics which ravaged the city, he founded Europe's largest hospital; horrified by the deaths due to lack of care on the battle fields, he established a training school for army doctors. His special interest in his underprivileged subjects resulted in a school for the deaf-and-dumb and a large orphan asylum.

Yet, despite his unrelenting attempts to better his world, one detects a sense of hopelessness, a constant bout against futility in the travails of a monarch who may have intuitively realized that his actions and ideals were ahead of his time and that another generation of Habsburgs was to nullify or at least modify most of his progressive innovations.

Like all Habsburgs before and after him he was deeply concerned about the succession of the royal house and, brusquely and with impatient severity, groomed shy retiring Franz, the son of his brother Leopold of Tuscany, for the throne. When in 1790 Joseph felt his end nearing he urgently appealed to his brother to come to Vienna and take the reins of royal office from his failing hands. But Leopold's sensitive nerves (or so he claimed) were unequal to the morbid proceedings, so he simply instructed his son Franz, who was conveniently at the scene and more or less familiar with the situation, to keep him posted of the unfolding events. The twenty-two-year-old, inexperienced young man bravely faced the tasks presented by his uncle's demise and his father's dalliance. Untrained in diplomacy and politics, he filled his day by signing innumerable documents in his father's name, without time or experience to study or comprehend them. An entire month elapsed before Leopold saw fit to leave his Tuscan estates for Vienna and look after the realm's affairs with suddenly awakened responsible sternness and circumspection. The effects, good and bad, soon radiated throughout the empire.

The first and overwhelmingly pleasant effect of Leopold's residence at the *Hofburg* was the reappearance of laughter with the arrival of his spouse and the hilarious horde of Franz's thirteen brothers and sisters. In the decades to follow some remarkable names were to emerge from that brood, among them Archduke Rudolf, Beethoven's pupil and patron to whom the *Missa Solemnis* was dedicated, and Archduke Karl, who led the Austrian forces to their only victory over Napoleon.

It soon became apparent that Joseph had left the realm with most of his innovations unsettled or unfinished. Leopold, not quite the "absolute liberal" his brother had been, but of a firmer hand and realistic mind, set out to pacify, clarify, implement, revoke. As if disorder in his own realm were not sufficient, he received the news that his sister Marie Antoinette and her husband were in mortal danger from the French revolutionaries. At that hour of trial by crisis Leopold fully matured. His anguish for his sister became submerged by the overriding considerations of the empire. While realizing that he might be forced to consign his sister to certain death, he gained stature as a ruler and statesman as he wrote to Marie Antoinette: "I can act only according to the interests of my people and not according to family interests." Fate unfortunately did not allow Leopold to grow into the role of the realistically enlightened ruler to which he had lately aspired. In 1792, after only two years of reign, he wasted away within two days. Historians generally attribute his death to either the plague or a ruptured appendix.

His father's sudden demise forced twenty-five-year-old Franz to ascend to the throne of Austria without fetters, experience, or friends, but with an earnest single-minded dedication to his formidable task once he had reluctantly decided to tackle it.

Cautiously but determinedly Franz inched into the illustrious position as Franz II of the Holy Roman Empire, only to find himself immediately threatened. The efforts of his grandmother, Empress Maria Theresia, to achieve an *entente* with France against Prussia had never really succeeded; worse, France now decided to declare war on Austria. Franz's self-confidence was to be sorely tested as a young Corsican upstart, Napoleon Bonaparte, headed the revolution and military campaign and in his first lightning thrust into Italy toppled crowned heads (mostly Habsburgian) like so many sheaves of grain. Austrian possessions shrank alarmingly until the young emperor, about the same age as the young conqueror, was left with only the province of Venetia, which he promptly lost in the course of Napoleon's next campaign. Franz turned to Russia for military assistance and promptly received it, only to see the combined armies decisively defeated at Austerlitz. It was there that Franz and Napoleon finally met. Napoleon, the upstart conqueror, was in high spirits; Franz, the emperor with barely an empire, the product of centuries of breeding, was icily cold. The subsequent Peace of Pressburg robbed Austria of Venetia as well as of a special jewel in the Habsburg crown—Tyrol.

Napoleon subsequently invaded Austria and settled at Schönbrunn, the summer palace of the Habsburgs. At that hour of trial the rotted pillars of the Holy Roman Empire buckled and fell. Traditions and glories of nearly ten centuries crumbled into dust between the millstones of conquest and realignment, and the once regal vestments became museum pieces. Franz II of the defunct Holy Roman Empire became Franz I, emperor of Austria, or what remained of it.

As Emperor Franz matured the picture of a dual personality emerged, deepened, and hardened. "People?" he answered his councilors stonily, "I know no People, only subjects." Yet, perversely, as Austria's defeats and Franz's idiosyncracies mounted, his popularity with the Viennese rose. They began to glorify and idolize the man who was to care for them less and less as the shadow of his reign lengthened. The Viennese did not mind. On Franz's birthday, 12 February 1797, all of Vienna sang the new *Kaiserlied*, the national anthem, freshly composed by none less than Joseph Haydn. In all theatres audiences rose to intone full throatedly and jubilantly, "*Gott erhalte Franz den Kaiser*" ("God keep Franz the Emperor"). In time of war (with France) the noble melody immediately filled and fired the Viennese with one emotion they had sorely missed—pride. Even Franz smiled sourly and, as a token of his imperial esteem, sent Haydn a gold snuff box. A snuff box as a reward for a patriotic act by one of the world's most renowned composers! But then Haydn had been snubbed before in Vienna by potentate, press, and public in like measure. The enemy, Napoleon, had much more appreciation. Although during the war Haydn could not accept a French invitation to conduct in Paris, his oratorio *The Creation* was performed there, nonetheless, and Napoleon, who attended the performance, considered it a memorable event and awarded the Austrian composer a medal.

To Franz anything that smacked of Napoleon was anathema. Never was the emperor of Austria to forget the snub of the "Little Corsican." Franz even avoided Schönbrunn after Napoleon had been quartered there. When Franz wanted to relax from the affairs of state gone awry, he and his pleasure-loving second wife,[1] Marie Thérèse of Naples, would repair to the delightful and secluded pleasure castle and large estates of Laxenburg, south of Vienna. There the entire household played games Marie Thérèse invented on the spur of the moment, then fished, boated, and above all, danced.

Dancing had become livelier as the first of the dance manias had begun to grip Vienna, and the imperial household did not abstain. Overnight the minuet had vanished from the ball room, the imperial salon, the dance floor, and had fled to the concert hall where it found temporary refuge in the symphonies of Haydn and Mozart. Beethoven was to banish it even from that last haven. The imperial pair and entourage now danced two imported dances, the polka and the *Schottische*, plus an early form of the waltz then danced in a peculiarly strenuous fashion devoid of the later graceful gliding turns. Adolf Bäuerle, a Vienna writer, vividly described the scene:

> It was the fashion to be a dashing dancer and the man had to whirl his part-
> ner with the greatest possible speed from one end of the hall to the other. If

---

1. Franz's first wife, Elizabeth of Württemberg, whom he had married in 1788, died in childbirth two years later.

one round of the immense hall would have been considered sufficient one might have allowed this bacchantic dance to pass. But the circuit had to be made six to eight times at top speed and without pause. Each couple endeavored to top the performance of the other and it was no rare occurrence for apoplexy of the lungs to put an end to such madness.

Dancing thus surpassed in Vienna all other pastimes, rivaled only by the attention of each sex to the other—half of Vienna's children were born out of wedlock. The gaiety, the loosening of fear and restraint, the light wine, the closeness of clinging bodies in a dance which was only a thinly veiled symbol of love-making, brought to Vienna in ever increasing measure an undesirable but inevitable part of the scene. Vienna's narrow streets near the *Sperl*, *Mondschein*, and *Apollo* dance halls swarmed with the denizens of the oldest profession; prostitution was rampant in Vienna. Installation of gaslights drove prostitution off the streets but did not alleviate it. Only a stiff ordinance from the chief of police forbidding the renting of rooms at the street level muted the blatant trade.

As he retired more and more from contact with his people, stolid, stoic Emperor Franz found only one place to relax, the realm of his family. There he joined in the games and dances arranged by his pleasure-bent spouse. In the best Habsburg tradition, which demanded that every member of the household either sing, act, dance, or play an instrument, the imperial family made music. The emperor played the violin passably, Marie Thérèse the string bass, daughter Marie Louise the harp. Even Prince Metternich occasionally joined the ensemble and exhibited admirable prowess on the cello. There was a surprising warmth of love within the daily life of the imperial family, with special consideration being given by all to mentally handicapped Prince Ferdinand, heir presumptive to the throne. When affairs of state carried the emperor away from his spouse he wrote repeatedly, ending his letters with "believe me to be throughout life your loving Franz." The empress reciprocated by beginning her letters "Dearest Best Husband." When she died in the premature birth of their twelfth child, Franz was inconsolable and had to be dragged from her body to which he tearfully clung. However, eight months later he married the beautiful, regal Maria Ludovica of Modena, young enough to be his daughter—and consumptive. That fact, unknown at the time of the marriage, was to cast a pall upon their lives. To conserve strength, she was bedridden much of the time and thus could not partake in Franz's beloved outdoor activities or satisfy him in her chambers. To that end the emperor had to avail himself of a mistress, a discreet affair known and acquiesced to by his helpless, loving spouse.

When Napoleon encountered trouble in Spain in 1809, Emperor Franz and his chancellor thought the time ripe for some quick backstabbing. But Napoleon was

Emperor Franz II. He headed an empire controlled by "a standing army of soldiers, a kneeling army of priests and a crawling army of spies." Mezzotint after a painting by Sir Th. Lawrence; the original hangs in Windsor Castle.

not yet to be brought to his knees. A vindictive French army again overran Austria. The only gratification was Austria's victory at Aspern (Napoleon's first defeat), quickly nullified by the defeat of the Austrian forces at Wagram. In that era of short-range missiles Emperor Franz and his staff had been able to watch the battle from a nearby hill. After witnessing the encounter in which hundreds of his brave men had been killed or maimed, Franz's only comment on the defeat was a dry, resigned: *"Jetzt können wir halt nach Haus geh'n"* ("All that's left is to go home").

Another pact and another brief, unstable peace followed, but with a new twist. This time both the Austrian monarch and the French conqueror were looking for a chattel to insure the peace or at least prolong the breathing spell. Napoleon thought he had found it in Emperor Franz's daughter Marie Louise. *"Eine solche Frechheit"* ("such insolence") muttered Metternich. How did the hated Frenchman dare to ask for the hand of the daughter of his enemy? But, for reasons of state the chancellor soon had second thoughts which prompted him to officially favor the *mésalliance.* For Metternich it meant insuring peace for his tortured Austria, for Napoleon it meant insuring an heir for France. Emperor Franz hesitated, for fatherly reasons. But affairs of state overrode all family consideration, and he gave his consent. War-weary Vienna heard the news with a sigh of relief, and danced. In March 1810 Marie Louise departed for Paris and her middle-aged bridegroom. As a bow to his Viennese bride Napoleon had taken time out from his duties in a vain attempt to master the Viennese waltz.

The bride's husband and her father were to meet only once more, two years later, in the Royal Palace in Dresden. If the Habsburg emperor had hoped to meet his son-in-law in a more cordial mood and atmosphere, he was bitterly disappointed. While Napoleon was considerate, even gallant to the emperor's ailing wife, he displayed all the traits of the boorish conqueror in the presence of the representative of the oldest crown in Europe. While Emperor Franz and his entourage stared in stunned, stupefied silence, Napoleon entered the hall of festivities before the Austrian monarch, the first time in history that anybody, even a monarch, had taken precedence over the emperor of Austria. Boldly Napoleon ensconced himself at the head of the table and, in a deliberate display of conqueror's arrogance, watched the Austrian party file in.

Wily Metternich, while he hated Napoleon with a vengeance, a feeling reciprocated with equal fervor and fury, did not let insults and provocations distort his judgment and plans. He bided his time. Time and the Russian wastes accomplished what no army had been able to achieve. Napoleon was brought to his knees, shunted into exile, and the world literally assembled in Vienna to celebrate, adjust, divide and reapportion that variegated succulent pie called Europe.

Suddenly everybody with a crown or a heraldic emblem seemed to have a claim, ancient or recent, on some part of Europe. Led by Emperor Franz of Austria, King Friedrich Wilhelm of Prussia, and Tsar Alexander of Russia, they assembled at the Congress of Vienna in the autumn of 1814. In their wake arrived ministers and armies of secretaries, households, families, retinues, mistresses, necromancers, and throngs of unbidden hangers-on, adventurers, thieves, and camp followers. Colorful costumes and customs, rapid tongues, and gay songs gave Vienna overnight an exotic atmosphere. Nor did nightfall quiet the city. On the contrary, colorfully attired servants, swinging their torches to lighten the darkness for their owner's coaches or sedans, ran on swift feet and added a flamboyant splendor to the nightly proceedings. The spectacle and tumult inside the imperial palace, the princes' palaces, the Spanish Riding School, and the *Apollosaal* belied the relative poverty of the emperor-host. Every night throughout every Congress session eight thousand candles burned in one conference hall alone.

Vienna also enjoyed musical splendor during this period. Prince Andreas Rasoumovsky (more prominent for his amours than his diplomatic prowess), a true patron of the arts, forever engraved his name in the annals of chamber music by commissioning from Beethoven the three quartets (opus 59) which bear the prince's name. The composer, who usually treated his forbearing Vienna princes with studied disdain, was to dedicate his fifth and sixth symphonies jointly to Princes Lobkowitz and Rasoumovsky. A lesser yet no less imposing Congress figure, Prince Charles de Ligne, coined the phrase which was to mirror the spirit of the assembly: *"Le Congrès ne marche pas, il danse"* ("The Congress does not march [achieve]; it dances").

During the Congress, for reasons of prestige, everybody wanted to be at the *Hofburg*. The vast complex of buildings, literally packed to the rafters, resembled an aristocratic ant hill rather than an imperial abode. All reigning sovereigns who attended, as well as their families, domestics, and assorted retinue, were housed there. The chores which demanded attention from a staff normally attuned to the needs of the imperial family and an occasional visiting potentate were staggering. Lighting and stoking hundreds of huge ornamental tile stoves, polishing hundreds of pairs of boots and emptying hundreds of chamberpots, setting forty enormous banquet tables each evening, were only a few of the demanding daily chores performed for patrons accustomed to luxury and to immediate attention to every whim. During the day seven hundred carriages (sleighs in winter) and fourteen hundred horses to pull them had to be in readiness at the imperial stables to take visitors to the Vienna Woods for an outing, to the opera, ballet, concert, ball, to Klosterneuburg, Grinzing, or Gumpoldskirchen for some light vintner's refreshment, to Laxenburg for the hunt, or the Prater for fireworks. Many went out simply to relax, more often from the strenuous pleasures of the previous night than from the daily strain of the conference table.

Emperor Franz, regardless of near bankruptcy and his consumptive empress, offered and partook of all entertainment. The populace was not solely restricted to watching the grandeur. On the anniversary of the battle of Leipzig a reunion was arranged for all soldiers who had fought there. They were fed and fêted, much to the displeasure of nobility who bitterly complained of torn dresses, lost finery, stolen medals and jewelry. Winter, with its confining temperatures, saw the heightening of three forms of Viennese entertainment—intrigue, amours, and dancing. Everyone, from crowned head to washerwoman, skipped, jumped, and turned in a joy which fitted the occasion, the Viennese temperament, and Metternich, who considered ballroom dancing the only "safe" assembly of more than three people. Although most of the nobility easily entered into the lighthearted equalizing spirit of Vienna's dance mania (even crotchety Lord Castlereagh engaged a dancing master for waltz lessons), not all approved. Talleyrand wrote to his sovereign Louis XVIII: "Wherever one looks one sees nothing but emperors and kings, empresses and queens, hereditary princes, ruling princes and the like ... At these assemblies royalty undoubtedly loses something of the grandeur which is its prerogative; the presence of three or four kings ... at the balls or tea parties of simple private people in Vienna seems to me incongruous."

Yet all was not ecstatic at the conference table. The matter of precedence erupted: who was to enter the conference room first? The problem remained unresolved until four doors were cut into the walls of the conference room so that all sovereigns and their delegations could enter at the same time. Later a fifth door had to be added because Talleyrand successfully argued that his French delegation should also be seated in the council.

All those comings and goings, wranglings and deliberations, were presided over by silken, mellifluous, shrewd Chancellor Metternich. One did not have to be Napoleon to hate Metternich. His "friend" the Tsar of Russia loathed him, and just about everybody resented his tight surveillance through secret police, who day and night shadowed even the most illustrious visitors and their retinues. It is said that the emperor and his minister spent many an amused hour sifting the reports after letters had been intercepted and steamed open, keyholes manned, and domestics prevailed upon to report in intimate detail on the comings and goings from morning waking to midnight embrace. However, no major plots or intrigues were ever uncovered, primarily due to the proverbial inefficiency of Austria's secret police.

All those alliances, dalliances, and amusements did little to move the avowed cause of the Congress of Vienna—justice and peace—closer to realization. The lead-

*Prince Clemens Metternich, Austria's mighty chancellor
and the wily spirit behind Emperor Franz, the Congress
of Vienna, and the Holy Alliance.*

ers of nations who assembled at the *Ballhaus* (only the Viennese would give this name to a chancellery) had hoped to produce concrete results within a matter of weeks, but nine months passed before a treaty was born, with everybody and everything becoming less glamorous as the time dragged on. Suddenly the food at the imperial table and the champagne from the imperial cellars had become "dreadful," and the gaiety at the balls appeared more and more strained. Overnight, it seemed, the Viennese barely bothered to turn a head to watch an imperial *equipage* pass. Yet, while all complained, few abandoned the free lodging, free food, and free entertainment provided by the Austrians. The cynically keen eye of the Viennese soon sized up the situation in proper perspective: "The Russian tsar makes love to all, the Danish king talks for all, the Prussian king thinks for all, the Württemberg king eats for all, the king of Bavaria drinks for all, and the emperor of Austria pays for all."

The news of Napoleon's escape from Elba moved all participants to a new urgency. What had taken months to plan and develop came to fruition within a short few weeks. The candles still shone, the music still played, but the party was over. The duke of Wellington was the first in the long subdued line of departure of stunned royalty and diplomats. Emperor Franz's coffers were bare but the borders of his realm had been extended again because the provinces of Tyrol and Salzburg, as well as the provinces of Lombardy and Venetia, had been returned to him. This joy and satisfaction at regaining territory was suddenly diminished and saddened by the death of his lovely consumptive wife at age twenty-nine. Apparently he could not bear the loneliness of his lofty office; less than half a year later he married his fourth wife, again a royal princess young enough to be his daughter. Sturdy, gay, and homely, Charlotte of Württemberg was the exact opposite of frail, regal Maria Ludovica. Her reign as Empress Karoline was sweet revenge on the crown prince of Württemberg, whom she had married when still princess of Bavaria. During the Congress of Vienna her husband had met his old flame, the Grand Duchess Catherine, sister of the Tsar of all Russia. And although Catherine, now hawk-nosed and eagle-eyed, was a far cry from her former graceful self, it was "love again at first sight" between Württemberg and Russia. Claiming that he had married Princess Charlotte under pressure and for political reasons and that the marriage had never been consummated, the crown prince appealed to the pope for annulment. After receiving it he left Charlotte, who later was more than comforted when she ascended the Austrian throne on the arm of Emperor Franz. But time, age, pressure of affairs of state, as well as three previous marriages and discreet mistresses had taken their toll. Although he dearly loved children, Franz either could not, or would not extend the Habsburg lineage consisting of five children from his second marriage.

With all the world occupied with Napoleon, whether in exile or in flight, Marie Louise, the French emperor's wife and the Austrian emperor's daughter, now returned to Vienna and receded into the wings. In the process of reapportioning Europe, the Congress had granted her the Duchy of Parma to which she retired with a small retinue which included her dashing aide, Albert von Neipperg, thoughtfully supplied, it was whispered, by Chancellor Metternich. The one-eyed, black-patched general became for the sensual Marie Louise a lively male antidote to Parma's sluggish and boring routine. Two illegitimate children, appropriately named Albertina and Wilhelm Albert, born while Napoleon was still alive, were the result. Marie Louise did not have the courage to disclose her extramarital panderings and issues to her imperial father until after her husband's death in 1821 and her lover's demise in 1829. Unbelievable as it may seem, the existence of her two bastard children had remained a secret from her father the emperor. When it was finally disclosed to him as a *fait accompli* of ten years, he forgave her and made the two children prince and princess of Montenuovo (an Italianization of the family name of Neipperg, originally Neuberg—New Mountain). He also arranged for the Vienna branch of the house of Rothschild to float a loan, disguised as a financial affair of state, for the children's future benefit. Napoleon's only legitimate offspring, now retitled *Herzog von Reichstadt* and outfitted with a new uniform (Austrian, of course), meanwhile lingered at Schönbrunn. He was kept under constant and close surveillance for fear that he might fan pro-Napoleonic feelings in millions of Frenchmen should he escape or be kidnapped by France.

Although Emperor Franz's days were filled with diligent studying, signing of innumerable papers, and presiding over endless conferences, he enjoyed his evenings with his grandchildren and with a palace full of Habsburg relatives who constantly came to visit. The quiet nights, however, were filled with an agonizing concern— the search for a suitable and effective heir to the throne. By then it had become obvious to all, including Emperor Franz, that his son Ferdinand should not be handed the reins of empire. His oversize head already gave indication of mongoloid development and innumerable tutors had been unable to fill the huge cavity with any knowledge whatsoever. Young Ferdinand would either stand and stare vacantly from his windows onto the palace grounds or reply haltingly to questions in phrases which had been drilled into him through endless repetition. He was in constant dread that his dedicated, demanding father would witness one of his violent epileptic seizures which occurred with alarming frequency, although he was never violent; on the contrary, when not held in terror by his racking seizures, he was as gentle and thoughtful as his mind would permit.

Franz thus turned to his younger son, not the brightest of men but at least not retarded. The emperor peremptorily paired Franz Karl with Bavarian Princess Sophie, who was destined to become the power behind the throne and the Habsburg succession, which she managed with cunning and determination. In that effort she was first aided by her charm and intelligence, later by flattery, shrewdness, and a steely will. Soon she made it her business to know her way about the court and its intricate protocol and to know it better than any of her relatives. She noted the loneliness of Franz and turned this to her advantage by catering to his desire to converse freely and intelligently, unhampered by protocol. She soon became a favorite of the aging monarch, who was now able to turn from stumbling Ferdinand and dimwitted Franz Karl to a charming and bright mind. With her he could even discuss affairs of state, including Ferdinand and the precarious position of the duke of Reichstadt. Fortunately for Franz worry and speculation concerning the young duke's ultimate fate was settled when the engaging young man obligingly died an early death from an "unexplained high fever" suspected to have been tuberculosis.

Archduchess Sophie's role at court, already prominent, was immeasureably enhanced with the birth of her first son in 1830. Emperor Franz had waited impatiently for six years for such an event. Little did he know when the twenty-one-gun salute rang out announcing the arrival of a male heir that Franz Joseph was destined to reign longer than any sovereign before or after.

The winds of change had ripped through France with the destructive power of a tornado. The kings of Württemberg and Bavaria had read the wind scale correctly and changed their regimes from absolute to constitutional monarchies. Austria's Franz had no such intentions. The inevitable explosion was delayed because the realm was shut off almost completely from the outside world. Vienna was confined to the limited tastes and vistas of the burgher who proceeded to apply his stamp on the city. That stamp was to be longingly remembered by another generation as the *"Gemütlichkeit* of Biedermeier Vienna." Finding no ray of light, no uncensored report of the world outside the empire, the Viennese turned inward and reveled. Since public meetings of more than three people were proclaimed unlawful, the Viennese found two places where they could congregate, entertain, relax, talk of scandal and of politics (in hushed tones): the coffee house and the dance hall.

The coffee house existed in innumerable varieties, from the low-ceilinged and smoke-filled intimate hole-in-the-wall, the quieter counterpart of the low-ceilinged inn, to the elegant establishments where aristocracy sipped coffee from cups made in the emperor's porcelain works at the *Augarten*. There newspapers with meager news were avidly scanned and politics whispered. There chess, *Tarock*, or billiards were played, friends received, business transacted, marriages arranged, and babies diapered. The coffee house had flourished since shortly after the second Turkish siege of Vienna in 1683, and had become all things to all people. There were specialized *cafés* whose implied segregation was tacitly but strictly observed; *cafés* for high and low aristocracy, the *Hofrat*, the court councilor of highly placed aristocracy, or the scribes of lower rank; *cafés* for the horse lover, for the chess specialist, the literary set, or the lowly burgher who would devour the papers over a *Schale Gold*, a cup of pungent golden brew, and innumerable glasses of water. A different atmosphere pervaded the dance halls where Lanner and Strauss reigned supreme. Forced flight from reality, release of pent-up passions, innate enthusiasm and love of life had turned the waltz, a gay uninhibited dance, into a mania.

Despite all of Metternich's edicts and spies, not all lines of communication with the outside world could be severed. The umbilical cord of the Danube still brought musicians, travelers, tradesmen, and sometimes clandestine news from up- and downstream, only now it arrived by steamboat. An occasional gesture towards the outside world was made, for example, when Metternich personally invited Niccolo Paganini to play in Vienna. The world's most famous fiddler made a belated appearance in Vienna in 1828, in time to be heard by Schubert before his untimely death. Schubert was the embodiment of the better side of the small-scaled life of Vienna's Biedermeier times. While deaf, ailing Beethoven had stopped roaming the palaces of the mighty and retired into an outwardly silent, inwardly volcanic world of his own creation, Schubert lavished his music on a small circle of friends, poets, painters, singers, and lower civil servants in the famed gatherings immortalized as the *Schubertiads*. It was typical of the times that his works should be performed in the confines of private homes or in the contemplative quiet of a favorite coffeehouse or *Weinstube* and that his greatest masterpieces, his *Lieder*, should be small-scaled. Yet such was the generally narrowing spirit of the times that, despite the appearance of Beethoven, Schubert, Paganini, Weber, and Rossini in Vienna, the city was reaching a low ebb of artistic doldrums.

Emperor Franz, through his chancellor, was anxiously looking about Europe for a suitable bride for the defective crown prince. After much soul searching Franz had definitely decided in favor of Ferdinand as a successor. While the decision defied all wisdom, statesmanship, and reason, the century-old bond of Habsburg hereditary tradition was still so strong that to replace Ferdinand, even with someone obviously healthier and more capable, would have bordered on treason in Franz's mind. The next in line would have been Archduke Franz Karl. Although not much of an improvement, he at least would have spared the court the sorry spectacle of an emperor-to-be pushed and pulled by servants through marble halls, stammering inane platitudes at public gatherings. Beyond Ferdinand and Franz Karl, Emperor Franz would have had to look to his own brothers for succession. Archdukes Karl and Johann were both competent men, eager to lead and to rule. However, their abilities earned them the strong dislike of the emperor who, through his chancellor, managed to bypass them.

Then, early in 1831 came the thunderclap: Metternich announced that a bride had been selected for Archduke Ferdinand. The hapless pawn in the desperate search for Austrian succession was Princess Marianna of Sardinia, no prize catch herself. But the naive, plain, virtuous, and extremely shy maiden was at least mentally sound. Even with such a shrinking, insignificant girl Metternich took no chances

The Father

Archduchess Sophie, the mother of Emperor Franz Joseph. Her patient scheming shrewdness secured Austria's throne for her son.

and did not let the bride see Ferdinand until she had arrived at Schönbrunn. Keen-eyed Archduchess Sophie read the girl's mind, her ashen whiteness, her trembling voice, and swallowed tears but did nothing to console her or attempt to prevent the shameful mockery of matrimony. The future role of Ferdinand's wife seemed preordained when Ferdinand, one year later, suffered twenty violent epileptic seizures.[2] She remained by his bedside throughout the ordeal which was to repeat itself innumerable times. Against all expectations, perhaps even his own, Ferdinand clung to life. Despite the obvious desperate plight and incongruous position the stubborn emperor's mind could not be changed. Incredible as it seemed, Ferdinand emerged as the heir-presumptive to the throne of Austria.

2. Ferdinand was not the only epileptic in the family. Sophie's first daughter, Anna, also had the disease, but her death at age five released her from a life of constant dread.

The one person at the Viennese court who had the closest and clearest view of the situation and thus was eventually able to maneuver herself into a commanding position was, of course, Archduchess Sophie. The painting of her by Josef Stieler, in the Historic Museum of the City of Vienna, shows her proudly holding her first-born in her arms. Her set, determined mouth is slightly mocking, but her eyes, clear, wide, strong, looking straight at the beholder, are more revealing of her personality. Shrewd, self-assured, skeptical and cunning, she was not to be embroiled in petty court politics, nor were intrigues allowed to spoil her long-range plans. Sixteen years were to pass before these plans were to come to fruition, but she had come a long way, she was young and determined, and she could afford to wait.

Emperor Franz was becoming increasingly feeble. The trying Vienna winters were beginning to prove too harsh for his weakened constitution. Pneumonia was to end the life of this dedicated, controversial ruler whose petrified reign and mellow family life bordered on the schizophrenic. In anticipation of his demise he had seen to it that the "rule" by Ferdinand was carried out by able men. Chancellor Metternich was his natural choice for the interpretation and execution of state and foreign affairs, and Count Kolowrat was to handle internal affairs. As the third of the ruling triumvirate Franz had selected the least qualified of his brothers, Archduke Ludwig, weak enough not to interfere. Thus, Franz had hoped, there would be assurance for perpetuation of a way of life which he and Metternich considered the only "virtuous" way of ruling the polyglot people of the empire. As was to be expected, the "rule" of "Ferdinand the Good" was a cruel farce perpetrated on the individual himself as well as on an entire empire. He shambled down the palace halls to the ridicule of the court and its diplomats who, behind their hands, mocked the "animal," and "idiot." However, it had been a wise move, under the circumstances, to leave the reins of office in the trained hands of Metternich.

Sophie's own four sons, Franz Joseph, Maximilian, Karl Ludwig, and Ludwig Victor were hale. Franz Joseph, presumably the next in line in Habsburg succession, received training in all the attributes expected of a future ruler. Although that task was mainly given over to tutors, Archduchess Sophie supervised all details and phases of his education, particularly his study of languages with special emphasis on French, the language of diplomacy; Latin, the language of the literati; plus Italian, Hungarian, and Bohemian, the prominent languages of the people of the empire; and the great writers and poets of German literature. At age thirteen he was dutifully made a colonel in a famous cavalry regiment. This pleased him because it meant a splendid new uniform and the right to "command" the regiment. Few future monarchs were as carefully groomed for their responsibilities as was Franz Joseph under the sternly benign eye of his mother.

The Father

"Every Constitution Needs Motion" (Metternich in flight). Vienna's first political caricature, from the year 1848.

As Emperor Franz had foreseen, Ferdinand's total incompetence in matters of state had to be constantly counterbalanced. The task fell to Metternich, who knew only one *modus operandi*, that of draconic decrees, an army of spies and police, and unrelentingly tight censorship. What aggravated the precarious situation even more was the constant tug-of-war between Metternich and Kolowrat, each attempting to outmaneuver, undercut, and subvert the other for supremacy in empire rule. But the easygoing Viennese could endure only a measure of incompetence and oppression. The suppressed working class, the censored bourgeoisie, and the maligned students had withstood all the punishment they were going to take. Overnight the tightly held lid of Metternich's Pandora's box blew off its hinges. Typically, the Viennese sought less a return to the administration of justice but rather the relaxation of tight regulations as had been promised through the "benevolent" rule of Ferdinand. "Viennese! Liberate your good Emperor Ferdinand from the bonds of his enemies!" was the slogan shouted. Metternich, who read the handwriting on the wall correctly, fled to Tory England with a Rothschild letter of credit hidden in his pocket.

Ferdinand, now acting on the advice of frightened incompetents, acceded to all of the people's demands—which included a constitution—and briefly basked in fickle adulation. As the emperor, together with Archduke Franz Karl and his son Franz Joseph rode through the streets, a jubilant mob unhitched their horses and proceeded to race the imperial carriage to the *Hofburg* while shouting Haydn's national anthem.

However, when demands were specified and definite dates for execution requested, when commitments such as free elections and a constitutional assembly were sought, the magnitude of promises given under duress overwhelmed the incompetents at the helm. Fright prompted flight, and the imperial household hastily hied itself to Innsbruck in Tyrol, the old capital of Maximilian I. It soon became apparent that their move had been premature because the Viennese were basically anti-Metternich, not anti-Habsburg. In a petition containing eighty thousand signatures the Viennese asked Ferdinand to return to Vienna. The emperor heeded the plea. But meanwhile, with Metternich's restraining hand removed from the wheel of state, events began to turn in directions unforeseen by all concerned. The Italian provinces, always outspokenly anti-Habsburg, had taken advantage of the momentary void and had revolted. Hungary and Bohemia had been ignited by this revolutionary spark and, in closing the cycle, had also ignited Vienna's latent revolutionary tinder. The court, barely returned to the capital, was aghast, leaderless, and totally without direction. Devoid even of makeshift planning the imperial household fled again like a flock of frightened bleating sheep, this time north to the city of Olmütz (Olomouc) in Moravia. Only the minister of war, Count Latour, remained at his post. Deprived of its main target, Metternich, a Viennese mob promptly sought out and killed the nearest available victim, Latour, whose death made flight for the imperial family seem like a well-timed idea.

If Ferdinand was incapable of a rational act concerning the fate of empire, the *Camarilla*, the court party, was not. Once safely out of reach of the Vienna mob, courage returned. Disregarding all recent lessons, it dispatched the empire's foremost generals to force peace and compliance on the rebellious provinces and capital. Field Marshal Radetzky crushed the Italians, Prince Windischgraetz and General Jellacic dealt the same fate to Hungary and Bohemia. But aroused, idealistic Vienna remained defiant. Again Windischgraetz was called upon the scene. He broke the gallant, ineffective resistance of Vienna within five days.

Even with the tenuous, brooding, and vengeful peace imposed by Windischgraetz's steely hold on the capital, the situation appeared clearly untenable, even to the *Camarilla*. At that tense moment of impasse and stalemate Archduchess Sophie made her move to garner the fruits of her long years of waiting and planning. Gossip began to seep through the imperial corridors: Ferdinand is incompetent ... Ferdinand must go ... Abdication is the only solution ... Franz Joseph is eligible ... Franz Joseph is ready ... Franz Joseph is a leader ... If Archduchess Sophie had not instigated the rumors, she certainly fanned them through silence and acquiescence until the entire court seemed to speak with one voice: "Franz Joseph."

With the inevitability of Greek drama the events which Sophie so shrewdly had set in motion took their preordained course. The morning of 2 December 1848 saw the entire imperial household assembled in the temporary imperial quarters in Olmütz. The officers' dress uniforms, complete with decorations, already hinted at the significance of the occasion. Emperor Ferdinand was led into the room and a hush fell over the assembly. History took its next to final turn for the Habsburgs as he haltingly read from the document handed to him:

> Weighty considerations have led me to the irrevocable decision of renouncing the imperial crown. The renunciation is made in favor of our beloved nephew, his serene Highness, Archduke Franz Joseph whom we now declare to have attained majority.

Franz Joseph knelt before his uncle, asked for his blessings, kissed his hand, was embraced, and rose as Emperor Franz Joseph I. Archduchess Sophie, now queen mother and a greater power than ever, proudly watched the realization of her years of planning. She stepped forward to embrace her imperial son. Ferdinand exited almost unobserved, his abdication a *fait accompli*. "We went to our room," his diary reads, "Afterwards I and my dear wife heard Holy Mass ... After that I and my dear wife packed our things ..."

Archduke Franz Joseph, age seventeen, one year before he ascended the throne. Elegant, gracious, and educated — but would he be able to govern? Lithograph by Franz Eybl, 1847.

2

The Father of IT All

A ballroom where Lanner played resembled a flower field moved by a melodic storm, so the heads of the flowers bent to each other in an innermost trembling of their souls ... The pairs touched and weaved in a sea of melody.

Simultaneously with the French Revolution and the death of the stately minuet, the *Langhaus*, the two-step forerunner of the waltz, reappeared and proved immediately popular with the populace. The authorities, however, for religious, health, and social reasons viewed it with a jaundiced eye. As early as 1572 a Vienna ordinance had specifically advised: "Ladies and maidens are to compose themselves with chastity and modesty and the male persons are to refrain from whirling and other such frivolities. Whichever man or fellow, woman or maiden will turn immodestly in defiance of this prohibition and warning of the city fathers will be brought to jail and fined 20 groschen by the city council each time it happens." A Dresden wedding ordinance of 1595 was no less specific: "The evening meals are to be served so that all can arrive at the dance not later than eight. Several honor dances are to be held, chaste, and without voluptuous turning, jumping, or running hither and yon. The ladies and maidens are to be led to and from the dance by the arm and without holding hands. The orders are to be announced and followed by whoever caters the wedding." Sermons from Vienna pulpits thundered forth: "God preserve pious young men from such maidens as delight in evening dances and in letting themselves be swung around and allowing themselves to be kissed and mauled about; indeed they cannot be honest while each entices the other to harlotry and offers a sop to the devil." Yet despite all warnings, threats, and admonitions the *Langhaus* craze spread, aggravating conditions such as heart failure and lung collapse. Deaths were so numerous in Vienna that the police had no choice but to forbid the dance.

The opera *Una Cosa Rara* by the Spanish composer Vincente Martin[1] occupies a place in waltz history. In 1787 it was performed to great applause in Vienna's historic *Theater in der Josefstadt*. The glare of history has shrivelled the work into oblivion, but in its day it was considered the worthy rival of *Le Nozze di Figaro* and its opening run actually overshadowed Mozart's earlier immortal creation. The innovation in *Una Cosa Rara* was the insertion of a waltz interlude. Although it had no influence on the development of the waltz, the interlude became the main attraction of the opera and kept the arid work on the boards for twenty-two years. History records that the word *Walzer* (from the German word *walzen*, to roll, to turn) had its first mention there.

A true ancestor of the waltz is the *Ländler*, a slow-turning alpine dance in three-four time. It took hold quickly and already during the time of Beethoven and Schubert had become a joyous household word. Soon all of Vienna was drawn into the exhilarating vortex of the *Ländler* and the waltz, and on 16 January 1827 the poet Bauernfeld reported in his diary: "Day before yesterday, Sausage Ball at Schober's, Schubert had to play waltzes." Those were typical, delightfully unpretentious affairs in the home, without pomp, ceremony, or fancy trappings. One simply moved the furniture out of one large room, and "if the food and the piano playing were palatable" everybody had a glorious time.

Again, not all received the dance with open arms. England's Lord Byron railed against it. France boycotted the waltz for a long time, but green-eyed envy lurks from the dance descriptions of Madame Genlis: "A young maiden, lightly clad, throws herself into the arms of a young man. He presses her to his heart with such vehemence that they soon feel the beating of their hearts and their heads and feet begin to spin; that is what is known as the waltz."

Long before Lanner and Strauss began their reign, Vienna had waltzed to the strains of its folk musicians. The sound was thin, the melodies monotonous and repetitive but Vienna was grateful for the meager efforts of her "beerhall musicians." A few names stand out: Faistenberger for the quantity of his output, about two hundred dances ranging from minuet to *Ländler* to waltz; Pfister for the comic titles he gave his dance pieces; and the one and only Pamer for the superior rendition of his music (when sober) and for his celebrated drinking bouts. In its early stages a waltz consisted of two times eight bars, twelve such selections constituting a complete waltz. Nobody thought of or cared for fancy artistic trappings—there was neither

1. Vincente Martin y Soler (1754-1806), successful rival of Mozart, with whom he shared Metastasio and da Ponte as librettists, was prominent in Vienna, London, and Russia. Catharine the Great personally wrote two libretti to be set to music by him.

introduction nor *coda*. The program simply announced "12 *Tänze!*," "12 *Teutsche*" (German dances), or "12 *Walzer*," and the composers proceeded to fabricate them *en masse* with a minimum of musicianship or invention. Yet such was the insatiable appetite of Vienna for dances that even prominent musicians such as Diabelli, Hummel, Czerny, Hüttenbrenner, and Lachner, far above the run-of-the-mill fiddlers and only a step below the immortals, began to write music for the dance hall. Needless to say, both Beethoven and Schubert wrote *Tänze*. However, they were more suitable to the concert hall than the dance hall.

True "Viennization" of the waltz was reserved for Lanner. His melodic inventiveness alone placed his waltzes far above those of his fellow musicians, and the balancing of brief introduction and *coda* soon began to appear in his dances. His creations, innately Viennese, were immediately understood, applauded, and cherished. Mendelssohn wrote to his friend, famed violinist Ferdinand David: "Enclosed find a masterpiece, *Die Werber* by Lanner. I suggest you study it." The young Viennese music critic Eduard Hanslick put Lanner into true perspective: "The best of Lanner sounds like an echo of Schubert. We who can recall Schubert's *Deutsche Tänze* will have no doubts about the relationship of the two Vienna masters, the great one and the small one; Lanner's violet-scented melodies charm not only the people but some of the greatest masters gladly bend down from their heights to be refreshed." Lanner's music was perhaps a shade more traditionally Viennese in its warmth, gentleness, depth, and melodiousness than that of Strauss Father, whose more daring, stronger rhythms appealed to a younger segment of Vienna just entering the age of dancing and courting.

The year 1801 records several important news items in Vienna. The Peace of Luneville brought the desperately sought temporary relief from the Napoleonic threat. Vienna jubilated and took advantage of the breathing spell by feasting, dancing, and gawking in wonder at the newly built brain-child of peripatetic Emanuel Schikaneder, the *Theater an der Wien*, destined to become one of the great theatres of Vienna and the world.

In the Vienna suburb of St. Ulrich a son was born to glovemaker Martin Lanner on 12 April and was baptized Josef. The life of a glovemaker at that time was one of hardship. Vienna swarmed with the French soldiers of the Napoleonic occupation forces whose bright uniforms could be seen everywhere, in the streets, the coffeehouses, the theatres, the bedchambers. Generally coexistence between conquerors and conquered was without incident; only an occasional flare-up pointed to the smoldering undercurrent, such as when the French, after the battle of Austerlitz, marched their prisoners through the streets to brash arrogant military music. While an uneasy peace prevailed and life slowly returned to its normal relaxed gait, the glove business improved sufficiently to enable Lanner to visit his favorite tavern, *Zur Goldenen Birne* (The Golden Pear). Sometimes he was accompanied by little Josef, who was exposed for the first time to what then passed for *Wiener Musik* with the Vienna burghers, the music-making of Ignaz Michael Pamer whose orchestra played there every night.

Pamer had attained a large measure of local success with his *Eipeldauer Teutschen* dances. It was typical of the kind of entertainment and the mental horizon of his nightly audiences that Pamer's most applauded success was a "feat" unique in the annals of music anywhere. The point of departure was a musical concoction entitled *"Selige Erinnerungen an das gute Hütteldorfer Bier"* ("Blissful Memories of the Good Hütteldorf Beer"). After having led his band in the piece Pamer would show his appreciation of the subject matter by downing a stein of that brew in front of the audience. Acceding to the audience's applause he would then repeat the performance anywhere from ten to twenty times before he was allowed to stagger through the rest of the program. Despite his immense capacity the quality of the remaining program was hardly impressive, even for innocents like little Lanner. But the fact remains that this was the level of musicianship offered to an undemanding Viennese drinking and dancing audience.

Despite such a horrible example as Pamer, little "Pepi" Lanner showed an early inclination for and interest in music. Due to the laxity of the parents and the stubbornness of the boy, general education was totally lacking—the youth could barely read or write. Soon a bigger problem arose. The down-to-earth father wanted Josef to learn a craft or trade, but the boy refused; he wanted to make music. Tension at home became so unbearable for the unhappy and frustrated boy that he began to drink secretly. When Lanner one day noticed wine on his son's breath, he administered a sound thrashing in typical Viennese fashion. That only worsened the situation. Finally the father relented, bought the boy his first fiddle, and allowed him to take lessons. Life instantly brightened again for the family as talented Pepi began to fiddle away to the delight of anybody who wished to listen. For reasons other than musical, however, this happiness was not to last. In 1811 the Vienna skies darkened into a nightmare. The financial picture of the city changed drastically due to Austrian bankruptcy and a sharp devaluation of Viennese currency. Thousands were wiped out; Lanner did not escape, gloves being the last thing on the mind of Viennese women at the time. To make things worse in the Lanner household, Pepi's sister Nettie was born.

The Father

The year 1815 saw Austria's economic fortunes on the upswing again. Peace had been restored and the Congress of Vienna was busily dividing — between dances — the patchwork quilt of Europe. That extended period when the great, near-great, and would-be great of Europe assembled and feasted in Vienna without a thought of replenishing the bankrupt coffers of Austria, nevertheless restored a measure of improved economy, even to the small merchant and craftsman. Lanner was among the fortunate who profited, although in small measure. The Congress's demand for fine gloves actually saved him from bankruptcy and starvation. More surprisingly, the arts also profited as is evidenced by the appearance of newspapers and magazines such as the *Theater Zeitung, Wiener Zeitschrift für Kunst, Literatur und Mode (Vienna Journal for Art, Literature and Fashion)*, and *Der Sammler (The Collector)*.

Despite small rations at home Pepi made solid strides on his chosen instrument and already made a modest living and contribution to the household by playing in the Pamer band. But having to watch Pamer's nightly drinking bouts disgusted the boy, who had been brought up in burgher strictness. The scene unfolded nightly with unfailing progression. Pamer at first would be the life of the party in forced, overly loud gaiety. The incredible amount of beer consumed each night as the program progressed would cause him to become, in turn, melancholy, cantankerous, and morose until, during the early morning hours, he would collapse into a crying spell. Barely able to move, he would leave his nightly drinking companions and, like an animal, crawl into a corner, whimpering until he fell into a stupor or some kindly souls dragged him to the hole he called home. Pamer also had an uncontrollable passion for gambling, which, with his drinking, made his eventual financial and physical collapse predictable. Despite these handicaps Pamer's innate talent was undeniable. The Vienna publisher Artaria at one time thought so highly of Pamer that he published his dances in the same album with works of Beethoven and Schubert. However, death at age forty-five felled a man who had squandered a talent and fortune but who, in the process, had also made the *Sperl* a household word in Vienna.

After leaving Pamer with regret and disgust, young Lanner began to look for an improved position. He had a vision, an ensemble of his own, with himself at the helm, of course. As luck had it he met at that important time the brothers Drahanek, talented Bohemians who played violin and guitar. The three boys decided to try it on their own as a string trio with Pepi as first violinist. The owner of the popular Café *Jüngling* chose to take a chance on the three clean-looking youngsters and, despite Pamer's wrath and threats, the trio settled down at the coffee house. Modest success was soon achieved although the café owner had given them no guarantee of income. But when the plate was passed around the "take" was usually considerable.

Josef Lanner, "The Father of the Vienna Waltz," whose violet-scented melodies elevated the waltz. Lithograph by Kriehuber, 1839.

The Father

The upgrading of light music was in the offing. Vienna had tired of the escapades of Pamer and the mediocrity of all others. Soon other musicians, poets, writers, and minor government officials began to frequent *Jüngling* to hear the young trio's brand of musical diversion. While Vienna "City of the Phaecians," as Schiller and Bauernfeld had called it, danced in nightly whirl at the *Sperl, Fortunasaal,* and *Apollo* to inferior fare, the time suddenly became ripe for the ascendency of Lanner.

Food was cheap again and available to all but the wretchedly poor, and a veal roast with a beaker of wine or a stein of beer was within reach of almost all. The small appreciative group which assembled at the *Schubertiads* also listened to young Lanner's music and loved it. Vienna lived for the dance, *der Himmel hing voller Geigen* (Heaven Was Hung with Violins). Nobody particularly cared what was going on beyond the venerable moss-hung bastions, except when a new dance hall opened in the suburbs or when the bush over the vintner's door signaled the arrival of the young wine in Grinzing or Sievering. In that relaxed aura of deceptive Biedermeier peace Lanner's fame gathered momentum. He left Café *Jüngling* to accept a better offer from the Café *Zum Grünen Jäger* (The Green Hunter). The swelling crowds who began to listen to the youthful trio with more than passing interest could not really put their finger on the source of the enchantment; better rhythm, better playing, yes, but it was more than that, it was in innate musicianship and modest artistry, in tune and in spirit with Vienna. Soon a dark-complected, blackhaired youngster with glowing eyes joined with his fiddle to make the group a quartet. This new member was Johann Strauss.

The day Strauss was born, 14 March 1804, dawned drearily. The heavens were drenching the city with a mixture of snow and rain when the mother, née Tollmann, gave birth to her son in the sparsely furnished apartment above her husband's inn, her cries in labor drowned out by the raucous songs of the men below. The inn was located in the Flossgasse in the district of Leopoldstadt, then an island in the Danube. It was not a safe place to live because of the constant danger of flooding, particularly in spring, but was inhabited by a lively, hardworking crowd of Bohemian tinsmiths, Polish artisans and craftsmen, and Jewish tailors and peddlers. Franz Strauss, Johann's father, was a man embittered by his unfulfilled ambition to better himself, to divorce himself from lowly tavern life and move into the bourgeois stratum of Vienna. The fact that he lacked the knowledge and drive to achieve his goal poisoned his life beyond endurance. One day he walked into the Danube and drowned himself.

If ambition had poisoned the father's mind it was to fire the son's dreams. Nobody knows when the latent talent of Johann Strauss began, but there could be no question that it was suddenly there. When stepfather Golder presented him with a cheap fiddle the boy, to the mirth of all, with unfailing ear scraped out the dance tunes, folk songs, and coarse limericks he heard in tavern and street. Schoolwork soon began to suffer as Johann's desire to be a musician grew stronger. The parents were shocked; *Wirtshausmusikant* (tavern musician) then rated on a par with street walker, a status barely above that of a beggar. They wanted their son to have "something better" than they had, an honorable profession, something that would earn a decent living removed from drunkards and fiddlers. Strauss was apprenticed to the bookbinder Lichtscheidl, but the boy rebelled against a milieu which provided no incentive and, worst of all, no music. He despised the smell of old paper, of linen and leather bindings, and the pervading stench of the glue pot. One morning he did not appear at the shop. A search failed to locate him; the boy had run off. At his age thoughts of the next meal posed no particular concern. Now that he had fresh air, and a fiddle, all was well.

Young Strauss roamed the streets, dance halls, inns, and vineyards, eating and sleeping wherever he could find a market for his music. He was hungry more often than not; he would curl up in some stable for the night, tired, lonely but determined not to return home. One sunny afternoon he climbed the Kahlenberg, one of the last gentle foothills of the Alps descending to the Danube and Vienna, in search of work at the inn at its top. He never reached the top. In the green Vienna Woods and the warmth of the sun, he gave in to his fatigue. A well-known Viennese musician, Polischansky, happened to pass by on his way to the casino and was startled to find the boy slumbering by the roadside, clutching a fiddle. He woke the youngster, engaged him in conversation, and made him play the violin. Something clicked; Polischansky divined latent talent and decided to take the young fiddler under his wing. He convinced the parents to end their opposition to Johann's musical ambition, promising that the young Strauss would receive at least a minimal education as well as musical instruction.

Encouraged by Polischansky the boy soon tried his skill in playing with the orchestra of thirsty Pamer. Despite the fact that Pamer was the antithesis of anything a Vienna burgher might aspire to, this young musician was fascinated. Strauss knew that Pamer was a drunkard, witnessed his wenching with any skirt that crossed his path, and watched his appetite which matched his thirst. Many a time young Johann was the target of Pamer's vicious temper, particularly when the older man had gone beyond the limits of natural thirst during the early hours of morning. But the boy also found that the uninhibited clown was a fine musician who, when sober, could play a *Ländler*, a *Linzer*, or a *Langhaus* with the best of them. Eventually Pamer's cheap showmanship and outrageous exaggerations disgusted even young Strauss. It was at that time that he became acquainted with Lanner and the Drahaneks. It was the ideal milieu for him, with only one drawback. The Lanner trio were professionals; they objected to Strauss's inferior instrument. Legend has it that an old *Musikant* advised the baffled young man to soak his instrument with beer. Supposedly Strauss poured beer into the instrument through the F-holes, swished it around, and let it run out the same way. The emergency treatment is supposed to have miraculously improved the tone-quality of the mediocre instrument. However no record exists of the odd procedure, nor did Strauss recommend it to anyone else. The members of the quartet complemented each other personally as well as musically, and Strauss grew from dreamy boy to gay blade to firebrand—with favorable effects on his music and on Vienna.

The friendship between the gentle Lanner and the impetuous Strauss deepened through their love of music as well as the leveling influence of poverty. They found joint quarters at the house *Zur Windmühle* (The Windmill) and became inseparable sometimes by necessity, as when they had to share a shirt, and one had to walk about with his coat buttoned to his throat because the other wore the shirt while performing. It may have been opposite qualities which attracted them to each other: Lanner was blond, quiet, and dreamy; Strauss was dark in hair and complexion, easily aroused, with a seeming inward raging which gaiety could not always dispel. On those occasions the "flaxenhead" had to use all his powers of persuasion to quiet the "Moor's head."

With growing success and demand for his type of music, Lanner decided to enlarge the ensemble to the size of an orchestra by engaging a cellist and a string bass player. Some original manuscripts of the time include the flute and guitar in the orchestrations, which indicates that Lanner must have further enlarged the group on occasion.

Again the group moved, this time to the prestigious Café *Rebhuhn* (Partridge), with a fine clientele of musicians and artists—Schubert, Schober, and Schwind among them. Schubert is said to have openly appreciated Lanner's music. Lanner reciprocated. When Schubert's opera *Die Zauberharfe (The Magic Harp)* opened at the *Theater an der Wien*, Lanner was among those who applauded vigorously. Lanner was known to love the musical theatre, but his own ever increasing activities allowed little time for the theatre or theatre music until late in life, particularly since he found it necessary in 1824 again to enlarge the group, which became a full string orchestra. It made its first appearance on 1 May 1824 at the First Coffeehouse in the Prater. It was a sensation because a salon orchestra consisting of strings only was a novelty in Vienna. So enthusiastic was the coffee-house audience that certain numbers had to be repeated as often as five times.

Vienna was growing impatiently and so was its appetite for music, diversion, dance, and food. As the Viennese looked about them they found the empire alarmingly shrunken, its influence and voice amid the concert of Europe barely heard and often ignored. In the wake of Napoleon's invasions a dull sense of defeatism was making dangerous inroads among a populace which could not ignore the maimed and crippled, the victims of Europe's interminable wars. What better way to forget than to dance and eat? Thus, by the turn of the century, the statisticians tell us Viennese had a yearly absorption rate of 454,000 barrels of domestic wine, 19,000 barrels of Hungarian wine, and 382,000 barrels of beer. That constituted only the liquid intake which aided the downing of mountains of *Backhendl* (fried chicken), *Schnitzel* (breaded veal cutlet), and *Gulasch* (Hungarian stew) to be counterbalanced at meal's end with cups of pungent coffee topped by heaping mounds of *Schlagobers* (whipped cream).

Suddenly the low-ceilinged *Weinstuben* and ale houses became too narrow, congested, and lowbrow for the expansive and growing Beidermeier bourgeoisie. They were joined by the growing working class and by a new monied aristocracy yearning for the escapist entertainment of their own dreams. While strenuously and awkwardly imitating the habits and mode of living of the highborn, they missed the simple, uninhibited pleasures of a milieu which they had abandoned in pursuit of wealth and station. The dilemma was compounded by their desire not to be seen in their former locales and with former companions but to search for new entertainment which previously had been barred to them or had been unattainable for monetary reasons. Therefore, since the choice of entertainments was limited, the bourgeoisie and newly rich created their own new places of amusement away from old friends and haunts. The *Sperl*, of course, remained one of the few dance halls where literally all strata could meet—from aristocracy, often incognito, to prostitutes, now in flamboyantly elegant finery. The vast establishment, opened in 1807, had become an immediate success, with the best beer, wine, food, and music. Although the barn-like *Sperl* presented no fancy exterior, inside it boasted famed Fortuna Hall where everybody who was anybody in Vienna, from Pamer to Lanner to Strauss, played.

But the establishment to eclipse all others for decades was the *Apollosaal*. The tales of its lavish luxury were carried far beyond Vienna and became the model to be emulated and envied in all of Europe. It was built by Sigmund Wolffsohn, an

The Father

Englishman (presumably of German extraction) who settled in Vienna at the age of thirty.

Wolffsohn was a versatile genius with an uncanny sense of timing for the needs of his era. He was also a modern man in that he foresaw the need for mass production to make things cheaply enough for the general populace. Although he was rumored to be a doctor and an orthopedic surgeon, nobody ever consulted him in either capacity. However, regardless of whether the titles were real or assumed, he had enough knowledge of the medical profession to allow him to found and maintain the only manufacturing plant, at the time, of surgical instruments. His products were of such excellence that the Austrian emperor conferred the mantle of imperial patronage on him. In 1801 the Berlin College of Medicine awarded Wolffsohn its highest honor, the Gold Medal, for his creation of a complete set of surgical instruments consisting of over three hundred components, all contained in one portable case. The tsar of Russia, after inspecting the surgical marvel, awarded its inventor a stipend of one thousand ducats.

Wolffsohn surpassed that feat with his most enduring creation—movable artificial limbs. The importance of his work in that field cannot be overrated at a time when the value of the individual lay mainly in quantity: the faceless taxpayer who underwrote the maintenance of a luxurious court; the faceless soldier thrown into the cauldron of war to achieve imperial ambitions of territorial gain. However, the returning soldier, once back in civilian life with an empty sleeve, trouser leg, or eye socket, was suddenly not only a fiscal burden, but, by the visibility of his war injury, a source of embarrassment to his sovereign, who also distrusted him as a possible source of future unrest. Thus European sovereigns welcomed Wolffsohn's invention of movable limbs as much as their subjects did. Also innovative was Wolffsohn's decision to produce the artificial limbs at only a small profit in order to make them available to the underprivileged.

His imagination next turned to "social work for the wealthy," and he produced beauty creams for the ladies of society. Again his intuition paid off. To have a cream or lotion from the great Wolffsohn, purveyor to His Imperial Majesty, socialites paid fantastic prices, and to own his inflatable "health couch" customers gladly paid a small fortune of three hundred seventy-five gulden. The wealthier Wolffsohn became the more restlessly his mind worked. His roving eye scanned the Vienna scene and promptly discerned the disparity between supply and demand in the field of entertainment. The lode of native talent, particularly in the field of music, never seemed to exhaust itself. On the contrary, there was such an overabundance of it and such a great demand for it by all strata of Viennese society that dancing space was actually at a premium. Suddenly there opened a new field worthy of Wolffsohn's genius.

A ballroom like no other dance palace ever was what Vienna needed, a true pleasure dome that was the epitome of luxury, that offered the finest in cuisine, wines, decorations, and music. The result was the *Apollosaal*. Nothing in Vienna, nothing in Europe was to compare with it. Whether it was a public dance festival or a private ball, to have it held at the *Apollo* became a status symbol in Vienna. Soon the demand for its services became so pressing that the public was advised to make reservations a month in advance, an unheard-of practice in Vienna. The *Apollo* opened on 10 January 1808, also, as it happened, the day on which Emperor Franz took his third wife, Ludovica d'Este. It seemed that the world came to see and be seen, to dine, to dance, to be dazzled. Although the ticket price for opening night was an exorbitant twenty-five gulden, over four thousand people managed to pay out and crowd in. The Apollo Hall, actually fifteen connecting halls, boasted of having the largest ballroom, the largest table service (worth sixty thousand gulden), the most kitchens, the best food, the finest service, and the foremost orchestras. In an anonymous pamphlet entitled "The Journey of the Goddess of the Dance to the Vienna Apollo Palace," probably masterminded by Wolffsohn, Terpsichore, the muse of the dance, reports to Clio, the muse of history:

> [The main hall is] a circular hall built to perfect proportions. At equal intervals Ionic pillars are placed against the blue background of the walls and between these are narrow mirrors with wall brackets. Below the cornices there are little cavities all around the hall which are ornamented with colored glass and illuminated from within. Pictures from mythology decorate the ceiling. Set around the hall are one hundred round tables, each with its own tasteful comfortable chairs. On each table there is a centerpiece consisting of either a figurine, a candelabra or a basin from which springs forth a fountain.

Count August de la Garde, one of Vienna's unofficial early chroniclers, described the *Apollo* as

> without contradiction the most remarkable building in Austria's capital. Throughout endless corridors one could find magnificent palace halls, gardens with real bushes. From the brightly shining colors of 'a Turkish garden one came to the hut of a Laplander. Wide avenues, planted with real grass, with rose bushes and aromatic flowers offered delightful change. In the middle of the hall where one supped there rose a gigantic rock. From it emanated murmuring fountains which united into brooks flowing along among flower beds, tumbling into a basin which teemed with fish. Many styles of architecture vied for decoration in these rooms, the capricious Moorish, the pure Greek, the decorative Gothic ... There sparkled a thousand wax candles in chandeliers of colored crystal, while elsewhere the soft magic sheen of alabaster lamps imitated the gentle stars of the night ... and

while the fierceness of winter enveloped the earth one luxuriated here in the gentle freshness of spring.

Music was, of course, indispensable for such a pleasure palace built for dancing. Again Wolffsohn proved himself knowledgeable of the Vienna psyche. He engaged not only the finest dance orchestras, but also one of the foremost musical names of the time: Johann Nepomuk Hummel, Mozart's pupil, Beethoven's friend, and one of the formidable pianists of his day. Wolffsohn commissioned Hummel to compose special music, and a new term appeared on the musical horizon. The concert waltz was an anomalous name since it was used neither in concert nor for dancing as Wolffsohn had expected. It was left to Lanner and Strauss to give the Viennese the waltz that was innately theirs.

The *Apollosaal* was everything to the pleasure-loving Viennese. Their near-frenzied dancing may have been a subconscious effort to shut out reality — the terror of Napoleon. The wars of 1794, 1799, and 1805 had taken a terrible toll, and the armless, the peglegged, the blind, and the one-eyed in the streets of Vienna were a constant reminder of the grim reality of battles in which Napoleon seemed invincible as his armies swept all before them. In 1809 his bloody name again rose on the horizon. For the third time Napoleon was to lead his troops into Austria. If Austria's army was not at all equipped to cope with the invaders they were no less brave and loyal. Napoleon's unexpected defeat at Aspern led him to shift abruptly from the military to the diplomatic front, and again he was victorious. While Europe gaped and gasped in surprise and outrage the conqueror asked for the hand of the daughter of the vanquished emperor of Austria. The choice of emissary on such a delicate mission was significant; no unctuous diplomat was delegated on this errand. It was Napoleon's chief of staff who arrived in Vienna, an unmistakable gesture signifying that not love alone had dictated the proposal. The very move, however, raised the possibility of peace; Austrians hoped the constant horrors of war would no longer flood the country. When the French emissary and his party called on the Emperor, Franz wished to show that the spirit of Vienna was far from crushed.

Where else was there a more convincing place to display that spirit than at the *Apollo*? Wolffsohn was equal to the occasion. When the emperor, with his daughter Marie Louise on his arm, and Marshal Berthier, with his retinue, entered the *Apollo* on a dreary March evening in 1810, they were received by a deferent Wolffsohn at the head of his own retinue of one hundred servants, all in splendid livery. Wolffsohn's many activities were not unknown to his sovereign. Emperor Franz congratulated him on his surgical instruments and his artificial limbs and expressed surprise that Wolffsohn still found time to supervise so vast an establishment as the *Apollo*. There was an introduction to the French guest of honor and another exchange of pleasantries before Wolffsohn guided the imperial party and their wide-eyed French guests through five huge ballrooms, seemingly endless smaller ones, through gardens, triumphal arches adorned with the sovereign's initials, right down to the thirteen kitchens which served twenty-course dinners and hot food throughout every night.

Because of the royal visit, the halls were more crowded than usual, and everywhere the visitors were received by men standing at attention and by the deep curtsies of the ladies, much to the barely disguised satisfaction of the emperor. Duke Berthier was sure to report to his sovereign that nothing in Paris or in the rest of Europe could compare to this wonder of the world. It was a victory of sorts for Austria and for the emperor, but it was triumph for Wolffsohn because now the *Apollo*, beyond any doubt, was *the* dance establishment in Vienna.

The craze was barely beginning. In 1809, when Strauss was a lad of five, the German conductor Reichardt reported that "Vienna's love for dancing is now intensified to the point of becoming a dance mania ... Festivities at the Apollo are evenings not to be missed ... everybody rushed to the entertainment with incomprehensible haste, lightly clad despite snow and harsh winds ... the number of waltz dancers in Vienna on a single evening including, besides the Apollo, the large and small *Redoutensaal* and the other dance halls, amounted to about 50,000 people ... every fourth person in Vienna could be found dancing."

In such a world, severe and lighthearted in turn, Lanner and Strauss gaily took life and poverty in stride, reading in wide-eyed wonder how Hummel, the same Hummel who had composed the concert waltzes for the Apollo, owned several diamond rings and ten dozen gold watches (usually from princely or female admirers). Both young men had sprung from decent stock, and despite their lighthearted living they never descended to the degrading level of "bohemians." They might be down to one white shirt between them, but when they stepped out they wore gloves, a sign of respectability among the Viennese. Their lighthearted pranks soon became the talk of Vienna as did their superior music making. People began to frequent the places where they made music: the Café *Rebhuhn*, the *Wällisches Bierhaus*, and the *Kettenbrückensaal* (Chain Bridge Hall), where both Lanner and Strauss shared in the popularity. The story made the rounds that even the musicians' creditors were charmed by the music. Having failed to collect, they stayed to enjoy the performance.

The height of Biedermeier. Lanner, standing, leads the orchestra; Strauss Father, to his right, leads the violins. Oil painting by Charles Wilda.

Lanner again enlarged the orchestra because it began to be invited to larger halls in which the sound of a sextet would be lost. The group now swelled to twelve members, with Strauss taking over as the leader of the violins.

Those larger concert halls had brought about a curious cycle of events. They attracted a new public which included officers of the Austrian and Hungarian armies. Such a clientele, having been reared in the music of Haydn, Mozart, and Schubert, having heard or even played the music of Beethoven, Boccherini, Cherubini, Handel, Kozeluch, and Mehul, demanded a higher level of performance and content even in their dance music. At that point the clientele and the dance hall proprietors, as well as the musicians, faced a peculiar and far-reaching dilemma. True, Haydn, Mozart, Beethoven, and Schubert had written *Tänze*, but these had been conceived as concert pieces, not dances, and thus resisted inclusion into the everyday dance repertoire. Lanner recognized that atrocious trash often passed for dance music. To take an eight-bar theme, devoid of spirit to begin with, repeat it five tones higher only to return to the original key, ceased to please the aspiring musician. Thus he began to compose his own dances. Strauss, listening to his friend's ambitious labors, at first nodded absentmindedly while making love to the innkeeper's daughter.

Those who assembled nightly in high spirits at the *Sperl* were hardly aware of it, but Lanner was nearly robbed of his rightful place in waltz history when Carl Maria von Weber, a romantic of a different, more dramatic breed, briefly dabbled in the *genre*. The result was *Aufforderung zum Tanz (Invitation to the Dance)*, a charmingly triumphant love story in waltz tempo. Weber rejected the tyrannic gravitational pull of the waltz's three beats as the dominant factor; when he headed the first dance theme of *Aufforderung* with the word *wiegend* (gently swaying), the musical and visual pictures, superimposed on each other, told the delightful Viennese love story. The sophisticated Weber was far ahead of all his Viennese *confrères* in the development of waltz composition. His addition of introduction and coda alone gave the waltz balance and body which was not to be achieved again until the day of the mature Johann Strauss Son. Weber was never to return to the charming style, apparently stimulated by his stay in Vienna.

Lanner, obviously unaware of Weber's concert achievement, went his own way, slowly raising the popular waltz from its banal repetitiousness. Not only the public but the publishers as well appreciated his work, and prominent men bought and published all the music he could create. Lanner's first sixteen waltzes were published by Diabelli[2] before diminutive Haslinger, an archenemy in the publishing field,

---

2. Beethoven undeservedly immortalized Diabelli when he deigned to participate in a competition to write variations on a trite theme by Diabelli. Beethoven's *Diabelli Variations* were the result.

plucked Lanner from Diabelli's grasp. Haslinger's beautifully engraved and appointed publications of Lanner's music did much to spread Lanner's popularity.

With public and publishers clamoring increasingly for more music, Lanner's work soon became too burdensome to handle alone. He decided to divide his orchestra into two and to put Strauss in charge of the second one. The new orchestra under Strauss's direction made its debut at the inn *Zum Grünen Baum* (The Green Tree) and was an immediate success. Strauss now began to view the elevation in rank with mixed emotions. He loved the idea of conducting rather than playing, but he soon realized that he was expected to stand in Lanner's shadow, conducting Lanner's orchestra and Lanner's music. Thus the opportunity for Strauss to be, in a sense, his own boss also proved to be the opening wedge in the eventual break-up. By now Strauss had written a few waltz compositions of his own, but these were also presented as Lanner's, thus giving Strauss no official opportunity to assert himself as a composer in public. If Strauss was beginning to be dissatisfied, Lanner at first was unaware of it. Soon, however, Strauss's unspoken but obviously changed attitude toward his friend could not pass unnoticed. When Strauss asked Lanner to release him from the organization, Lanner had no choice but to agree to the ending of their partnership and expressed the hope that they would remain friends. However, there is no room for calm discussion with a smoldering volcano. Strauss had been champing at the bit too long, wanting to be master of his own fate. The last night of their partnership they were playing in the ballroom of *Zum Bock* (The Ram). Toward the end of the engagement in the early morning hours Lanner took the stand to give a brief farewell speech to his friend. But tiredness and inebriation had deprived the normally gentle Lanner of his customary charm and control. The intended farewell speech became more and more abusive as Lanner rambled on. Strauss did not take the belaboring kindly. Equally tired he let his proverbial temper flare into attack. Almost in reflex motion his bow lashed out at Lanner who was quick to retaliate. Within minutes the ballroom was in an uproar as, after a moment of surprised silence, the musicians took sides, going at each other with their bows and, after they had been broken, with their fiddles and clarinets and after that with chairs and anything throwable while the many pairs of dancers, still in tight embrace on the dance floor, watched in wry amusement. Suddenly the *Bock's* giant mirror, the pride of the establishment and famed throughout Vienna, disintegrated under the impact of a chair which had missed its intended victim. The ugly splintering crash, mingled with the screams of the frightened and injured, had a sobering effect on crowd and combatants alike, all of whom vanished quickly into the night.

Lanner was disconsolate. He had not really intended to hurt his friend. He sat down in the deserted hall amid the shambles of combat and, with tears in his eyes, mourned the sorry event and the loss of a friend by playing his *Trennungswalzer* (*Separation* waltz). Strauss, explosive but good-natured, did not hold a grudge. On the occasion of the wedding of Lanner's daughter he made an unscheduled appearance to congratulate the bride. As fate would have it, the wedding party took place in the same ballroom in which the final fracas had occurred. As Strauss appeared in the door all movement and conversation stopped. The music died away after a few hesitant bars as all eyes turned to the two men, Lanner and Strauss. The spirit of the happy occasion prevailed. Lanner's face lit up and he opened his arms to the unexpected but most welcome guest. The two rushed towards each other and embraced amid shouts and tears of joy. The artistic separation, however, remained.

That "fever of the soul" was to carry Strauss far beyond the suburbs where he had started, far beyond Vienna. Lanner, on the other hand, disliked travel and seldom moved beyond the limits of his beloved city. And although he truly bemoaned the separation from the friend of his youth, he was no less in demand without him. History gave the laurels to Lanner as the true inventor of the classic Viennese waltz. His "violet-scented" gentle melodies flowed from his quill, epitomizing the love for his city, reaching its apex in his most famous waltz *Die Schönbrunner*. He had begun writing his ingratiating waltzes while Strauss had made love to Anna Streim, the innkeeper's daughter, destined to be a historic Viennese figure in her own right. Lanner continued to compose after he married and, later, in discreet seclusion with his charming mistress in the suburbs, while Strauss roamed the city, driven by his insatiable desire for lights and acclaim. Just as Schubert and Beethoven had shared the same Vienna yet had remained worlds apart, so Lanner and Strauss, although sharing the city musically, went their own ways.

If Lanner and Strauss, joined, had made a fascinating pair through visual and temperamental contrast, their separation made life even more interesting in the musical Vienna of the 1800s. Lanner continued in the circle of admirers, honored, acclaimed, fêted. In 1842 he was judged superior to Strauss. "Lanner's music has more spirit and soul ... It not only moves the feet, but also the heart and soul." His fame continued to grow as he was honored to conduct the ball music at the coronation of Emperor Ferdinand in Milan. It was his only journey far away from Vienna, and he left the Viennese dancing his Biedermeier-inspired waltzes with such typical Lanner titles as *Hoffnungsstrahlen* (Rays of Hope) and *Terpsichore*.

Strauss was finally his own master. No longer was he to watch in tacit indignation while some of his own compositions passed as Lanner's work. On the occasion of his abrupt exit from the Lanner orchestra, sixteen musicians had walked out with him. That was truly an act of faith on their part. Although their friendship to Strauss assured him a ready-made ensemble, employment for either him or his group was not at all assured. Unworried, he went ahead with his marriage to Anna, now pregnant with his child, and set out to find work in music- and dance-hungry Vienna.

Strauss's exit, at first, had a consequence distressing for Lanner. Lanner's growing popularity and increasing flood of engagements brought about a tight schedule now compounded by Johann's absence. In 1826 the situation became so demanding that Lanner had to employ a *Fiaker* on a standby basis in order to commute swiftly from one hall to another (each having announced in large letters the "personal appearance" of Herr Lanner), conduct two or three selections, take his bows before rushing to the next ball where the procedure would be repeated, and so on till dawn. Like many men in his profession Lanner was a night worker, in music-making as well as in composing. Upon returning from a ball, a concert, a dance, Lanner settled down to an unvarying routine. After changing into a comfortable robe and indulging in a final "nip," he would light his favorite *Meerschaum* pipe and reach for a sheet of music paper. First to appear in the corner were the words *"Mit Gott, Josef Lanner"* and inspiration would begin to flow rapidly and neatly, in perfectly shaped rounded notes, with hardly a correction or pause.

What further compounded the dilemma of time was Lanner's marriage in 1826 to Franziska Jahns, the daughter of a glovemaker. It had been love at first sight. The wedding was a social event and an overflow crowd attended the ceremony at St. Josef's Church. Many a heart was broken when the handsome twenty-seven-year-old Lanner took Franzi for his bride. The festive air was heightened by the presence of one of the most prestigious men in Vienna's dance world, the owner of the *Sperl*, who honored Lanner by being his best man. In 1829 Lanner received his highest accolade, his appointment to the coveted post of imperial music director. This made domesticity a seldom tasted way of life, despite the birth of Kathi. Lanner's life now totally revolved around late concerts and balls, nightly composition, sleep until noon, followed by rehearsals, conferences, and afternoon appearances, after which there was only enough time left for a hasty meal, a change of clothes, a brief kiss, and the rush to the first evening appearance. If Lanner thus was allowed little family life, he was responsible for family needs and obligations. Toward that end, as well as for reasons of prestige, he applied for membership in the *Wiener Tonkünstlersozietät* (Vienna Tone Artists Society) since that organization provided pension rights and death benefits to its members and their families. Despite his fame and popularity he was refused membership; the society felt that his popularity in light music was beneath the dignity of the society's lofty aims. That Haydn, Mozart, and Schubert had also been refused membership before him was of scant comfort to

Lanner, whose dizzying pace must have concerned him and his family. A look at the main events in his engagement calendar confirms the speed with which everything in his schedule—eating, sleeping, composing, rehearsing, concertizing—had to be performed.

Sunday	— Dance at Unger's *Kaffeehaus* in the suburb of Hernals
Monday	— Ball at the well-known dance establishment *Paradeisgartl* (Garden of Paradise)
Tuesday	— Soirée at the *Weissen Engel* (White Angel), forerunner of famed Dommaier's Casino
Wednesday	— Rehearsing new waltzes, conferences with publisher Haslinger, concert at Wagner's *Kaffeehaus*
Thursday	— Open air concert at the *Volksgarten* (People's Garden)
Friday	— Garden concert at the establishment *Zu den Zwei Tauben* (The Two Doves) at the *Wasserglacis* outside the city walls
Saturday	— Dance at the *Schwarzer Adler* (Black Eagle)[3] in Baden, the famed spa near Vienna

The fact that such a weekly schedule was duplicated by dozens of other dance orchestras bespeaks the joy of music and dance in Vienna.

In 1833 a new dimension widened Lanner's artistic life. Raab, balletmaster of the *Josefstädter Theater* and an ardent admirer of Lanner's music, suggested to the composer that he extend his talents into the field of ballet. Lanner had always been an admirer of the theatre, with and without music, although his tight schedule gave him little opportunity to enjoy it. He hesitated to venture into the field of ballet. But Raab was adamant and eloquent. "You say dance music is your field? Well, what is ballet but dancing out a story?" Lanner assented. The *Josefstädter Theater* had only recently emerged from a period of neglect and downdrift. The new management was eager to return to the previously high standard of the theatre by devoting itself again to a repertoire of drama, ballet, and opera. Thus Vienna became acquainted with such favorites of the day as Meyerbeer's *Robert der Teufel (Robert the Devil)*, Auber's *Fra Diavolo*, and Kreutzer's *Nachtlager in Granada (Night's Lodging in Granada)*. The management hoped to revitalize the ballet *genre* and at the same time to fill its depleted coffers by offering Lanner's art at their theatre exclusively.

---

3. Such colorful names as "Two Doves," "White Angel," "Black Bear," and "Black Eagle" for inns, coffee houses, and even ordinary dwellings remind of medieval days when streets had neither names nor numbers, and dwellings were identified only by the sign they displayed. Some of these famous signs remain to this day in rural Austria and Germany.

Thus, on 24 October 1833 the following announcement appeared:

Zum 1. Male
"Policinello's Entstehung"
Pantomime in einem Act
von der Erfindung des Herrn Raab
Musik von Herrn Josef Lanner
Vorher:
"Der hölzerne Säbel"
Singspiel in einem Akt
Musik von Mozart'schen Motiven arrangiert von
Herrn Ignatz Ritter v. Seyfried

For the 1st Time
"Pulcinello's Creation"
Pantomime in one Act
In the invention of Mister Raab
Music by Mister Josef Lanner
Preceding:
"The Wooden Sabre"
Musical Play in One Act
Music from Mozart's Themes arranged by
Ignatz Count von Seyfried

The premiere proved profitable as a musical as well as a social event, with Lanner's music the drawing card of the evening, as the management had fervently hoped. Despite the flimsy plot Lanner's contribution received repeated ovations. The *pièce de résistance* was the *pas de quatre* in waltz time—Lanner at his best—and the final tableau again evoked stormy applause. The press was less enthusiastic. *Der Spiegel* ("A Newspaper for Art, Elegance and Fashion") expressed the opinion that "Lanner's music is melodious and corresponds to the character of the pantomime without being particularly outstanding." But the public continued to flock to his performances. When Lanner gave a special benefit ball and performance at the *Römischer Kaiser* (Roman Emperor) under the heading "Homage to Womanhood," his female admirers swarmed in to hear such beguiling waltzes as *Die Unwiderstehlichen (The Irresistibles), Verlockungs Walzer (Allurement* waltz), and an added feature, the first performance of the *Paris* waltz, dedicated to the Empress of France. This was followed by a garden fête for which Count Ferdinand Palffy graciously opened his famous garden in deference to Lanner. It was entitled *Ein Mittsommernachtstraum* (no allusion to Shakespeare) and was attended by six thousand dancers, strollers, and onlookers. To make the Lanner festival an outstanding occasion the count even opened his renowned art gallery to the public and also consented to a fireworks display on his palace grounds. The dance was held in a specially erected tent of gigantic proportions. It was the custom on such a gala occasion that a new waltz be premiered. Lanner's *Die Abenteurer (The Adventurers)* had to be repeated ten times. The memorable evening was brought to a close with a torchlight procession which, in turn, became a spontaneous homage to Lanner.

In 1833 Strauss had visited Budapest, the Hungarian capital, and had triumphed. This may have given the reluctant traveler Lanner the impetus to do the same a year later. His visit was no less a success and his *Pester Walzer* became an immediate favorite with his Hungarian admirers. The joyful Hungarian experience lived on and found an echo in one of his most famous waltzes, *Die Werber (The Suitors)*, which opens with a gypsy strain before the Viennese mood takes over. A Budapest newspaper aptly discerned the basic difference in approach of the two greatest waltz composers of the time: "Both Strauss and Lanner shine like two stars in the same heaven, only the light that shines from their compositions is different. The first dazzles, the other illuminates ... Strauss speaks through the spirit to the heart, Lanner through the heart to the feet."

The initial Budapest success encouraged Lanner to return a year later. The journey required six especially hired express coaches to accommodate the orchestra. Again a new waltz, *Abschied von Pest (Farewell to Pest)* graced the occasion. One special waltz, dedicated to the Countess Appolonia Belcznay, was acknowledged by the Hungarian aristocrat with a gift of fifty ducats.

When Lanner returned to Vienna in March 1835, much of the *Fasching* was already over but the owner of the dance emporium *Zum Schaf* (The Sheep) lost no time in engaging Lanner and his ensemble. The *Schaf* at that time shared popularity with the *Sperl* and the *Apollo* for the oddest of reasons; it was the very antithesis of the *Apollosaal*. Where the *Apollo* was the epitome of the luxury establishment, the *Schaf* was a barn-like building constructed of plain planks, totally bare of any ornamentation except the crude image of a black sheep over its gigantic door. Only tallow candles lit its cavernous interior. But in its warm, cozy dimness which hid and tolerated, the burgher could remove his jacket, chat and joke, eat and drink, kiss and flirt, and above all dance in shirt sleeves and open collar. Cigar smoke was layered in such heavy clouds that the many candles of the hall could barely penetrate it. Lanner was playing lustily the night of 1 May 1835 when a police officer entered the hall escorted by a troop of burly policemen. Burghers and their partners for the night stared in disbelief and the inevitable ladies of the night, fearing the worst, faded discreetly into the impenetrable cigar smoke. The police officer walked through the dancers, who obediently opened a path for him, straight to the podium where Lanner was conducting.

"You are herewith ordered to cease playing immediately."

"But why, my permit has been issued and is in order. *Ich bin der Lanner.* I have the permit right here ..."

"I know who you are—and never mind the permit. All music must cease immediately. The Emperor is dead."

Vienna mourned and went without music for six weeks; even the street musicians were forbidden to ply their trade. Finding themselves on the threshold of starvation, the wretched creatures found a way to take advantage of the mourning period. With their faces reflecting tragic grief, they would silently occupy a street corner, their instruments in full view but silent and draped with black crepe; the street musicians had temporarily turned beggars.

In 1836 another unpretentious stage work with music by Lanner was produced: *Der Preis einer Lebensstunde (The Price of an Hour of Life),* "a romantic fairy tale with songs, in two acts and introduction." Despite its naive libretto, or perhaps because of it, the play was heard innumerable times with the applause mostly directed at Lanner's musical interludes and songs.

Since the second journey to Budapest had not yielded the same gratification as the first one, Lanner in 1837 turned his gaze southward and accepted an invitation to Graz, the capital of the province of Styria. The reception there was all a famous man could ask for. The elite of Graz society, in their finest carriages and finery, met his coach en route, escorted him into the city and showered him with kindness during his stay. A Graz newspaper reported, "Lanner is here, that dear genial Lanner with the melancholy minor notes in his gay tunes. Lanner, who makes the feet jump, whose melodies sound on the banks of the Seine and the shore of the Neva, whose name is called in the icy north and the blooming south, Lanner is here." During his Graz sojourn Lanner received offers to concertize in other major cities of the realm, Klagenfurt, the capital of Carinthia, and Triest among them. But the composer, disliking prolonged travel and fearing undue hardship for his men on a stagecoach trip through the Alps, declined. But the splendor of his visit to Graz was again recalled in his *Graz Soirée* and *Alpen-Walzer.*

A new breeze seemed to blow excitedly through Vienna's ballrooms in 1837 and 1838. The *Sperl* started its famed champagne balls, where bottles of French champagne could be won by the dancers in games and dance competitions. Lanner again provided his share of the innovations with his *Champagner Knall Gallopade (Cham-*

pagne Cork Pop Gallop). Another novelty was the sudden popularity of the French and British custom of masked balls, the most famous of which was held on 22 April 1838, in the *Redoutensaal* for the benefit of the victims of the disastrous Budapest flood. Its main feature was a musical extravaganza entitled "Coronation Festival" which included a massed trumpet choir of fifty players, a number of choral groups and, of course, of Lanner's combined orchestras. That particular evening, however, was only a small part of the festivities surrounding the coronation of Emperor Ferdinand and the crowning glory of Lanner's life. To insure Austria's presence in the Italian provinces, the coronation was scheduled to take place in Milan, and Lanner was chosen to conduct the festival dance music on that occasion. Even before departing for Milan, Lanner and his orchestra had become involved in the festivities which were in full swing months before the actual event and were a marvelous excuse for dancing. There was a feast at the *Augarten* which had as its highpoint the allegory *Ariadne auf Naxos,* or *The Triumph of Love* with Lanner conducting his full orchestra. So great was the demand that the spectacle had to be repeated three times and was witnessed by ten thousand Viennese. Those present at the last performance noticed with disappointment that a substitute conductor was in charge of a somewhat reduced orchestra. Lanner had already departed with the elite of his ensemble—twenty-three musicians—for Milan.

Lanner later delighted in recalling an incident which bordered on comic opera. To take full advantage of the long journey, Lanner had arranged for concerts en route in Linz, Innsbruck, and Triest. On the way from Salzburg to Innsbruck one sunny day, the company decided on the spur of the moment to stop, stretch their legs, and wander a bit into the magnificent alpine landscape in a small alpine village. Thus resplendent in Napoleonic-like dress—red cutaways, white trousers, two-pointed hats, and ceremonial swords—they climbed down from their carriages and leisurely sauntered through the village. What they had not anticipated was the fact that, except on French troops, the villagers had never seen such uniforms. At first startled, then frightened, they took their women and children and fled into their houses amid shouts that "The enemy is coming." Only the most strenuous persuasion in Austrian dialect by Lanner kept the villagers from going for the muskets to fight off "the enemy." After drinks had been passed around, Lanner and his gallant gang departed amid handshakes and laughter, and proceeded, via Innsbruck, Triest, Verona, Brescia, and Bergamo to Milan. Lanner's party had been given protected passage from Vienna to Milan. (Lanner's passport for the journey is in the archives of the *Gesellschaft der Musikfreunde.)* However, despite the honor and excitement of the coronation ball, Lanner counted the days until his homeward journey. But his fame had preceded him and he eventually granted requests to give concerts in

Venice and Graz. Needless to say, he and his men were feted and plied with an abundance of food and drink in both cities.

Lanner's occasional overindulgence in Vienna's light young wine was well known and humorously tolerated, even by the imperial party. When he once arrived for a court festivity in slightly inebriated condition, a princely chamberlain suggested that he "rest" and let an assistant conduct but Lanner, swaying, steadfastly refused. However, soon after the opening waltz nobody, including the imperial party, could ignore Lanner's condition. Goodnaturedly the emperor dispatched his chamberlain, Baron Kutschera, to diplomatically save Lanner from falling off the podium. Not all members of the court were as indulgent and understanding. Archduchess Sophie approached Lanner once between dances as he was wiping the perspiration from his face. "That must have been strenuous," she addressed the conductor, indicating her approval by the very fact that she deigned to address him. "You're so right, Your Highness," was Lanner's reply instead of the silent bow of gratitude expected from him. Wishing to emphasize the extent of his strenuous activity, he proceeded to open his tailcoat to display his sweat-drenched shirt. "There, you can see for yourself how I'm sweating." Scandalized by the vulgar display, the duchess recoiled, held her handkerchief to her royal nose and with a haughty shake of her royal head turned in disgust. Fluttering her royal fan rapidly to indicate her royal annoyance, she reported the indignity to her royal person to the royal chamberlain in charge of royal court balls. Lanner, in disgrace, was suspended for months before being restored to his honorary post.

The incident is typical of this relaxed, honest, sentimental arch-Viennese. Easily persuaded, he was easy prey to almost anyone who approached him for a handout. Remembering the poverty of his childhood, he would be moved by even the most improbable stories of suffering, particularly when he was mildly under the influence of alcohol. A household name in Vienna, he could be seen, in his rare free moments, walking the streets, nattily dressed, his beloved *Meerschaum* pipe absentmindedly held between his teeth. However, once musical matters were involved the picture changed abruptly. Unlike his many musical *confrères* in Vienna, he permitted no indulgence in execution; the gentle Lanner could explode in vulgar Viennese dialect when things sounded sloppy or not precisely to his liking. "Would you like me to spread some sand so you won't slip and slide?" he hurled at a violinist whose intonation was not up to Lanner's idea of perfection. To the detriment of his family, the highlights of Lanner's life revolved about the conductor's podium. Whenever he appeared on the podium a storm of applause would arise. After acknowledging it with a slight bow, he would pirouette towards his men and, with his violin at his left hip, would conduct with his bow. But his eager audiences really waited for the moment when he would tuck his violin under his chin and play with his men. Then even the dancers would halt their graceful turns and succumb to Lanner's magic sound. The most moving moments came on the occasions during intermission when Lanner sat among his men and played his violin. With a far-away look in his eyes, he would improvise, usually in high register. The huge ballroom would listen in silence with faces lifted toward the spot on stage where a single man sat and dreamed on his violin. Eventually the flute-like tones of Lanner's violin would subside, and as he rose, as if awakening from a dream, the hall would resound with thundering applause.

Lanner's appearances outside the concert hall or ballroom were rare, but when he did perform in his official capacity as *Kapellmeister* of the Second Burgher Regiment of Vienna, huge crowds gathered to hear and see him. The importance of those military corps of the city, constituted from among the Vienna populace, had of course greatly diminished, and their functions were reduced to participation in ceremonies, parades, processions, and concerts. Consequently, Lanner's position and functions within the regimental band imposed few obligations upon him but he loved to conduct them because he knew he looked handsome in his smart uniform. He even composed a *Bürger Marsch* for his outfit. Strauss also conducted a regimental band of burghers. Artistic competition flourished and was heatedly discussed in Vienna, particularly when Johann Strauss Son entered the Vienna musical arena conducting yet another regiment. As late as 1839, only four years before Lanner's death, the matter of musical preference among the Viennese remained unresolved, with many still handing Lanner the palm. The Viennese press reported: "Lanner is superior to Strauss in the technical handling of his instrument and in the versatility of his presentation ... the tones flow from his strings lovely and gently but soon swell with penetrating power which imbues the entire orchestra with stormy passion to suddenly make them jubilate or weep in melancholy ... Lanner makes the Viennese laugh and cry."

The opening of the railroad to Brünn (Brno) and a personal invitation from Count Ugarte brought Lanner to the lovely Moravian capital in 1838. For the occasion Lanner produced the loudly acclaimed *Brünner Walzer*. Later, however, it was found that it was not new but was his *Liebesträume* waltz retitled. Under pressure of business Lanner had resorted to the shabby trick of simply changing the title and presenting the little known waltz as a new composition.

Other pressures had begun to throw their shadow on Lanner's life. The graceful girl with the golden hair whom Lanner had married had grown into a stout, shrewish, overdressed, neglectful woman who made Lanner's life nearly unbearable, particularly since she was aware that she never had been Lanner's artistic equal or partner. Lanner's absences and night work aggravated Franzi's jealousy. His absences and the frequency of ugly scenes increased. According to reports Frau Lanner's jealousy was not without cause. Eventually she was observed sneaking into the places where her famous and adulated husband concertized. She then would sit, overdressed, stony-faced, and unapproachable, watching her husband's flirtations yet unable to interfere without creating a scene. When one specific female's name began to appear with increasing frequency, it provided the breaking point which brought about separation.

Despite his elevated position in Vienna's life, Lanner had found his *paramour* again among the ranks of Vienna's burghers: Marie Kraus, a butcher's daughter. After settling a substantial alimony on Franzi, Lanner moved to the suburb of Döbling where he built a new home and life. Marie was the opposite of Franzi. She was to devote her entire life to the master in love and adulation. Even before she openly became his mistress, nothing had meant as much to her as his presence and well being. During cold winter nights, while he was busy concertizing or playing at a ball, she would wait for him in a *Fiaker* near the ballroom entrance, either reading by candle light or shivering in darkness until he joined her in the gray dawn at the end of the engagement. Soon their liaison became an open secret, and the tolerant Viennese delighted in their undisguised fondness for each other.

By then Vienna's choice of first-class dance musicians had narrowed to two names—Lanner and Strauss. True, there were others who played respectably, such as Phillip Fahrbach, a former associate of Strauss, but none of them were artistically as good. Lanner, not surprisingly, had the heavier work load of the two because, unlike Strauss, Lanner was not fond of prolonged absences and thus was more readily available for the major dance events. Thus the Viennese magistrates chose him for their masked ball, as did the Austrian army officers for their elegant dance, an event of the highest rank.

Another milestone in Lanner's career, his first appearance, in purple dress uniform, as *Hofkapellmeister* at the imperial court ball, occurred on 16 January 1840. He was not allowed to rest on his laurels, because a few days later the city of Pressburg (Bratislava) claimed his presence. There one of the great lights on the musical horizon—Franz Liszt—was present. Liszt rushed up to Lanner after the performance to shake his hand in congratulation. Two days later Lanner was back in Vienna, no mean feat in view of the rutted roads of his day. The imperial *Redoutensaal* clamored for his presence, and he was delighted to oblige. A year later, the Imperial Opera did Lanner the honor of including his *Steirische Tänze (Styrian Dances)* in their ballet *Die Macht der Kunst (The Power of Art)*. But more important in the annals of the dance was one of Lanner's most enduring waltzes, *Die Romantiker*, which he dedicated to Tsarina Alexandra Feodorovna of Russia.

The house which Lanner had built for himself and Marie had now all the aspects of a museum, although he was barely forty years old. It was filled with presentations, prizes, wreaths, and medals which had been pressed upon him by emperors and potentates, cities, organizations, and individual admirers. A special place of honor was reserved for Lanner's collection of pipes, as famous in Vienna as his waltzes. Lanner possessed literally hundreds of pipes in precious and aromatic woods, clay, *Meerschaum*, and porcelain from many parts of the world, many carved into fancy shapes of heads, animals, musical instruments. Such was his passion that if he spied an interesting pipe at a dance or in the street he would rush up to its owner and offer considerable amounts of money on the spot to acquire it.

By that time another innovation of dubious musical or entertainment value had crept into the Vienna waltz tradition—the sung waltz, the waltz with a text. Some musical hack had discovered that a waltz with words was more saleable than one without. Few waltzes had been composed for piano alone; one generally needed a trio, preferably a salon orchestra. But to sing a waltz, however inane the words might be, and they usually were, only a piano was needed, and often a harp or guitar sufficed. Almost without exception the words, usually applied to an already finished instrumental waltz, were so innocuous, so outrageously stupid that they destroyed the artistic value of the piece. This became glaringly apparent because the text, regardless of its own meter, was bound to be subservient to the relentless three-quarter waltz time. Thus it came about, when a Vienna vocalist presented Lanner's lovely *Abendstern (Evening Star)* waltz with words added, that the opening phrase was completely dismembered into inane nonsense and was sung, "Ich hab' sie - nur auf die - Stirne ge- küsst." In translation the phrase would mean "Her forehead I kissed, that was all," but the German dismemberment of the phrase cannot be carried over into English. Later Millöcker was to use a similar phrase in his operetta *The Beggar Student*, but he had learned a lesson and tailored the music to the words.

Unfortunately composers had no recourse against such demeaning of their artistic material. Anything a composer wrote was unprotected and immediately usurpable by any dilettante or pseudo-professional who wished to make a fast gulden, often without even bothering to mention whose material had been appropriated. The worst offenders in that respect were those who were among Vienna's most popular entertainers. Even talented men, like the folk singer Johann Baptist Moser, had no qualms about fashioning words to Lanner's (or others') waltzes and presenting them as individual songs together with songs by Schubert and other, minor, Viennese song composers. Soon an entire new breed of composers would arise to bring to Vienna a new style of music, the Viennese folk song, which celebrated everything for which Vienna was justly famous—its women, its wine, its waltzes. New names such as Krakauer, Sioli, Siczynsky, and Pick would endear themselves to Viennese everywhere with songs that were to be known the world over, for example, Siczynsky's *Wien, Wien, nur Dū allein (Vienna, City of My Dreams)* and the most famous of them all, Pick's *Fiakerlied*. First with the dance melodies of Lanner, Strauss, or Fahrbach, later with Vienna's famous folk songs, the folk singers would take the town and public by storm. This was by no means entertainment solely for the lower strata. Artists like Moser, Johann Fürst, or Milly Turrececk [4] were invited to sing in the palaces of Viennese nobility, and when those true folk artists sang in public, fashionable carriages could be seen lined up for many blocks near the establishment that advertised their names. Regardless of where those artists began their performance—on the stage or near a piano—the traditional highlight of the evening would find them atop a table in the center of the hall, singing with an abandon that had the audience usually on their feet, demanding more.

No less in demand were the instrumental quartets which usually performed in the inns. Theirs was an even older tradition, going back into the middle ages when music (and news) was transmitted for entertainment all along the Danube's banks. Their arenas were the open air beer gardens and especially the small inns in the suburban vineyards. The quartets usually consisted of two violins, accordion, and guitar. The most famous of all folk quartets was the Schrammel Quartet (two violins, clarinet, and guitar), which became such a favorite of Emperor Franz Joseph that all Viennese folk quartets have been named "Schrammel Quartets" ever since. And when in a Grinzing inn Schrammel played and the young wine flowed, then tongues loosened and inhibitions vanished to reveal the best of the proverbial Viennese *Gemütlichkeit* in waltz and *Wienerlied* (Viennese song).

Lanner's effect on the development of the waltz was outstanding. Unlike all his contemporaries save Strauss, he made a conscious effort to free his music from the tyranny of the three-quarter beat. In one of his earliest compositions, the *Terpsichore* waltz, opus 12, he had attempted a brief introduction, something unheard of among the purveyors of cheap dance music who only wanted to get the dance underway quickly. Elaborate waltz introductions would have to wait until Strauss Son, however, the *coda*, or closing section, was to achieve elaborate treatment from Strauss

4. Or "Fiaker (Fiacre) Milli" as she was called in Vienna. She was immortalized by Richard Strauss in his opera *Arabella* with libretto by Hugo von Hofmannsthal.

A rare contemporary photograph of the original Schrammel folk quartet, the favorite of Emperor Franz Joseph. (Courtesy of the Historic Museum of the City of Vienna.)

Father. In his opus 31, the "Magic Horn" *Ländlers*, Lanner contributed another unique innovation to waltz literature—the program waltz, the waltz with a story line. The opening portion was devoted to "The Dancers," part two to "The Lovers," part three to "The Drinkers" (a logical Viennese continuity), and the finale, true to its alpine dance form, to "Memories of Upper Austria." Another innovation in the same *Ländler* sequence was that of ending the "Magic Horn" on a whispered gossamer pianissimo instead of in the expected fortissimo melodic whirlwind. Other waltzes featured such story lines as "Stormy Night" (in waltz tempo!), "Day Break," "The Herd in the Alps," "Shawm Call and Song of the Herdsman," "Evening Bells," "Country Feast," and "Peace and Rest." When we notice how akin Lanner here was in spirit to Beethoven, we will understand Mendelssohn's comment "Praise the masters, large and small."

With his waltz *Hoffnungsstrahlen (Rays of Hope)*, opus 158, Lanner entered upon his most mature and prodigious period. There followed waltz after ingratiating waltz in a profusion of inspiration. Opus 161, *Hofballtänze (Court Ball Dances)*, abounds in gaiety, melodious charm, and syncopations which leapfrog with seemingly naive abandon. Schubert smiles through the pages of *Steirische Tänze (Styrian Dances)* while *Die Romantiker* and *Die Werber* exude full-blown romanticism. *Die Flotten (The Lively Ones)* lived up to its name, *Abendstern*, opus 180 was the exact opposite with its lyrical bent, and *Die Vorstädter (The Suburbanites)*, opus 195 had the brash vivaciousness of Vienna's famed saucy washerwomen. Unquestionably the highpoint of Lanner's claim to the title "Prince of the Waltz" was his *Schönbrunner* waltz, his apotheosis of beloved Vienna, mirroring the beauty of Vienna's women and the charm of the city epitomized in the Habsburgs' summer palace, Schönbrunn.

Lanner's themes were not the only ones which he wove into his waltzes. If a melody was ingratiating and adaptable to dancing, he made it part of his musical fabric, always giving credit to the composer. As could be expected, the melodies of the violinists of his day greatly attracted Lanner. Thus the Viennese could hear Paganini's or "Ole" Bull's [5] melodies either in virtuoso rendition or as transcribed by Lanner for his orchestra. Lanner was also taken with the melodiousness of the Italians, and during almost any concert the tunes of Bellini, Donizetti, or Rossini were bound to appear. Surprisingly, he borrowed from only one German composer, Lindpaintner, to whose opera *The Vampyre* Lanner repeatedly returned for inspi-

---

5. Borneman "Ole" Bull (1810-1880) was a Norwegian violinist, popular throughout Europe with a great following in the United States to which he made five concert tours. Somewhat arrogantly he restricted himself to the playing of his own compositions.

ration. Although praised by Mendelssohn, Peter Joseph von Lindpaintner (1791-1856) is completely forgotten today.

It is generally assumed that *Der Traum (The Dream)* was Lanner's last composition. However, in 1919 an untitled program composition by Lanner was unearthed. Had the story line survived it would have provided a fascinating journey through Lanner's musical imagination and invention as Spanish themes mingle with Viennese waltzes; the popping of champagne corks is woven together with the rattle of drums and the roar of muskets; the whistle of a railroad train is counterpointed with a *Schnellpolka* until the dream-like fantasy sequence ends with an immediately recognizable beloved refrain: *"S'gibt nur eine Kaiserstadt, s'gibt nur ein Wien"* ("There's only one emperor's city, there's only one Vienna"). If a program is missing, the date is not: "5 Jänner 1843" clearly stamps the work as Lanner's last. Why it remained unpublished when publishers were fighting over Lanner's compositions will remain a mystery. Lanner may have waited for the outcome of the tug-of-war between publishers Haslinger and Mechetti, or he may have simply put it aside and forgotten about it in the rush of activity.

One of the specialties of any dance composer in Vienna had to be the gallop, certainly the most spirited and most strenuous of dances. Gallops were danced in two versions, either sideways in a straight line called *Gallopaden,* or with brain-scrambling rapidity in whirling motion. Lanner's awareness of the gallop's popularity, despite the many deaths its rapidity caused among Vienna's overweight population, prompted him to turn them out in great numbers. His always neatly written manuscripts bore such titles as *Schnellsegler (Fast Sailor), Jagd Gallopade (Hunt Gallop), Tarantel Gallop,* and, the one most indicative in title of the speed and strain involved, *Bruder lauf, Bruder spring (Brother Run, Brother Jump).* Here again Lanner was prone to reach into Bellini's, Meyerbeer's, or Rossini's musical pockets. On the evening of performance he would simply announce a gallop on the tune of this or that composer, opera, or melody. Although this was common practice, even among the greatest of classical composers, it caused the less inspired of Lanner's competitors to discredit him and cast doubt on his inventiveness. His not-so-private life was of course the repeated target of his critics. This he took with serenity. However, when his competitors went so far as to assault his professional honor, cast doubt on his artistry, even disrupt his performances, and instigate fistfights, he became extremely agitated and during one such incident was known to take to bed with high fever. Strauss, who was totally free of professional envy as far as Lanner was concerned, never condoned such petty attacks. The Viennese did not seem to take the disruptions seriously, although such happenings were eagerly discussed in newspapers and in public. When paid *agents provocateurs* would briefly disrupt a dance, the dancers themselves would watch in good humor and amusement then swarm back to the floor. Lanner remained an undisputed Vienna idol, and on the evening when he unveiled his greatest waltz and his swan song, *Die Schönbrunner*, enthusiasm reached heights never before attained and he was forced to repeat the waltz twenty-one times.

By then Lanner's coffers were filled to overflowing and he could indulge in such luxuries as a housekeeper, a cook, a valet, and his own *Fiaker* to be on call at all hours of day or night. It was his hectic schedule which bore within itself the seeds of death. Other incidents and professional hazards contributed: the heavy perspiration while performing in drafty halls and his bouts with Vienna's clear wine. He began to complain of ailments but refused to change his schedule or mode of life. Dommayer's Casino applauded him for the last time on 22 March 1843. By the end of the evening he felt "bone-tired" and friends accompanied him home, where Marie immediately put him to bed. Typhus made short work of the weakened body, and inflammation of both lungs aggravated matters beyond the meager knowledge of medical assistance available. On Good Friday, 14 April 1843, Lanner was dead.

Thousands upon thousands followed Lanner's flower-laden casket and cortege to its resting place. In a dark corner of its conscience Vienna had always hidden a troubled tear over the treatment it had accorded some of its greatest sons—Mozart and Schubert, for example—in life and in death. Tears flowed freely in the knowledge that "the prince of the waltz" had been irretrievably lost. The reporter of the newspaper *Der Wanderer* touched on a sensitive nerve in his eulogy: "Do not take advantage of the occasion to slander the dead by reprimanding the living who gathered *en masse* for the funeral of a dance fiddler, while other more deserving men in the service of nobler higher music went to their grave with barely a notice. Remember, there are few who value the nobler, higher music, while a waltz will touch many thousands at first sounding."

After Lanner's death there developed a faithful Lanner cult which lasted for years. On his name day—Josephi, 19 March—Vienna and its musicians devoted the evening to Lanner's music, and every prominent performer in popular music—Morelli, Fahrbach, and later Carl Michael Ziehrer—adhered to the tradition. On this occasion in 1885, Fahrbach, although ailing and forewarned not to work too strenuously, did not wish to relinquish the honor of conducting the opening of the concert dedicated to his late friend. He opened with Lanner's famed *Schönbrunner* waltz; it was also to be Fahrbach's swan song. In the midst of the waltz, violin and bow dropped from his hands and he collapsed into the arms of his son.

One of Vienna's famous parks embowers the monument to the two friends and great masters of the waltz, although, Lanner's gentler tunes were later overshadowed by those of the more temperamental Strauss. But Vienna did not forget:

> Wenn Wien zurück in jene Zeiten schaut
> Die es mit Herzensfreudigkeit genossen
> Da werden auch die Töne wieder laut
> Die einst aus Lanners Liederschatz geflossen
> Ein Schatz der Heiterkeit, Humor, Gemüt
> Von Blumen deren jede duftig blüht
>
> > Elmar

> When Vienna recalls the day
> Enjoyed to heart's delight
> Then tunes will have their way
> That flowed from Lanner's treasured flight
> A trove of humor, heart and cheer
> Of fragrant flowers without peer.

3

Poets and Politics

Reminiscences on *Alt Wien* or Old Vienna, a period lasting roughly from the end of the Congress of Vienna in 1815 to the fateful year 1848, conjure up its most pernicious label — Biedermeier — and the names of the immortals, such as Schubert and Raimund, who most poignantly personify that "Golden Age of Vienna." The term "Biedermeier" stemmed from a series of humorous verses by Ludwig Eichrodt published in *Fliegende Blätter*, a magazine dedicated to humor. Dissection of the term reveals the mentality of the times; *bieder* — honest, upright; *Meier* — peasant, farmer. It extends in historic context to mean narrowminded, stagnant, stolid, staid, and rooted in a morass of mediocrity seldom breached by the light of genius or even achievement. Only in rose-tinted retrospect does it represent the joyful laissez-faire, the happy-go-lucky mood so innately the hallmark of the Viennese. To describe Vienna's Golden Age with the term Biedermeier, as some historians have attempted, is to misjudge the ingredients — political, social, artistic — which went into the making of Vienna between the two dates which changed the face of Europe, 1815 and 1848. When the writer and historian Josef Weinheber describes Biedermeier Vienna as "escapist stagnation-in-cosiness," he comes closer to its true meaning.

In those fateful intervening years Vienna's middle class had reached a level of comfort unknown before and smugly refused to "achieve" any further. Happy in their small-scaled status quo, barely interested in the musical landmarks of Beethoven, Schubert, or Weber, they frequented the cheap, vulgar magic plays. Thus middle-class life in Vienna proceeded — polished, pompous, and policed. The poet Bauernfeld described it aptly: "A Dutch still-life where no noise of the outside world, no ray of daylight penetrates." It took the 1848 revolution to shake them out of their fatuous feather beds.

That such geniuses as Grillparzer, Ferdinand Raimund, Johann Nestroy, Adalbert Stifter, and Ludwig Anzengruber could exist, let alone create — even during Emperor Franz's gray medieval regime and Metternich's devious and dedicated searches for "subversion" — bespeaks the latent artistic health and strength of

Vienna. Raimund, although he suffered during the difficult war years until peace was established with Napoleon in 1815, mirrored the finer aspects of early Biedermeier. Beethoven, deaf, cantankerous, wrestling with the musical titans of his silent world, retired into himself and away from most contact with life. Schubert, part of the first half of Vienna Biedermeier, truly began to blossom artistically after the drought of war. Yet his own strength of character, and of art, was often suffused with a false show of gaiety and sentimentality, a hallmark of Vienna in general and of Biedermeier in particular, and of which Schubert often seemed a personification at its best.

The escapist attitude of Biedermeier Vienna can be understood in the light of a postwar period in which the desire to forget past horrors became paramount. Schubert elation, Strauss ecstasy, and Rossini fever offered just such relief from the painful memories of the last eighteen years, which had been a calendar of horror:

In 1797 the Treaty of Campo Formio, in which the Habsburgs had lost Lorraine, was signed. In 1800 Napoleon defeated Austrian forces at Marengo. Tuscany was lost in the Treaty of Luneville. Only five years later, the French besieged and occupied Vienna. Another peace treaty signed at Pressburg resulted in the loss of Venetia and the cession of Tyrol to the Elector of Bavaria. In 1809 another occupation of Vienna and yet another flaming war against Napoleon ensued, producing Napoleon's first defeat and Austria's only victory at Aspern, promptly nullified by the defeat at Wagram. A peace dictated from the very steps of the pleasure palace of the Habsburgs, Schönbrunn, resulted in the loss of Carinthia, Dalmatia, and Galicia. In such a time of defeat and spirit of defeatism the Viennese harked with a passion bordering on frenzy to the sounds of Schubert, the fairy tales of Raimund, and the dynamic rhythms of Strauss.

In 1800 another genius, worthy to play the title role in Raimund's *The Spendthrift*, appeared on the Vienna scene; Emanuel Schikaneder. Schikaneder had made and squandered a small fortune with his "magic play" *Die Zauberflöte (The Magic Flute)* with music by one Wolfgang Amadeus Mozart. Now he requested imperial renewal of a privilege to build a theatre. It was granted, the wording of the privilege and grant opening a significant window onto the thinking of the Austrian regime: "The political consideration cannot be overlooked that those spectacles have become a need for a large part of the public in this city, and that a refusal of license would cause great discontent, particularly among the lower class of the public."

It was not through his extravagances or his libretto for Mozart that Schikaneder was destined to be engraved in the annals of Vienna's history, but for the theatre he built. He set out to build it in 1801, in the prevailing "Napoleonic" style, the new vogue, even in Vienna. Originally it boasted seven hundred seats and standing room for fifteen hundred. Soon it became Vienna's favorite and was destined to be its most

Vienna's famed Theater an der Wien, built by Schikaneder. Here Mozart,
Beethoven, Schubert, Strauss, and Lehár triumphed.

historic theatrical landmark. The new *Theater an der Wien* was located close to the
trickling, reeking rivulet misnamed *Wienfluss* (Vienna River). In that theatre history
was to record the resounding successes and failures of Beethoven, Mozart, Schubert,
Strauss, and Lehar. However, Schikaneder's reign in the sumptuous theatre was
short-lived. True to form, he presented everything from the sublime to the ridiculous,
interposing Kotzebue and Iffland with Schiller, Shakespeare, and Mozart.
Schikaneder, the flamboyant showman, was to share the fates of Mozart and
Mozart's other famed librettist, Lorenzo da Ponte. Like da Ponte, whose librettos

The Papageno Door at the Theater an der Wien. This charming group on the right side of the building, above the carriage, commemorates Mozart's Magic Flute to which Schikaneder wrote the libretto.

Emanuel Schikaneder. Actor, impresario, librettist, spendthrift, he ended, like Mozart and da Ponte, in an unnamed mass grave. Etching by Philipp Richter.

for *Cosi fan Tutte, Le Nozze di Figaro,* and *Don Giovanni* inspired Mozart, and like Mozart himself, Schikaneder vanished into a pauper's grave, having died in insanity in 1812.

As Vienna expanded, its artistic liberty was curtailed. Censorship harassed authors, poets, writers, and theatre impresarios alike. Beethoven's Spanish villain in *Fidelio* was judged unacceptable to Metternich's henchmen, as were Schiller's *Maria Stuart* and the rebellious *Don Carlos,* and Goethe's *Goetz von Berlichingen.* Whenever and wherever criticism of the Habsburg regime, implied or real, was suspected, whenever rebellion against the establishment was noted, the play was either refused outright or left to gather dust in the censor's pigeon hole. Surprisingly, the French conqueror loosened the bonds which had held Vienna in an intellectual straight jacket. The Viennese, suddenly enjoying a measure of intellectual freedom, were torn between loyalty to Austria and indulgence in French laissez-faire, so akin to the Viennese temperament. Yet the grating sight of flamboyant enemy uniforms in the streets, the inns, and the theatres was softened by the relaxation of censorship and the permission to perform plays which had been deemed controversial in Habsburg eyes. Haydn enjoyed the special esteem of Napoleon. Two years after its Vienna premiere, his oratorio *Die Schöpfung (The Creation)* was performed in Paris despite the hostilities. When Napoleon invaded Austria and headquartered in Schönbrunn he ordered a French honor guard posted at Haydn's modest home, and Austrian and French officers united in forming an honor guard as Haydn's body lay in state. It was a French officer who, upon hearing Beethoven's Piano Concerto in E-flat at its premiere gave it its enduring subtitle by exclaiming *"C'est l'Empereur parmi les concerts"* ("This is the emperor among concertos"). Thus, while Beethoven had to flee in rage into the cellar of a friend, covering his sensitive ears with a pillow to block out the terrifying sounds of the guns of the man he hated, the Viennese reluctantly acknowledged the unshackling of music and drama under Napoleon's occupation.

In some musical aspects, however, Vienna remained a pauper despite its first wave of musical giants who either lived or performed there. Thanks to Habsburg example, the city was one of talented musical dilettantes. Consequently none of the compositions of those greats received competent professional performances until 1842, when Otto Nicolai[1] founded the Vienna Philharmonic Orchestra. This lack a professional competence, then, is especially surprising in view of the fact that

1. Otto Nicolai (1810-1849) was a prominent composer and conductor. He made his first appearance in Vienna as *Kapellmeister* of the Opera. His most lasting work is the comic opera *Die lustigen Weiber von Windsor.* Wishing to give the symphonies of Beethoven first-rate performances he founded the Vienna Philharmonic orchestra. An annual performance of Beethoven's Ninth Symphony memorializes his name as "Nicolai Konzert."

music and the theatre provided the only outlets for society to meet openly in the presence of Metternich's everpresent spies.

Another name, difficult to pronounce but destined for fame, began to appear on the Vienna literary horizon. Franz Grillparzer was eighteen when the French occupied his native city. He came from an illustrious literary Viennese background—his mother the sister of Josef Sonnleithner who had coauthored the libretto for Beethoven's *Fidelio*. Grillparzer's home was filled with the sounds and conversations of the theatre, music, and poetry. Nonetheless, the man destined to become Austria's only claim to classic drama fame wandered through a youth as sunless as his parents' apartment. Franz's anticlerical father, a stern, stoic lawyer at the Vienna courts who always remained the model of citizen loyalty and rectitude, was appreciative of the arts. The son's first artistic impulse was, surprisingly, musical and not poetic. Although poetry and drama ultimately became the fulfillment of his life, music always remained part of him. He was a prominent member of the *Schubertiad* and amorously attached to one of its most charming members, Kathi Fröhlich, one of the delightful Fröhlich sisters whose home was always open to anything musical in Vienna. It was the arrival of the French which proved disastrous to the Grillparzer family, as Franz's unfinished autobiography shows:

> Then came the war events of 1809, the lost battles, the bombardment of the town, the entry of the French in Vienna, the paralysis of business, the billeting, the war tax and contributions; above all [my father's] patriotic heart was suffering torment under all these humiliations ... While expenses continued to mount with rising prices, incomes gradually fell to insignificant levels, until in the last months the entry [my father] made in the ledger, with an uncertain hand was *Nihil*. He was even forced to take out a loan, he to whom the terms contractor of debts and thief were synonymous. The knowledge that the city was occupied by the enemy was abominable to him, and to see Frenchmen [in the streets of Vienna] was like a knife thrust ...

Inflation became rampant. Prices tripled between May and July 1809. The peace treaty of Pressburg ceded one third of the monarchy to the French and was almost directly responsible for the death of Grillparzer's father. Yet throughout the Napoleonic suppression the ideals and attempts at ideals instituted by Emperor Josef lived on subconsciously until they bore violent fruit in 1848. Unwittingly, Emperor Franz contributed to the perpetuation of Josef's memory. He wanted to remind the Viennese during their most troubled times of the achievements of the past—although these had mostly vanished in his own time and due to his doings. But although the Viennese revered the office more than the man, and although they hated the regime

The Father

Franz Grillparzer. Austria's greatest poet and its claim to German classical greatness.

and its ministers, they smiled gratefully and nostalgically; they understood when they looked up at the equestrian statue of Emperor Josef II which Franz had placed at the *Josefsplatz*, a nobly subdued square in front of the equally subdued splendor of Fischer von Erlach's National Library.

Grillparzer, who had held himself aloof from public activity and agitation, may have surprised even himself when in 1809 he began to actively participate in the student defense of Vienna against Napoleon's onslaught. When questioned he was nonchalantly noncommittal about it. While Grillparzer's father viewed Napoleon with unremitting hatred, the son half despised, half admired him: "I had hatred in my heart ... yet never missed one of his (troop) reviews at *Schönbrunn* or on the parade ground known as the *Schmelz*. I can still see him before me ... running rather than walking down the open-air steps of Schönbrunn ... and then standing there, as if cast in iron, hands folded behind his back, to survey his armies or their march past him, with the unmoved look of the lord and master ... He put me under a spell as a snake does a bird" (from Grillparzer's autobiography). The conflict remained, the hatred and the admiration, the desire for heroism and the hero worship of the hated, fascination with the image of total power and the self-mockery of that very fascination. This was no unconscious reaction; Grillparzer was well aware of the conflict within him, particularly since the conflict reached out in other directions, with local authorities, for instance, where the seesaw tension of mutual distrust persisted. Censors either rejected his plays, destined for immortality, because of the poet's subtle or open criticism of the regime, and left them to gather dust (as one censor commented, "because one never knows"); or Grillparzer himself, aware of the censor's attitude, purposefully left his plays in his own desk drawer. His grudging admiration of Napoleon may have stemmed from his bitterness towards the total inefficiency of the Austrian bureaucracy and the military which contributed greatly toward the Austrian debacle in the field. Although he was cheered by the Austrian victory at Aspern and although he considered himself a staunch Austrian patriot, despite his loathing of officialdom, Grillparzer could not bring himself to celebrate in poetry Napoleon's downfall as Beethoven did in "Wellington's Victory" in 1813 and in anticipatory measure in the funeral march of his *Eroica* Symphony.

"Wellington's Victory," or the *Battle* Symphony, perhaps Beethoven's shoddiest work, nevertheless had a curious effect on Vienna as well as on the composer's career. The war-weary, amusement-hungry Viennese were so enamoured of the blatant pageantry, the trumpet fanfares, the rattle of muskets, the obvious programmatic content of the work, that they suddenly desired to hear more of Beethoven's music. Thus his Seventh Symphony and even his often spurned and neglected opera *Fidelio* rose to sudden, surprising success on the coattails, so to speak, of the *Battle* Symphony.[2] Grillparzer wavered between hatred and fascination for Napoleon, but Beethoven was cast of a different mold. He, the staunch republican and composer of the revolution, had envisioned mankind's hope in Napoleon's rise, had dedicated his *Eroica* Symphony (which revolutionized symphonic writing) to the French consul. When Napoleon crowned himself emperor, Beethoven was revolted. In a fit of rage he attempted to efface the dedication, tearing the page in his furious attempt. (Beethoven's original *Eroica* manuscript, complete with torn title page, is in the

2. When it was performed on 24 May 1814, it could not have sounded worse even if it had been performed in Maelzel's Panharmonium, for which it was intended. The cream of Viennese musicians and composers had assembled for the occasion, a concert for the widows and orphans of Napoleonic wars. The famous violinist Louis Spohr led the violin section, composer Ignatz Moscheles clashed the cymbals, composer Antonio Salieri commanded the guns offstage, composer-pianist Hummel pounded the bass drum, and Meyerbeer was in the orchestra, as was Dragonetti, the most famous string bass player of the time.

possession of the *Gesellschaft der Musikfreunde* in Vienna.) When years later he was informed of Napoleon's death he icily remarked: "I have already composed the proper music for the catastrophe," referring to the funeral march of the *Eroica*.

But even before St. Helena, Austria found reason for rejoicing in the fact that the military seas were becalmed after the Napoleonic ravages, and Vienna celebrated the outbreak of peace with the Congress of Vienna, and for a brief span the music capital of the world became also the diplomatic capital of Europe. However, trouble was brewing from other directions and crowding the conservatism which Metternich espoused and wished to impose on all German states in his subtly devious ways. More and more young intellectuals wished to make themselves heard. Metternich was aware of that trend. In a memorandum to his confidant, collaborator, and principal adviser, Friedrich von Gentz, he stated as early as 1819: "I feel certain that an entire generation of revolutionaries is inevitably bred [at the universities]— unless the evil is contained ... This impression will prompt me to intervene from above and the only measures I deem feasible have already been taken ... the greatest and therefore most pressing evil today is the press." Control of the universities and censorship was espoused and attained.

The barefaced hypocrisy and steely will of this supreme chancellor, in charge and command of foreign affairs as well as internal security, is further attested to by yet another comment to Gentz: "The severity of our censorship has up to a point ... protected our monarchy from being invaded by this pestilential poison [journalistic criticism]. If it cannot be stopped, it will be difficult to determine, judging the future from the present, to what degree of depravity even the state may come, which so far has remained so calm and happy, in the paternal care of our virtuous sovereign."

Calm and happy, indeed—in a country noted for its "gray medievalism," controlled by "a standing army of soldiers, a kneeling army of priests and a crawling army of spies." That deceptive happy calm, so often the hallmark of Biedermeier Vienna, was musically personified by two men, Franz Schubert and Johann Strauss Father. But even with placid and loyal men disagreements and schisms could not be glossed over. In 1816 Schubert composed the cantata *Prometheus*, hiding his own protest behind the mythological defier of the gods. When corresponding with his brother Ferdinand, Franz disguised his dislike of the clergy by using the dialect expression *Bonzen* (bosses). Schubert, who wrote Masses as a matter of course (because his mentor Salieri had hammered into his mind that music began and ended with operas and Masses), also testified in another indirect way to his indignation. He never indulged in open criticism but displayed it by leaving out entire passages of the traditional Latin text in which he did not believe. That conscious stand, extending into the artistic and creative field, is doubly amazing in a mind of which Josef von Spaun, one of Schubert's close friends, remarked: "His artistic achievement is unconscious, hardly revealed to and understood by himself." The years from 1825 to his untimely death in 1828 plunged Schubert into despair. He suffered from severe illness, presumably from venereal disease. The *Death and the Maiden* Quartet and the somber despairing song cycle *Winterreise* in 1827 attest to his misery when "Each night ... I hope not to wake and each morning only recalls yesterday's misery." The impulse of despair, the subconscious premonition of death, a sudden wave of creative impulse—one or all of these may have driven Schubert in his last year to new creative heights in songs, the "Great" Symphony in C, the Mass in E-flat, the String Quartet in C (all of them, surprisingly, in major keys despite the downward curve of his life), funded only by the income from a first concert and the first reluctant nibbles from publishers. But on the threshold of success he was struck down by typhus which his body, weakened by wine and sickness, could not withstand.

Typhus was taken in stride in Vienna despite the terrible toll it took with each outbreak, the worst of which occurred in 1806 when as many as sixty people died from it each day. The Schubert family was ravaged. Of the fourteen children which the father sired only three survived, and of the twenty-five children from brother Ferdinand's two marriages more than half died. In the great epidemics of 1815 and the 1840s Vienna's population was decimated as much as ten percent. Half of the victims were younger than twenty years old. Only the constant influx into the capital of workers and their families from the provinces and the empire, undaunted and unabated by repression, hardships, and epidemics, accounted for the steady growth of the city.

The increase of the lower classes within the city walls was viewed with a jaundiced eye by Emperor Franz, his chancellor, and the military. The lesson of France was still a vivid memory, and cavalry and infantry were always ready to disperse, squelch, or shoot on orders of Metternich but in the name of the emperor. The sudden end of the Congress, triggered by Napoleon's escape from Elba, had torn away the smiling mask of opulence which the city wore. Increased misery, starvation, unemployment, and the demise of the trades were glaringly evident. Yet the thought of providing relief for his miserable subjects either never entered the minds of Emperor Franz and Metternich or was impossible due to the emptiness of the treasury. Haunted by the specter of the Paris of 1789 they were blinded into repressive measures. The only solution they could devise was to reinforce the garrison of Vienna and to keep out as many of the distrusted proletarians as possible. So blindly intent was the ruling clique on retaining a petrified *status quo* that even the building of factories and apartment houses, cynically called *Zinskasernen* (rent barracks) by the people, was forbidden in order to deprive the newly arrived workers of housing and employment, thus forcing them out of Vienna. The fact that Vienna's industrial growth was thus stunted had no impact on the court's lingering fears. History inevitably was to channel the workers' ambitions and dreams into different, hostile detours despite the court's frantic attempts to the contrary. In the end Franz reverted to a variation of the Roman idea that if bread could not be made available, let the circus thrive. Police were advised that "in times like these, when the character of individuals is affected by so much suffering, the police are more than ever obliged to cooperate in the diversions of the citizenry by every moral means. The most dangerous hours of the day are the evening hours. They cannot be filled more innocently than in the theatre." Raimund, Nestroy, Lanner, and Strauss were the ideal men to fill that need with their special brand of genius.

Ferdinand Raimund was fourteen years old when his father died. Apprenticeship to a confectioner had put an end to his meager early education. But fortune smiled at him in an odd way. He helped make cookies during the day, then sold them at night in the gallery of the old *Burgtheater*. Prohibited from hawking his wares during the performance, he would sit on the steep steps, chin in hand, drinking in the make-believe world, imagining himself in some of the roles he witnessed. Soon reality was overwhelmed by dreams, and he ran away to join a traveling group of actors who performed drama and comedy in the provinces. Although Raimund had dreams of being a tragedian, he ended up as a comic with a small suburban Vienna theatre. His reputation grew with his experience, and at age twenty-eight he had established himself as a subtle character actor in the Viennese comic repertoire.

But as he found himself on the road to success in his chosen profession, his personal fortunes deteriorated. The very fact that he was a *Schauspieler*, an actor, gave him an ominous reputation of lewdness and lechery among parents of marriageable daughters, because the occupation carried with it the automatic connotation of a shiftless, low-character bohemian unfit to marry a Biedermeier burgher's daughter. Actually Raimund proved to be the opposite. He was a gentle yet passionate man and, above all, a poet. His love for the daughter of the owner of a coffeehouse was ardently reciprocated but rejected by her parents, who could not see the man for his profession. A trumped-up scandal which forced him into brief marriage did nothing to improve his reputation, but could not dampen his love for Toni. His divorce had little effect because Raimund was a Catholic and his church would not recognize such a separation. Thus the two lovers faced what seemed an insurmountable dilemma. Johann Strauss Son was to face a similar situation in later years. He solved it by turning Protestant. Raimund could not even contemplate such a step and, in near despair, thought of suicide as the only solution open to him. By then

Ferdinand Raimund. Actor and Austria's greatest folk poet of the theatre. His beloved fairytale comedies, in which he always reserved a part for himself, reached an unsurpassed peak.

he was a mature adult of thirty-one and, with Toni's understanding and determination, love triumphed, in a fashion. Defying custom and tradition, Raimund and Toni went to *Neustift am Walde*, a little village in the Vienna Woods and there, before a wayside shrine of the Virgin, knelt and swore to each other eternal love. In the solemnity of the quiet green of the forest they repeated their marriage vows in the face of God, a vow which God's Viennese representatives would not honor. The lovers' fortitude was to be sorely tested. Peace of mind continued to elude them and only years later did Toni's parents relent and receive the then famous poet into their home. Raimund continued to write his splendid plays in which good always triumphed, and he became one of Vienna's most famous playwrights of folk poetry. His abiding love for Toni, the steadfastness with which she reciprocated, and the suffering which ensued over the years may have fortified his character and artistic endeavor because shortly after their forest vows in 1823 his lasting success was assured by a series of fairty-tale comedies in which he always reserved a substantial part for himself. These plays, *Der Diamant des Geisterkönigs (The Fairy King's Diamond)*, *Das Mädchen von der Feenwelt oder Der Bauer als Millionär (The Maid*

from Fairyland or The Peasant as Millionaire), Der Alpenkönig und der Menschen-
feind (The Mountain King and the Misanthrope), and *Der Verschwender (The*
Spendthrift), his most famous and most enduring work, became the rage of Vienna and forever assured him a place of honor in Vienna's literary annals. His
private life of torment, disillusion, and tragedy culminated in suicide. After being
bitten by a dog he thought to be rabid, he chose death rather than possible insanity.

For seven years Raimund was aided in his triumphs by a Silesian-born actress,
Therese Krones. She was a friend of the *Schubertiad* as well as of Raimund's theatre
family. Her portrayal of the Vienna girl, charming, graceful yet possessed by a wild
streak earned her an early fame in Vienna's *Leopoldstädter Theater*. She gave herself to her early fame and wealth with lavish passion and reckless abandon. She
became the image of the *Wiener Mädl*. On the stage Raimund and Krones became
the very image of Vienna personified, bright and brilliant before the footlights,
doomed in real life. Krones soared to fame and was dead at the age of twenty-nine.
Her only last wishes were that eighteen Masses be read for her soul, and that she
have a grave of her own. The ghosts of Schikaneder, da Ponte, and Mozart haunt
those last requests.

Despite Raimund's efforts on stage, the political, intellectual, and artistic atmosphere of Vienna became more oppressive. Grillparzer was all but unknown (although Byron, after reading his work, had paid him a left-handed compliment:
"The world will be forced to remember this outlandish name"). Beethoven found
himself in a similar position, having been swept aside by a flood of Rossini adulation; Schubert hardly existed as far as the world of music was concerned. Had
it not been for the joyous new strains of Lanner and Strauss, Vienna would have
enjoyed no active native music. The fact that Metternich looked benignly on
dance music as a diversion made Lanner and Strauss the men of the hour and
reinforced the deceptive air of surface tranquillity and contentment. The state of
education, except for religious matters, created a purposeful mediocrity. And,
despite keyhole spies and commissions, it was estimated that every ten children
born in wedlock were matched by an equal number of illegitimate ones. So complete was Metternich's internal control that the English biographer Peter Turnbull,
in 1840, could state with innocent ignorance, "[The Viennese are] frugal, cheerful
and contented, they seek not alteration in their conditions ... they dread change
of any kind as fraught with evil."

Eight years later Metternich would be unable to hold down the lid of his Pandora's box any longer and "dreaded change" would manifest itself with shouts "to
the barricades." When that time arrived Strauss, always loyal to Habsburg, ebullient,

almost demoniac, fitted well into that environment of contradictions so akin to him, a man of near-schizophrenic tendencies. Strauss Son, on the other hand, was not quite as clear-cut in his loyalties during the 1848 revolution, and this became another item to contribute to the father-son rivalry. In 1844, when the younger Strauss made his famous debut, and his parents became separated, the rivalry between father and son was not the only one Vienna could boast about in the artistic field. Of equal importance and significance in mirroring the changing image of the city was the competition in the theatrical arena between Raimund and Nestroy. As in the case of the Strausses, opinions were divided, some people leaning toward Raimund's gentle, pictorial laissez-faire Viennese humor, others preferring the near-venomous satire of Nestroy, clad in seemingly innocent comedies.

Johann Nepomuk Ambrosius Eduard Nestroy saw the light of Viennese day in 1801. He was slated by his lawyer father to study law but he started on a theatrical career instead, which brought him—surprisingly—to the Court Opera as a bass baritone. His must have had a superior voice, because he was successful in a magic fairy tale, of sorts, singing Sarastro in Schikaneder's *Zauberflöte*. While Nestroy was busy gaining prestige but little else, his wife ran off with her aristocratic lover. In disgust Nestroy left Vienna to find less prestige but better salaries in theatres in the Austrian provinces. In the process he changed from singer to comedian. Eventually he settled again in Vienna, but as a highly paid character actor with sharp, deep insight into human foibles in general, and those of the Viennese in particular.

There was a parallel of sorts in the marital troubles of Raimund and Nestroy. The latter, also unable to obtain a divorce from the Catholic authorities, took a mistress who became his wife in all but name. A singer before meeting Nestroy, she became a perfect artistic companion as well as an attentive "wife" and mother and, equally important to an aspiring actor, a successful manager of his business affairs. Nestroy's year, 1831, saw his artistic ascent to fame as well as that of the *Theater an der Wien*, his showcase for his brand of Offenbachian satire and cynicism. Magic and fairytale plays, with the exception of Raimund's, went begging. Raimund had all but retired from the stage and Therese Krones was dead. Hacks with their shoddy wares dominated the Vienna theatre, which was in a state of paunchy decline. Nestroy became an overnight sensation, either acclaimed or reviled. In the mire of stale comedies and thinly veiled adaptations of French imports, his characterizations, etched in acid, exposing human frailties with relentlessly biting humor, were a fresh wind blowing through faded scenery.

Another beloved figure of the Vienna stage entered into the limelight at about that time. Fanny Elssler, Vienna's first famous ballerina, was the antithesis of Therese Krones. Where Krones had been flamboyant and lavish with her favors, Elssler

The Father

Fanny Elssler. Vienna's first ballerina of international fame.

seemed the model of the Biedermeier era; shy and modest, she remained the life-long companion of historian-diplomat Friedrich von Gentz. Her warm companionship lent an afterglow to his old age in their May-December relationship. She came from a family tradition steeped in music. Her grandfather had been a violinist in the court orchestra of the princes Esterhazy under Joseph Haydn, and her father had been Haydn's faithful factotum who accompanied the aged master on his two journeys to London. Contemporaries described Fanny as graceful rather than beautiful, her mien quiet and her face, under hair tightly brushed into a dark gloss, altogether natural and simple, devoid of mannerisms. Her entire personality changed when she danced one of her fiery folk dances or the dance creations of the great Noverre,[3] who then reigned supreme at the ballet school of the Vienna Court Opera. Additional training in Naples provided the final touches to make her a prima ballerina of the Vienna *corps de ballet* at age twenty. She embarked on international tours (one of the few Vienna artists to do so), including the United States, no mean venture in the 1830s. She entranced the world for twenty years before retiring in 1851.

As Raimund and Nestroy reigned supreme in the suburban theatres, the focal point of the classic repertoire remained the imperial *Hofburgtheater*. Although the old house was modest in structure and smaller than the *Kärntnerthortheater* (devoted to opera), it was destined to hold a supreme position among the German-speaking theatres. Its rise was aided by a man whose name is indelibly engraved in the annals of the *Burgtheater*—Joseph Schreyvogel. In the face of a pusillanimous administration, caught in the web of its own bureaucracy, and despite his non-aristocratic background, he succeeded brilliantly. He presented not only the noblest of classic stage works but even controversial ones, no mean task at a time when the censor's office shelved anything that even faintly smacked of new thought or controversial spirit. As *Intendant* of the *Burgtheater* he staged the outspoken plays of Schiller *(Wilhelm Tell, Don Carlos)*, Goethe *(Goetz von Berlichingen)*, Kleist, and Lessing. He also presented a number of great French and Spanish plays. His most enduring achievements, however, were performances of Shakespeare in German, and of Grillparzer. The appearance of Shakespeare in German was a phenomenon of the utmost literary importance. The trend and desire to acquaint Germany with the great literary creations of other nations had begun in 1781 with Johann Heinrich Voss's translations of Homer's *Odyssey* and *Iliad* (1793). J. G. Robertson writes in his *History of German Literature:* "In Voss's translation, Homer passed over into German literature as Shakespeare was later to pass over into it in the translation of Schlegel."

The translation of Shakespeare was done between 1797 and 1810. August Wilhelm Schlegel provided the lion's share, seventeen plays, in the so-called Schlegel-Tieck translations, and, to quote Robertson again, "he made Shakespeare a national hero of the German people, and no higher tribute could be paid to any translator." *"Sein oder nicht sein"* ("To be or not to be") became as immortal a phrase in German as it is in English. Part of Schreyvogel's success must surely have been his foresight in using these supremely poetic translations in his uphill fight to present Shakespeare

3. Jean George Noverre (1727-1810) was a Paris born ballet master and dancer who staged the ballets of Gluck and Piccini in a new revolutionary manner. For a time he was ballet master at the Vienna Opera, where he was engaged by Empress Maria Theresia; later went to Paris as ballet master upon the request of Maria Theresia's daughter, Marie Antoinette.

at the *Burgtheater*, which previously had heard only Schiller's translation of *Macbeth*.

An even more daring contribution to contemporary German poetry was Schreyvogel's staging of Grillparzer's dramas. He presented in successive years *Die Ahnfrau (The Ancestress), Das Goldene Vliess (The Golden Fleece), König Ottokar's Glück und Ende (King Ottokar's Fortunes and Death), Ein Treuer Diener seines Herrn (A Faithful Servant of his Master), Des Meeres und der Liebe Wellen (The Waves of Sea and Love,* also known as *Hero and Leander).* Through Schreyvogel's excellent staging Grillparzer became universally recognized as a powerful German dramatic force sharing literary olympic heights with Goethe and Schiller. The artistic void opened by Schreyvogel's death may have contributed to the near catastrophic reception of Grillparzer's only comedy *Weh dem der lügt (Woe To Him Who Lies).* It was one of those monumental failures when everybody concerned was grateful for the *Burgtheater* tradition forbidding anybody to ever take a bow, be he poet, director, or actor.

Politically there was little to applaud in Vienna. After the death of Emperor Franz, his regime was placed in the slack hands of feeble-minded Ferdinand, with the actual strings pulled by Prince Metternich in foreign affairs and Count Kolowrat in domestic matters. Despite inefficiency, intrigue and counter-intrigue, despite censorship and enforcement, new ideas inevitably began to filter into Vienna. The philosophical influence of a Goethe could not be ignored or censored away. Just as inevitably, the first great names of the later famous Vienna school of medicine appeared. Ignatz Semmelweis found the cause of the rampant puerperal fever in the lack of cleanliness in the dissecting and maternity wards of the Vienna hospitals. He urged his colleagues and students to cleanse their hands thoroughly with soap and water and then dip them in solutions of chlorinated lime water. His innovations reduced maternity deaths from a disastrous 12.24 percent to 1.27 percent within two years. Carl Rokitansky was the founder of Vienna's pathological anatomy. His *Handbuch der pathologischen Anatomie* was his crowning achievement in which his experiences of examining three hundred thousand post mortem cases were documented. Joseph Skoda was the first of the great diagnosticians; together with Rokitansky he was one of the few who supported Semmelweis's theory. Later Theodore Billroth became a surgeon of world renown and pioneer in gastro-intestinal operative care; in his house much chamber music by his friend Brahms had its first performance. (Hanslick called it "Billroth's *jus primae noctis*") Later still another illustrious name was to join the splendid array of Vienna greats of medicine; Sigmund Freud.

The presence and magnitude of Grillparzer's literary achievements unfortunately overshadowed another figure who, in the mid-1800s, under the guise of entertainment, began to voice slight opposition to the *status quo*, the parasitic aristocracy, the schemes of unscrupulous promoters, and the regime itself—Eduard von Bauernfeld. Bauernfeld was not censored because Metternich failed to see public laughter in response to such satire as the people's critical response to conditions they knew existed but dared not touch upon in any way other than a knowing, laughing nod. Instead Metternich saw such outspokenness and the laughter it evoked as "diversion" to be categorized with the innocent gaiety of Lanner and Strauss waltzes and gallops. His failure to perceive that such laughter could, and would, change to fury overnight only tended to embolden the growing but still tacit opposition.

On the surface, and under Metternich's "benevolently fatherly" eye, Vienna danced nightly in orgiastic abandon to Lanner and Strauss. Censorship might tighten, internal disaster loom, repression strangle, but Vienna danced. Bauernfeld sensed the inevitability of the coming clash, but he believed in justice, a common meeting ground, and a happy ending. Grillparzer also was aware of the gathering storm but publicly kept a stoic, disgruntled silence. Thus, as the workers, the students, the burghers, and the soldiers eventually took to the streets and the barricades, their leaderless revolt was doomed and crushed. It did serve, however, to leave the wedding-cake image of Biedermeier Vienna crumbled; the saccharine conception of the city's peace and contentment lived on only in Schwind's nostalgic, lovingly conceived pictures.

Even at that critical impasse the regime knew only one way to respond—with inflexible discipline, with make-shift day-by-day decisions, with wishful thinking, and especially with the continuance of the policy of "divide and conquer, wait and see." The February declaration proclaiming France a republic sent shudders through the ruling aristocratic ranks of the *Camarilla* but served only to stiffen an already petrified regime. Thus even the mild protest of 13 March 1848—by students flamboyantly attired in their fraternity costumes, blue-collar workers, and respected citizens in high hats—before the lower Austrian *Standhaus* (Guild House) and the equally moderate demands, stopping short of a constitution, were hastily and nervously met with a soldier's volley into the crowd which killed a number of students who were in the forefront of the demonstration. Such hysterical reaction served only to fan the orderly and restrained demonstration into open defiance. Students broke into the arsenal and began to arm themselves. The city, following a plan of long standing, closed the massive city gates, hoping to cut off blue-collar support from the suburbs and quickly deal with the insurgents inside the walls. But the deciding factor was to come, to the surprise of all including Metternich, from inside the walls. The workers, the forgotten men in Vienna's social structure, over-came their traditional distrust of students and bourgeoisie and at that historic moment joined hands in common cause with the students to force the regime's hand. Metternich suddenly found himself at the end of his rope. Perplexed and suddenly irresolute he resigned and fled.

The revolution gained momentum within itself. Success had been unexpected at that early hour, and consequently progress was ill-planned, haphazard, impulsive, and idealistic. What worked in favor of the revolutionaries in those opening skirmishes was the fact that the opposition found itself equally disorganized and leaderless. Only this lack of governmental strength made possible the proclamation of a constitutional monarchy two weeks after the first bloody encounter. However, the leaderless revolution was unaware that it bore within itself the seed of defeat once the reactionary forces, temporarily benumbed, recovered from their initial shock. While it lasted, the uprising was exhilarating and awe-inspiring in the virginal purity of its idealism. Grillparzer was to remember in later years the unbelievable sight of students in their romantic, colorful costumes, facing three ranks of unsmiling grenadier regiment's muskets. They impressed him as "heroic children." In typically Viennese fashion Grillparzer added, "Incidentally, it was the gayest revolution imaginable. Favored by spring weather, the entire population filled the streets all day long." Others saw the event in its true context. The poet Gottfried Keller gave Vienna its due: "City of pleasure, city of music, morning-happy, proud Vienna ... We have sinned when resenting your gaiety and your apparent self-indulgence. It is true, you floated on the waves of your dances and pretended luxurious ease even while the storms were gathering. But as icy gray, dead guardians kept watch outside your tune-filled houses, you sent noble fighters into the rosy dawn, singing ... "

After an abortive attempt to crush the revolution, a second round of revolt en-gulfed Vienna in May of the same year. Barricades rose again, and again students and workers mounted the parapets in joint vigilance. This time they were inflamed by a poem from an opera conductor in Dresden. The poem was *"Gruss aus Sachsen an die Wiener"* ("Greetings from Saxony to the Viennese"), the poet was Richard Wagner. In the poem, running to fourteen stanzas, he praised the Vienna "heroes" for having "drawn the sword."

But as the Habsburgs gathered their wits about them, the freedom promised in undue haste failed to materialize, and the few concessions made in frightened sur-prise were watered down or nullified. While looking about the empire, however, the ruling clique realized that the danger had not passed. Hungary, which had also revolted under the fiery leadership of Louis (Lajos) Kossuth, had yet to be dealt with. The move by Count Baillet von Latour, the minister of war, to send troops against the rebellious Hungarians kindled the third, and final, disastrous round in Vienna's 1848 revolution. At the railroad station from which the troops were to depart for Hungary, the soldiers and their cavalry escorts were attacked by the revolutionaries. The soldiers refused to obey orders to shoot into the crowd. Other troops were hastily called to restore order but were also attacked and routed. Now the crowd, drunk with its unprecedented success against the military, spilled inward toward the center of the city and the war ministry. With Metternich in flight the shout changed to *"Nieder mit Latour."* "Get Latour" quickly became a battle cry. The minister of war, the only official courageous enough to remain in the capital after the court and government had fled, had been forewarned of the crowd's approach and battle cry. He attempted to hide in the vast recesses of his offices but was sought out, seized, dragged into the court yard of the ministry and lynched. His naked body was then hung from a lamp post. A vision, a dream had turned into a nightmare. Unknown to the rebels, Emperor Ferdinand had acceded to the pressure of the *Camarilla.* And now, reaction, organized, steeled, bent on revenge, was on the move. The Imperial General Prince Windischgraetz was dispatched to move his army against the emperor's own capital. Vienna, ill led, ill fed, ill armed, was soon helplessly pinned within its walls by an imperial army of forty thousand soldiers. Windischgraetz demanded unconditional surrender; Vienna defiantly decided to fight. Windischgraetz thereupon ordered the shelling of the capital. Hungary dispatched a force which arrived too late to relieve the city and which was annihilated within sight of the walls. Vienna's leap from unquestioning subservience to defiance had been too sudden. It had had no time to prepare and develop leadership to guide it beyond its initial outburst of delirious defiance into ways of governing, arming, and defending itself. Yet, the fires of revolution burned on. Vienna gallantly fought on for five days before Windischgraetz pounded and smashed his way into the city. Within one year after the capitulation twenty-five persons were executed for their part in the revolution and over two thousand arrested.

Conservatives dismissed the 1848 events with a wave of the hand as "unprincipled fickleness," but those who understood the underlying historic causes and developments knew better. Said the historian Heinrich Friedjung: "If one compared the conduct of Vienna with that of Berlin or Budapest which surrendered noiselessly ... it becomes impossible to dismiss those five days of fighting as contemptuously as had been done so often" (Österreich von 1848-1860). It was Karl Marx who summed up the events most aptly: "We would not wish to exchange all the glamorous victories and glorious battles of the Hungarian campaign, for the spontaneous, isolated uprising and heroic resistance of Vienna."

The Father

As the human desire to be free affected history in the days of 1848, so history, in turn, affected the individual. None were more affected than the sensitive minds and *métiers* of the artist, the writer, and the musician. The Strauss household was no exception as the explosive Vienna situation deepened and intensified the rift between father and son. While the father, undaunted by threats and demonstrations, composed the marches extolling the men who had stamped out the Italian and Hungarian revolts, the son was caught in the fires of the revolution which kindled his spirits. While the father remained true to the black and yellow of the Habsburgs, Strauss Son took his band to the barricades to play the *Marseillaise* and his own "March of the Student Legion," "Song of the Barricades," and "Freedom March." But one day as he was standing guard duty, an exchange of musket fire came too close. Overcome by sudden fright, he leaned the musket against the sentry box and vanished to safety. His participation was an act which Emperor Franz Joseph, young but long of memory, was not to forget for decades to come. Yet so revered was the name of Strauss that, despite ruthless military reprisals in similar cases, no severe action was taken or even contemplated against the young Johann. Anna Strauss did not take any chances, however. When government soldiers entered the Strauss home in search of evidence of antigovernment activity, Mother Strauss, forewarned, took the uniforms of her sons into the cellar and buried them there.

While Strauss Son was mildly prorevolution and Strauss Father openly pro-Habsburg, the more complex Grillparzer, although fervently prorevolution and anti-Metternich, kept silent. The effect of that silence was strongly felt in Vienna. Austria's greatest poet, a complex and superior mind, a personality of fame to whom the intelligentsia looked with awe and reverence for spiritual leadership, for direction and guidance, did not commit himself. The reasons for his failure to speak out were never explained, but they emerge in historic retrospect. Grillparzer wished for order; he abhorred disorder and violence. While he was an implacable foe of Metternich and his devious rule, he desired the continued smooth sailing of the ship of state. Thus, incongruously, he even came to extol the virtues of Field Marshal Radetzky, the man for whom pro-Habsburg Strauss had composed his most enduring melody, the conqueror of the insurgent Italians. Grillparzer admired him not because he approved of crushing the Italian uprising but because he acknowledged the order and discipline which had been restored by Radetzky's victorious campaign. In an unintentional turn-about, in the poem "Feldmarschall Radetzky," with its famous line *"In deinem Lager ist Oesterreich"* ("In your camp is Austria"), Grillparzer contradicted himself by seemingly pointing to army discipline as truly Austrian, comparing it with the undisciplined heroism of those who had fought at Vienna's barricades for freedom. To the superficial observer he had forsaken the ranks of the intellectual revolutionaries for the Habsburg camp, dismaying his friends and admirers. Disappointment, despair, and bitterness deepened when Grillparzer, through the strength, popularity, and impact of the poem, found himself honored and courted by the very people he despised and distrusted. While it did not attach a stigma to him (on the contrary, it made life with the censors a bit easier), it nevertheless carried him farther from the worker, to whom he felt intuitively akin but with whom he had had little in common. At times he had actually loathed their disunity and ineffectiveness.

As the constitution became a worthless scrap of paper soon to be discarded, the lonely poet addressed himself directly to the young emperor: "I am loyal to you as before, but the reason is different; once I was loyal out of love, now, from loathing of the opposite side." But the despair of his soul remained misunderstood. Repression was rife, reaction rampant with the connivance of the clergy, which, through the Concordat of 1835, pointedly claimed its loyalty to the ruling house and saw to it that educational trends were reversed to come under the supervision of Catholic influence once again. In the face of repression, regression, and stagnation in the ranks of progressives and liberals alike, it was not surprising that the legend of the "good old days" of merry Biedermeier again gained credence. But 1848, despite its shortcomings, lack of leadership, and defeat, was to leave its indelible stamp on all strata of Vienna, mentally, physically, and temperamentally. With the recall of those bygone "good times" there also returned the now exaggerated tales about the moving spirit of that day, Emperor Joseph. Rosa Mayreder, the poetess (who was to prepare the libretto for Hugo Wolf's ill-fated opera *The Corregidor*), recalls in 1858 a story told by her old nursemaid of the "wonderful Emperor Joseph" who would mingle with the Viennese in disguise, dispensing justice and, at the height of happenings, would shed his disguise to reveal the splendor of his imperial garb. *"Ich bin der Kaiser Joseph"* ("I am the Emperor Joseph") were the words which he was supposed to have uttered on those awesome occasions. The tart Viennese tongue, detecting the ludicrous hypocrisy behind the legend, promptly recoined the phrase: "You will never learn my name, I am the Emperor Joseph."

As could be expected, Nestroy exposed the ridiculous side of the revolution. It is said that he and a fellow comedian actually wore fake arms from the prop room of the *Carltheater*, much to the amusement of their fellow national guard members. It was his way of showing his sympathy with the revolution and at the same time mocking its failings and incompetence. Nonetheless he kept undiminished his belief in the essential rightness of the cause even at a time when the aspired-to freedom and its limited achievements had been crushed. Thus his impudent plays *Freiheit in Krähwinkel (Freedom in Krähwinkel)* and *Die Dame und der Schneider (The Lady and the Tailor)* reflect his views and feelings at a time when police censorship had again become the law of the land. He lashed out in equal measure at Metternich and at the incompetence, muddle-headedness, and the self-seeking motives of the other side. To nobody's surprise the most outspoken of his plays, *Der alte Mann mit der jungen Frau (The Old Man with the Young Wife)*, written in 1850, which speaks most freely of the ideals of the revolution, never received the censor's stamp of approval and never saw the stage lights in Nestroy's day. Needless to say, Nestroy, although he used his plays to express his political views, remained first and foremost a man of the theatre. Nor did he forget his role as actor when writing a play. Like Raimund, he always reserved a rewarding part for himself. One of the reasons for Nestroy's immense popularity in Vienna was his affinity to the art of Offenbach. His most masterful parody, worthy of Offenbach, the parable of *Judith and Holofernes*, unassailable due to its mythological guise, furiously lampooned Hebbel's play and the establishment yet always remained delightful theatre.

Johann Nestroy. Unlike Raimund he endeared himself to Vienna through sarcastic and satiric comedies in which he also acted.

Freedom of thought was not the only notion which moved the stale air of Vienna. Mobility and living space had also become important in the minds of the Viennese, tightly hugged by their medieval walls. Some went so far as to suggest that Vienna stop being a quaint medieval city and begin to play its role as the capital of an empire by razing its ancient walls. Oddly enough it was not the city planners who suggested it but a group of Vienna's influential bankers who thought in progressive terms of expanded housing, trade, and industry in so important an empire and European crossroads as Vienna. If anything, the importance of Vienna's location had increased, as a center of trade for the East as well as the seat of an empire. These progressive thoughts, as expected, were opposed by the military, not because the walls would check a foe from without — they had already proven inadequate for that — but because they provided a means of controlling the populace.

The military wanted to divide and conquer, to keep the university students and the burghers of the inner district separated from the "unruly" workers so as to hold an explosive situation in uneasy check. Only after seven years of contention did a joint effort by the Ministry of Public Works, industrialists, and the banking community overcome the arguments of the military ("the citizens of the Inner City should not have to be unnecessarily exposed to bullets in case of civil strife") and the hedging of hesitant Emperor Franz Joseph.

While the Viennese, in maudlin sentimentality, tearfully watched the walls which had withstood two Turkish onslaughts and had kept Europe Christian, crumble under the wrecker's hammer and pickax, a new Vienna emerged. The liberal ideals of the 1848 revolution had failed, but the medieval spirit which had long possessed the Habsburgs, Austria, and Vienna had also come to an end.

4

The Father of THEM All

Da schmaust und zecht um die Wette	There vies in feast and carousal
Beim Sperl und horcht auf ihn	At the Sperl, and listens in bout
Der Falstaff der deutschen Städte	The Falstaff of German cities
Das liebe, dicke Wien	Vienna, old and stout.
Es huschen die Feen und Nixen	The Fairies and sprites they scurry
Im Mondenschein vorbei	On pale beams of the moon
Sie lachen und tanzen und knixen	They laugh and dance and curry
Bei lieblicher Melodei	To lovely melody and tune
Das ist ein Geigen und ein Blasen	There is a fiddling and tootling
Ist eine tönende Flut	A flood of sound and flow
Die Männer und Frauen, sie rasen	The men and women are raging
In stürmisch jubelnder Glut	In stormy jubilant glow
Rasch sind die Nixen gezogen	Quickly the sprites have vanished
In ihr kristallenes Haus	Into their crystalline house
Es schreckt sie der Fiedelbogen	They fled in wide-eyed terror
Des Walzer-Tyrannen Strauss	Before the bow of waltz tyrant Strauss.

Eduard von Bauernfeld

About a year and a half before his separation from Lanner, Strauss had met Anna Streim, the dark-haired daughter of the innkeeper of *Zum Roten Hahn* (The Red Rooster) where Lanner and he had taken up quarters. The innkeeper's daughter could not resist the dashing Strauss's ardent charm, and she was soon "heavy with child." Marriage was imperative, and the wedding took place on 11 July 1825. Their first child, baptized Johann, was born on 25 October 1825. While, on the one hand, Strauss had forgone an assured income when he explosively resigned from Lanner's ensemble, his initial burden now was vastly increased to a wife, a child, and sixteen musicians who loyally had thrown in their lot with him after his separation from Lanner. Strauss had to find employment for the musicians, a heavy burden at age twenty-one. Unfortunately the musical efforts of the young man had not yet taken wing, and the meager income from occasional engagements had to be supplemented with music lessons which Strauss found boring and soon detested.

Strauss was eager and determined to succeed, and he and his band of musicians soon had their first engagement at the *Gasthaus zu den zwei Tauben* (Two Doves Inn). For them he wrote his first orchestral waltz, the *Täuberlwalzer*, under his own name. We can reconstruct the ensemble from the music which was scored for three violins, a flute, two clarinets, two horns, a trumpet, two drums, and a double bass, with cellos and violas conspicuously absent. While the composer must have lamented the balance lost by the absence of cellos and violas, financial considerations at that time may have forbidden a larger ensemble. Strauss thus had to use his meager capital to emphasize the violins, which throughout his life were to remain his chief interest. It was the violin he played best; from it he could coax that *Schmiegsamkeit*, the pliancy and suppleness which the waltz demanded. In 1826, in an upswing of activity, Strauss played at the hotel *Schwan* as well as at open-air concerts at the *Zwei Tauben*, which during the summer months became a beer garden. Open-air concerts by prominent salon and military ensembles at coffeehouses and beer gardens were among the most delightful evening and Sunday features in Vienna. The populace—fathers, mothers, children, and dogs—went to hear them, and often stood five deep outside to listen and applaud if they could not afford the price of a glass of beer or a cup of coffee inside. Brahms is remembered as having been fond of those outdoor places and their concerts and could be seen beating the time on the table with his walking stick or umbrella.

Strauss, although now gainfully occupied, was too meticulous a professional not to realize that his natural talents had to be supplemented with additional musical knowledge if he wished to rise above the musical trash which, at the time, passed for dance music in his native city. Too proud to admit his shortcomings he decided to take secret lessons from the well-known conductor Ignatz von Seyfried, one of the few musicians in Vienna who was on friendly terms with Beethoven and Schubert. While Lanner continued his own triumphs with public, publishers, and potentates, Strauss determinedly went his own exploratory way.

Thus, unknown to them, the crowds at The Swan and The Doves were the first to hear Strauss's own compositions. These took the public's fancy so swiftly that publisher Haslinger immediately approached Strauss for the publishing rights. But Strauss did not attain wide popularity until he played his new *Kettenbrückenwalzer (Chain Bridge* waltz), named after the café near that famous bridge where he had found a new engagement. Overnight his name was in the forefront of waltz composers. Once exposed to the limelight which he had sought so fervently, Strauss quickly attracted a following. He remained at the *Kettenbrücken* Café for an entire year, not because he was particularly eager to stay but because he had found out too late that his inexperience had allowed the owner to tie him and his musicians to the café for a year by the contract he had signed without bothering to read the fine print. Soon Vienna divided into "Lannerianer" and "Straussianer," but Lanner was generally considered the better of the two, as is seen in a Vienna press critique: "Lanner is the Mozart of dance music. So far no one has attained his level in the field; though many have tried, no one has succeeded in approaching him. Lanner has no rival, not even Strauss. Lanner is a waltz poet, Strauss a waltz composer."

In 1830 Schubert had been dead two years, Beethoven three years, Weber four years, and Haydn twenty-one years; Mozart had vanished from the Vienna scene thirty-nine years before. Schubert had hardly been known during his lifetime, Beethoven had been neglected in the heat of Rossini fever, Haydn and Mozart had become relics of the past, and Wagner was to be snubbed for years to come, even after his first visit to Vienna in 1832. Only the waltz mattered. Chopin rightly detected a lack of seriousness among the Viennese: "Lanner and Strauss and their waltzes overshadow everything." Wagner, on the other hand, viewed the same spectacle with awe: "[Strauss waltzes] are originals with full-blooded productivity ... the magic forces of the suburbs ... the Strauss ecstasy. The waltz is a stronger narcotic than alcohol. The listeners are aflame with the first stroke of his bow. Strauss ... drunk with music, sees the enthusiasm which borders on frenzy. And the 'magnificent Strauss' himself, the magic violin leader, the demon of the musical spirit of the Viennese trembles (with anticipation) at the opening of each waltz ... Vienna's hot summer air is impregnated with Strauss."

Strauss ruled supreme and absolute. In the application of such power Strauss went from one extreme to the other. When a member of his finely honed orchestra missed a cue in Beethoven's *Fidelio* overture, Strauss harbored a grudge against the culprit for years. On the other hand, he was not averse to introducing circus tricks of the coarsest variety into his programs. He once engaged a counter-tenor to sing Rosina's *cavatina* from Rossini's *Barber of Seville* because it was a crowd-pleasing stunt. As usual, he had gauged the public reaction correctly. The audience climbed on chairs, tables, even trees to get a look at the singer from whose bearded throat emanated such beguiling falsetto tones, trills, and coloraturas. To have fireworks go off while he played a *Schnellpolka* was another of Strauss's novelties. Not even the 1832 cholera epidemic was able to curb Vienna's thirst for the dance. If anything, it had the opposite effect; with everybody aware that they might die any hour, what better way to expire than while dancing?

Also in 1830, the owner of one of Vienna's most prestigious dance establishments, the *Sperl*, was searching for a new musical ensemble. Lanner had conducted there in 1829, but his appointment as music director for imperial balls, a new family addition, and a hectic schedule threatening to become unmanageable, had prompted him to relinquish the position. Six of the most prominent Vienna orchestras had applied for the position, and the owner, wishing to be fair, auditioned them all on six consecutive evenings. As expected, Strauss's ensemble was the winner for the coveted engagement.

There, at the *Sperl*, began that climax of Vienna's dance craze with "The Tyrant of the Waltz," Johann Strauss. The sobriquet applies because lighthearted, jovial Strauss when leading his orchestra became the strictest of task masters who would under no circumstances permit the sloppiness which pervaded many other ensembles and was passed off as *Gemütlichkeit* or tradition. Strauss's regimen, which started with the first rehearsal, paid off in precision playing unheard of before his day, except with Lanner. Strauss's mania for precision in rhythm and intonation became a terror for another reason; Strauss had an excellent memory, and a player's blatant mistake remained unforgotten sometimes for as long as he played with the orchestra, which might not be long if excessive drinking or other nocturnal escapades caused repeated playing offenses. It soon became apparent that Strauss, through his engagement at the *Sperl*, had stepped into the limelight of Vienna and the world as he led a nightly orgy of dancing. Heinrich Laube[1] in 1833 gave a vivid picture of dancing Vienna:

> The entire Sperl Garden in the Leopoldstadt is blazing with a thousand lamps, all its dance halls are open. Strauss conducts; fire balls fly, all the bushes come alive and whoever possesses a Viennese heart steers himself there in the evening ... This is no assembly of high society but mixed company; the ingredients are respectable and the brew is classic Viennese. One evening and half a night at the Sperl, when the place blooms in all its voluptuous exuberance, is the key to Vienna's sumptuous life. Under illuminated

1. Heinrich Laube, 1806-1884, although German-born, knew Vienna and the Viennese well, as his travel journal *Reise durch das Biedermeier* illustrates. Together with Schreyvogel he was the creator of the great tradition which made the *Burgtheater* the foremost theatre in the German-speaking world. His greatest achievements were the creation of a universal repertoire, bringing the bourgeoisie into the theatre, and the second revival of Grillparzer.

trees and open arcades ... men and women are seated at innumerable tables, eating, drinking, gossiping, laughing and listening. In the center of the garden is the orchestra from which emanate those seductive siren tones, the waltzes ... which, like a tarantula's sting, incite the young bloods to riot. In the middle of the garden at the helm of his orchestra stands Austria's modern hero, the Austrian Napoleon, music director Johann Strauss. What Napoleon's victories were to the French the Strauss waltzes are to the Viennese ... the father points him out to his child, the Viennese girl to her out-of-town lover, the host to the traveler: "That's him."

They are gaily sensuous people, these Austrians. Napoleon cost France many sons and brothers and fathers before they could say "Voici l'homme." The Austrians have to pay only with a few gulden and sleepless nights. For that they have an exotic looking bird with colorful, enticing feathers for the ladies ... and they exclaim with delight "This is the Strauss." [The allusion to the bird is lost in translation. But in German the name for ostrich is Strauss, spelled like the composer's name.]

I was very eager to see the Austrian Napoleon and I was glad to have found him on the battlefield. He was in the process of fighting the imperial battle of Austerlitz when I arrived ... There he stood before me ... violin in one hand, beating time as if possessed by invisible forces. All eyes were on him, it was a moment of worship. They will ask you, I said to myself ... future generations will ask: "What does he look like, that Strauss?" I watched closely; one poetizes when standing before a person of historic importance ... maestro Strauss is ... exultant with life and sunshine, modernly bold, restlessly fidgety, passionate in an unlovely way ..."

The man is as black as a moor. The hair is curly, the mouth melodious and enterprising and he has a snub nose. One regrets that he has a white face ... otherwise he would be the perfect moorish king from the Orient ... Balthasar brought the vaporous incense to envelop the senses, and thus it is with Strauss; he too drives the devil from our bodies with his waltzes which is modern exorcism, and he too envelops our senses in sweet ecstasy.

Exotic also is the way in which he conducts his dances. His limbs are not his own any longer; when he lets loose with the thunderstorms of his waltzes, the fiddle bow dances with the arm ... the beat jumps with his foot, the melody waves champagne glasses in his face ... the entire Strauss bird takes a stormy run into flight, the devil is abroad in the land.

And this passionate procedure is received by the Viennese with an enthusiasm without parallel and they attentively remember their hero and his musical ideas ... One potpourri which he performed was strewn with some of his waltz themes and that vast mixed audience recognized the smallest Straussian melodic shred and greeted each waltz with thunderous jubilation.

It is a potentially dangerous power which is given into this man's hand; it is fortunate that music can give rise to all kinds of thoughts, that censorship cannot interfere with the waltz, that music ... stimulates our senses in

Johann Strauss Father (1804-1849). Exultant—restless—passionate—possessed.

a direct way. I do not know how much he knows aside from notes, but I do know he could do much harm were he fiddling Rousseau's ideas; the Viennese would go through the entire *contrat social* with him in one evening.

It is remarkable that Austrian sensuality is never coarse, it is naive and no sinner ... The variegated crowd surges hither and yon, the girls, warm, laughing, squeeze through the merry groups of lads; their hot breath reached me, the friendly stranger leaning against a pillar, like a perfume of tropical flowers, arms pressed me into the turmoil—nobody apologizes; at the Sperl no pardon is asked or given ...

Now preparations for the actual dance are made. To keep the unrestrained crowd in line, a rope is spanned ... to separate the dancers from the rest. But this border is constantly fluctuating and yielding; only the rhythmically whirling heads of the girls are noticeable in that dancing stream. In bacchantic abandon the pairs waltz ... joyful frenzy is on the loose, no god checks it ... The beginning of each dance is characteristic. Strauss intones his trembling preludes, longing to pour forth fully ... the Viennese girl snuggles deep in her lad's arm, and in the strangest way they sway to the beat. For a long while one hears only the long-held breast tones of the nightingale with which she begins her song and enchants the listeners, then suddenly the piercing trill bubbles forth, the dance itself begins with whirling rapidity and the couples hurl themselves into the maelstrom of gaiety.

I have never witnessed excesses there, the unfortunate magic word of the north, brandy, is absent ... the dumbly drunk, the senseless are not to be seen. The light Austrian wine only makes the senses aware, and the Viennese have big stomachs but narrow throats. Those orgies last until early morning, then Austria's musical hero, Johann Strauss, packs up his violin and goes home to sleep for a few hours, to dream of new battle plans and waltz themes for the next afternoon. The flushed couples stream out into the warm Viennese night, and the love-making and the giggling recede into all directions. This is the Sperl in bloom.

Watching such a gay fatalistic way of life, Wagner commented "Nobody dreams of altering his outlook and places of amusement are crowded (despite the plague). I visited theatres, listened to Strauss, went for excursions and all in all had a wonderful time."

Another German journalist, Kurländer, vividly described one of those dance occasions and its orgiastic frenzy led by pied piper Strauss: "Over forty thousand people were gathered in the Brigittenau [a suburban district]. There were green tents made of branches, lanterns radiated their colored lights and the moon shone on the spectacle with magic brightness ... a rotating movement had seized the meadows and the surroundings as far as the eye could reach. The masses of people waltzed over hill and dale, stumbled on the grass but went on dancing."

Vienna suddenly was too narrow a space for Strauss. The world beckoned. He had already been to neighboring Budapest and, as expected, had been ecstatically received. One Budapest newspaper reported: "The genial composer was received with jubilation and his performances were accompanied with such storms of applause that the entire hall roared." Now Prussia had extended an invitation, and that was an altogether different matter. There had always been, even in times of peace, a multi-level tug-of-war, politically, culturally, and religiously: North against South, Hohenzollern against Habsburg, Protestant versus Catholic, stern responsible outlook versus "let's live today, for tomorrow we die," the military march versus the waltz. Austria and Prussia, despite their common language, history, and cultural background, had fought each other bitterly in the past (and were destined to do so again in 1866), with Austria usually on the losing side.

To the surprise of all, Prussians and Austrians alike, except perhaps the self-assured Strauss, Austria scored one of its rare victories on Prussian soil. Despite the chill of autumn the Berliners melted before the warmth of Viennese music, its fever pitch, its fervent presentation. The Prussian delight was contagious. Tsar Nicholas of Russia and the Tsarina, present at a Strauss concert during their state visit, attempted in vain to lure the musician back to St. Petersburg with them. Strauss, although flattered, had to decline due to prior commitments. Enthusiasm for the waltz and for Strauss repeated itself in Dresden, Munich, Augsburg, Stuttgart, Wiesbaden, Heidelberg, Frankfurt, Leipzig, Magdeburg, Braunschweig, Hannover, Hamburg, Bremen, and Düsseldorf. Wherever he traveled, he swept his public before him and they responded with jubilation, laurel wreaths, flowers, adulation, and avowals of love. That lure of adulation soon was to carry him beyond German confines to Amsterdam, the Hague, Liège, Brussels, and back again to beckoning Germany. The waltz had "arrived." Whereas centuries before it had been condemned as the ploy of devilish forces and fair maidens were warned against close embraces and whirling motions, the waltz now, in its most romantic aspect, outshone such sparkling dances as France's quadrille, Bohemia's polka, and Poland's mazurka. Strauss, of course, did not remain untouched by these sparkling foreign dance creations. He was adept at using them in his own works. Furthermore, to include the quadrille and the polka in an evening's program was to be *au courant* and also to inject variety into an evening which might last from nine o'clock until dawn.

Five years after this separation from Lanner, Strauss commanded nearly two hundred musicians, usually divided into as many as six orchestras each evening, as the demand might dictate. While Lanner and Strauss remained life-long friends, their artistic and commercial rivalry was keen. Strauss could not match Lanner's appointment to the imperial balls at the *Redoutensaal*, but he had a bourgeois triumph of his own, a six-year contract at the *Sperl*. The *Sperl* had a special attraction for Strauss because there, twelve years earlier as an obscure boy of fourteen, he had fiddled under Pamer's sodden direction. Now he had returned in triumph at the helm of one of the finest dance orchestras Vienna had ever heard. It was to be there that Strauss's magic exploded and ignited Vienna into dance mania. Besides the *Sperl*, six other establishments were constantly vying for Strauss's services. Since each announced its "special event" in large print "under the personal direction of Herr Strauss," the composer, particularly during the *Fasching* season, had a *Fiaker* on call, as did his friend Lanner. More than once Lanner and Strauss must have passed each other in the night as they hurried to engagements. Their competition had an overall beneficial effect on Vienna's musical life, because minor purveyors of dance music either were forced to strain to improve their level of nightly offerings or leave the field. The art of the Viennese waltz which had started with two *Gasthausmusikanten* (inn musicians) had been elevated to ballroom, concert hall, and palace. The slow but inevitable disappearance of the *Cholerakapellen*, so called because Viennese wit felt that their music was bad enough to induce the sickness, served only to close tighter a cycle of sorts. The prominent names—Lanner, Strauss, Morelli, Fahrbach—were thus called upon even more frequently to feed Vienna's voracious appetite for dance music. For Strauss the situation was especially trying because of the additional honors bestowed upon him. In 1834 he was appointed *Kapellmeister* of the First Vienna Burgher regiment, and in 1835 he finally became Music Director of Imperial Court Balls—the supreme honor. Those honors added the palaces and salons of the mighty to his itinerary. To top it off Strauss was again assailed by *Wanderlust*, that traveling fever which is the hallmark of all true romantics. Off he went in 1835, leaving wife and family behind, to gather laurels in Munich, Augsburg, Ulm, Stuttgart, Heilbronn, Heidelberg, Karlsruhe, Mannheim, Wiesbaden, Frankfurt, Nuremberg, Regensburg, and Passau. Munich proved especially enjoyable because Strauss and the poet Raimund met and quickly became friends. The triumphant return to Vienna was short-lived because Strauss, having tasted anew the acclaim of non-Viennese audiences, longed for more of the same. He had begun to thrive on adulation, and no amount of it was excessive. He watched his home fill with laurel wreaths, honors, and souvenirs. Soon he roamed again, ranging from Amsterdam and Brussels in the west to Prague in the east and Dresden and Leipzig in the north on a four-month tour which proved as strenuous as it was exhilarating.

Having conquered the stolid and once hostile Germans, Strauss's musical ambitions led him to venture even further, across the Rhine into France. Germans had greedily absorbed Vienna's sentimentality, if for no other reason than because they longed for its warmth, so alien to Prussian sentiments. Would Strauss be as successful in a country where music was part of life, where opera was presided over by such masters as Bellini and Cherubini, where their ravishing *bel canto* was balanced by the massive French Grand Opera at its height led by the German with the Italian first name, Giacomo Meyerbeer? Strauss had reason to feel perturbed as he and his twenty-six musicians, a grotesquely small number with which to conquer the critical French, prepared for the journey.

Strauss had realized that he could take no chances with whims or foibles in such an undertaking. Slowly he had begun to find out if the most dependable musicians within his organization were available and willing to travel even more extensively. He had left no detail to chance. He had inquired into the members' financial status and their ability to support their families from abroad despite the hardships involved on both ends. Having laid the groundwork, he entered into negotiations with the musicians he wanted, and, with an eye on the future, accorded them higher salaries than they had received in Vienna. On 4 October 1836, Strauss and his carefully selected musicians left for Paris. News of the impending departure had spread swiftly, and when his ensemble arrived at the stagecoach depot a huge crowd had gathered around the express coaches, especially decorated for the momentous occasion, and three cheers went up as the caravan started. To break the monotony and, incidentally, earn travel money, shrewd Strauss had also arranged for concerts en route in Munich, Ulm, and Stuttgart. Thus advance money and publicity were assured.

Two weeks later, on the gray day of 19 October, Strauss and his "army" crossed the Rhine into Strassburg. In view of the total rearrangement of the global map of our day, the Strassburg concert is noteworthy because of an incident which preceded it. Strauss was about to begin when a messenger approached him offstage bearing a note from the prefect of police requesting a military fanfare before the actual opening of the concert. Strauss was puzzled but obliged. In the silence which followed, the prefect rose and proudly announced that the important city of Constantine in Algeria had fallen to the French colonial troops under the command of General Damrémont. The audience rose in jubilation. Thereupon the prefect signaled for a second fanfare and, in a voice trembling with emotion, announced that the general had fallen in battle. While a wave of emotion swept the hall, a third fanfare sounded and the prefect exhorted the audience to join him in the singing of the *Marseillaise*. Again a wave of pride and emotion swept the theatre. The last note of the stirring national anthem had barely echoed away when Strauss raised his bow and the concert began. Borne on the emotional wave which had preceded it, the concert was a tumultuous success the news of which, in turn, preceded Strauss to Paris.

The Father

After another nine days of travel, they entered the French capital. The Paris newspapers greeted the "Austrian Apostle of Joy" with flattering editorials of welcome and watchful anticipation. The triumph in provincial Strassburg did little to alleviate Strauss's insecurity in Paris, because now he became aware of his mistake of bringing only twenty-six musicians with him on so important a musical foray. How was he to compete with the illustrious Musard or with Dufresne who, like Strauss, included Haydn, Mozart, and Beethoven in his programs? Besides, in Paris the quadrille was queen. How could the waltz, not nearly as popular, succeed when thinly played by an ensemble of twenty-six? Actually the quadrille was something of an antithesis of the people's round dance which the waltz represented in sublimation. The Paris bourgeoisie, having been deprived of the dance of the highborn, the minuet, yet unwilling to totally forgo past pleasures, had devised a sequence of dance steps of their own, obviously less rigid than the minuet but with a surprising dash of elegance far removed from the bacchanalian round dance. Despite all outward signs of welcome, French success for Strauss was not nearly as assured as his cocky mien led Paris to believe. Paris too had become a musical center. Among the wealth of composers, conductors, and musical organizations in the field of superior light musical entertainment, the name of Phillipe Musard—Napoleon Musard, the Parisians called him—stood out, as did the names of Lanner and Strauss in Vienna. Adam Card comments: "Musard in Paris, Jullien in London and Johann Strauss Father in Vienna were the first conductors who by their own skill and personality were able to draw audiences to their concerts at which they were conducting, quite independently of any other attractions that were offered ... and quite regardless of what music they heard." Musard, fiery, temperamental, rightfully famous, proudly conducted an orchestra one hundred strong, all of them well-trained musicians. Their number and reputation alone must have given Strauss some sleepless nights.

If up to that moment nervousness and uncertainty had tugged at Strauss's sleeve, it was forgotten as he stepped in front of his men on the stage of the *Gymnase Musicale* on the premiere date of 1 November. The house was filled to capacity, and the greatest musical minds of Paris—Adam, Auber, Cherubini, Halévy, Meyerbeer, and, of course, Musard—were there. Before an audience abounding in gala uniforms, lavish gowns, and glittering diadems, Strauss opened with a bow to France, the overture to the opera *Les Faux-Monnayeurs (The Counterfeiters)* by Daniel François Auber. Paris understood the gesture and applauded appreciatively. However, beginning with the *Gabriellenwalzer*, the emotional climate in the hall changed abruptly. Paris had never heard the like. There was no conductor stiffly beating time with a baton, there was a master fiddler, conducting with head, arms, bow, and body, drawing his bow across the violin, his head thrown back in ecstasy. The precision and the élan were not lost on the illustrious Parisians who applauded wildly for minutes on end. Vienna had conquered Paris also.

Four days later Strauss played a command performance at the Tuileries before the king of France. There he witnessed a paradox which he was long to remember. Louis Phillipe, the "bourgeois king," was the antithesis of all that surrounded him — the past splendor of tapestried and mirrored halls, the elaborately uniformed lackeys, the gleaming chandeliers. Again Strauss easily hurdled all obstacles. Soon French aristocracy, the king and his entourage, the king of Belgium, the duke of Orléans, and wealthy industrialists mingled with the Viennese musicians and drank a toast to them. The king paid Strauss a supreme compliment: "Your waltzes have been familiar to me for a long time, my dear Strauss. It gives me all the more pleasure that you have done me the honor of appearing personally." The effect of the king's cordial reception was not lost on the Parisians. Reinforced by a royal gift to Strauss of two thousand francs and a diamond stick pin, the royal reception became the signal in Paris for a change from enthusiasm to adulation.

If both Strauss and Musard were excellent musicians, they were shrewd businessmen as well. Musard knew a good waltz when he heard it and wished to be part of the attraction of the Viennese novelty in Paris. Strauss wished to have Musard as a friend rather than a competitor and also wished to share in Musard's deserved fame and popularity. An understanding was soon reached whereby their respective organizations would combine in thirty concerts, with each man to entertain for half a concert. Having already had the opportunity to hear Musard repeatedly in the past, the public often left the concerts in droves after Strauss, the musical novelty, had performed. Thereupon Musard shrewdly arranged the programs so as to have Strauss occupy the second half of the program.

By now the urge for constant and renewed signs of success had become a mania with Strauss. "Tomorrow we are leaving for Rouen," was his peremptory order one day, given without prior consultation with anyone in his orchestra. Success stories had preceded him like wildfire, fanned by the winds of press reports. Next he went to the port of Le Havre. The performance there was such a success and champagne flowed so freely that the Strauss company was barely aware of being ushered into their carriages at dawn and thence back to Rouen where a sumptuous champagne breakfast awaited them. Inevitably the strain of concertizing and traveling was beginning to take its toll on the company, particularly since it was now 23 December, and the men were shocked into the sinking realization that this was to be the first Christmas which their families were to celebrate without them. Strauss was aware of the gloominess and depression among his men, and he could not ignore it. He promptly arranged for a lavish banquet. The misgivings and melancholy soon evaporated in the mist of spirits. That night's masked ball at which the Strauss ensemble was to provide the music was especially noteworthy for the orchestra's high morale. The musicians barely took notice that they were to return to Paris that same night.

Carnival in Paris began earlier than in Vienna, and more of it could be observed in the streets than in Vienna, where most of the dancing and merrymaking was an indoor affair. Thus Strauss's men curiously eyed the shivering figures of masked harlequins and Colombines, maharajahs, Turks, Spaniards, and Moors huddling around the flaming barrels put in the streets to provide light and heat. The high flickering flames drew an eerie picture across the darkened wintry streets, more like a witches's sabbath than a carnival revelry. But only a furtive glance was grudgingly allowed by Strauss. "We have work to do, there's no time for frivolities." He led his orchestra on for another two whirlwind months with concerts nearly every night in concert halls, the palaces of French nobility, and the equally imposing palatial homes of the *nouveau riches*, followed by the inevitable feting until dawn. Now the Vienna picture was repeating itself and the Paris *haute volée* were vying for Strauss's services, with Count Apponyi, the Austrian ambassador to France, leading aristocracy to Strauss's doorstep.

Among the many parties, the most memorable was the one given on New Year's eve by Maurice Schlesinger, editor of the *Gazette Musicale* and the man who was the "open sesame" to everything musical in Paris. Everybody was there. Cherubini paid Strauss what he considered the supreme compliment; "You play like an Italian." Meyerbeer called him "modest although unequaled in your own sphere." Skeletal, taciturn Paganini stared at Strauss from the sidelines before walking up to him, shaking his hand, and departing without murmuring a word. Jacques Fromental Halévy, famed composer of the opera *La Juive*, joined the long line of congratulators. When an age-wrinkled hand joined his, Strauss looked into the once steely eyes of ancient Talleyrand, their fire banked by age.

Neither the strenuous work, nor the inevitable nightly bouts, nor the kindness of Parisians in high and low places swayed the Viennese from the standard which they had set themselves. Both Strauss and Dufresne were invited to play at the City of Paris ball, the feature costume event of the season. In keeping with the motif and the tradition of the event, black dominos had been laid out for the musicians, who were expected to wear them while playing since everybody entering the ballroom was required to be in constume. Dufresne's ensemble complied as a matter of course. Strauss gave the costumes one startled look, then refused in his name and that of his orchestra to wear them. The ball committee immediately was in high dudgeon; tradition could not be flouted. The Austrian ambassador was called upon to intervene in the "crisis." Strauss refused: "We are musicians, artists, not clowns." Gasparin, the French minister of the interior, then approached Strauss and argued that it would be impolite for the Viennese guests to disregard French custom and that he feared unpleasant consequences in the diplomatic field should the Strauss company refuse to comply. Strauss demurred: "White tie and tails have been accepted throughout the world as the height of elegance." He had no intention of wearing or having his musicians wear buffoons' costumes, tradition or no. The official departed shaking his head, and the committee, fearing the worst, wrung its collective hands. But Strauss carried the evening. After a surprised glance and a wry smile, the sophisticated Parisians accepted the musicians' evening attire and went on dancing.

If Meyerbeer, Cherubini, and Halévy found pleasure in Strauss's music, one man of music found it extraordinary—the man who, with César Franck and Claude Debussy after him, was to break the dominance of opera in French musical life—Hector Berlioz. Berlioz saw in Strauss, his music, his precision, and inspiration a typical example of German musical excellence and an opportunity to lash out at France's petrified state of musical affairs. In his famed and feared *Journal des Débats* he proceeded to make his point:

> It is remarkable that in a city like Paris, where the foremost virtuosi and composers of Europe are heard, where the study of music is so advanced in many respects, the arrival of a German orchestra which lays claim only to present a good waltz should develop into an event of such importance. But this is the case. The fact becomes clearer when we examine the style of these foreign artists and their effect, on first presentation, upon a public about whose impartiality there cannot be any doubt. We know the name of Strauss thanks to music publishers who spread his waltzes in thousands of copies and thanks to Musard who presented some of them to us. But that was all; of the technical perfection, of the fire, the intelligence, and the rare rhythmic feeling which distinguishes this orchestra, we had not the slightest notion.
>
> Strauss brought only 26 musicians from Vienna ... 4 first violins, 4 second violins, 1 cello, 2 contra basses, 2 flutes, 2 clarinets, 1 oboe, 2 horns, 2 trumpets, 1 bassoon, 1 cornet, 1 trombone, 1 timpani, 1 harp, one bass drum. But since most of these artists possess two or three instruments between which they are able to switch back and forth with great rapidity there emerges an interchange of the most variegated shades ... so that the small orchestra appears twice as large as it actually is.

Berlioz continued to remark on the versatility of the players, discussed the ingenious use of the instruments in general and bemoaned the fact that in the entire city of Paris neither a bass trombone nor a contrabassoon was to be found which, in turn, made it impossible to perform such works as Mozart's *Requiem*, Haydn's *Creation*, or Beethoven's Fifth Symphony.

> But back to Strauss! Not only the ability of the brass seems remarkable. The clarinets achieve nuances of extraordinary tenderness without losing in purity of tone. The oboe received applause after a tasteful solo passage. The flutes were rather mediocre, the violins by contrast, despite their small number, possess a tone faculty of exquisite modulation which can only be ascribed to the finished training of the artists and the precision of their bowing technique. However, their noticeable superiority, to my mind, is not the main achievement of the Vienna orchestra. Although they are not a daily occurrence (in Paris) it would not suffice to evoke such great interest as the Paris attendance of the Strauss concerts indicates. There is in music a field of immense importance, yet equally neglected by all creative artists. Although rapid progress can be noted in almost all fields in the realm of art, one can barely find the beginnings of one development ... I am referring to rhythm.

In a review of rhythm, its history, development, difficulties, and neglect, Berlioz proceeds to point up its importance, calling on Gluck, Weber, and Beethoven to prove the significance of rhythm in symmetry—or the lack of it—the development of new rhythmic patterns, their difficulties, before returning to the subject at hand.

> The musicians of Strauss are much more trained to overcome difficulties of this sort than our artists; the pieces they execute, those charming waltzes in which the melody, self-intoxicated, incites and whiplashes the beat in a thousand different ways, are often against the grain; but they overcome them with such playful rhythmic coquetry and bravura that those piquant rhythmic flirtations are enriched with an irresistible charm. That is the reason why I look at the local success of Strauss as a good omen for the development of music in Paris. That great success, in my opinion, must be attributed to a much greater degree to their rhythmic accent of the waltz than to the grace of melody or the brilliance of instrumentation ... Strauss operates in a field first opened by Beethoven and Weber. That is the great field of rhythm.

Berlioz may be forgiven for a wrong assumption, because it was the triumph of Lanner and Strauss to have infused melodic grace into a dance form which, before them, had been dominated almost exclusively by rhythmic "whirling and stomping." Nevertheless, so monumental a compliment by so prominent a musical personality as Berlioz only added to Strauss's stature. He, in turn, reciprocated graciously by dedicating his waltz *Der Diamant (The Diamond)* to Berlioz, who commented again in his Memoirs: "Strauss is an artist whose influence is not fully appreciated ... In the *Redoutensaal* Vienna's youth gives their passion for the dance full rein, a true and delightful passion which enabled the Viennese to perfect the salon dance to a true art which stands above the routine of our balls as high as a Strauss waltz stands above the polkas and the fiddling of our Parisian dance floors ... I spent entire nights watching those thousands of incomparable waltz dancers whirling, the choreographic order of those contra dances of 200 persons arranged in only two rows and to admire the piquant figures of those character dances."

Strauss attended Musard rehearsals to acquaint himself with the intricacies of the quadrille, which he, in turn, was to introduce to Vienna. Aside from his arrangement with Musard, Strauss also combined musical forces with the other prominent member of Paris light music—Dufresne. They would appear jointly at the masked balls of St. Honoré, with Dufresne conducting the quadrilles and Strauss the waltzes with the mighty combined orchestras of one hundred forty players performing for both. The total of eighty-six Paris concerts was to prove a great source of satisfaction and income to Strauss. Yet surprisingly little money was actually left in his pocket because of the vast expenditures necessary to keep his musicians in good spirits and to maintain the high degree of perfection which evoked admiration and applause everywhere. Strauss spared no expense to maintain that level. A member of the orchestra reported to his family in Vienna: "Wherever we go Strauss rents the finest hotels, orders the best meals ... Every comfort is attended to, not even wealthy travelers would live better. In Paris we rented an entire hotel for fully four months ... [during] a terribly hard, cold winter Strauss had to have all rooms heated. In short, Strauss earned much honor but damned little money. Yet all he did was done with the greatest willingness and he never found himself in financial difficulties ... In short, Strauss cares for his people like a tender father for his children."

That view was disputed both by his own family—he cared for his children only in the most tyrannical manner, or left them unattended for months—while he was on tour and by some members of his ensemble, four of whom deserted him and returned to Vienna and their families. Those men spoke angrily of being overworked (an obviously justified complaint) and underpaid (perhaps equally justified, considering the trying circumstances).

On 28 February Strauss finally left Paris. But no thoughts of returning to Vienna assailed him. Rather, the tour was extended to Amiens, Lille, Antwerp, and Brussels. In the Low Countries the exhaustion of the ensemble was eased due to the extensive rail network which afforded better and faster transportation than crammed, drafty stagecoaches. But Belgium was only a way station in Strauss's lofty plans, which reached beyond the continent. Fortified with his Parisian triumphs, Strauss issued another one of his commands: "We are going to England." He was bluntly rebuffed, to his surprise, by a mutiny in his orchestra. Nobody had told them when they had left Vienna that they would stay away from their families and their city for months on end, nobody had told them that they were to leave the continent or how many weeks they were to spend in foreign-speaking lands where they had no friends. Suddenly Strauss was met with cries of "dictator," "adventurer," and "tyrant." Regardless of whether he considered the epithets true or not, they all applied.

Strauss had decided on the spur of the moment that the coronation of sixteen-year-old Princess Victoria as Queen of England was the ideal moment to concertize in England. In his feverish haste to realize the plans once he had made up his mind (without further consultation with anyone), he executed slipshod contracts without guarantees, convinced that his Parisian triumphs and English wealth would make English success almost mandatory. But his men did not agree or approve. They refused to be drawn into Strauss's whirlwind; they were not interested in further success; they did not wish to become pawns in his quest for British conquest. They wanted to go home; they did not have to travel hundreds of miles to be well paid since musicians of their caliber, Strauss musicians, could find engagements every day and night of the week. Besides, success in puritan England was not assured, despite triumphs in Paris and wealth in London. Upon closer scrutiny success seemed particularly distant in the light of Lord Byron's railings against the waltz. Lord Byron claimed impropriety in the waltz, but two other ingredients might have colored his views: his anti-German feelings against a dance that could be construed as being of German origin, and the fact that he could not dance because he was lame. Yet his poem on the matter was bound to command respect and might adversely influence the reception in England despite Strauss's renown:

> Round all the confines of the yielded waist
> The strangest hand may wander undisplaced
> The lady's in return may grasp as much
> As princely paunches offer to her touch
> Pleased round the chalky floor how well they trip,
> One hand reposing on the royal hip;
> The other to the shoulders no less royal
> Ascending with affection truly loyal
>
> Thus all and each, in movement swift and slow
> The genial contact gently undergo;
> Till some might marvel with the modest Turk,
> If "nothing follows all this palming work?"

Something does follow at a fitter time;
The breast thus publicly resigned to man;
In private may resist him—if it can.

Luck, however, was still with Strauss. Victoria did like the waltz. If Strauss were to be present in England at her coronation, she would be secretly delighted to have him there. But first he would have to calm his orchestra, which was not at all inclined to be soothed. Tempers flared and voices rose, but in the end Strauss prevailed. The men's fears and objections overcome, the company embarked upon a bright moon on 11 April 1838 on the *Princess Victoria* and arrived on English soil the next day and in London soon thereafter.

The vast, teeming metropolis made Vienna appear like the provincial city it still was, particularly since London was feverishly and joyously preparing for the coronation. Strauss first called, of course, on Prince Esterhazy, the Austrian ambassador to England, who expressed his pleasure that the Austrians, through Strauss, were to play a part in the coronation festivities. The two men also agreed that it would be fitting to have the first concert on English soil at the Austrian embassy "Under the Patronage of His Serene Highness, Prince Esterhazy." The prince, elegant, charming, extravagant, and uninhibited (it was rumored that he had sired one hundred children), advised Strauss to read all contracts carefully before signing them to protect himself against excesses and law suits. This advice, coming from a man hardly qualified to issue it, was nevertheless sound. But Strauss, equally uninhibited and extravagant, threw caution to the wind, to his immediate regret.

Soon after his arrival in London it became apparent that Strauss had contracted with a hotel which was far inferior to the lodgings to which his men were accustomed. The food was as bad as it was overpriced, and the rooms were unclean. Strauss promptly informed the proprietor of his dissatisfaction and his resolve to leave the premises. Thereupon, the innkeeper, taking advantage of Strauss's unfamiliarity with English customs, promptly hauled him into court. Brought before the solemn, bewigged magistrate, Strauss, who spoke no English, delegated his trusted friend, the violinist Reichmann, to represent him before the British bar. But soon Reichmann's command of the English language also proved inadequate, and he was grateful for the intervention on their behalf of a stranger from the courtroom audience who translated and interpreted. After a lengthy investigation the court decided that Strauss had acted with propriety and owed only the actually incurred cost of their brief stay, a total of twenty-nine pounds to the delinquent hotel owner. But then the court declared Strauss responsible for cost of court proceedings—one hundred forty pounds. He was speechless. Before he could recover from the blow he was approached by the clerk of the court and informed that, unless he paid the court costs immediately or posted bond, he would be put in jail. "But my name is Strauss, Johann Strauss, *the* Strauss, I am here to play at the coronation, the Austrian ambassador knows me personally." The clerk remained unmoved. Strauss sent for his valet to bring the necessary funds to the court. The messenger returned empty-handed. The valet had absconded with nearly one hundred pounds, all the money Strauss had had available at the moment. Strauss was frantic. Where was he to secure such a sum in a country where he knew practically nobody? Of course there was still the ambassador, but, under the circumstances, to involve him would have been embarrassing to both sides. Strauss then received permission to communicate with his Viennese publisher who was told of his London predicament and his resolve, under duress, to sell some of his new compositions to the London publisher Cocks to extricate himself from his precarious position. The Viennese publisher had no choice but to accede or lose Strauss as a client. The London publishing house, on the other hand, was so delighted with the unexpected windfall that they gladly paid a purchase price which more than covered Strauss's unexpected London debts.

Strauss's fortunes then soared. Soon advance notices and fliers announced that his performances were "Under the Patronage of Her Majesty Queen Victoria and His Serene Highness Prince Albert." Although hardly needed, this brought him to even more prominent attention of London audiences. Now there was no end to the court balls, dances, soirées and musical receptions at which the Strauss orchestra was prominently featured. In "English Impressions of Strauss Sr." Ignatz Moscheles, the famous composer and pianist, recalled that Johann Strauss's music "is like an Oberon horn, all are dancing, all must dance when he fiddles. In the concerts which he gives with his small orchestra, you dance sitting down ... At the most fashionable of subscription balls all aristocratic feet jump to his tune, and we were fortunate to dance to his melodies at a soirée and we old married people felt decidedly rejuvenated. He himself dances with body and soul while playing, not with his feet but with his violin which moves up and down constantly while the entire body gives the beat. All the time he is a genial Viennese, not cunning like some men of the world of which we have seen enough sorry examples, but amusing and always gay."

Madame Rothschild, Prince Esterhazy, and Princess Schwarzenberg also honored Strauss at special soirées. The Russian ambassador, not to be outdone, engaged Strauss and his ensemble for a ball; for the occasion, the palace of the Russian embassy, especially the ballroom, was "a sea of light." But the outward Slavic splendor had a tactless and crude side. Strauss and his ensemble were not permitted to enter the palace through the main staircase used by aristocracy, nor were they allowed to use the servants' entrance. They had to reach the second-story ballroom via a ladder leaning against the outside of the building. There were muttered curses as the double bass and the harp were heaved upward and through a window. A significantly different treatment was accorded Strauss at the ball of the Austrian Prince Schwarzenberg. There the prince and Ambassador Esterhazy linked arms with Strauss and the three walked the entire length of the huge ballroom as Schwarzenberg exclaimed: "Now that we are all merry Viennese together we will show those English what we are capable of."

The coronation of Princess Victoria took place on 28 June. The occasion was the perfect excuse for the English to enjoy feasting and festivities. Peers of the realm, monied aristocracy, and foreign potentates and ambassadors for weeks had provided an unending parade of balls, garden parties, and receptions. Strauss, as he had correctly calculated, found himself at the vortex of that happy maelstrom, sometimes to the tune of three performances a day. All previous adulation paled before his English triumph. For a while even the closely guarded class lines seemed to vanish. Never before, not even at the court of France, had such a spirit of congeniality prevailed outside Vienna, never before had Strauss observed such an unostentatious display of the fabled wealth of imperial England. It was thus no surprise that the thought of returning to Vienna, at least in the near future, held little attraction for the ambitious composer.

Only a few days' rest was allowed his musicians before Strauss set out to fulfill contractual obligations made while concertizing in London, to quench his unending thirst for adulation and to satisfy the public's voracious appetite for his music. But a few days were hardly enough rest for either conductor or orchestra after they had presented eight concerts before the queen, thirty-eight public concerts, plus another twenty-six concerts in aristocratic homes and for special occasions. Since no concerts were permitted on Sundays or holidays, the task emerges as superhuman. Additional strength was now needed by all to go on the extended tour which Strauss suddenly (and in near-secrecy) had added to their itinerary: Birmingham, Liverpool, Manchester, Dublin, Cheltenham, Bath, Southampton, and Brighton. Wildly ("heedlessly" his men called it behind his back), he rushed his orchestra across England and Scotland sponging up applause and pocketing large amounts of money which were immediately spent on hotels, provisions, and comforts for his musicians, and on advertisements on huge billboards, placards, and handbills for their seemingly interminable one-night stands.

As summer waned, as leaves blazed in autumnal splendor, and as an early chill pervaded the English countryside, memories of Vienna rose to the surface again and dissension among the small and generally docile group began to ferment again. One day they simply refused to go on. By then their reasons were painfully obvious even to Strauss, although he continued to be driven by a force seemingly beyond his control. But he would heed no advice, no request, no protest. The eyes glittered in the pale face crowned by wild black hair, and night after night he cajoled his men, goading them into musical battle, fighting colds, fatigue, and mounting murmurs of mutiny. Minutely at first but soon in ever-increasing measure, Strauss's behavior and schedule became erratic; he crisscrossed England seemingly without formulated plan. Life became more and more burdensome for all concerned. The English autumn fog played havoc with breathing as well as with instruments, and the English culinary fare disrupted stomachs. Stringed instruments were nearly impossible to keep in tune, woodwinds constantly threatened to sound flat, some even developed cracks which were difficult to repair in a country whose language the Viennese commanded only in brief broken phrases for everyday use. Only their foresight in bringing extra instruments with them saved the situation as far as music-making was concerned. Worst of all, the men, accustomed to well-done meat in their *Schnitzel*, *Rostbraten*, and *Gulasch*, could stomach the "rare" meats of England only with liberal libations of English wine—even though the best vintages did not appeal to the Viennese taste. All those circumstances combined to turn their stomachs as well as their dispositions sour, and in consequence they turned on Strauss in open revolt. To stay the inevitable, Strauss promised his men an immediate return to the continent. He did keep his promise, but he intended to continue his erratic schedule through France. Once the men felt continental ground beneath them, however, the bubble of belligerency burst. The pox on Strauss's commitments, be they in England, France, or anywhere else except Vienna! They had no desire to go anywhere but home. Ugly scenes followed in the wake of their meticulously played concerts. His players even accused Strauss of having abandoned his family and therefore having no desire to return, ever. To make matters worse, somehow his musicians had found out about his plans for a journey to America, and the news had become grossly exaggerated; Strauss wanted to shanghai them to America ... they were never to return again ... Strauss did not care whether he ever saw Vienna again because he had broken with his family ... he wanted to settle in the New World.

History did not record what sorcery Strauss wrought that time. Suffice it to say that, with the assistance of the faithful Reichmann, Strauss so imbued them with his spirit that, unbelievable as it seems, they followed him back to Southhampton! A monthly salary raise of ten florin per man had helped, of course, to raise spirits and lower tempers. Strauss, victorious on all fronts, raced on to Reading, Cheltenham, Worcester, Leicester, Darby, Sheffield, Nottingham, and Halifax. Nothing was to stand in his way. In Halifax the weather was so inclement that only seven people appeared at a soirée for which he played. Money was promptly refunded, and the evening was a great financial loss to Strauss. Nonetheless, he was undaunted. Beneath the charm and grace mysteriously fringed with a diabolic gleam, beneath that show of urbanity and amiability to his men, Strauss remained flinty. Yet if he had been under the illusion that the storm had passed, he was to be rudely awakened. In Halifax the orchestra's most serious mutiny was triggered partly by the fact that it was the anniversary of their departure from Vienna, and partly because they were not allowed to rest after the concert but were required to travel in lumbering coaches, hastily engaged, to Edinburgh. The night and the road were as miserable as the men. The coaches were drafty and poorly hung, the night cold and foggy. After one of those week-long rains the coaches often sank axle-deep into the mud, and the cries of the coachmen spurring on the horses did nothing to improve the disposition of Strauss's men during the slow and miserable journey.

Upon arrival at Edinburgh the entire ensemble was sick. Strauss promptly commandeered a doctor who prescribed hot red wine "strong enough to wake the dead," to be mixed with ginger and nutmeg. The perspiration induced by the pungent remedy apparently aided all but Strauss, whose worsened condition of influenza continued to demand rest and proper medication. What was equally painful and dangerously obvious to Strauss was the fact that the musicians' contracts were up for renewal. Their refusal to sign on again could embarrass him artistically and ruin him financially since he had again contracted with more cities in anticipation of his ensemble's continued compliance. Without waiting for a move from his men he called a meeting. In the face of dour reluctance he wheedled, cajoled, promised; a raise in pay, a trip to the south of France to relax, an early return to Vienna. After an ominous beginning he was again able to calm aroused tempers. His charisma prevailed. Feverish, coughing, wheezing, and bleary eyed, he continued the tour to Newcastle, Leeds, Hull, Wakefield, and Derby. None of the places was likely to add to his fame or fortune, but on he went, driven by applause, adulation, and ambition.

By now his illness had become too bothersome and intense to be ignored. In the chill Scottish November air Strauss stayed close to blazing fires and heated wines, hoping to cure or at least ameliorate the coughing and the increasing chest pains. In Derby, however, the condition of his health had become so threatening that Strauss secretly visited a doctor who may have been more quack than physician. To dull the pain, the doctor prescribed a dose of opium large enough to have killed the patient had he taken it in full. But neither heat, toddies, nor opium could now keep the realization from Strauss that there were, after all, limits to his strength and that rest was the most needed medicine. Looking at his schedule, however, Strauss decided against resting; on he went to Leicester. There the inevitable occurred; Strauss was unable to conduct the second half of the concert because a racking cough and rising fever shook his body beyond control. Abruptly, after the concert, Strauss told his men to pack. Within the hour they were on their way to Dover and thence to Calais. Strauss had hardly set foot on continental soil when he was approached by an entrepreneur suggesting a local concert. The composer, although incredibly sick only the night before, suddenly decided that he was much improved and promptly arranged a farewell concert to be held under his personal direction. But the body, totally drained of its physical resources, refused to be subjected to further torture. To the horror of the packed house Strauss collapsed during the third number of the concert. At that point the total lack of comprehension of Strauss's motives by the English is astounding. Reported the *Musical World* sanctimoniously, "The hero of the waltz lies stretched on the bed of sickness in Calais ... As the hour of sickness is held to be a good time for the inculcation of a little morality we shall [offer] a word of advice to those who are disposed to make money too fast, and damage their constitutions, their fame and worst of all—music itself by a horrid greediness ... Be warned in time, ye itinerant speculators, observe ... the fate of Strauss and tremble."

Leaderless, exhausted, demoralized, the company, with Strauss in tow, dejectedly proceeded to Paris. There Strauss hastily summoned physicians to restore his health without delay, since he intended to continue the tour as quickly as possible. The doctors' diagnoses were unanimous: Strauss was to stop all tour activities and return immediately to Vienna for rest and recuperation. Strauss remonstrated stubbornly but his flesh was unwilling, and so was the orchestra. With the composer standing by, weakened and helpless, his men decided that they had neither the financial resources nor the patience to await Strauss's recovery but had to return to Vienna. The orchestra was formally dissolved on the spot. Strauss could, of course, have returned to Vienna as advised. His reasons for not doing so were threefold: he was not sure whether he would be able to travel in his weakened condition; he felt that it would hurt his image should he return a sick, weakened man; and, finally, despite his momentarily debilitated health he expected to "snap back" quickly, recall his musicians, continue the tour, and return to Vienna in triumph. He still believed in the Strauss magic and expected it to return his men to him at a snap of his fingers. At present, however, only one member, ever-faithful Reichmann, remained with his master. This was fortunate for Strauss, because, contrary to expectations, his health did not improve; for reasons beyond the French physicians' ken it began to deteriorate to an extent that the promptest possible return to Vienna was mandatory.

Stagecoaches lumbering on rutted roads were not the ideal vehicles to transport a near-invalid and the journey had to be interrupted again at Strasbourg because Strauss was sinking so fast that Reichmann became afraid the master might die en route. For several days Strauss remained unconscious in his hotel room while local doctors stroked their beards. Eventually, one doctor's suggestion to Reichmann that Strauss return to care in Vienna as quickly as possible induced them to continue the trip. The wisdom of that advice was questionable since other doctors had felt that Strauss might not survive such an arduous journey. But Reichmann, seeing only a choice between a strange city with mediocre doctors he could barely understand and patient care by the family in Vienna, decided to risk the gamble, packed Strauss into a special coach to Munich and, despite freezing temperatures, set out on the difficult trip home. From Munich other coaches were to take them to Vienna via Linz, in intervals to be determined by the patient's condition.

Upon arrival at Linz Strauss showed the first surprising signs of improvement. Reichmann, hard pressed during recent weeks of constant vigil, engaged attendants to watch over the patient while he visited relatives in the capital of Lower Austria. However, during the night Strauss suffered a relapse and, while his attendants were asleep, he wandered in a delirious state out into the icy hotel corridor. Upon returning to the hotel Reichmann found Strauss unconscious in the hallway, clad only in his nightshirt. With the situation now desperate, Reichmann acted on his own without bothering to consult a doctor. In the middle of the night he hunted up a comfortable express coach and whisked Strauss to Vienna.

Two days later the tattered hero and his faithful companion arrived back in the city from which they had set out triumphantly over a year earlier. Upon Strauss's repeated insistence nobody, not even the family, had been informed of the state of his health. But the news had preceded him nonetheless. Only the children were at home, and they were in tears when their incapacitated father arrived. The mother had gone to the theatre, and Johann, the oldest, hurried away to give her the news. When she arrived, Strauss had already been put to bed. He remained in delirium for several days, tended by his wife and a doctor more competent than his Paris and Strasbourg colleagues.

Not only his health but also his position in the musical life of Vienna had deteriorated during his prolonged absence. Emperor Ferdinand, despite his naivete, looked askance at the man who had conducted music for the coronation of an English monarch in preference to that of his own emperor and who had played at the Paris carnival rather than at the Vienna *Fasching*. Ignoring Strauss, the emperor had appointed Philip Fahrbach to the coveted post of music director of imperial balls and accorded Lanner the supreme honor of conducting the coronation music in Milan. The fact that Fahrbach at one time had been a member of the Strauss orchestra was calculated to be an added affront to the renegade. Faced not only with the loss of popularity, but also with a considerable loss of income, Strauss, in a desperate gamble after only four months' convalescence, decided to concertize again. As soon as the joyful news that *"Der Strauss spielt wieder auf"* ("Strauss is playing again") echoed through the city, Vienna's foremost establishments vied for his services and all but threw money at him. The *Sperl* won the honor of his first appearance. A description appeared in the Vienna Press:

> The halls were packed with humanity, who awaited their darling with grow-
> ing longing and rising impatience. Finally there appeared on the podium
> the pale master with the thick black hair and a storm of applause greeted
> the creator of Viennese cheerfulness, with shouts and applause which abated
> after several minutes in sheer exhaustion only to break loose again with
> new force and seeming never to end. Strauss was so moved that his entire
> body trembled and tears ran over his hollow cheeks. In the hall, too, all
> were touched with deep emotion, everywhere one saw moist eyes and sob-
> bing women and girls who constantly dabbed at their charming faces.
> Finally Strauss began the first waltz after whose ending the jubilation
> started all over again.

Strauss had composed a new waltz, *Freudengrüsse (Greetings of Joy)*. Despite his incomplete convalescence he would not relinquish the podium, and he conducted the concert throughout the entire evening. Within a matter of days the slim signs of recovery evaporated as Strauss conducted throughout the *Fasching*, but he held on grimly. Now he was driven by more than applause; the fully recognized paucity of his finances had deteriorated to the point where even Anna Strauss's meager savings had been exhausted. The small amounts which Strauss had irregularly sent home from his extensive travels had been barely enough to run a household and keep three active boys and two girls in food and clothing. (A fourth boy, Ferdinand, born 1834, had died at the age of two.) Thus, although only half restored and with even that small measure of improvement threatening to diminish, he could not resist the tempting offers of an insatiable clientele. His need for money was the one over-riding thought that now constantly filled his mind. His health again hanging on a thread he nevertheless agreed to conduct on the last day of *Fasching* at the ball at the Russian embassy, one of the more prestigious dances in Vienna and one of the highlights of the season. The concerned ambassador, noticing Strauss's paleness, personally urged him to use his energy sparingly, to conduct only a few highlights and leave the balance of the program to his capable concert master. Strauss only replied with a tired smile and expressed his appreciation for the princely concern and consideration with a deep bow. Summoning all his strength he conducted the entire ball. The festivities ended, he collapsed, and news of his impending death made the rapid rounds of Vienna. Hastily summoned doctors detected an advanced kidney infection and expressed doubt to Anna as to whether her husband could ever conduct again. His recovery was painful and slow for all concerned. Confined to his room and his bed, Strauss missed all he had ever longed for: lights, music, excite-ment, adulation. Instead he was forced to listen to the prosaic noises and smells of the huge apartment building, the *Hirschenhaus*, tenanted by seventy-seven families; all day he heard the out-of-tune Italian hurdy-gurdies and street singers in the court-yard, the street noises of carriages, the cries of street vendors, the fighting of his children, and he suffered from the kitchen odors invading the stale air of his room. He came to despise the noises and smells, all magnified by the sensitivity of sickness. Towering above all those minor inconveniences was the ever-present and intensified calamity of finances. What had happed to the fabulous sums Strauss had earned on his European tour? Little enough had found its way home. Besides the expenses in-curred by the orchestra, much money, it was whispered, had been squandered on his "dear friend" Emilie Trampusch, an ardent admirer. Aside from that, concerts abroad had proven more expensive than expected. One account of a Strauss con-cert reveals that of a receipt of twenty-eight hundred gulden, after expenses for illumination, bandstands, musicians' salaries, police protection, traveling expenses, posters, and advertising, only three hundred gulden had remained in Strauss's pockets.

Money earned in Vienna had been handled differently. No-nonsense Anna Strauss had sought the advice of a fellow tenant, Carl Friedrich Hirsch, a Jewish banker and talented musician who worked in the accounting office of the war depart-ment. Hirsch's relationship with the Strauss family was truly unique. As the years went by he was to become the close friend and honorary financial adviser of Anna Strauss, and also one of the very few confidantes of Johann Strauss. Steadfastness had become Anna's standard despite a wasteful, truculent husband. The children had to be considered, especially the first-born Johann, now fifteen and studying at the *Schottengymnasium*, as well as his brothers Josef and Eduard. All had to be fed and clothed and, with their father's reluctant permission, given some musical in-struction. It had been decided that all three should take lessons on the piano, the instrument which all sons and daughters from well-bred homes should be able to master to some degree.

But then, one afternoon, the convalescing father heard a fiddle being played in a distant room of the apartment. He left his bed and stealthily moved closer to the sound of a waltz tune. Gingerly he opened a door. Looking into the room unobserv-ed, he saw his son Johann playing the violin before a mirror, scraping and weaving. The father could literally watch a miniature issue of himself as the son ended his solitary rendition and bowed into the mirror to the applause of an imaginary audi-ence. Strauss was outraged; his own son, and behind his back, a professional *Musi-kant!* Fury personified, Strauss tore into the room, leaped at the boy aghast in wide-eyed terror. He tore the violin from his son's hand and smashed it to pieces on the floor. Only then did he inquire into the meaning of the boy's performance. Soon the obvious became clear, even to the father. The love for music had unknowingly been instilled and nurtured by the father in whose dwelling there was a constant coming and going of musicians. Instruments of all shapes and ranges were stored in cupboards, in closets, in all corners of the apartment where music resounded in rehearsal day or night. So the boy had borrowed one of his father's discarded violins and had been taking secret lesson from Herr Amon, one of his father's best string players. "Where did the money for the lessons come from?" Hesitatingly the boy admitted having given secret piano lessons to a neighbor's daughter. Despite his anger the father could barely suppress a smile at the boy's ingenuity. He knew that both Johann and Josef were excellent musicians for their young age and he had often taken pleasure in hearing them play from memory his own compositions in the four-handed piano style so popular then. But to play for fun was one thing, to play professionally another. "Out of the question," was his stern order. He wanted no dog-eat-dog rivalry, one-night stands, drunken insults, or insecurity for his son. Johann was to be apprenticed to a banker friend, and that was that. Little did the father know that the mother was to "borrow" another of his violins for Johann the following day.

It took Strauss another four months, until May 1839, before he was again able to leave his sickbed under his own power and for extended periods of time. To celebrate his recovery he promptly arranged for a concert at the Augarten park, the former imperial retreat now open to the public. For Vienna, which had so little occasion for joyful celebration, the return of Strauss was a festive event. As news of the impending concert spread, entire trainloads arrived full of eager people who had seen the announcement posted all over Vienna and adjoining districts.

> Le sousigné a l'honneur de faire a la haute Noblesse
> sa très humble invitation pour la Soirée musicale
> Dans les Salons J. et R.
> De L'Augarten
> qui aura lieu
> Tous les Jeudis
> après midi
> ****
>
> La musique sous la direction personelle
> de
> Mr. Strauss

The announcement in French was more than mere snobbery. It was an indication of something new in Viennese dancing as Strauss introduced the quadrille to his admirers. Strauss had returned to concertizing with trepidation. He need not have worried. Shouts of joy greeted the thin, pale man with the fierce eyes as he stepped onto the podium. His triumph was complete, his hold over his public was undiminished, his pride and confidence were restored.

The frosty attitude of the Austrian monarch was thawed by the glow of Strauss's waltzes and the ecstasy with which they were received, and Metternich shrewdly used both for his own ends. Vienna seemed peaceful as long as it danced. Between Metternich's draconic edicts and Strauss's pulsating music the dissenters seemed silenced. And, most important to Metternich, there could never be any doubt as to Strauss's loyalty to the Habsburgs.

Anna Strauss had ominous premonitions. Strauss's strong dispostion had enabled him to return to concertizing after a much shorter period than had been expected. With the irascible, tyrannical father back in the world of night concerts, peace and quiet had again descended upon the Strauss household. Strauss, on the other hand, spent less and less time with his family. Anna therefore disregarded her husband's edicts and planned the life of her children according to her own vision. Vienna shook its head and murmured "Emilie Trampusch."

Emilie, a little *modiste*, a hatmaker, who during the day occupied herself with hats and artificial flowers, in the evening had only one thought and focal point— Johann Strauss. He was the idol for whom she frantically waved her handkerchief and clapped night after night. During intermission she would approach the bandstand or stage and chat with the musicians, but she raised her pretty little face adoringly only to the swarthy, domineering man on the conductor's podium who physically and socially stood so high above her. Such adulation was the very essence, the lifeblood of a man like Strauss. It became his habit to look for her, exchange pleasantries with her. This soon led to midnight *Fiaker* rides and suppers in secluded inns or *chambres séparés*. While Anna and the family scrimped, Emilie began to blossom out in fashionable finery. It is a moot question as to what attracted the romantic master to the mediocre milliner who had nothing to recommend her save a young, pliant body, pretty face, and unrestrained adulation. It seemed enough. Strauss, equally unrestrained, accepted her modest charms and reciprocated fully. Soon Vienna knew that Emilie was with child.

Anna Strauss held her breath and her tongue. After all, it might turn out to be no more than previous flames, nor was it the first time that a man of Strauss's charm had attracted and ignited more than just admiration. This too would pass, she hoped. It did not pass; soon the first-born son from the liaison was christened

The Father

Johann. The fact that Strauss had brought shame on his family had now been intensified a hundredfold by the insolence of giving the bastard son the same name as his legitimate first-born. It was an insult which Anna was unwilling to accept without battle. She confronted Strauss with facts, fury, and an ultimatum— leave Emilie or leave home. Strauss stared at her, wordless, for minutes on end, then turned and walked out. The next day he rented an apartment in the Kumpf-gasse for himself, Emilie, and his second family. It was to be his home until his death. A marriage, entered forcibly and too soon, now less than meaningless, an albatross, had ended in all but name.

To everyone's surprise Strauss remained in Vienna for two full years. But his restlessness ran unabated. First it had manifested itself in feverish travel, then in composing. The haste inevitably brought with it a carelessness which was obvious only to the more knowing observer. With the public Strauss could do no wrong. Like most others in his field, he had always waited until the last minute before composing; now a flightiness and superficiality in invention and particularly in orchestration became noticeable. Fahrbach, long a faithful friend and collaborator, related the often incredible lassitude which Strauss exhibited during that period.

> Strauss had promised the committee [of a huge benefit ball] a new waltz premiere. The opening of the festivities was set for nine o'clock in the evening ... but at seven in the evening not a single note had been composed. Strauss just smoked his pipe and waited for me for whom he had sent. I arrived at eight and work began. Apparently Strauss was able to work out a waltz in his head before putting it on paper because now the waltz was sketched without hesitation or delay and we feverishly began to work on the orchestration. By then it was eleven o'clock at night, the ball was already into its second hour with the *Primgeiger* leading the orchestra. While I completed the conductor's score Strauss leisurely dressed, then we collected the music, called for Strauss's driver and at 11:30 Strauss appeared amid the jubilation of the vast crowd. With the ink barely dry the music was distributed. The musicians took one look and smiled at each other, knowing that the hour of creation had just passed; then Strauss raised his fiddle bow, the players their instruments and played the waltz fluently by sight to great applause from the throng of dancers who, transfixed into motionless stillness at its first rendition, had no idea of the feat of composer and players.

Once, in London, Strauss had procrastinated so long, despite reminders and harangues from festival officials and publishers, that the dilemma threatened to become a public scandal. Strauss had promised them not only a new waltz in homage to the queen, but also a souvenir copy of it to each lady at the ball. Due to his negligence and tardiness all the ladies received was a slip of paper inserted into their ball program reading: "Mr. Strauss respectfully informs those ladies who honor the ball with their presence that they will each receive, as a souvenir, a copy of his new waltz, entitled 'Homage à la Reine de Grand Bretagne,' in presenting this note to Messrs Cocks and Cie, Music Warehouse, 20 Princess Street, Hanover Square."

Few among his contemporaries or even among later historians realized the intuitive friendship and mutual musical understanding between Strauss and Fahrbach. Strauss possessed the gift of immediate melodic inspiration; Fahrbach, in equal measure, represented the "compleat" collaborator who was able to enter promptly into the spirit of Strauss's inventions. Their usual process proceeded in almost set pattern, with Strauss sketching the waltz in pencil, usually in a piano score. After correcting it, he personally wrote the part for the first violins and handed it to Fahrbach who then proceeded to write the flute part which often paralleled that of the violin. The orchestration thereupon began to flow swiftly, with Fahrbach writing a harmonic viola part to Strauss's second violin; Strauss proceeded with the double bass to which Fahrbach matched the trombone part. Consecutively Strauss sketched the first clarinet, Fahrbach the second, and the same procedure followed with the horns and trumpets. While Strauss put the finishing touches to the percussion parts, Fahrbach prepared the additional copies for the violins, and promptly the waltz, in its orchestral entirety, was ready for Vienna's acclaim. Only after Fahrbach had decided to strike out on his own and assemble an orchestra did Strauss employ professional copyists to do the work which for years had been entrusted to his friend.

Vienna continued to idolize him. A contemporary newspaper gushed, "His waltzes ferment and boil, hiss and foam, they rush and roar in fullness of melody, like five hundred champagne corks, popping one after another. Only these melodic corks ignite like rockets which develop lightning fast and descend upon our ears as light flashing sheaves of color ... fire of light. All explodes, nothing fizzles, all ignites." Waltz after waltz exploded before an insatiable multitude which enthusiastically received each one: *Das Leben ein Tanz (Life's a Dance)*, opus 49; *Bajadere*, opus 53; *Die Temperamente*, opus 59 (its score running to an unheard-of length of thirty-eight pages); *Frohsinn mein Ziel (Cheerfulness my Aim)*, opus 63; *Erinnerungen an Berlin (Memories of Berlin)*, opus 78; *Künstlerball Tänze (Artist's Ball Dances)*, opus 94; *Pilgrim am Rhein*, opus 98; *Pariser Walzer*, opus 101; *Londoner Saison Walzer*, opus 112; *Tanz Rezepte (Dance Recipes)*, opus 119; *Elektrische Funken (Electric Sparks)*, opus 125.

As he progressed and matured, Strauss also attempted, not always successfully, to free himself from the tyrannical rhythm of the waltz. Syncopation, off-beat accents, and graceful antiphony served only to alleviate the matter, not eliminate it. But Strauss was in no way committed solely to the waltz. Although it always remained the main fare of his concerts and balls, he found equal pleasure and success in fashionable, often imported, dances such as the quadrille and the gallop, both much sought after in Strauss's day, which, together with the polka, were performed primarily to bring variety into a ballroom or concert program. Another genre, in great demand and explored by Strauss for his concert repertoire was medleys of other composers' works. Strauss excelled in writing potpourris, particularly of the fashionable operas of his day, mainly those of Auber and Meyerbeer.

It is intriguing that, despite his spreading fame and even at its summit, a certain inbred personal frugality never deserted Strauss. Unlike Lanner, who was prone to overindulgence, Strauss was at all times sparing in both food and drink. This extended to his household as well as to his musical organization. At no time did he allow his orchestra members to drink before or during a performance or a ball; any member caught in the act of taking a nip while working faced immediate dismissal. The drink Strauss recommended to his men for its cooling and quenching qualities was lemonade. But even that recommendation was coupled with a constant reminder that the water used in that refreshing drink be boiled before use. Regardless of his nearly schizophrenic behavior—tyrant to his family, ardent lover to his mistress, taskmaster to his men, charmer to his public—Strauss never let his dissolute private life enter into his business affairs. In his dealings with publishers and players, he was known to be the soul of rectitude. His men were always paid well and on time, even if on occasion he had to borrow or pawn to pay their salaries. Waltzes might be conceived at the last possible moment but were always delivered for the designated occasion. Strauss expected the same musical discipline from his men. Their musical response had to be swift and sharp, a necessity since they were obliged to play waltzes night after night from manuscript without prior rehearsal or even reading; their attire also had to be equally correct at all times.

Besides having destroyed any kind of family life, Strauss's frenzied schedule had produced another lamentable side effect. With the exception of Fahrbach and the devoted Reichmann, Strauss was seldom known to have had friends. And even with those two men it was merely a musical bond which cemented a friendship of sorts. Throughout Strauss's entire life there was only one man with whom he was known to sit down in friendly discussion, to share a meal, a glass of wine, engage in a game of cards or billiards. That friend was none else but Karl Friedrich Hirsch, the same man on whose judgment Anna Strauss relied in equally heavy measure. It is not known whether the apartment building was named by him or after him but he was a tenant there and a neighbor of the Strausses. Despite his main activity in the war department, he was known throughout Vienna, where his nickname *Lampl* Hirsch (Lantern Hirsch) had become a household word because of his genius with anything related to lights. When fireworks, illuminations, or light decorations were called for in a celebration, Lampl Hirsch was automatically called upon, and he invariably shone.

One day Hirsch had been called upon to arrange lighted decorations for a Strauss gala. Strauss admired his handiwork, and in time they became close friends. Hirsch became Strauss's confidant and adviser, the only individual Strauss ever fully trusted. The fact that Hirsch was also a fair musician in his own right and, according to his claim, a former pupil of Beethoven, only served to cement their friendship and mutual trust. At concerts Hirsch would hold forth at the boxoffice to see to it that nobody lined their pockets at Strauss's expense. At the end of the evening he would report "the take" to Strauss while the two men engaged in a rare moment of relaxation over a leisurely pipe and a glass of wine. Not even Emilie, despite her obvious physical attraction and undisguised adulation, could equal or break the close and trusting understanding between the two men which her narrow horizon could not comprehend but could only distrust as a threat to her relationship with Strauss. Her undisguised dislike for the Jew Hirsch did not seem to affect the two men or their friendship.

In 1834 Strauss saw his friend Lanner laid to rest, but he had no time to brood about it. He had caught "road fever" again, and was soon en route to the eastern parts of Europe, Bohemia, and Moravia. He returned in expected triumph. In eastern Europe the polka rivaled the waltz as the quadrille had in Paris. Strauss promptly entered into the spirit. His *Sperl-Polka*, opus 113, *Annen-Polka*, opus 137 (his most famous), and his later *Mariannen-Polka*, opus 173 had to be repeated at least three times at each concert as he visited Raab, Pressburg, Olmütz, Troppau, and Teschen. But that was by no means the end of the tour. On he went to Prague. From there Germany beckoned again and back he went to Dresden, Magdeburg, and Berlin. Until Strauss's arrival in Berlin, Joseph Gungl, the self-appointed "Berlin Strauss," had pompously held forth. Gungl (1810-1889), a prolific composer of march and dance music, was music director to the king of Prussia. However, he found himself consigned to oblivion after the first Strauss concert. Berlin streamed to Strauss soirées which were attended by the king and the royal princes. At one performance a slender young man with bohemian hair and beard but attired in exquisitely tailored clothes inched his way through the crowd to shake Strauss's hand. "My name is Mendelssohn," he said, barely audible in the din of noisy wellwishers. "Thank you for the splendid artistic pleasure you have given me tonight." Strauss had to prolong his intended three-day stay in Berlin to three weeks to fill the demand for his music under his personal direction.

The Father

In 1845 Strauss's life reached its zenith and its nadir. The Austrian court again deigned to prove its understanding of his artistic contribution to Austria's musical life and his world standing by appointing him *Hofballmusikdirector*. The inspired *Wirtshausmusikant* had reached the pinnacle of his fame. Yet the step he had taken in another direction bore within it the seeds of disaster. Strauss's sudden departure from his family to move in with Emilie constituted an open affront to Vienna's hypocritical social surface, which preferred its scandals and liaisons delicately handled, particularly when its famous personalities were concerned. Grillparzer's friendship with Kathi Froehlich was looked upon benevolently. When Raimund loved his Toni without the blessings of the church, when Lanner set up house with his Marie, and when Fanny Elssler provided splendid sunset years to Court Councillor von Gentz, Vienna understood and accepted tacitly. But for Strauss to choose Emilie? Vienna would have charitably understood and forgiven a liaison with a famous actress or singer, a titled damsel, or an otherwise artistically or socially congenial partner. But Emilie ...? Explanations failed but avid second guesses suggested that stony compliance or outright refusal in the marital bed had driven Strauss into the ever-open arms of the comely hatmaker. What had begun as one more tryst developed into a "close friendship" and ended in ruttish embraces. The move away from the family had obviously been dictated by sexual motives because in so doing Strauss, inexplicably and perversely, traded a comfortable home and care for dark, cramped quarters which he had to share not only with Emilie but with a miniature zoo of assorted birds, dogs, monkeys, and eventually five illegitimate children, the fruits of his affair and the cause of his death. History can only surmise whether it was a subconscious desire for self-punishment that drove Strauss into such quarters when he could have afforded luxury—a hair shirt to atone for the abandonment of his world of yesterday. Socially his behavior was scandalous. This, plus his political stance, was to bring temporary disgrace at home and trouble abroad.

Strauss had always been at odds with his wife as to the future of their sons. When his oldest son Johann had approached him with the request to join the father's orchestra as a violinist, the older man came close to a tantrum. "No, no, you will never become a musician, you must look for an honest way of making a living. The lot of the musician is very hard—and one thing I've found out long ago, you have no talent." The last statement was an arrogant effrontery on the part of the father, who knew better than anyone else that all his sons had musical talent. The sober thinking and plans of the more stable mother eventually prevailed, and in 1844 her oldest son was to give proof of his musical prowess denied him by his father. The father had had ample notice of his son's musical intentions, as had all Vienna, through reports from musicians and later from public announcements. But the father was not going to stand idly by "while the boy made a fool of himself." To prevent the son's debut he sent his old friend Lampl Hirsch out on disruptive action. Hirsch actually went from establishment to establishment, dance hall to dance hall, cajoling, threatening, "Strauss will never play here again if you allow that boy to play." Many were cowed, but not Vienna's foremost establishment in the elegant suburb of Hietzing. Johann's debut was to take place there at Dommayer's Casino, which risked the father's ire and boycott to contribute to the son's triumph—and to its own claim to immortality. Strauss, although in no way financially threatened or musically embarrassed by his son's appearance in the field, could not forgive the "upstart." The fact that another excellent ensemble, his son's, had entered the Vienna arena became secondary to the fact that the son had defied the father's strict order and, worse, to the father's realization that he was powerless to reassert his hold over the boy or the mother who stood behind the son's successful professional career.

For two years father and son did not speak to each other. This was found to be embarrassing because their paths constantly crossed, in a sense. As was the custom in Vienna, both conducted regimental bands, the father at the helm of the First *Bürgerregiment* in red uniforms, the son conducting the Second *Bürgerregiment* in blue uniforms, high shakos, and white patent leather bandoliers crossed over the chest. As was the custom, they conducted with batons. During the changing of the guards before the emperor's palace or in front of the war ministry they might concertize at the same time, one either pausing while the other was playing or far enough apart so as not to disturb each other, and smartly saluting each other with a barely suppressed smile as they marched off in opposite directions.

The son was deeply disturbed by the father's totally negative attitude. Seeing the father leave home for his mistress had been a traumatic experience for all. However, Johann's future plans had practically been preordained. Despite the father's punctually paid monthly alimony, the family soon found itself financially hard-pressed. The deteriorating situation crystallized Anna's plans, tentative until then, and all but drove Johann to music-making in order to aid in the support of the family on whose side his sympathies and loyalties always remained. Thus one day, Strauss, returning from an engagement, found a letter waiting for him which he opened with misgivings.

The Father

Dearest beloved Father!
In the knowledge that the loving son would lack strength and fortitude in the face of the father and in the difficult struggle of the heart, wherein a son's love could not reconcile with feelings of right and wrong and feelings of gratitude, and wishing to choose the truly good and noble, I have decided, after employing all my strength of heart and spirit needed for such a decisive step, to use my small talents which, next to mother nature, I owe my mother whose betterment, under the present circumstances, depends on you. Thus she would remain unprotected and helpless and deserted on all sides unless I show my small thanks by at least using my small strength for earning purposes.

Neither you, dear father, nor the world, after mature consideration, will disapprove of my decision to remain at the side of my mother.

With respect and love
Your devoted son
Johann

The boy of eighteen came to his métier well prepared. His mother had scrimped to give him the best musical education she could afford. Johann had studied theory with Josef Drechsler, choirmaster of the church *Am Hof* and a composer in his own right, best remembered for his lilting melodies in the incidental music to Ferdinand Raimund's plays.[2] The devout mother also felt that Johann should receive a strong, basic education in, of all things, church music. Again it was Drechsler who labored with his reluctant pupil. People passing the church would occasionally stop in wonder as the solemn polyphony of a *Benedictus* or a *Sanctus*, minutes after the teacher's departure, dissolved into lighthearted homophony in the Viennese vein. Drechsler, undismayed, proved a relentless taskmaster, and under his prodding guidance Johann managed to compose a gradual, *Tu Qui regis totum orbum*, for four voices and brass, in G-major. Drechsler was so pleased with his student's musical creation that he personally performed it at his church as the beaming mother and the scowling young composer listened. Little did Drechsler, or Johann, for that matter, realize the importance which that gradual would soon assume in the young musician's life.

After having written that fateful letter of love, loyalty and independence to his father, Johann, at the age of nineteen, applied for a license to perform music in public. Normally such licenses were refused to minors, and even adults had to submit proof of musical background and prowess. There was no question as to Johann's

---

2. Nearly a hundred years later he was to be immortalized in an operetta by Leo Fall. Fall chose for its title Drechsler's best-known melody—*Brüderlein Fein*—which, incidentally was also to be the last melodic utterance of Johann Strauss before his death.

abilities. In the end the name of Strauss, Drechsler's reluctant recommendation, and the gradual carried the day. Johann was issued a license; he was on his own.

In Vienna the inn and hostel The City of Belgrade was known as the gathering place of musicians between engagements. There Johann went and auditioned musicians for his venture. Normally musicians would have looked with a jaundiced eye at a nineteen-year-old lad without capital to fund such an undertaking, but again the Strauss name apparently proved guarantee enough for them, and Johann ended up with fifteen musicians for his initial orchestra. He then began the feverish, painstaking task of honing them into an ensemble and assembling the all-important repertoire for the opening which might decide his future in a city where this type of music was tasted by gourmets equally adept in recognizing *Schmiss und Schmalz* (verve and melody) in a waltz and the correct bouquet in a new wine from Grinzing. Johann was confident; after all, from earliest youth he had been acquainted with every instrument and every waltz, and at age six he had written his first waltz, *Der erste Gedanke (The First Thought)*. The program for the premiere concert had to be prepared with special care. First of all, it could not consist of dances only. There had to be a bow to the serious repertoire before coming to the meat of the musical matter. Secondly, one had to give proof of one's composing skills by presenting a varied program. Thirdly, it could not be a skimpy program because that would immediately be interpreted as a lack of inspiration which was inexcusable for a composer of dance music in Vienna.

Finally the day dawned. Practically the entire populace waited in anxious anticipation for the event and its consequences for Strauss and Vienna.

ANNOUNCEMENT

Invitation to a dancing soirée which will take place, even in inclement weather, at Dommayer's Casino in Hietzing, Tuesday, 15 October 1844. Johann Strauss (son) will have the honor to conduct his own orchestra personnel for the first time and will present, aside from overtures and opera selections, also several of his own compositions. Johann Strauss Jun. humbly recommends himself to the goodwill and favor of the highly esteemed public.

Sides formed even before Johann had played a note. One man went so far as to disrupt the concert by causing a disturbance. He was none other than *Lampl* Hirsch, Strauss Father's trusted friend. He was not the only one who attended with mixed feelings ranging from professional interest to a wish for failure. There were many who had a vested interest in the *status quo*. Vienna had a wealth of orchestras—so who needed another Strauss? Therefore they were all there, every

Dommayer's Casino, the scene of Johann Strauss's (Son) first triumph.

orchestra leader worth his name, Bendel, Fahrbach, Morelli. Was it going to be an unveiling or a funeral? A feast of joy, a public scandal, or a wake?

Johann had thoughtfully made an excellent choice for his debut; Dommayer's Casino was the epitome of suburban elegance. It is again a moot question whether another, equally talented youngster without a celebrated family name would have been able to open at Dommayer's. The concert had been announced for six o'clock in the evening. As early as three in the afternoon police had been called out to regulate the traffic because it seemed as if all of Vienna wanted to hear the "new Strauss." Even the police detachment sent to the scene was barely able to keep a narrow path open for the prancing horses and carriages who wished to make their way to the casino. If possible, the situation was even worse inside. Waiters had long given up serving anybody because it had become impossible to get through the aisles between the tables, now accommodating five or six where usually two people leisurely sipped their wine or coffee. The frantic picture of people thronging the foyer to partake in a musical repast, literally throwing money at the cashier for the privilege of gaining entrance and standing throughout the performance in a hall which normally held one fourth the people, was indicative of the prevailing spirit of Vienna.

Word had spread throughout Vienna from "reliable sources" that Chancellor Metternich personally took great interest in the Strauss debut. Yet few knew that his interest was far removed from musical considerations. Times were difficult for the regime. Thunder and lightning could be observed on the political horizon although it would take another four years before the storm broke. In a Europe where the word "constitution" was shouted from land to land, the medieval trappings of an anachronistic, overly paternalistic regime, desperately fighting a rearguard battle through spies and censorship to maintain standards and a role long rendered obsolete in other countries, were both ludicrous and explosive. Thus, aside from musical import, an event like Johann's premier performance was the best thing that could happen at the moment in Vienna — and to Metternich. As long as the Viennese swung in dance, they would not swing clubs; as long as they were inspired by music, they would not fire muskets.

The day broke brightly. Overnight Johann Strauss the boy had grown into a man. And now the hour, the moment was at hand. As he stepped out in front of his orchestra in the best finery his mother could afford, he was greeted by polite applause tinged with a few boos from the hostile section led by *Lampl* Hirsch and the publisher Haslinger. Johann looked in vain for the reassuring sight of his mother hidden somewhere in the recesses of the vast hall. All he saw was a sea of expectant faces, all he heard was a sweaty smoky silence made doubly oppressive by the roar in his ears and the hammering of his heart. The brief outburst of expectant applause over, he turned to his men and lifted his bow in a silence now turned oppressive.

The strains of the overture to *La Muette de Portici (The Deafmute of Portici)* by Auber wafted through the hall. He did it reasonably well, as expected, and was rewarded again by polite applause. By now the anticipatory tension in the vast packed hall could be tasted; the Viennese had not come to hear an overture by a minor French composer, they were primed to cheer or jeer a waltz, a Viennese, a Strauss. The point of no return was at hand. The next composition might tip the balance toward either fame or oblivion.

Gunstwerber (Favor-Courters), as its title indicated, was intended to court the favor, the acceptance, the acclaim of his fellow Viennese. And the Viennese knew from the first phrase that this was indeed a Viennese waltz in the finest tradition, and they responded with a storm of applause that forced three repetitions of the work. Johann was still far from success; however, his *Debut Quadrille* gave further proof that he was on his way. Then came the unexpected, the explosion

which took everybody, audience and artists alike, by surprise. The waltz *Sinngedichte (Epigrams)* was not just another waltz, it was the waltz that took the imagination, the spirit of the Viennese soaring into a new sphere, caught it and carried it
like a flaming torch into a new era of Vienna. The spark ignited the hall. If applause
had been enthusiastic before, it was now frenzy which gripped all. A storm of shouting, a delirium broke loose as Johann intoned the final strains of the waltz. The
audience which thronged the vast hall rose as one to cheer the "new" Strauss. Women cried, men shouted themselves hoarse, and, as is the case in Vienna at emotional
moments, there was a white wave of fluttering handkerchiefs telling the young
composer-conductor how deeply his fellow Viennese felt about the moment.

Johann bowed to the right, to the left, over and over again to acknowledge the
joyous storm, but there seemed to be no end as wave after wave of applause forced
the composer to repeat the waltz nineteen times. Other selections, such as the waltz
Herzenslust (Heart's Delight), only reenforced the impression that Vienna had found
a new idol, Johann Strauss, the son. Despite the oppressive heat, the absence of
food or drink, the impossibility of dancing or even moving, nobody left; perhaps
they sensed a historic moment which was not to be missed. And yet, amazing as it
may have seemed, the high point of the evening had not been reached. Sometime
during the early hours of morning Johann ceased to bow, his smile gave way to a
serious mien as he bade the audience be silent, only to return again to his men, his
bow raised. The strains which next emanated from his ensemble first stunned the
audience, then stirred the storm of adulation to its highest pitch. The sounds which
now flowed from his violin were not his own. They were *Loreleyklänge (Sounds
of the Loreley)*, the luring, beckoning melodies of Johann Strauss Senior, his father's
greatest waltz. The message of homage was clear, and many years later Johann was
to put it into words: "I am not a new competitor, I am one of you, I am my father's
son and always will be, I am a Viennese, a Strauss." The audience understood and
was grateful to the son for his loyalty. Vienna had a new idol in Johann—no one
doubted it. The poet Johann Nepomuk Vogl, influential critic for the *Oesterreichis-
ches Morgenblatt*, wrote on 19 October 1844:

> It was a grand festival evening for the dance world in Vienna, it was hoping,
> wishing, fearing as if on the eve of a major battle which was to decide the
> fate of many thousands of people, but Strauss Junior, around whom those
> hopes and fears swirled, appeared and with the first stroke of his bow the
> thousands of eagerly waiting people were soothed, yes even enthused, be-
> cause talent is not the monopoly of only one but can, as in the case at hand,
> be passed on from father to son. I heard only the overture and the *Gunst-
> werber*, because only a superenthusiast would allow himself to be knocked,
> pushed and stepped on in such heat, and on top of all would have to risk

going to bed without supper, but from those two selections I gathered well that Strauss was possessed by a smart talent for conducting and that, in the matter of composition, he could not be accused of being an imitator.

In the newspaper *Der Wanderer* the critic Wiest reminisced: "I am glad to have found the Viennese at Dommayer as I had seen them ten years ago ... in such masses ... as only Strauss Father could assemble ... And there he was ... Strauss's son! ... now he swings his bow, now he touches the strings, now, one, two, three beats, now he flashes through us like an electric current, from head to toe, now he throws sparks like a battery ... now a shout reverberates through the hall: "Yes, this is Strauss Son, this is the worthy successor of his father."

Neither one of the two critics was able to last the entire concert. Wiest stayed to hear *Sinngedichte*, but nineteen repeats were too much for him. On his way home through the early dawn Wiest passed the former home of Lanner, now dark and empty. It had now been two years since the father of the waltz had died. In deep mourning all the bands of Vienna had followed Lanner's coffin to its last resting place: Johann Strauss and his orchestra, Phillip Fahrbach, they all had been there to serenade their friend for the last time. And now, in the stillness of night, looking up at Lanner's empty-eyed windows Wiest was to compose the phrase that was to make him immortal: "Good Night Lanner, Good Evening Father Strauss, Good Morning, Strauss Son."

Hirsch, Haslinger, and their cohorts, whose misguided loyalty to the father had prompted them to come to disrupt the concert, had been swept up in the jubilation and in the end were among those who stormed the podium and carried Johann off into the night on their shoulders. With a wry smile of satisfaction the eyes of an elderly woman followed them from a far corner of the slowly emptying hall. In the enthusiasm of the crowd she had been largely ignored. Yet it was she, Anna Strauss, whose foresight, energy, thrift, and unwavering belief and determination had brought her son to this day. Against an absent father's disapproving authority she had set her own determined mind, had recognized her son's talent and, first secretly, later openly, had guided him along a path of solid musical development until the day when he had begun to realize all his ambitions and all her dreams.

The father, nearly oblivious to his family's plight, continued to shower his mistress with expensive trinkets and finery. Aware of her naive joy yet blind to her avarice, he heaped luxury on her in exchange for her pliant adulation.

During all the upheavals in the lives of the family Johann never left his mother's side. What hurt him equally and personally as much as his mother's painful dilemma and hardships was his father's stubborn refusal to acknowledge his son's artistic presence. After his son's debut, Strauss refused to speak to him for two years. It was the son who found a way back to the father and reestablished a mode of communication. On 23 June 1846 Johann assembled a group from his orchestra beneath the father's windows and played the elder Strauss's waltzes. The older man was touched by the serenade. At first he appeared only at the windows but later he stepped out, and father and son embraced. But even then, despite his son's established fame, the father attempted to eliminate the competition he himself had spawned. He had already been relieved of his strongest competitor through Lanner's death, and he now proceeded to invite the son to join his own orchestra. In deference to the mother Johann rejected the proposal, but the two men remained on friendly terms.

In 1846 and 1848 the restless father again went on tour. In Berlin Strauss had a gratifying experience. For a concert at the Prussian court he had composed his opus 209, the *Defiliermarsch (Parade March)*. The Prussian monarch was so taken with its martial crispness that he personally approached Strauss with the request to dedicate the composition to him. Strauss was only too happy to accede, and the piece became known as the "Prussian Army March." Hamburg was not to prove as friendly. There Strauss wanted additional players for his opening concert. Due to a cabal of envious local musicians he was unable to engage a single player. Strauss, seeing through the stratagem, rose above the unprofessional attitude and had his noble revenge. After the tremendously successful concert he announced in the presence of the shamefaced musicians that he was donating the entire evening's proceeds to the poor of Hamburg.

The year 1848 started in splendid fashion, and Strauss was hard-pressed to fulfill all the concert and ball dates. But then the ever-threatening, blindly ignored thunderclap fell on the city, engulfing all, changing all: the Revolution of 1848. Instead of waltzes, polkas, and quadrilles it was marches and harangues, musket shots, and cannon roars which enflamed the populace. The abortive revolution brought an end to the Biedermeier era; that dancing, docile false front was shattered forever. Bloodily suppressed, the revolution had to wait until 1918, when, after one more disastrous war, the walls of a long-crumbling Habsburg empire came crashing down. Despite their reluctance to discuss politics publicly, the Strausses, father and son, were on opposite sides of the conflict. With the father the sentiments blossomed musically into what was to become his most enduring composition, the *Radetzky* March. It was unveiled at a feast on the *Wasserglacis*, a vast area where the Medieval moat that had ringed the city was filled in and used for carnivals, military parades, or evening and Sunday strolling. There, at the annual autumn festival in which Strauss participated, the *Radetzky* March was first heard by a large crowd sprinkled heavily with officers, national guardsmen and soldiers. The concert, musically pre-

The regimental band of the K.K. Hoch und Deutschmeister regiment,
Austria's most famous.

sided over by the elder Strauss, opened with the overture to Halévy's *The Mus-*
keteers of the Queen, followed by a variegated program in which Strauss waltzes
were interspersed with pieces such as Beethoven's *Leonore* Overture. The *Radetz-*
ky March was the closing number on the program. The spirited rousing march
had a tremendous impact on the massed audience who refused to leave until it
had been repeated four times. Field Marshal Joseph Radetzky, the conqueror of
the rebellious Italians, was the man of the hour. Even the liberal Grillparzer,
disillusioned with the valiant but inept and abortive attempts at revolution in
Vienna, had reluctantly come to recognize Radetzky as the champion of law and

order and, to the consternation of his liberal friends and admirers, had written these famous lines:

> Glück auf, mein Feldherr, führe den Streich
> In deinem Lager ist Oesterreich.
>
> Good luck, my general, strike the blow
> In your camp is Austria.

To the men assembled, strongly devoted to the cause of the Habsburgs, the march was a spark, it was the stuff that inspires deeds and victorious battles. What Berlioz had said of the Rakoczy march, "As long as there are marches like this one there will be wars," applied in equal measure to the Strauss march. To those assembled it had immediate meaning; the middle section of the march is the melody of a ditty which was sung or whistled by the men as they departed to war, a Viennese *Gassenhauer* (street song) adopted by the soldiers for their tearfully bittersweet departures.

Meanwhile the revolutionary students had found a mildly enthusiastic champion of their cause in Strauss Son and had arranged a festival of their own in the suburbs to listen to his revolutionary airs such as his *Barrikadenlieder (Songs of the Barricades)*. Although suppressed for the moment, the tide was decidedly running against the old order, not only in Vienna but over most of Europe. Strauss Father, openly the supporter of *schwarz-gelb*, the Habsburg colors, now was often hard-pressed to appear as the "Apostle of Cheer" because wherever he turned in his travels the liberal student element came to protest his presence. He even received threatening letters. Yet, despite the unfavorable political climate and against the advice of his informed friends, Strauss decided on yet another European tour in 1849, convinced that his legendary charisma would overcome all adverse feelings. As was to be expected, in university towns such as Heilbronn, Heidelberg, and Frankfurt, Strauss experienced painful moments as he was harangued by students. In Frankfurt the concert was actually interrupted by protesters who demanded that the *Radetzky* March be replaced by another selection. When Strauss, resentful of such interference, demurred, an angry demonstration ensued. Only when he was on Belgian and English soil did tranquillity return to his concerts. When he concertized in Tory England, he was received with gracious cordiality, and his concerts again became veritable social and musical triumphs. As was to be expected, the first invitation to be tendered to Strauss upon his arrival was that of Prince Metternich, the ancient exiled Austrian chancellor, now residing in England. Memories of their beloved Vienna were still so vivid that the prince and his daughters were overcome by tears at hearing Strauss's *Donaulieder (Danube Songs)*. So enthusiastic was the English reception that Strauss remained there from late April to early July, giving more than thirty public concerts in addition to playing at innumerable private balls and soirées. The final farewell from England was one of the most moving London had ever witnessed. A committee headed by the duchess of Gloucester arranged for an aristocratic farewell benefit concert. The performance in the crowded hall was both an artistic and a financial triumph; wave after wave of enthusiastic acclaim, a rarity in reserved England, broke at Strauss's feet. He was deeply moved but could do no more than bow innumerable times to acknowledge the honor. Handkerchiefs waved emotional farewells and dried the tears of parting. Meanwhile an English orchestra had assembled before the hotel where Strauss was staying. As the conductor and the orchestra arrived they were serenaded. The most touching moment occurred when Strauss boarded the boat to return to the continent. The orchestra intoned one of Raimund's most moving songs *"So leb' denn wohl du stilles Haus"* ("Farewell then, thou quiet house")—from the play *Alpenkönig und Menschenfeind (King of the Alps and Misanthrope)*. While forebodings and deeper meanings escaped the serenaders as well as the serenaded, emotions nonetheless welled over as Strauss, through a thicket of outstretched hands bidding him farewell, moved up the gangplank. As the boat slowly moved out of the harbor, he waved his last goodbye to England.

On 15 July Strauss, back in Vienna, was giving a concert. The joy of his admirers was undiminished, and they demanded innumerable repetitions of his newest creation *Waldfräulein's Hochzeitstänze (Forest Maiden's Wedding Dances)* and his most famous *Loreleyklänge*. An incident, considered insignificant to most but deeply disturbing to Strauss, marred the occasion. As Strauss raised his bow to signal the upbeat of his overture, the bow broke and for a second hung limply from his raised hand. The first violinist promptly handed him his and the overture proceeded. Although the incident had barely been noticed by the audience. Strauss blanched at the sight of the broken bow dangling limply by its horsehair, and dire forebodings assailed his mind. "Something terrible is going to happen," he murmured over and over again. A new honor soon made him forget the omen. At a court concert the emperor requested, as a special honor to the composer and a sign of the emperor's appreciation of Strauss's loyalty, a repetition of the *Radetzky* March. On 16 September the premiere of yet another martial composition, the *Jellachich* March,[3] took place. During the concert which lasted four hours, Strauss began to feel weak, and feared a recurrence of collapse from exhaustion. Although the uncomfortable feeling persisted and worsened through rising fever, he kept an

---

3. Count Joseph Jellachich, Austrian general and Croatian nobleman and governor, fought on the Austrian side during the 1848 revolution against the rebellious Hungarians. His victory suppressed the revolutionary Kossuth regime.

engagement at the *Sperl* the next day. Heavy perspiration drenched him during the performance and brought on weak spells which he overcame only with a supreme effort. He finished the performance, hoping in vain that the perspiration would remove the toxin. Despite continued fever and weakness he accepted an invitation to head and direct the musical portion of the festivities honoring victorious Field Marshal Radetzky and prepared to write a new march for the occasion. By then the burning sensation seemed to consume his body and forced him to take to bed. A hastily summoned doctor immediately diagnosed the dreaded cause of Strauss's dilemma—scarlet fever. The source of the infection was only too easily traced. Strauss's youngest daughter by Emilie had recently returned from school complaining of fever and headaches. Not suspecting the cause, Strauss had held the sick child in his arms and comforted her. When Emilie was informed that the father had contracted scarlet fever from his daughter, she reacted in a way typical of her. She thrashed the innocent child mercilessly until her cries prompted aroused neighbors to call the police.

The doctor initially had not expected any complications, but when the sick man took a turn for the worse, the doctor decided to call in another colleague for consultation. The second practitioner, Dr. E. Raimann, promptly decided to apply leeches to ease the blood pressure. When, despite the application, the patient showed no signs of improvement the doctors were forced to view the case with the utmost gravity. A priest was called to give Strauss the last sacraments. On 25 September in anticipation of the imminent arrival of Dr. Raimann, the other attendant, Dr. Innhauser, left after having spent the earlier part of the night with the patient. Dr. Raimann was to arrive at two o'clock. The night was still as Emilie sat by the sickbed in the miserable hole Strauss had called home for the last four years. A small window barely lit the room even in summer daylight. There was hardly room for the piano, which had to do double duty as a desk. As Emilie bent over the unconscious suffering man, Strauss opened his eyes, took a deep breath, and then lay still, his glassy unseeing eyes still open. A few minutes later Dr. Raimann arrived. His verdict to the dumbfounded woman was death through brain paralysis brought on by excessively high fever.

The next morning a breathless messenger knocked impatiently at the door of the Strauss apartment. Frau Strauss opened the door warily. The boy, wide-eyed, his obvious fright mixed with excitement, could only blurt out, "Come quickly; it's terrible." "What's the matter? what's happened?" Anna demanded. The boy only shook his head in breathless terror and motioned her to follow. Anna gathered her children, threw a scarf over her shoulders and followed the messenger, forebodings as well as the rapid pace taking her breath away. When they arrived at the Kumpf-gasse, the abode of the estranged father and husband, Anna Strauss stopped short. She had no intention of going into "that house" and meeting "that woman." But the messenger ignored her hesitation and hurried up the dark stairs, tore open the apartment door, and awaited their arrival. Reluctantly Anna ascended, followed by her sons, and hesitantly walked through the bedroom door. There was an air of horror, of emptiness, of ... Anna did not dare to even think the word, but one look into the bedroom confirmed her fears ... death. In a bare room, in a house devoid of everything living, devoid even of furniture, lay the naked corpse of her husband on a bare bed without linens, on a bare sack of straw. Emilie Trampusch, upon realizing the death of her lover, in panic, terror, and avarice, had packed her children, monkeys, cats, birds, furniture, dishes, linen, everything movable, and in the dead of night had vanished into the lower strata of Vienna from which Strauss had lifted her.[4]

Anna stared in horror and pity from which she was recalled by the silently comforting hands of her sons. Slowly her gaze fell on Johann. The twenty-four-year-old elegant young man, so much alike in looks to his father, stared at the body with undisguised terror. The mother gathered her wits about her and turned to her oldest son. Suddenly he broke away from his mother's comforting arm, ran out of the apartment, down the hall, and down the street. Two days later he returned to his mother's home, dishevelled, hollow-eyed, unshaven, exhausted. Never again was he to lose the specter of death he had witnessed, and in his long, fruitful, and joyous life he would forever flee from the haunting vision of his dead father's corpse and from any occasion relating to death.

The funeral had been an outpouring of sentiment, love, and pain in Vienna. After an initial priestly blessing at the place of death, members of the Strauss orchestra carried the coffin past huge placards announcing the festivities for Field Marshal Radetzky, which Strauss was to have led, to the cathedral of St. Stephan. The interior of the huge cathedral was illuminated by innumerable candles and a group of torch bearers surrounded the coffin in an eerie setting. From somewhere in the organ loft high above the mourners the choir moaned as princes of the church performed the last rites in somber chant and ritual. Afterwards a gala cortege escorted the coffin, pulled by four black horses, to the city limits at the ancient gate of the *Schottentor*. There the orchestra members received the coffin and escorted it in a simpler and swifter cortege to the cemetery at Döbling. Anna Strauss and two

4. After Strauss's death, Emilie soon receded into even darker recesses than the ones from which she had emerged. All belongings soon disappeared. Despite occasional support from a surprising source—Johann Strauss, the legitimate son—she drifted even lower until she was forced to earn money as a water carrier. Dubious reports even told of her stealing the flowers and ornamental lanterns from her lover's grave.

of her sons (Eduard was sick in bed) stood at the grave. Josef, the younger, wept. Johann stared in vacant horror. The red-and-silver embroidered uniform, complete with two-pointed gala hat and dress word, which Strauss had so proudly worn at all court functions had been spread over the coffin. White-haired Amon, Strauss's first concertmaster and Johann's first teacher, carried the master's violin on a velvet cushion, tears streaming down his haggard face. Military and civic bands, all wearing black armbands, solemnly marched in the procession playing funeral marches composed for the occasion by Strauss's most prominent colleagues, Fahrbach, Haslinger, Morelli, Suppé. The *Wiener Männergesangsverein*, one of Vienna's foremost choral societies, sang two chorals at the grave side. En route a flood of people, with hats removed, thronged the streets in total silence. Many windows and portals had been draped in black in reverence and mourning as the greatest funeral since Beethoven passed. After the coffin was lowered, a large laurel wreath was placed upon it before the earth began to cover the remains of one of Vienna's most illustrious men. Strauss's resting place had been thoughtfully chosen by the side of the friend of his youth, Josef Lanner, who had preceded him in life and in death.

Strauss's body had been laid to rest but the vision lived on.

> A good deal of the electrifying force of Strauss's dances died with him. The slender pale man with the moorish facial features was the truly vital spirit of his well-rehearsed orchestra; when he with his violin victoriously sounding above the masses of tone at highlights, waved his bow like a Field Marshal's baton, one could observe how his melodies vibrated through his limbs ... The classic era of dance music, which he almost personally represented, closed with him. But the world went on and demanded something new. Johann Strauss the younger stepped into his father's place ... the younger Strauss has some of the talent of his father and written some pretty music ... The model is superior, but the copy has merit.
>
> A. W. Ambros, *Kultur-Historische Bilder*, 1861.

5

The Father of the Realm

While liberal and reactionary forces were locked in deadly battle, one political figure had remained in a steady, pivotal position. Archduchess Sophie had watched and appraised the scene with a shrewdly calculating eye, and her plans, laid over the span of many years, had come to fruition. She had calculated correctly that neither her husband Franz Karl nor his hapless brother Ferdinand would be capable of occupying the throne; nor did she have to look far for the successor. The new emperor was standing by her side: her oldest son, Franz Joseph, just turned eighteen, handsome, charming, well educated, trained in his imperial task by his mother's hand-picked tutors.

With the voices of liberalism and liberation temporarily silenced and an ominous peace restored, the imperial family had returned to its palace in Vienna. Franz Joseph might now bear the title of emperor, but it was his mother who took the reins firmly in hand. Since poor Ferdinand had been barely able to attend to himself, the palace had fallen into a shabby disarray which aroused all the Viennese *Hausfrau* instincts in the imperial mother. The palace was scoured from loft to servants' quarters, the main halls refurbished, the walls recovered with new silk, broken or dull mirrors replaced, furniture reupholstered and regilded. But Sophie did not stop there. The world would have to be informed that the new "tenant" of the palace was alert, vigorous, and up-to-date. Palace guards shed their worn uniforms and paraded in new attire complete with silver helmets. A new coach was ordered and the coachmen's outfit proudly displayed the Habsburg colors of black and yellow.

Archduchess Sophie looked with pride at her elegant, suavely courteous son, the model of imperial and diplomatic polish. "Breeding tells," she assured herself as she watched his flawless performance. Government had not yet been entrusted to the handsome youth. For that function Sophie had personally selected a coterie of men ranging in their viewpoints from conservative to reactionary, headed by an absolutist prime minister, Prince Felix Schwarzenberg, who promptly set out to "restore order." That was not an easy task, because the atmosphere was still restive

Schönbrunn, the summer residence of the Habsburgs. Here Empress Maria Theresia introduced folk dancing, Franz Joseph romped as a child, and Napoleon reviewed his grenadiers.

although actual fighting had been drowned in various bloodbaths and innumerable arrests.

On the surface all seemed splendid. The *Hofburg* had been restored to its former elegance, as had the summer residence, Schönbrunn. *Fasching*, the gay pre-Lenten period, witnessed one of the grandest imperial balls Vienna could recall. The place was the Grand Gallery in the palace. The magnificent evening was tinged with nostalgia because it was to be the last ball before Lent, and it would be nearly a year before *Fasching* was proclaimed again. The opening cotillion, rehearsed for weeks under the watchful eye of the imperial master of the ballet, was a feast for the eyes. An inner circle was formed by Hussar officers in brilliant scarlet and gold uniforms. Young ladies of the court in white gowns formed a circle around them. Beyond them the dashing officers of Austria's famed Uhlan Lancers formed a larger circle, only to be ringed again by a circle of girls in pink. All of them were encircled again by officers of the *Kürassier* regiment, their gold-embroidered white uniforms and black patent leather boots gleaming in the light of a thousand candles reflected in a hundred mirrors. After the opening dance, the floor was open to all, the couples formed and waltzed while court pages dashed between them delivering messages and *billet-douxs*. When the clock moved dangerously to midnight the orchestra launched into a last *Schnellpolka*. Everybody who could dance rose from his seat and joined in the last dance of *Fasching*. Close to midnight the music grew slower and softer until the chiming of the midnight bells mingled with the fading music. Everybody stopped —*Fasching* was over.

However, glamor could not gloss over the political situation, as jailings, hangings, firing squads, and repression of civil liberties restored Metternich's old "order." The young, inexperienced monarch, trusting the distorted, censored reports of his mother's handpicked advisers, was to have a rude awakening. On 13 February 1853 Franz Joseph strolled on top of the spacious city walls from which he could observe teeming Vienna on one side and the suburbs and the Vienna Woods on the other. As he bent forward to observe a regiment drilling on the *Wasserglacis*, a shadowy figure flung itself at him and with a sharp knife inflicted two neck wounds before being thrown to the ground and disarmed by an adjutant and a bystander. Apparently nobody had thought it necessary to protect the ruler of the realm with bodyguards or secret police. Only the high stiff collar of his officer's uniform saved the emperor from severe wounds and perhaps death. That attempt on his life must have shaken Franz Joseph's belief in the sacredness of the emperor's person and the abiding verities of absolutism. The incident actually was the beginning of a series of disastrous events which were to stalk Franz Joseph all his life. He was to watch helplessly as his charming brother Maximilian, "Emperor of Mexico" by sufferance of France, died (1867) before Juarez's firing squad and as Maximilian's wife went mad. Few happy moments were spent between the suicide (1889) of his son Rudolf, heir to the throne, and the death (1898) of his wife, Empress Elizabeth, at the hands of a fanatic. In 1914 he listened in stunned disbelief to reports of the assassination of the successor to the throne, Archduke Franz Ferdinand and his wife, at Sarajevo. And finally, two years before his death at age 84 he found himself tricked and trapped into a declaration of war which was to spawn World War I and was to destroy the last vestiges of Habsburg's three-hundred-year-old reign.

Archduchess Sophie, imbued with the images of Emperor Franz and Metternich, did not read the signs. She saw the unaccustomed calm not only as a welcome change but as a chance to arrange something joyful and useful at the same time—a marriage. Austria's political fortunes, through thoughtful marriages, had become proverbial throughout Europe: *"Tu felix Austria nube."* [1] Looking about, Sophie decided upon Helene—the daughter of her sister Ludovica—as her son's future spouse. Helene was quiet, obedient, and easily led; thus, in Sophie's eyes, she was an ideal future empress who could be counted on to bear successors to the throne but not to interfere with her husband's rule or Sophie's schemes. The sisters were in full agreement about the excellence of choice but had forgotten to consult with the groom-to-be. Franz Joseph had other plans after he had met Helene's younger sister, Elizabeth, fifteen years of age. Sophie raged in disapproval, but for the first time Franz Joseph, much to his mother's dismay, was adamant, and he prevailed. Thus in April 1854 a flower-draped ceremonial boat brought Elizabeth von Wittelsbach down the Danube from her native Bavaria. At Vienna, before the boat had even been secured, the impatient emperor leaped abroad to embrace and kiss his bride, much to the delight of the Viennese and the disapproval of his etiquette-minded mother.

Elizabeth's official entry into Vienna was straight out of the fairy-tale books. Cinderella could not have wished for a more dream-like setting. The golden glass ceremonial coach of state, drawn by eight of Vienna's famed white Lippizaner stallions, slowly proceeded to transport the radiant young princess, all dressed in blushing pink with a diamond crown in her raven hair. Young Viennese maidens strewed rose petals in her path and the Viennese bade her welcome with jubilation and a sea of fluttering handkerchiefs. Shy Elizabeth, who had been allowed by her indulgent father to roam the Bavarian countryside unchaperoned on horseback, was overwhelmed by so massive a display of friendly welcome. That impression was reinforced by a dazzling array of gifts from her fiancé's family including a new diamond crown for the wedding day, a new tiara, and a necklace of opals and diamonds. Soon the great day, 24 April 1854, had arrived. The traditional Habsburg church, *Augustinerkirche*, its dark medieval edifice now lit by a thousand candles for the joyful occasion, had been chosen for the wedding of the twenty-four-year-old emperor and his seventeen-year-old bride.

If the queen mother had been stymied in her choice of the bride, everything else had been efficiently arranged by her. First of all, Elizabeth had to be isolated from all persons familiar to her. None of her entourage accompanied her to Vienna, and her present court of elderly ladies-in-waiting had been carefully chosen by Archduchess Sophie. To make things worse, the word "privacy" was to

---

1. The much quoted line of a poem: "Bella gerant alii! / Tu, felix Austria, nube" (Let others make war! / Thou, happy Austria, wed").

be a thing of the past to Elizabeth. Even the bridal bedchamber was subject to imperial ritual. On their wedding night, after the seemingly endless wedding ceremony by Cardinal Rauscher, after stiffly receiving the court and diplomatic corps at the Ceremonial Hall at the *Hofburg*, after the traditional family supper, the bride was led into the bridal chamber by her mother and readied for the wedding night. However, this was not the end of the ludicrous ritual to be observed in the bedchamber. Next Archduchess Sophie ushered her son, the emperor of Austria, into the chamber. Then the mothers beamed at their "children" and at each other before leaving the chamber.

Archduchess Sophie, despite the marriage of her son, had no intention of relaxing her grip on any phase of court life. The wing of the *Hofburg* which the young couple was to occupy had been redecorated under her supervision without consultation with the bride, and daily life, from sunup to sunset, was under her constant control. Sophie had fashioned the Habsburg mold which had yielded an emperor and was now to be used to shape an empress. The result, unexpected by the Archduchess, was a clash of two strong characters. Sophie won the battles but lost the war, because the young empress could not be pressed into the Habsburg straightjacket. Perceiving the turn of events, Sophie's fiendishly scheming mind resorted to stronger measures. Since Elizabeth's individualistic instincts could not be curbed, the children had to be removed from her influence. The nursery for the first-born, also named Sophie, was installed in her grandmother's quarters, half a palace length removed from the mother; the attending physician and nurses and, later, the governesses were again hand-picked by Sophie, and the palace, in due time, mockingly referred to the infant as "Sophie's child." The procedure was repeated with a second daughter. Even when the marriage finally produced the longed-for son and heir in 1858, Archduchess Sophie assumed control over his upbringing in so thinly disguised a tyrannical manner as to outrage any sensitive court member. She openly took advantage of the young empress's shyness. If Elizabeth had one shortcoming it was a retiring, trusting, sensitive nature which was not suited to the task of being empress of Habsburg, a task made exacting to the point of being unbearable by the relentless criticism of her mother-in-law, who went so far as to burst into Elizabeth's chambers for no other reason than "to see what she was doing."

The expected remonstrations of Elizabeth to her husband fell, not surprisingly, on near-deaf ears. How was any man to act when he found himself unexpectedly in the midst of a vicious dispute between the young wife he adored and the domineering mother to whom he owed his position as emperor? Despite the fact that venom was spewed in the refined manner and rarefied atmosphere of the high-born, it was no less vicious nor less obvious to the palace. Sentiments may have been with the young empress, but when Elizabeth darted across the court lawn to eagerly receive her husband returning from the hunt and was sharply and publicly reprimanded by her shrewish mother-in-law, everybody may have winced but everybody also held his tongue. There was no sense or future in offending the power behind the throne. Even if one's position was not endangered due to one's title, royal vindictiveness could poison one's life. It was not difficult to understand why the young emperor did not wish to be drawn into the palace battle—his major attention had to be given to Austrian affairs, then in a precarious state and threatening to become worse. On that point Archduchess Sophie's shortcomings became most glaring. It was one thing to run the imperial household on a smoothly rigid schedule and to have one's emperor-son cut an elegant figure. It was quite another task to administer to an empire racked by dissension and beset with difficulties from within and without. His concern with distressing affairs of state added to Franz Joseph's reluctance to become involved in the clash between wife and mother. The task of the inexperienced sovereign, struggling to make day-by-day, makeshift decisions, was not eased by the intransigence and arrogance of reactionary advisors, holdovers from the previous regime or handpicked by Sophie. Compared to them, absolutist Metternich, who had returned from London exile to die in his beloved city, was still the superior statesman who advised moderation.

Others—Bismarck and Napoleon III—realized the present helplessness of Austria and began successful forays into the Austrian vacuum. Soon the French wrenched the Italian provinces from Austria's feeble grasp. Franz Joseph hoped to repeat Radetzky's victory over the Italians ten years earlier. In a gesture of medieval chivalry which was to pervade his life, and to bolster the morale of his troops, he journeyed to the Italian front and personally took part in the battle. But gestures did not suffice when incompetence carried the day. Austria was defeated at Magenta and Solferino. Meanwhile the Prussians, watching from the wings for the moment to strike next, wryly commented on the Austria troops: "Lions led by asses."

The opportunity to strike at Austria presented itself in 1866 when Franz Joseph blundered into war with Prussia, who made short work of the Austrians at Königgrätz (Sadova). In a surprising display of tact and statesmanship the victors did not pursue their advantage. Actually, they did not need to. Austria had lost its last footholds in Italy, the provinces of Lombardy and Venetia. Moreover, Austria had failed in regaining the leading role in the German-speaking world, a role which the Austrians, as leaders of the now defunct Holy Roman Empire, had always felt was inherently theirs. With the last vestige of Austrian leadership irrevocably removed, Prussia saw the time ripe to move into the void

Emperor Franz Joseph (seated, white uniform) with his brothers, Maximilian (seated beside Franz Joseph), Karl Ludwig (with book), Ludwig Viktor (standing).

and assume leadership. The result was historic because Prussia succeeded in uniting and dominating the numerous small German states under its leadership; *Deutschland* was born.

Faced with dissension within his own family and derision from a hostile, defeated, deprived populace, some of whom even intimated that he should abdicate in favor of his brother Maximilian, and disheartened by crushing defeats abroad, Franz Joseph matured rapidly. The first task now before him was to shore up his empire of around fifty million souls, a conglomerate whose forces worked centrifugally from Habsburg rule. In such a situation it was important to establish and realize what actually were the motives which held this multi-lingual, fiercely nationalistic community together. The picture soon became obvious. The territory was a vast area of free trade and travel; from the borders of Russia to the westernmost provinces of Austria trade flourished. It was aided by an increasing network of roads and railroads fanning out from Vienna, the capital; this in addition to the age-old vast waterway, the Danube, the umbilical cord which tied Austria to eastern Europe and brought eastern influences and trade. However, the overriding factor, which lasted until the holocaust of 1918, was the binding link of Catholicism, practiced devoutly from the emperor down to his lowliest subject. Later, the figure of Franz Joseph himself was to become another common bond.

In the face of defeat and unrest Franz Joseph grasped the facts with increasing rapidity. Hungary, straining against absolutism, had to be dealt with first. The emperor's task was not made easier by the fact that Empress Elizabeth openly sympathized with the truculent Hungarians. Her own spirit of revolt against the confinements of Habsburg court rule had identified itself with the Hungarian cause. She endeared herself even more to the chauvinistic Hungarians by learning to speak their difficult language fluently and by adding Hungarian noblewomen to her entourage. Her repeated visits to Hungary were viewed with a jaundiced eye by Vienna and with satisfaction in Budapest. If in 1851 young Franz Joseph could write to his mother that Austria had thrown the constitution overboard, nine years later he had to concede: "We are going to have some parliamentary life, to be sure, but the power remains in my hands." Seven years later was to find him, with the beautiful empress at his side, kneeling in Budapest to be crowned king of Hungary. The Magyars had reached their goal—autonomy and a parliament of their own—but they had to concede in turn that the armed forces and the matter of foreign policy remained in Austrian hands.

Hungary's avowed loyalty to the empire had curious repercussions. Having achieved autonomy, its powerful aristocratic circles successfully fought to exclude other minorities from the same status. Thus Franz Joseph reigned almost intuitively, a monarch of limited capabilities, benevolent, solitary, and remote—the upholder of the remnants of imperial privilege but, above all, imbued with a spirit of responsibility toward his subjects, whose father he considered himself in the best sense of the word. His subjects, equally intuitively, understood and responded. Their esteem, respect and love seemed to grow in inverse ratio to his defeats. Even after the blunder into World War I, there was no revolt or mutiny among the many nationalities within the realm. All fought bravely until the final dismemberment of the empire, a disaster Franz Joseph was to be spared by his death in 1916.

Empress Elizabeth, the Bavarian
wildflower strangled by the Habsburg
hothouse.

Emperor Franz Joseph at age 45. His
eyes had seen defeat—yet more was
to come.

Imperceptibly a reversal of the roles in the *Hofburg* had evolved. While Elizabeth, elated by her role in achieving Hungary's autonomy, seemed to grow in stature,
Archduchess Sophie never recovered from the crushing blow of her son Maximilian's
death in Mexico. As Sophie's influence lessened, Elizabeth, at least for a limited
time, was more Austria's empress than she had ever been. She accompanied Franz
Joseph on inspections and parades and, an excellent horsewoman, she rode to the
hunt with her husband. But Elizabeth's days as empress and mother were numbered
as fate held its crushing blow for her also, in the death of Crown Prince Rudolf.

Rudolf, a precocious, immensely gifted child, grew into a manhood which was
not of his making. Soon he found himself at odds with one and all: his father, the

147

establishment, and after May 1881, with his newly acquired wife, Princess Stephanie of Belgium, one of the few Catholic princesses available and eligible to marry the heir to the Austrian throne. The marriage between the twenty-three-year-old, sophisticated roué and the bland, retiring Stephanie, who had barely reached puberty at the time of her wedding, was destined for disaster. "My illusions were shattered by the horrible experience of the wedding night" she was to state drily in her memoirs of 1937. Soon rumors grew of Rudolf's renewed roamings, and one name appeared with increasing frequency—Marie Vetsera. Widowed Baroness Helene Vetsera, her two daughters, and one son were relative newcomers to Vienna. Little was known about them except that they seemed to enjoy a measure of affluence and that the two girls were lovely. Seventeen-year-old Marie Vetsera in particular drew appreciative glances from everyone for her soft, luminous beauty. It is said that Edward VII, Prince of Wales, brought the young girl to Rudolf's attention. From then on the bittersweet, brief affair gathered relentless momentum with the preordained fate of a Greek drama rushing toward its macabre finale of double suicide at the hunting lodge of Mayerling in 1889.

Despite or perhaps because of total censorship imposed by the court and Prime Minister Taaffe, wild rumors spread throughout Europe and eventually settled on the romantic theory of a love affair with tragic ending. This has been found to be only partially founded in fact. Marie Vetsera certainly died because of her love for the crown prince. Rudolf's motives, however, seem to have centered in affairs of state and his precarious political position, constantly at odds with official circles and policy, and with his father the emperor. He had no illusions concerning the empire his father led: "The monarchy ... a mighty ruin which might last today and tomorrow but which will ultimately disappear altogether. It has endured for centuries; as long as people were willing to be led blindly, all was well; but now the end has come ... the next conflict will bring down the ruin ... graft, theft, rabble in high places, the crudest despotism, hand-to-mouth makeshifts. The state is sliding towards ruin ... a great powerful upheaval must come, a social revolution from which, after long illness, a new Europe will blossom."

It is significant that he left no suicide note for his father. Thus a seemingly untenable position may have brought on the sudden decision to end his life. The effect of the tragic news on Franz Joseph was described by an eyewitness: "He entered like a youth, he left the room an old man." Yet so imbued was Franz Joseph with the spirit, the dignity, the image of empire that, regardless of rumor, tragedy, and consequences all the means of imperial court machinery were set in motion to cover the tragedy with the mantle of total official silence. But even then conflicting statements could not be totally suppressed, and they added fuel to the mystery. The prestigious

Neues Wiener Tagblatt had first announced: "the hope of the Empire, the darling of all the people of the monarchy, is dead. A hunting accident has robbed Austria of its idealistic heir to the throne!" That announcement was in ominous contrast to the communique of the official *Wiener Zeitung* stating that the crown prince had succumbed to a heart attack. But even that announcement was countermanded two days later by the terse statement in the same official newspaper that the crown prince had committed suicide while suffering from severe mental strain, perhaps the statement which approximates the truth most closely. A Catholic burial ceremony—denied to suicide victims—was secured. Nowhere was there a hint of Marie Vetsera's presence and her suicide at the same time and place. Her body was whisked away in the dead of night by relatives who had been ordered to do so. If one wanted to read the lurid details, mostly either romanticized or distorted, one had to secretly consult the foreign newspapers that exploited the story to the fullest.

If Franz Joseph's mind was diverted from the catastrophe by daily affairs of state, Elizabeth had no such solace or diversion. She had not been able to bring herself to attend the funeral, had instead taken to visiting the imperial burying place, *Kapuzinergruft*, the Capuchin Crypt, in the dead of night, calling her dead son's name over and over again. Signs of deepening melancholy were soon apparent. In a desperate attempt at escape she resumed her travels, accompanied only by her trusted lady-in-waiting, the Hungarian Countess Sztáray. Like eccentric King Ludwig of Bavaria she had a castle—Achilleron—built for her on the island of Corfu. But when it was ready to receive its imperial occupant in 1891, her restless loneliness found no pleasure in it, and she continued her aimless wanderings, which she interrupted only briefly and irregularly to appear at her husband's side at a court function for no other reason than to squelch the constant rumors of her insanity. She would depart as unpredictably as she appeared. In the autumn of 1898 she was on her way back to Vienna for one of her infrequent appearances when she decided on a brief stop-over in Geneva, Switzerland. After shopping for her grandchildren she decided to take a lake excursion with her lady-in-waiting. While approaching the landing leading to the waiting steamer she was suddenly accosted and thrown to the ground by a wild-eyed young man who had seemingly materialized from nowhere. The assailant, the Italian anarchist Luigi Luccheni, was subdued by bystanders and the empress helped to her feet. With the utmost exertion of willpower she walked aboard the steamer and collapsed. The attack had so taken everybody by surprise that nobody had noticed the stabbing motion of the attacker the moment he had pushed the empress to the ground. The stab had pierced her heart; she died within the hour.

During those days, when Franz Joseph was bowed down under another crushing blow, his mother's early steely training began to bear fruit. Whatever charge may be leveled against Archduchess Sophie—her antiquated views, her relentless drive to achieve the aim of her scheming—her preparation and education of the eventual heir to the throne of Austria was tough, foresighted, determined, and thorough. Innately a shy, quiet, retiring man, Franz Joseph had been steeped in a spartan way of life, totally dissimilar from the sumptuous, often uninhibited life of other courts. Thus he was prepared to bear the ever increasing burden of his reign: the change from absolute to constitutional monarchy, the split into dual monarchy, and the personal and diplomatic defeats. The image he thus presented won him the unreserved admiration not only of his people but of the world.

Yet all the careful mental and physical preparation had left Franz Joseph unprepared for the overwhelming task of ruling an empire shaking in its foundations. Steeped by his mother in authoritarianism, he was inept in negotiation, diplomacy, and intrigue. Worse, he had never anticipated that authoritarianism was destined to give way to the give-and-take diplomacy of constitutionalism. Thus he lacked the conciliatory skill and spirit needed to deal with and conquer the critical situations confronting the house of Habsburg. Only after disastrous trial and error did Franz Joseph achieve and convey that sense of true authority which, even after the change to constitutional monarchy, enabled him to decide important issues concerning the empire with a sense of balance and a spirit of conciliation. In his mother's limited vision, Franz Joseph had been a worthy representative of the realm. At age seventeen he had acted mature enough to be sent to Pesth as the emperor's representative on a minor mission of state. He shone beyond anyone's expectations. And when he addressed the Hungarian parliament in flawless Hungarian, enthusiasm for him and indirectly for the Habsburgs rose. Yet he was not happy with the prospect of ruling at an early age. Faced with the prospect he exclaimed: "Am I to have no youth at all?"

Even after ascending the throne Franz Joseph was not immediately aware of the difficulties in store since the clique of the previous regime of Emperor Ferdinand continued in their set course. Soon Franz Joseph found himself in the midst of seething jealousies and struggles for supremacy within the empire. The charge was most often leveled at the German segment of the population, and Franz Joseph was constantly called upon to pass judgment, to use imperial prerogative, to cajole, and to appease. The ever-present case for or against Germanism was fought with a special bitterness and continued unabated although its actual influence receded from a high of sixty-five percent in 1873 to forty-seven percent in 1896. Since even at the lower percentage it was clear that close to half the population of the empire either spoke or preferred German, it came to be regarded as the logical language of the empire, particularly in matter of commerce and diplomacy, since the other fifty-three percent did not represent any solid language block but a conglomerate of splinter groups dominated by the Hungarians. Yet all non-German nationalities repeatedly joined forces to prevent a proclamation which would decree German as the official language of the realm. Only with the armed forces did Franz Joseph succeed in establishing German as the official language.

Hungary had always opposed Habsburg rule. The fiery Magyars, in their disagreements and disenchantment with Habsburg rule, had brought the Turkish menace to the very walls of Vienna in 1683. Some fifty years later the young Empress Maria Theresia had to undertake a personal journey to appear before the Hungarian assembly to insure their loyalty. Under emperors Ferdinand and young Franz Joseph the Hungarians had joined Vienna and the Italian provinces in revolt under the leadership of Lajos Kossuth and had declared their independence from the Habsburgs. It was soon realized that the reign of the young monarch would never be secure if such insurrection were permitted. Worse, it would always encourage other minorities to attempt the same. The situation had to be stabilized, but the fact that the Austrian army was fully committed did not permit a campaign against Hungary. To withdraw Radetzky's forces from Italy or Windischgraetz's from Vienna would only tend to rekindle the still smoldering fire of revolt in those places.

Prince Schwarzenberg found a solution. He approached the Tsar of Russia, always agreeable to the disposing of insurrections, with the request for help in Hungary. The Russian monarch was only too happy to restore the situation to "normalcy" on the side of the crowned heads of Europe. Forty-thousand Russian troops marched into Hungary and on 13 August 1849 the Hungarian general Artur Görgey was forced to surrender to Russian Field Marshal Count Ivan Fedorovich Paskiewitch at Villágos.

For some anxious months the specter of the "friendly ally," Russia, taking possession of Hungary loomed on the horizon. The aftermath of terror and repression which followed the suppression of Kossuth's rebellion was surely the saddest chapter in Franz Joseph's early reign. Angered by Russia's arrogant presence as well as its intention to stay, and eager to restore the Habsburg presence in Hungary at all costs, the commanding Austrian general, Julius Jakob Baron von Haynau, suggested to the inexperienced monarch steeped in absolutism the most ruthless measures against anybody in authority at the time of the revolt—officials, politicians, officers. The blame was placed not on the advisors but on the youthful emperor and his medieval attitude of sternly avenging humiliations to the image of the imperial house, and his belief in the emperor's God-given right to do so. Baron von Wessenberg, one of the staunchest supporters of the imperial role, sadly commented in a private note: "[Franz Joseph] is forced to establish his power by means of scaffold and gallows." But Franz Joseph had not yet learned the lesson of the time. Having "punished" Hungary he set out to put his house in order. He elevated the reactionary prime minister, Prince Felix von Schwarzenberg, to minister president. All attempts at liberalizing the regime which had been wrung from Ferdinand were abolished with the total suppression, by imperial decree, of the constitution on 31 December 1851. The Diet was dissolved. Absolutism reigned recklessly and German was proclaimed as the national and official language of the empire exempting only the (soon to be lost) Italian provinces. Under the guise of strengthening the basic idea of monarchic rule through "enlightened absolutism," a term which evoked hollow, helpless laughter in the trampled realm, reactionary Schwarzenberg reigned secure.

Prince Schwarzenberg's death in 1852 only tended to further Franz Joseph's regressive plans. His intent to appoint another reactionary as minister president was eventually foiled by the strong opposition of his advisors, ancient Prince Metternich among them, now mellowed and repeatedly consulted by Franz Joseph. Without a minister president to head the government, the twenty-two-year-old monarch decided to take on the awesome duties and responsibilities of that office also, a task to which neither his youth nor his inexperience were equal. Yet continued falsified optimistic reports and reactionary counsel remained his guiding influences. And even those were often distorted in transit by malicious court gossip related to him as fact. All these influences only tended to affirm his tenet that a strong hand was needed at the helm. This was translated into continued and relentless authoritarianism. Only Austria's increasing isolation from other nations, particularly after her expulsion from the German Federation, made Franz Joseph painfully aware, at long last, of the need for constitutional change. The process of change was a slow one. The first two attempts to provide a constitution, one the "October Diploma" and the other the "February Patent," were promptly attacked as either giving too much or surrendering too little. Only with agonizing slowness did the emperor's views and the sentiments of the realm toward him change for the better. The Prussian military attaché in Vienna, Count Lothar von Schweinitz, a clear-eyed observer with a penetrating eye, followed the turn of events and sentiments with astute assessment.

> When I came to Vienna, I could see how the Emperor, who was unpopular in the highest degree ... won the good-will and soon the love of the capital's populace ... The straightforward devoted efforts of the Emperor have found their well-deserved recognition late but completely. In those days only a few greeted him when he went about the streets ... All possible sins were attributed to the poor sovereign, who was already at work every morning

at 5 o'clock, who was surely the best husband and the most conscientious official of the entire realm. The Empress was also not beloved, neither by the nobility nor by the populace; with the former she had not had a friendly reception from the outset, while she had won the hearts of the masses by her radiant beauty without taking the least pain to hold them. Only later, when she became gravely ill, did the sympathy of all classes turn to her.

Life was made even more difficult for Franz Joseph by the limitations of his intellectual horizons. The gruelling task of holding together his empire offered few releases. Books, with the exception of those on military subjects, were closed to him. Unless a new gallery requested his presence at its opening ceremonies, art was seldom viewed by him and opera equally seldom welcomed him. The *Burgtheater*, for personal reasons, was unquestionably his decided favorite. Through studies during his youth he was familiar with the classical repertoire including Shakespeare in German. With the presence of his favorite actress on stage, however, he enjoyed the comedy repertoire as well. As the years progressed, hunting, audiences and receptions, parades and maneuvers as well as politics demanded most of his time, and only the *Burgtheater* remained a matter of intense personal interest. Until he became too old for strenuous activity, horseback riding and hunting were another means of relaxation, and Franz Joseph was both an expert horseman and hunter. In his younger years he was accompanied by Elizabeth, an accomplished horsewoman from earliest youth. They seemed closest when riding, one of the few points of interest they shared.

A special corner of Franz Joseph's heart was reserved for the art of another man of about the emperor's age—the music of Johann Strauss. That preference had not always been acknowledged. The revolutionary notions of the younger Strauss, his playing at the barricades for the 1848 rebels, his antiregime marches had not escaped Franz Joseph. Consequently, during his early reign Johann Strauss was deprived of many court positions and appointments by his sovereign, who was slow to forget and forgive. But as Strauss piled success on success and Franz Joseph's failures and disappointments were compounded, he found solace in the lilt of Strauss's genius and the typically carefree ways of the "Emperor of Vienna." There could be no doubt that, at the height of his success, Strauss's popularity was surpassed only by that of the monarch. Actually, many a man in the emperor's entourage felt that Franz Joseph ceased to partake of life, ceased to reign with the death of the musician in 1899. He actually seemed to retire from the still gaily throbbing life of his beloved Vienna and devote himself more and more to affairs of state in his frugally furnished *Hofburg* suite, finding solace only in his visits and correspondence with actress Katharina Schratt.

Kärnthnerthor, one portal of the ancient Vienna city walls.

Truly at no time during his life and reign did he find an extended period of re-laxation. Constant adversities with his political and private family applied pressure, putting him constantly on guard. Thus the retiring, inhibited, poorly advised mon-arch could steer the ship of state toward moderation only through supreme effort and self-discipline. Constant plots and intrigues, actual or imaginary, the attempt on his life, and the Viennese, Hungarian, Bohemian, and Italian uprisings were not designed to aid him along a path of moderation. Only age and maturity inevitably

*The Stadtpark. The razed city walls gave way to parks, a wide boulevard, **and** magnificent buildings. In the center background, the spire of St. Stefan's. Oil painting by Franz Alt, 1866.*

brought about a desire, and with it piecemeal plans, for reform. They came in slow stages because they were not prompted by an inherent idealism but by a desire for self-preservation and fear of more dire consequences if no signs of relaxation were to be observed. The first and most conspicuous innovations came in the Ministries of Justice and Labor, notably in the abolition of forced labor among agricultural workers and peasants, in the face of total opposition from landed gentry and aristocracy. Next came assistance to industry which, during decades of dark absolutism, had fallen upon bad days. Boundaries between the states of the monarchy were abolished, thus making the Austro-Hungarian realm an economic entity, a tremendously beneficial achievement to commerce. Next came training in newly established trade schools and, most important, an improved railroad network, giving the theoretical entity of empire practical application. Ghega, in a marvel of engineering, built the first alpine railroad over the *Semmering*, finally connecting Vienna with the southern provinces and with the Mediterranean harbors of Trieste and Fiume. It was an awesome accomplishment and drew much favorable comment, so rare in Franz Joseph's life.

Finally came the long overdue crowning glory, the supreme moment for Vienna, a moment which by a stroke of the imperial pen was to transform Franz Joseph's capital from quaint medieval city to resplendent metropolis, the "December Decree" of 1857:

> It is my will that the extension of the inner city of Vienna with regard to its approximate connection with the suburbs should be begun as soon as possible, and that consideration should be given to the regulation and styling of my residence and Capital at the same time. For this purpose I give My permission to abolish the surrounding walls and fortifications of the Inner City, as well as the surrounding moats.[2]

Thus, unnoticed by most but belabored by the hard-core doctrinaire reactionaries, Franz Joseph, who would have shunned the label, driven by forces and impact of time and events, turned liberal. He could point pridefully to internal achievements in the face of external adversity. As Heinrich Friedjung aptly noted, "The social development continued unhindered on the road once taken."

2. Johann Strauss Son was to musically memorialize the event with his *Demolition Polka*.

6

Die Freundin

Madam
My Dear Madam
Dearest Friend
My Dear, most beloved Friend

Your devoted admirer
Your devoted Franz Joseph
Your faithfully devoted Franz Joseph
Your most affectionally devoted
Your deeply loving
Your most fondly loving
In most affectionate friendship your faithfully devoted
Your endlessly loving
You are loved immeasurably by your truly devoted Franz Joseph

Thus opened and closed the letters of Emperor Franz Joseph to actress Katharina Schratt. Katharina Schratt—*Die Freundin*, as she was known within family and court circles—was born in the spa of Baden bei Wien on 11 September 1853. Theatrical desire and talent were apparent at an early age, but this ambition as well as successful recitals were studiously ignored by the parents. Katharina was not to be denied, however, and with the help of a nursemaid had herself smuggled into the theatre and performed her first brief stage role. Unfortunately her father had decided, by sheer coincidence, to see that particular play. "The nursemaid had hurried to the stage to take me quickly to safety. She came too late, my father had already discharged his duty. These blows of fate are numbered among the most painful memories of my youth." Such blows of fate, as Katharina tactfully called them, could not hold her either. Relentlessly she followed her calling, continued in amateur productions, implored her parents, and finally was allowed to study under famed

*Die Freundin—Katharina Schratt
in stage costume.*

Alexander Strakosch. Her talent did not remain unobserved, and suddenly she found herself besieged by requests for three important auditions. Heinrich Laube, one of the great names in the German theatre, wanted her for the *Stadttheater*, Dingelstedt for the famed *Burgtheater*, and Ascher for the *Carltheater*. Katharina Schratt auditioned for and received offers from all three, but instead went to Berlin for a year before returning to Vienna and to Laube at the *Stadttheater*. Her premiere appearance in Vienna in the title role of Kleist's *Das Käthchen von Heilbronn* was a sensational success. Despite her second triumph in *Der Widerspenstigen Zähmung (The Taming of the Shrew)* her fortunes in Vienna were ended due to the catastrophic stock market crash. She went to St. Petersburg in Russia and signed with the German *Hoftheater* there. When Laube summoned her to Vienna again, she gladly accepted. On 25 September 1879 she married Nicholas Kiss von Ittebe. Lavish habits of spending large amounts on sudden whims cost him a fortune, and they soon separated due to incompatability, but without rancor or divorce.

It was in the Shakespeare play that Franz Joseph first saw the actress. Their initial meeting took place ten years later during an audience when Katharina Schratt unsuccessfully intervened on behalf of the Kiss family. Again two years elapsed before the emperor and the actress met at the Industrial Ball. But ultimately it was Empress Elizabeth who, deeply concerned about her husband's loneliness due to her prolonged absences, took eyebrow-raising steps. To ease her husband's painful solitude, she searched for a compatible, conversational companion for him. Elizabeth wisely did not look to the ladies of the court to find that companion because it would have given that woman immediate and immense influence, if not over the emperor, certainly within various cliques within the court. It would have to be a sensitive, cheerful, intelligent woman, unconnected with the court. Her eye fell on that charming, bright, cheerful actress whom she had met and engaged in intelligent conversation on several occasions and who had also attracted the emperor's fleeting attention.

The first truly personal meeting between Franz Joseph and the actress took place in the studio of the Viennese portrait painter Heinrich von Angeli. The circumstances which brought the meeting about reflect the thoughtfulness of the empress. The actress was greatly in demand in the theatre, and much of her time was occupied with rehearsals, fittings, readings, and performances. To partially compensate Franz Joseph for the actress's absences, Elizabeth decided to have a portrait made of Katharina in her favorite role and have it hung in the emperor's private chambers. Franz Joseph was much surprised upon entering the studio because he had not expected to view the original. Franz Joseph's first note to the actress two days later was the beginning of a friendship of thirty years. The moment of the start of their friendship was an auspicious one. Franz Joseph had been forced to mature without the needed transitional span between boyhood and manhood. Faced with an overbearing mother on one hand and warring, intriguing, and bickering parties and personalities on the other, he had had nobody in whom he could confide or put his trust. For a comparatively brief span the void had been filled by young Elizabeth's radiant personality, but she too soon found herself the victim of palace intrigues and chose to withdraw into travel. The result was that Franz Joseph's outward regal bearing covered his loneliness, shortcomings, and indecision, but inspired deference in most people who came in contact with him. Thus the empress' choice was an inspired one. Needless to say, it stimulated gossip in the palace and in all the world's newspapers although no secret had ever been made by any part of the friendship. To squelch inevitable rumors the empress repeatedly invited the actress either to the *Burg* or to the imperial villa in Ischl and other places, wherever the emperor and the empress were vacationing.

As was to be expected, defamatory letters concerning the relationship between Frau Schratt and the emperor cropped up from time to time. One especially unfortunate one was sent in the autumn of 1892 to Toni von Kiss, Frau Schratt's young son, then a student at the military academy Theresianum. When they learned about it, the imperial pair was shocked and, to counteract the impression on the twelve-year-old boy, Empress Elizabeth invited mother and son to their summer villa, where the empress had a long conversation with young Toni, one of the many occasions when she showed her personal esteem for *Die Freundin*. For Katharina Schratt herself the friendship of the emperor often posed a quandary. Despite avowals of mutual love and frank interchanges of opinions on all matters of life, theatre, politics, and diplomacy, Frau Schratt in her correspondence never forgot her position vis-à-vis the emperor. Note the formality in the draft of a letter (approximately 1895) despite nine years of friendship.

> My Most Gracious Lord and Emperor!
> A thousand thanks for the kind, gracious letter which I received yesterday here in Paris.
> Unfortunately the rush in Vienna was so great that it was impossible for me to write to your Majesty. The last day was especially strenuous. The reading was canceled, to be sure, but *Minna von Barnhelm* could not be canceled ... Tomorrow we are going to Bayonne, stay the night there and Monday we travel farther to Lourdes. There I shall pray very fervently for E.M. und I.M. [abbreviation for Your Majesty and Her Majesty] ... I am glad that your Majesty is having fine weather ... I kiss your hands countless times.
> Please deliver my *Handküsse* to I.M. d.K. [handkisses to her Majesty the Empress].

On the other hand, Katharina seems to have been exactly the foil for all the worries and tensions which beset Franz Joseph's life, as can be gleaned from his letter dated 21 April 1887:

> ... I can only be grateful to you for talking away quite openly and frankly. When one has so much work and trouble, so much to look after as I, then a free-flowing, frank and cheerful conversation is a real joy and therefore the moments I spend with you are of such infinite value to me. My friendship for you is so firm and sincere that you must drop every apprehension about not appearing to me in a sufficiently favorable light—in short, above all, drop all shyness. Forgive me for troubling you with my views about the

nature of our friendship and about the gossip of well-meaning fellow creatures ... Your honor and reputation are sacred to me...

1 October 1887

For my taste you could never write me saucily enough, for this so-called pertness is indeed my greatest pleasure ...

Thus the friendship between the monarch and the actress deepened. She became more and more aware of his kindness and thoughtfulness, his high sense of chivalry, but also felt drawn into an awesome world not of her making in which that mortal, although emperor of the realm, played an ever greater role in her life. Franz Joseph also, more and more, looked forward to spending precious time, sometimes minutes, sometimes hours, with that charming woman who knew no sham, who was kind and understanding, unsophisticated except for the theatre, irrepressible and unpredictable, and surprisingly undemanding. Thus a mutual deepening of their feelings seemed inevitable. In that light, the letter from Katharina Schratt to Emperor Franz Joseph on 12 February 1888 and his reply on 14 February must be considered significant in their entire relationship because in them they bared their souls to each other, defined their views, but alas, also had to come to grips with reality. From Franz Joseph's reply we must assume that Katharina had spoken of her love for the emperor freely and for the first time.

> *Der Gedankenbrief* [the letter of thoughts] made me infinitely happy and if I did not know that you are always truthful to me, I could hardly believe its contents, especially when I look into the mirror and my old wrinkled face looks back at me [Franz Joseph was then 58] ... That I adore you, you surely know or at least feel, and this feeling has also grown constantly with me since I have been fortunate enough to know you. So, now we have spoken out mutually, which perhaps is good, for the burden had to be lifted from our hearts.
>
> But at that it must remain and our relationship likewise must be the same in the future as it was before if it is to last, and it should, for it makes me so truly happy. You say you will control your feelings—I shall do likewise, even though it will not always be easy for me, for I will do nothing wrong. I love my wife and do not intend to misuse her confidence and her friendship for you ... I shall keep your *Gedankenbrief* as a precious treasure and as proof of your love ...
>
> If I did not have the *Gedankenbrief* I might be jealous, but now jealousy need no longer plague me, that is also the advantage of this letter ... *Ich bete Sie an* [I adore you] but in the future I dare say no more, but yet, it is said ...
>
> Your faithfully devoted
> Franz Joseph

The Father

Days later Katharina was overcome by apprehension at having been too forward in her expression of sentiments and hurriedly wrote another letter to Franz Joseph who, in turn, calmed her fears.

> Ofen, 18 February 1888
>
> ... You have qualms and a dreadful fear that I might regard you as a temptress and might be angry at you ... you are indeed so beautiful and so beloved and good that you could become dangerous for me but I shall always remain strong and since I have your *Gedankenbrief* and know your feelings I am just as happy since I am put at ease ... How often I have already read the dangerous letter, I do not know. With the request that you lock away this letter of mine as well as the last one ...

Despite the intensity of his feelings, Franz Joseph's consideration for her, her name and good fortune never lessened during their entire friendship.

> Schönbrunn, 7 June 1888
>
> ... Since you seem to have decided not to go riding regularly with (Count Baltazzi) I can frankly tell you that I prefer it that way, for in the first place I am not at ease in my mind as to whether the horses he would give you to ride would be safe enough ... and there is something else which I ask you to keep to yourself, however, Hektor Baltazzi ... does not have an entirely correct reputation in racing and money matters, so that in former times he dared no longer appear on English race tracks ...

To shield, to protect was always uppermost in his mind, be it *Die Freundin*, the empire, or his family.

On 5 February 1889 the emperor wrote, "Today I have before me a grievous task; to accompany the best of sons, the most loyal of subjects to his last resting place." What exemplary loyalty on the part of the father. In life Rudolf had neither been the best of sons nor the most loyal of subjects. On the contrary—his mature views in the face of day-to-day makeshift policies had revolted and exploded into ugly scenes between father and son, particularly when rumors became rife that Rudolf had begun to conspire with Hungarian dissidents against his father's established course. Rudolf was totally bereft of illusions concerning the empire or its future. The dead son's personal feelings were borne out by the fact that he left a farewell note to his mother and his wife but not to his father. "I know very well that I was not worthy to be his son," reads a phrase from his note which speaks for itself. Thus, despite all romantic film fare and printed pulp about the tragedy of Mayerling, the facts emerge that the successor to the Austrian throne chose death by his own hand either to escape political entanglement and embarrassment or possibly in a fit of insanity, but definitely not because of ill-fated love which seems to have been the motive of Marie Vetsera, an almost incidental co-victim. Jean de

Bourgoing goes so far as to conjecture complete disorder of the nervous system from a hereditary trait (Franz Joseph and Elizabeth were cousins). Refusal to acknowledge that fact may have been only out of consideration for the empress, who was not deceived about having transmitted a diseased mind to her son.

Political near-insurrection in Hungary repeatedly demanded Franz Joseph's prolonged presence in Buda and Gödöllö. There he had to pit his personal prestige, integrity, and imperial power and prerogative against what he termed lack of patriotism and lack of able men. But even at such distance, in free minutes, he concerned himself with the empress's travels and poor health and with Katharina's infrequent letters and the anticipation of the free and easy as well as confidential exchanges with her.

> Ofen, 16 February 1889
>
> ... the Empress wants me to give you a key to a small door through which you can reach our garden without having to go through a lane in Ischl ... Oh! if it were only summer and we were already in Ischl. Or if there were even now a place where one could forget! But there is no such place and so one must bear one's sorrow in patience and submission to God's will.

> Ofen, 29 March 1889
>
> ... Perhaps I can get away day after tomorrow ... but in any case I am coming to Vienna because I cannot wait to see you again ...
>
> The Empress greets you cordially and I remain in longing constancy and deepest love
>
> Your truly devoted
> Franz Joseph

So free was the exchange of ideas, feelings, and information that no subject was removed from the course of their conversations.

> Ofen, 31 March 1889
>
> Your political information interested me very much, all the more as it is obtained from a source surely very well informed ...

> Ischl, 1 August 1889
>
> Dearest Friend:
> If it is not too inconvenient for you I beg to make the bold request of you to have the kindness to come at half past six [in the morning!] through the little door in our garden ...

> Kisbér, 17 September 1889
>
> Yesterday ... I rode to maneuvers of the 5th Corps, which went very satis-
> factorily. The troops were especially handsome[1] and excellent and were very
> fresh despite a rather strenuous march.

The strict regimen of life, the mores and manners with which his mother had imbued
him never deserted him, nor was he afraid to rile against it in his own gentle yet
unwavering manner.

> Ofen, 21 February 1890
>
> Yesterday the Taxis Fiancé [Prince Albert of Thurn and Taxis, 1867-1952]
> finally arrived, but I have not seen him yet. He could come no sooner be-
> cause he had to attend still another costume ball at Regensburg. In my time
> one used to rush instantly, without regard to balls and festivals, if one knew
> that the beloved betrothed was expecting one.

Nor did Franz Joseph attempt to suppress his thoughts if and when he felt that Katharina needed a stern warning, or rather a warning as sternly as this gentle man could
deliver it — innumerable reproofs were blithely ignored by the actress.

> Villa Hermes [Vienna], 6 June 1890
>
> I cannot refrain from sending you proof in the enclosed clipping that I was
> quite right about silence to the newspapers ... You ascended [in the balloon]
> at nightfall, at your urging and actually against Silberer's[2] wish. How in-
> discreet. And you thought not at all of your friends down on the ground.

So upset was Franz Joseph about the balloon ascent, its inherent dangers and its
reception in the press that one day after his first epistle he sent another to Katharina.

> The balloon trip lingers in my mind. In the several years that you have
> favored me with your friendship, this is the first time that I could be angry
> with you, but I am not and cannot be, I am only hurt (but not offended).
> I have already told you that the air trip was a great folly ... I also expressed
> to you at once the apprehension that the newspapers surely would not be
> silent, and I sent you the first proof ... When I arrived here ... I found pub-
> lished in ... the Pester Lloyd a telegram from Vienna dated 5 June, thus sent
> the very evening of the balloon trip. In the *Neues Wiener Tagblatt* ... is the
> description which I enclosed likewise; only the *Freie Presse* handles the mat-

1. That medieval conception of "troops looking especially handsome" bore within it the seed of disaster
at a not-too-distant date in history, 1914, when Austrian troops marched into battle in their dress uniforms, flowers tied to their rifles, preceded by their regimental bands. They thought war was still a game
not unlike maneuvers, and brave Hussars on horseback, their lances cocked, attacked machine guns.
2. Victor Silberer (1846-1916) was a Viennese jack-of-all-trades, promoter, newspaper man, and theatrical backer who also built several theatres in Vienna. One of his passions was the furthering of Austrian
aeronautics.

ter briefly and bluntly ... I know you well enough to know that, as far as you were concerned, it was only done ... to satisfy your curiosity, but the way in which the newspapers seize upon the thing ... a harmless pleasure [takes on] the appearance of a publicity stunt.

I should like to raise still another point ... I have never objected to your association with Alexander Baltazzi [uncle of Marie Vetsera who died with Crown Prince Rudolf] ... on the contrary, I was thankful that in a way I learned from you so much that was important to me to know during difficult times ... It is immaterial to me that you undertook the aerial trip under his auspices, but in the eyes of a malicious world it will harm you, this fact emphasized by the newspapers, that the Baltazzi family is not welcome in all circles since our disaster ... I should like to request you to mention it to me sooner if sometime again you wish to perform a foolish trick.

But there was no end to Katharina's adventurous spirit. Whether it was a special treatment of the thyroid gland, *Pfarrer* Kneipp's special cure through health foods and cold water baths, or a mania for a Tyrolian hay bath, the adventurous actress had to try them all. The lateness of the information received annoyed Franz Joseph most; she would duly inform him, blandly and without apology, of her latest adventure and endure his gentle wrath.

Gödöllö, 8 November 1890

Perhaps your passion for experimental medicine will induce you even to try this rustic treatment sometime ... I can only express my happy wonder ... at your robust constitution which withstands all these baths, waters, liquid medicines, cold and warm treatments. God protect you!

When perusing Franz Joseph's letters one cannot help the feeling that beneath his chiding of the irrepressible actress there was a silent chuckle and a wink at her indefatigable vitality, perhaps even a trace of envy at her free spirit so alien to his and so unthinkable in his position.

21 March 1893

I congratulate you on the moderate winnings in the gambling hall and hope that your luck held and brought you ample enough means for a visit to the Holy Virgin [at Lourdes?]. Here one can really say *"Der Zweck heiligt die Mittel"* [The end justifies the means].

27 March 1893

[You] make continual excursions and lately go every day to Monte Carlo and instead of enjoying the fresh air spend time in constant excitement in the dense unhealthy atmosphere of the gambling hall. Besides, the disastrous intention of absolutely winning must irritate your nerves and keep you under constant tension, even if the sums involved are not large; and at last the familiar result, that everything is bungled.

The Father

Yet nothing could diminish the love of the imperial pair for the actress.

> 31 December 1893
> To Katharina Schratt
> Our dear friend
> Wishes for good fortune and blessings
> for the New Year
> from her most faithful
> > Friend
> > Elizabeth

But if the emperor wished for the company of the charming, vivacious actress, he had to accept her on her own terms, always eager to start an unexpected, perhaps dangerous adventure to satisfy her eagerness to enjoy life to the fullest, regardless whether loved ones were annoyed, concerned, or angered. Her alpine ventures thus became a constant source of vexation to Franz Joseph.

> Schönbrunn, 20 September 1895
> I had believed that I surely could trust your given word and therefore was unworried about your *Dachstein* [famous alpine peak] excursion, but now I see that even that was an illusion. How anxious I will have to be about you in the future ... now that you undertake the most dangerous ascents in spite of promises and your given word. Your having ordered [mountaineer] Klauner to Hallstadt proves to me that you were already planning to climb the peak ... if you meant to think of me and to keep your word, you would not have eyed the difficult climb ... you can surely do as you wish ... but I still remain quite wretched.

Despite the *Gedankenbrief* other qualms also entered his mind.

> Cap Martin, 5 March 1896
> When I related the contents [of your letter] to the Empress, who greets you most warmly, she observed at once that Count [Philip] Eulenburg [German Ambassador to Vienna] will be a threat to me. I have already long feared that, as you know, for the ambassador is very *amiable*, much more witty and amusing than I, and will all too soon have displaced me in your heart ... So I am being constantly pursued by gloomy thoughts.

Besides, the state of health of the first woman in his life left much to be desired.

> If you should be shocked at [the empress's] unfortunately very bad appearance please do not show it, also do not talk too much with the Empress about health but if it cannot be avoided, encourage her, but above all do not recommend any new cure or remedy. You will find the Empress quite exhausted, very much in pain and in unbelievably depressed spirits.

Fortunately there were other topics of lesser import which could be discussed and were certain to receive a willing ear — such as scandal.

Cap Martin, 16 March 1897

[Princess] Louise Coburg [Saxe-Coburg-Gotha, involved in marital scandal] is avoided here by all the nobility and only her niece Taxis and her husband frequent her. To console herself she has had a Viennese coachman come with two pairs of horses, two carriages and goes riding with her daughter. Poor [husband] Philip goes around alone and in most depressed spirits.

Soon Franz Joseph had to worry about himself more than about others.

Totis, September 1897

I had a fall with my horse while galloping over the deep ruts of a field path; it did not hurt me at all and I was pleased that despite my great age I have not yet entirely forgotten how to fall with skill.

The untimely death of Empress Elizabeth brought many more difficulties to Katharina than the loss of a true friend and patron. There arose a misunderstanding over an order the emperor had given which prompted her to resign from the *Burgtheater*. However, that misunderstanding was not the only reason she left. A decided change in the repertoire, from Austrian poets to the contemporary writings of the German theatre (Hauptmann, Ibsen) plus a veering away from the drawing-room fare which had been Schratt's forte were also factors in her decision. Added to this was the inevitable Viennese intrigue and a marked resentment by the imperial family of her role in the emperor's life, now that the veil of protection, provided for so long by Elizabeth, had been removed. All this could produce only one effect, a cooling, an estrangement in the relationship between the actress and the monarch. Needless to say, the cooling trend was decidedly from the actress's side because Franz Joseph felt that "all possible intrigues and plots will not make me stray from my true friendship for you and my lasting gratitude." But the situation only deteriorated further.

I cannot give up hope that yesterday's black thunderclouds will disappear and the old happy relation of friendship will be restored again. You rejected so obstinately and passionately my earnest well-meant remonstrances and pleas, made in our mutual interest, that I let myself be overcome by vehemence that I regret and for which I ask your forgiveness with all my heart. I also mean to forget the hasty, insulting and to me deeply painful manner of your departure yesterday. But ... you will find that we can by no means part, that we must find each other again ... If all this should change, I should be lonely in the days of my old age; give me a sign which will let me hope that all can be well again.

His illustrious title could not keep Franz Joseph from pleading with the woman he loved and whose cooling ardor toward him led to demeaning scenes which

167

stripped the man Franz Joseph of the emperor's trappings and left only a wretchedly miserable, longing human being. However, towards the autumn of the same year, 1900, there seemed to reappear a semblance of the old feeling and understanding on both sides.

> Ischl, 30 August 1900
> The tower clock is just striking six o'clock. I left my room 24 hours ago for the last walk to see you, my *heissgeliebter* [passionately loved] angel.

But troubles of one kind or another simply would not stop. On 1 July 1900, Archduke Franz Ferdinand, the heir to the throne, with the emperor's reluctant permission, had married beneath his rank. His wife, Countess Sophie Chotek, was later to be elevated by the emperor to princess, then duchess, but she remained always beneath her husband's station.

> 6 September 1900
> My nephew Franz [Ferdinand] presented his wife to me, at my invitation. It went off very well, she is natural and modest, but appears to be no longer young.

> 17 September 1900
> The Press Congress also seemed a great fraud to me. The men spoke so unctuously, so idealistically, so moralizingly, while the newspapers proceeded in their meanness, lies and slanderous baiting—look at the Louise [Coburg] scandal ...

> 12 November 1904
> On a boar hunt ... I missed two boars ... and killed only two pigs with one shot. Because of my increasing weakness of old age, I just won't be able to shoot steadily any longer ...

> Gödöllö, 20 November 1904
> First of all my sincerest thanks for your good, long, and interesting letter of the 14th, as well as for both your telegrams, the second of which made clear to me that the great industrial project you are planning, according to the newspaper report, is the tobacco business of which you spoke to me ... I did not think then that you were in earnest about the matter and our conversation included nothing at all about a trip to the West Indies. When I read the news in the *Fremdenblatt* it gave me a nervous shock, as I could not at all imagine that you would engage in a magnificent swindle venture ... the business in which Tewele means to involve you is certainly just a sort of swindle in which you would risk your fortune and would experience many annoyances and disappointments ... The journey to the West Indies is nonsense, would injure your health, and I really do not know what you intend to do there, as you would certainly make a very bad businessman.

One marvels at the diverse interests Franz Joseph developed while strictly attending to daily, weekly, monthly schedules which would have put a man thirty years younger to shame.

> 29 May 1905
>
> A whole series of wearying events awaits me in June ... troop inspections ... reception for a fishing congress and one of botanists, a church foundation stone laying ... a trip on the Danube to Schlosshof for inspection of new dikes, and a three-day visit by the Shah of Persia ...

And that was not all:

> 13 June 1905
>
> The month of June is especially strenuous for me this year. I have already gone through the visit of Prince [Nikita] of Montenegro and the Khedive [Abbas II Hilmi] with a dinner at Schönbrunn ... the Shah of Persia ... had a retinue of more than forty gentlemen, not counting the servants, and all of them will be lodged in the *Burg*. There will be three dinners ... and a ballet performance at the Opera, and a visit to the Schumann Circus. On the 20th and 21st the King of Rumania and Carmen Silva [pen name of the Rumanian Queen] will come for a day; on the 23rd and 24th I shall inspect troops at Bruck, on the 27th in the Prater and on the 29th on the *Simmeringer Heide* [Simmering Heath].

By 1905 the relationship between the emperor and Katharina seemed to have been strengthened.

> Ischl, 9 July 1905
>
> ... I close with the request that you arrange for the little door of your garden to be left unlocked tomorrow morning [for a 7 A.M. visit].

> 16 March 1905
>
> Medical science has obviously made a new discovery through your illness, for I have never before heard anything of a rash brought on by bad luck in gambling ...
>
> I am very sorry that you have been treated so badly by the gentlemen [croupiers?] at Monte Carlo and I just hope that you will not attempt to recover the spoils of reckless gambling ...

> 18 March 1907
>
> Your having rented an automobile delights me less, since I will be constantly worried ...

> 7 April 1907
>
> It is also disquieting that you had an auto accident, but it was to be expected ...

But aside from all idiosyncrasies, so annoying and exasperating, Franz Joseph never lost his trust in the woman with whom he could discuss everything from the

Emperor Franz Joseph arriving at the Schmelz parade grounds.

latest *Klatsch* (gossip) to political and diplomatic matters, often with tongue in cheek but also in the safe knowledge of Katharina's absolute discretion.

> 23 February 1888
>
> Allow me to send you seven photographs of the Brotherly Friend [Prince Ferdinand of Bulgaria] ... From twenty-five different poses I have selected for you the most interesting, because I thought they might amuse you. Note the picture where the great statesman sits meditating at his desk and the one where the commander-in-chief gives orders to his adjutants, and the incredible mass of decorations placed on the dress uniform ...

> Ischl, 17 August 1888
>
> The Portuguese [King Louis I of Portugal 1861-1904] arrived duly yesterday

afternoon with a large retinue and at half past 7 we had a rather large dinner which was very hot because of the smallness of the room which you know ... It was magnificent but not nearly as *gemütlich* as our little supper ...

By far the most persistently troublesome spot in the emperor's monarchic life had always been Hungary and Hungarian politics which were seldom relieved by a bright spot.

Ofen, 26 February 1890
For several days again, things have been brisk in the House of Representatives here; the Deputies of the opposition say the most extraordinarily rude things to the Prime Minister [Koloman von Tisza] and the uproar is colossal at times. But now there is nothing to do but to observe quietly and wait ...

Székelyhid, 14 September 1890
My visit to Debreczin went off very well ... I made my entry in a municipal *Fünferzug* [a carriage drawn by five horses] ... the reception was incredibly enthusiastic, which pleased me very much in this typically Hungarian city, headquarters of the Calvinists ... Coming back from the festival, I rode through the city in a *Dampf Tramway* [steam streetcar] for the first time in my life ... Irksome days now remain ahead for me in Silesia but then comes the reward for all effort ... seeing you again ...

With Austria's "umbilical cord" to the east—the Danube—opening up commerce, political and trade alliances, one of Franz Joseph's main occupations remained the contact with the East and Eastern potentates.

Gödöllö, 8 November 1890
The visit of the Russian Imperial Heir [later Tsar Nicholas II, 1868-1918, victim, with his family, of the Russian Revolution] went off according to plan ... The Grand Duke has grown somewhat ... but he is still not large and very ill at ease, nevertheless a quite sensible and friendly man.

Ofen, 5 January 1892
The King of Rumania did not arrive until three o'clock ... I received him ceremoniously in dress uniform at the station ... The King was in good humor with regard to the successful formation of his new cabinet, in which your friend Ghermani is again Minister of Finance ...

Ofen, 21 March 1892
Consul General Burian of Sofia came to see me ... He left Sofia [Bulgaria] at the moment of ministerial crisis which began due to a rather sharp difference of opinion between our Bulgarian friend [Prince Ferdinand] and his Prime Minister (Stephan) Stambulow. At this moment a change of ministers would be quite calamitous and so Burian hopes, and so do I, that Petit Ferdinand will master his nerves and irritation and reach an understanding with his minister ...

The Father

The dismissal of the "Iron Chancellor" Otto von Bismarck after the ascendency of Emperor Wilhelm II of Germany caused a European sensation, socially as well as politically. So deep was Wilhelm's detestation of Bismarck that he went so far as to contact Franz Joseph by letter requesting him not to receive the "disobedient" subject.

> 17 June 1892
>
> I sent a letter to Kaiser Wilhelm, short and reassuring. Whether the wicked old *Reichskanzler* will likewise be satisfied is of course another question. I fear that he will fume. Yesterday ... there came the official request of Prince Bismarck and his son for an audience with me. I arranged it ... so that he will have it refused in writing, and there the matter rests at present ...

But there the matter did not rest.

> 22 June 1892
>
> I was informed by the new President of Police about the tumult at Bismarck's arrival. This was again a *Schweinerei* [piggishness, an ugly affair] and you can imagine how angry I was about the unpatriotic demonstrations of the adherents of Schönerer [leader of the German nationalistic party in Austria] ... Prince Bismarck, who should have left yesterday, is still in Vienna ...

Shortly thereafter the letters were filled with Eastern gossip.

> Gastein, 9 July 1893
>
> Our friend [Ferdinand of Bulgaria] has once again comitted an actual folly. When two of his best and most loyal officers would not follow etiquette and the order of precedence ... he not only had them placed under house arrest, which would have done no harm, but also dismissed them from the service. You are right, he is still ... a petty tyrant and harms himself by such frequently laughable pettiness.

> Gödöllö, 18 October 1896
>
> I have survived the visit of the King of Serbia, but it was quite tiresome, with his constant questions [the king was then eighteen years old] and although he repeats them ten times he confuses one and I had to make an effort not to be disagreeable to him.

> Ofen, 2 October 1896
>
> In all of Rumania and particularly in Bucharest the welcome was just as splendid as it was hearty ... The King was the most amiable host imaginable. [Queen] Carmen Silva was charming, almost too charming and occasionally tiresome in her exuberance ... The Crown Princess [Maria] is bewitching ... the Crown Prince [Ferdinand] a good fellow, but insignificant ...

> Ofen, 12 May 1896
>
> Yesterday I had 127 audiences ... and I shall also give 108 audiences today ...

Whether it was diplomacy, politics, court life, or the theatre, a very enjoyable and integral part of the conversation and correspondence between emperor and actress was gossip.

Ofen, 2 October 1896

Count Badeni's duel [with German Radical Deputy Karl Hermann Wolf] came off luckily, comparatively speaking. Perhaps it will bring about some moderation in the more than vulgar air of the noble *Reichstag* and perhaps it will contribute to bringing the so-called moderates, whom I think the most horrible of all, to their senses and to making them somewhat less cowardly. Moreover, I think that Count Badeni has done Representative Wolf too much honor in fighting him, for such people deserve only a caning ...

Vienna, 6 March 1898

The Bulgarian ... was with Goluchowski the day before yesterday for 1½ hours, first with the utmost vehemence and quite domineering, then servile, lastly, at the close of the lively conversation, a downright comedian. The outcome was that he expressed the wish to be received by me. I am curious as to what pose he will assume towards me. I am now enjoying the delight of a cabinet crisis again ...

Schönbrunn, 23 September 1900

We still have the Shah [Muzaffer ed Din, of Persia] in Vienna but he is leaving us tomorrow evening, to travel to Budapest and Constantinople. Since he is a sick man and needs a great deal of rest, his visit was less irksome than I had feared.

26 September 1900

I accompanied the Shah to the *Staatsbahnhof* from where he traveled on an enormously long train to Buda-Pesth in eight hours. He cannot endure rapid travel ... thus the train often stopped in the middle of the stretch so he could rest. In general resting seems to be his principal activity.

Vienna, 11 February 1901

King Milan of Serbia lies dying here in his private residence ... He fell ill with influenza from which pneumonia developed. That will be a huge funeral for people to catch cold at. Boris of Bulgaria is very ill in Philippopolis with abdominal typhus. I telegraphed my sympathy to the Bulgarian yesterday with a request for information and received a very touching reply.

In 1901, despite all efforts of Franz Joseph, the actress's feelings visibly cooled again, much to the monarch's distress.

Vienna, 27 February 1901

You have prolonged your stay in Berlin and I am curious as to where you will wander from there. Unfortunately I know so little about you and receive news so seldom ...

The Father

> 9 March 1901
>
> I do not know whether you arrived in Frankfurt or where you are stopping otherwise, and as I do not even know your Frankfurt address I can neither telegraph you nor send you a letter ...

> 17 March 1901
>
> Your lines yesterday grieved me very much. I shall annoy you neither with letters nor with inquiries and shall wait in patience ... for you to allow me to see you ... Perhaps you will even be so compassionate as to notify me of your destination and ... let me know if I may write to you ... to remain completely out of touch with you ... would be just too cruel ...

Thus the aging monarch, bereft of friendship and love, became just another lonely man pleading for understanding and friendship, presently lost. The estrangement and Katharina's absence from Vienna lasted over a year. Not until 19 June was Franz Joseph informed that he would be received at Frau Schratt's residence at the *Glorietgasse*. Yet coolness from her side persisted, and in his letter of 2 July Franz Joseph literally pleaded for "charity" toward him. During the summer at Ischl, he was a miserable, lonely man haunting the paths which he and Katharina had walked in earlier happier days. His letters followed her in early 1902 as her absences from Vienna became longer during her tour to Berlin, London, and the United States, much to the distress of Franz Joseph. Her impending return in the middle of 1902 was received by the monarch with great expectations for their future.

> Ofen, 12 May 1902
>
> Let us hope ... [that] I can spend some happy moment near you. I need ... some cheering up so very much, for I am especially melancholy and tired and you will find me quite aged and mentally enfeebled. I think a great deal about the past and a great deal about the dead, hopeless future and about death ...

Personal misfortune and difficulties seem to have had a curious effect on Franz Joseph; they made him adhere to principle and tenets of the past in which he strongly believed, not realizing that some of them had outlived their day.

> Ofen, 26 August 1903
>
> I have received some of the so-called leading politicians each day. I have not grown wise thereby, only my nausea at all this desultoriness and cowardice has increased. The assertion of my wishes should still have some effect ...

He asserted himself strongly and clearly in an army code of 16 September against intrigue and dissension and separation, a proclamation which was enthusiastically received by his always loyal troops: "My Army in particular ... may wish to know that I shall never renounce the rights and powers that are warranted for its Supreme Commander. My Army is to remain united and uniform as it is."

The constant seesawing of Hungarian politics, always a thorn in Franz Joseph's side, reached a thundering climax in 1904. With Franz von Kossuth's Independent party chipping away at the government of Premier Tisza, the premier issued an edict dissolving parliament and calling for new elections. The elections turned out to be a disaster to Tisza's aspirations. His conciliatory United party lost and the radical Magyar party, which demanded, among other things, Hungarian as the official langage within the army and civil service, gained the upper hand, to the despair of the other nationalities in that part of the realm—Slovaks, Croats, Serbs, Rumanians, Germans.

With a swiftness generally alien to his deliberate ways Franz Joseph decided to eliminate the bickering politicians and to entrust a Hungarian military man, General von Fejérváry, with the formation of a new cabinet. Despite stirrings of unrest, Franz Joseph stood by his decision, relying on his loyal army. Unfortunately, the general was unable to come to an understanding with the opposition and form a cabinet. Franz Joseph, angered by the opposition's intransigence, summoned the politicians in question, some of Hungary's most illustrious men among them. On 25 September 1905 he read to them his stipulations for the formation of a government. Without allowing questions or debate he dismissed them without a further word. When nothing came of it, he once more entrusted Fejérváry with the formation of a cabinet. This infuriated the pro-Magyar politicians. Thereupon Fejérváry, after receiving assurances from the army and the emperor, peremptorily summoned the Hungarian parliament on 18 February 1906 and appointed a general from one of Hungary's most famed regiments, the Honvéd, as royal commissioner. Promptly at the end of the session Honvéd officers and troops occupied parliament and a decree was read dissolving the *Reichstag.* To stabilize matters Franz Joseph had made the best of a bad situation which threatened to split the empire. The lightning speed of his decision and action had taken all by surprise. The effect, however, was not long-lasting.

> Ofen, 5 September 1905
> I am sitting here again in the hot room to put together a cabinet if possible, which is hard work, as I yield nothing on the army question ... [then] I shall journey to Galicia according to the maneuver schedule. On the 18th Kaiser Wilhelm is coming ... to Vienna for a three-day stay ... and on the 30th the Tsar of Russia who will go at once with me to Mürzsteg for a three-day hunt.

> Schönbrunn, 2 October 1905
> My hunt guests have left ... Unfortunately I must stay and worry and fret on account of Hungary, but I shall not yield.

Emperor Franz Joseph at about age 80.

Schönbrunn, 2 May 1906
The so-called solution of the Hungarian crisis occurred with the naming of
the new cabinet, which will not please you nor me either ...

Age began to weaken his hand but not his mind or devotion to his imperial task
which, in times of crisis, would take precedence over his longing for Katharina's
company.

Schönbrunn, 21 May 1908
Unfortunately ... I am absolutely not in a position to ask you to visit me ...
because of the trouble, excitement, and rush these days when the most important matters will be discussed and decided ... I beg you earnestly not to
get too excited and consider how very busy [Foreign Minister Count Alois]
Aerenthal is these days, with the most urgent and weighty affairs, which I
have already called to your attention [i.e., the consideration of annexation
of Bosnia and Herzegovina].
Excuse the scrawl; I cannot handle the pen any longer.

Buda-Pesth, 26 May 1910
I thank you most heartily for your intention to pray for me and I commend
myself to your prayer during the entire Bosnia expedition ...

Schönbrunn, 7 May 1912
Just a few lines, for writing is growing quite difficult for me ...

Regardless of all other topics of conversation, whether of a general or confidential nature, personal, diplomatic, political, or familial, the one topic which held
top priority between Franz Joseph and Katharina Scratt was the theatre. From
earliest youth Franz Joseph had been steeped in the classics of Germany and Austria
as well as foreign countries, and he knew them well, although in German translation.
Fortunately he had become acquainted with them through the tutors of his youth;
from early manhood until old age Franz Joseph was never again to read a book other
than the army manual. Knowledge of Goethe, Schiller, Grillparzer, and Shakespeare
was engraved in his mind, although he consistently preferred lighter fare and had a
penchant for drawing room comedy. While he occasionally visited another theatre,
mainly perhaps to inaugurate it, he was a steady and surprisingly knowledgeable
visitor to his beloved *Burgtheater*. The *Burgtheater* was, of course, one in a beloved
string of pearls created and hovered over by him, the *Ringstrasse*. After the fall of
the ancient, confining bastions, Franz Joseph, in his most ambitious plan, set out to
create in "his" Vienna a boulevard worthy of his seat of empire. It was to be the pride
of Vienna, magnificent, wide, destined to become one of the most famous in the
world. There he had set down in architectural profusion and confusion the Roman-
esque opera house, the neo-Gothic city hall, the neo-Grecian parliament, the new,

poorly designed wing of the *Hofburg*, the new university, the stock exchange, the Academy of Arts, the Ministry of Education, the Museum of Natural History, and the Museum of Art History, flanking the majestic monument to Empress Maria Theresia surrounded by her marshals and councilors, and the new *Burgtheater*.

Interspersed between the new there remained splendid reminders and remainders of the old: The *Burgthor*, the entrance to the court complex in the old wall; the *Mölkerbastei*, part of the old proud bastion which had withstood the Turks; above the *Mölkerbastei* the massive glowering Beethovenhaus, one of the many the titan of music had occupied; next to it, in exquisite contrast, the *Dreimäderlhaus*, the Rococo house of Schubert fame.

Sprawling splendidly with its impressive wings (for use by the emperor, aristocracy, and assorted "carriage trade"), next to the *Stadtpark* with its seas of roses, lilacs, and forsythia, the *Burgtheater* was Franz Joseph's personal pearl among the many indiscriminately strewn along the horseshoe-shaped boulevard. Here he could relax, indulge in a suppressed chuckle, watch the most impressive generation of great German actors strut and emote, and adore *Die Freundin*, Katharina Schratt.

23 November 1866

I admired you very much as a sailor in *Schach dem König* and was immensely pleased at the decorous male costume. I am curious as to how you will manage the uniform in the next production in which you will portray a cadet ... I am much happier seeing you play in woman's attire, as for me the favorite among your roles remains always that of Claire in *Der Hüttenbesitzer* [*The Mine Owner*].

18 January 1887

I regret very much that your petition to [*Burgtheater* Director] Willbrandt was unsuccessful. I certainly wanted to speak recently to [the general manager of the imperial theaters] Baron Bezecny when I had an opportunity to say a word concerning your affairs but I did not dare since, as a matter of principle, I have never interfered until now in the scheduling of plays or the casting of roles ... Also I feared bringing you into a false light by my protection, harming you rather than being of use to you. But now, for your sake, I intend nonetheless to take the next opportunity to propose your wish to him.

Ischl, 19 May 1887

How did you hold up at the banquet with the dramatic performance and ball [marking the 25-year jubilee of famed Burgtheater tragedienne Charlotte Wolter]? Is it true that you recited [Schiller's] *Jungfrau von Orleans* [*Maid of Orleans*]? I hear that the youthful Charlotte danced until 4 o'clock in the morning and at 10 o'clock she was already here with me to express her thanks and after all her exertion looked fresher than in the role of [Grillparzer's] *Sappho*. Truly remarkable ... I was sorry not to have seen you in your favorite role as Miss Lucy ... You play this small role with such distinction, and blond wig and glasses look so well on you ... what you told me about Fräulein Hohenfels's coquetry made me very happy ...

In discussing the *Burgtheater* Franz Joseph indulged primarily in two topics; a knowledgeable discussion of authors, direction, interpretation, performance, and gossip. He could never get enough of backstage *Klatsch* which he would gleefully discuss with the trustworthy actress.

> 30 May 1887
>
> [concerning the Wolter Jubilee] I am already eager for your account ... of the candid sentiments of the audience and ... of the dear colleagues ... Recently I encountered [fellow actress] Fräulein Hohenfels in her carriage ... She greeted me affably, indeed, but with a partly displeased, partly melancholy expression. It would surely have amused you if you had seen it. [A doubtful statement because Fräulein Hohenfels was obviously "making a play" for the emperor.]

He did not want to miss any theatrical detail of the *Burgtheater*, be it onstage or backstage.

> 14 June 1887
>
> It would also have interested me to see Frl. [Babette] Reinhold in the role of our friend ?? Hohenfels. I read in the newspaper that a hissing claque operated at that performance, which clearly enough will be attributed to the latter's influence ... In [Kleist's] *Käthchen von Heilbronn* the youthful guest pleased me very much. She was very charming and simple but she still has much to learn. A house across the street burned during the Sunday performance. Were you very frightened? ... Did the recent experiment with the window opening in the cloak room fully succeed, and if necessary, would you be quick enough to be able to jump out?

> Vienna, 31 December 1887
>
> The day before yesterday I worried to no purpose because of your hasty study of the role in *Marquis de Villemer* [by George Sand]. It was a splendid performance indeed ... The play itself ... did not please me. I found it almost stupid despite the famous gifted author ... The Empress was very happy to see you perform on the last two evenings; unfortunately she always remains for the first act only.

Needless to say, Katharina Schratt had at all times the ear and interest of her imperial admirer, who followed her fortunes, suffered her intrigues, and rejoiced in her triumphs.

The Father

Vienna, 11 January 1888

When I read Frln. Tondeur on the playbill in your role, I was really shocked at the thought that she should be in a position to substitute for you, and only at the performance did I calm down, when I saw that you had not lost much in the role ... In general the entire performance was brilliant, mostly because of its tasteful, historically authentic costumes and decorations, and was played very well on the whole. Frau Albrecht ... was excellent ... It was pathetic to see with what devotion husband [Count Thomas Nyary] and admirer [Marquis von Bacquehem] watched her, and both even sat together for some time in the superintendant's box. Our dear friend Hohenfels played splendidly, as usual, looked younger and prettier than ever and sang a ballad quite horribly ... Recently I also saw *Unsere Freunde* [by Max Ring] ... The performance was sloppy ...

1 February 1888

You played very well again in *Galeotto* [by José Echegaray]. Your bearing was distinguished and elegant, all movements beautifully plastic, the swoon in the third act enchanting ... I found the play interesting but laborious ... particularly the third act ...

Vienna, 15 May 1888

Today I had to arise at half past three to be able to send you these lines ... I was not so satisfied with your appearance yesterday ... therefore my first question: How are you, are you really quite well and how is the *Weltschmerz*? I think so much of you and am worried at once if your eyes do not shine as gaily as they should ... What you write me about the gods [an "in" reference to the leading actors of the *Burgtheater*] amused me very much. I did not know at all that you have an entire Olympus ... I find the assignment of the names very apropos, the Diana [wife of Burgtheater Director Adolf von Sonnenthal] especially amused me ... Jupiter [Sonnenthal] will attend a gala dinner I am giving tonight for quite a company. Perhaps it will incline him more gently in your favor.

24 May 1888

Yesterday I inspected the new *Burgtheater* again. Artistically it is exquisite but on the practical side [Joseph] Levinsky may be correct in many of his antagonistic remarks. The artist's boxes are particularly frightful ... On the other hand I found my box more comfortable this time and with a better view ...

Gödöllö, 1 November 1888

I am already very eager for your report of Forster's [the new *Burgtheater* Director] first appearance. You make me especially happy when you write theater talk to me. It is perhaps neither noble nor proper for me but true ... You should see Sarah Bernhardt perform [the famous French tragedienne often guest starred in Vienna] ... I would also wish for an opinion from you.

The death of Crown Prince Rudolf left Franz Joseph inwardly deeply shaken. Outwardly life for the ruler of an empire went on, with audiences, conferences, receptions, affairs of state and the *Burgtheater*.

> 28 February 1889
> You see I am again concerned with the *Burgtheater*, also a step forward toward a normal life. Why I do it, you certainly know best ...

> Ofen, 28 February 1889
> I must tell you that I was astounded that Countess Nyáry had received your role in *Letzte Liebe*, for if she had not had an especially lucky day with her make-up, she would not have looked young enough, even otherwise she does not seem to me suitable for the role ...

Deeply religious, Franz Joseph had a shrine erected at the scene of his son's death, yet surprisingly, despite his devotion to Catholicism he questioned some of its aspects.

> Schönbrunn, 5 November 1889
> I was actually in Mayerling ... the Chapel [in memory of his son] is really very lovely ... First I heard Mass in the chapel and then inspected the cloister ... The nuns are pleased ... there are even some pretty young novices there. What a decision ... to bury themselves for their entire lives within these stern cloister walls. In each cell and also on the nuns' dining table stands a stone skull ...

Newspapers, his only reading material aside from the army manual, also acquainted him with the innovations of his day and time and whetted his curiosity, although he never became as daringly inquisitive as Katharina.

> Gödöllö, 5 November 1889
> Herr Wagmann brought me the famous Edison phonograph which is just as astonishing as it is interesting. I heard Bismarck speaking quite distinctly, a "Hurrah" shouted for me in Berlin ... our national anthem played by the band of the Railroad Regiment and the Radetzky March; a declamation by Sonnenthal in his most affected style made me laugh; a song by [singer and voice coach] Frau [Rosa] Papier was especially clearly and beautifully reproduced, as was a piano number played for Kaiser Wilhelm ... and a trumpet fanfare sounded for the Grand Duke of Baden ...

So absolute was Franz Joseph's confidence in the discretion of Katharina that he had no qualms discussing with her the sensitive subject of her fellow actors.

> Ofen, 22 June 1890
> My opinion of the acting of Frau X is also well known to you. It is so harsh that it is impossible to give it to her husband, and so I daresay there is nothing for me to do but to corrupt you into telling a lie ...

Ofen, 8 September 1891

I was at the *Burgtheater* again ... partly out of curiosity to see Frau X. Actually a beautiful blond woman, but what acting!! I have never seen the like in the *Burgtheater*. Unnatural, affected, always in motion, mincing about, mispronouncing, lamenting, shrieking, moreover almost wholly unintelligible ... The entire performance, given to empty seats, was bad in general.

Gödöllö, 8 November 1890

I had to go to the opera where I sat with the Grand Duke [Nicholas of Russia] at *Die Afrikanerin* [by Meyerbeer] until I accompanied him to the *Südbahnhof* [Southern railroad station]. During the performance my thoughts were at the *Burgtheater* ...

Ofen, 17 February 1891

Yesterday [theatre intendant] Prince Hohenlohe received the following telegram from Bezecny: "Revised manuscript by Carmen Silva [pen name of Queen Elizabeth of Rumania] just arrived in which all changes proposed from here are accepted. The play [*Manoli*] now goes to the management with the order to prepare the performance for May ... I am curious as to the results ...

21 March 1893

[I went] to the Burgtheater to see *Kriemhilde*. The play is tiresome but it was so excellently played that it is good to see it once. It would have had a splendid ensemble if you would have taken the role of the nun. Her costume does not offend religious feelings because it is more that of a Protestant deaconess. Wolter looks remarkably well in gorgeous clothes. Frln. Reinhold again produced some fashionable clothes without bodice which make her thoroughly ugly.

On a par with the *Burgtheater* and often even more to Franz Joseph's taste was the light fare of Vienna's operetta.

9 April 1895

In the evening I drove to the *Theater an der Wien* ... and attended the entire performance of *Die Karlsschülerin* [operetta by Karl Weinberger] which was very good and amusing. Palmáy was *en verve* and your friend Girardi made me laugh a good deal ...

14 December 1895

I went to the opera again where after *Cavalleria Rusticana* I saw *Amor auf Reisen* [*Cupid's Travels*, by Heinrich Berté] which I liked very much. Frl. Schlesinger looked charming in a shockingly scant costume ...

12 May 1896

In the evening I will go to the Opera House because the one-armed [pianist and composer Gèza] Zichy wants me to hear his new opera which is said to be quite boring ...

15 May 1896

I was duly at Count Zichy's opera which pleased me better than I had expected. A lively ballet in it kept me from falling asleep.

13 April 1897

I was at the *Burgtheater* performance Saturday ... It was less than so-so, actually quite depressing ... Frau X looked terrible and played with unspeakable vulgarity, hardly possible even in the suburbs ... the entire performance was downright sloppy. What are we coming to, if this continues??!!

11 March 1898

I went ... to the *Burgtheater* where *Die Versunkene Glocke* [*The Sunken Bell*, by Gerhart Hauptmann] was given. I stayed until 9 o'clock ... Frln. Medelsky was incomparably better than our friend Devrient Reinhold ... Herr Löwe who, unfortunately and I don't know why, played instead of Levinsky, was a frightful frog. You probably knew that the indisposition of Frau Devrient is that she is pregnant ... I also called on poor Phillip [Prince Coburg] ... He is depressed by all the indecencies of his wife and has already begun divorce proceedings ...

12 May 1898

High Court Marshal Count Cziráky was here to repeat to me in detail about the Louise Coburg affair. Everything has proceeded smoothly beyond expectations ... After First Lieutenant Mattatich had been arrested, the Princess submitted to urgent entreaties and herself expressed the wish to go to a sanatorium ...

But all did not proceed "smoothly beyond expectations," as the emperor had hoped. Thus one of the lustiest stories involving titled personages made the rounds of all European newspapers, which dealt with it in lurid detail. Crown Princess Louise of Saxony, the granddaughter of none less than Grand Duke Ferdinand IV of Tuscany, had set Europe on its ear by running off in December 1902 with her language teacher. She was thirty-two years old at the time. King Georg of Saxony promptly rescinded "all rights, honors and privileges," and Emperor Franz Joseph followed suit. After giving birth to a daughter in May 1903, the now Countess of Montignoso fell in love and married Italian composer Enrico Toselli (known for his famous "Serenade"). After a divorce from him she again changed her name to Comtesse d'Ysette. Two years later she scandalized titled Europe again. After having been interned in a sanatorium at Meissen, she fled from there to a spa, Bad Elster, where she met Lieutenant Geza von Mattatich. Gossip had it that she had known him before but that their acquaintance had lapsed when he was sentenced to six years in prison for forgery. After his release they met again and moved to Paris where she lived as his companion.

The assassination of Empress Elizabeth brought Franz Joseph again face to face with disaster. As he resumed the functions of his office, the theatre, which he loved so dearly, again helped soften reality.

> Ofen, October 1898
>
> Next Thursday I shall resume the regular audiences, and so I return gradual-ly to life as it was. Asking you to give news often and not to forget the repertoire of the *Burgtheater*. I remain with most affectionate greetings and with sincerest gratitude for your kindness, care and indulgence.
>
> Your most fondly loving
> Franz Joseph

> 18 October 1898
>
> I was twice in the Empress' rooms where I found everything unchanged, even decorated with flowers as of old ... It was quite sad and yet rather comforting ... In my last letter I forgot to write you that all the streets in Buda-Pesth are still decorated with hundreds of black flags ...

> 8 November 1898
>
> I shall accompany you in thoughts to the *Gruft* [the Capuchin Crypt, the traditional burial place of the imperial family, in Vienna] to the sarcophagus of the dear, beloved, unforgettable one and join you in prayers. I thank you with all my heart for keeping our *Verklärte* [transfigured one] in such faith-ful remembrance ...

> 13 April 1900
>
> I was at [Eleanora] Duse's entire performance of *La Gioconda* [by Gabriele d'Annunzio]. The theatre was sold out, the public very elegant, the per-formance really very good, if one gets accustomed to much that is strange to us; the Duse, rather old, without make-up, with mixed gray hair, without corset, acts remarkably well and perhaps exaggeratedly natural ...

Katharina Schratt had challenged Franz Joseph's sense of propriety by gambling, mountain climbing, adventurous business deals, and even driving an automobile. Despite all the derring-do she outlived her admiring monarch by nearly twenty-four years. In 1929, at the age of seventy-four, she ventured on her first airplane ride despite the rigors of early air travel. How Franz Joseph would have shuddered!

Her death on 17 April 1940 brought to the forefront again all the rumors which she had had to endure during her lifetime. French newspapers called her *l'amie fidèle de l'Empereur;* the Italians called her *La dulca Catarina* while condemning Empress Elizabeth as *La vagabunda Emperatriz.* Some German reports even described her as "the morganatic wife of the emperor." The American press was by far the fairest and kindest. *The Journal American* described her as, "The last of the historic sweethearts of emperors and kings, also the least vain, least selfish and surely the most close-mouthed of them all," *The New York Times* paid her gentle tribute: "Cheerful, warmhearted, unaffected, she brightened and amused by her conversation her guest elsewhere condemned to be essentially solitary and friendless ... Katharina Schratt's influence on Franz Joseph was good. She seems to have been incapable of intrigue, disinterested, kind. Like most stage folks she was generous ... she was as genuine as she was gracious."

Part II

The Sons

7

The Other Johann

As his fame grew apace with that of his father, Johann allowed neither himself nor anyone else, professional, publisher, or public, to demean his senior or to inject a spirit of competition into their relationship. Yet Vienna could not stop comparing and wondering. What caused constant wonderment was the obvious fact that the personification of the Viennese waltz looked anything but Viennese with his flashing eyes, wild black mane, and "moorish" features.

Eduard, the youngest son of Strauss Father, relates in his memoirs the legend of his mother's ancestry as it had been told to him as a child:

> A wealthy Spanish grandee dared not only to actively oppose the court but in zealous opposition challenged the crown prince to a duel. When he killed the prince he was forced to flee for his life. There was no time to dispose of his wealth and he had to flee with his wife and children, hiding by day and traveling by night. Miraculously, despite the hazards of traveling and the large size of his family, he escaped to France, from there to Germany. His flight finally ended in the palace of the Grandee's friend in Vienna, Duke Albert of Sachsen-Teschen.

According to Eduard's recollection, the duke promised help under the condition that the Spanish nobleman renounce all titles, forgo any mention of his birth and former rank, and assume the name of Rover. The refugee had no choice but to accede. He became a cook in the duke's service. Although the grandee and his wife died soon thereafter, the family secret was kept by their children. One daughter, Maria Anna, married Josef Streim, who later became proprietor of the inn *Zum Roten Hahn* and subsequently Strauss's father-in-law. One of their daughters, Anna, inherited not only the mother's Spanish features but also played the family guitar with great competence. The guitar was something of a relic in the family because it was reputed to be the only link with the past, the only thing which had accompanied the family on the flight from Spain.

The Sons

Close scrutiny gives little credence to the story. There is no mention in the annals of Spain of such a duel. It is doubtful whether a well-known Spanish nobleman traveling on foot with a large family could have escaped the court's swift and vengeful cavalry. Assuming that he did escape to France and Germany, the royal heads of those countries certainly would have jailed and extradited the grandee or, in case of hostilities, held him for ransom. Assuming that the Spaniard, family and all, had reached Vienna and the refuge of Duke Albert's palace, would the brother-in-law of the emperor have treated a fellow nobleman so shabbily? On the other hand, would he, as an Austrian Field Marshal, have risked the rebuke of the court for harboring a Spanish criminal? Would the duke have been able to keep such a monstrous secret of state from his household or from the court? It seems unlikely.

Ernst Decsey, the Vienna music historian, presents a more plausible explanation. He reminds us that dark skin and raven hair, heavily lidded, deep-set eyes, and dexterity on the guitar are equally common among Spaniards and gypsies. Thus the possibility exists that it was not a grandee of Spain being downgraded but a gypsy attempting to upgrade himself into respectable society by joining the duke's kitchen staff. Wishing to disguise his lowly background, which would have aroused distrust and animosity, he invented the story of the Spanish nobleman, the flight, and all the gory delectable details so dear to the minds of the wide-eyed kitchen help, and displayed his precious guitar as the only salvaged treasure from past wealth. Rumors were always rife in Vienna about the dark-skinned troubadour of the fiddle. Hadamovsky expounds the theory that the mother of Johann Strauss Father had brought Jewish blood into the family, not from southern Europe but from Pressburg in the East. The belief was reinforced by Fahrbach, collaborator and competitor of Strauss, who told how the dark-complexioned boy was often called "The Jew with the Fiddle," and by Eduard Kremser who reminds us that Franz Strauss's hostelry was called "Jew Inn." The usually haphazardly kept records of the eighteenth and nineteenth centuries offer no clues to differentiate facts from fiction. However, there can be no doubt that the mass of raven curly hair, the dark, flashing eyes, the mercurial temperament, the Mediterranean complexion, particularly in the father, indicate more than a drop of foreign blood in the family history. Add to that the easy-going charm of the Viennese background and the bewitching artistry and personality and a figure to excite the imagination emerges.

Johann apparently put no stock in those implausible tales. To him his father was very real, and the memory of him vivid and treasured:

> Father lived in a special wing of the apartment, separated from the family, which, considering his strenuous life, was the only possible way. During the *Fasching* he worked with no less than three orchestras, commuted from

one to the next, conducted a few numbers and then left the balance to the orchestra conductor. Of course that activity took up a great part of the night. After that he usually sat up with some friends. Thus it usually became quite late [until he returned] and he slept deep into the morning. The day was also filled to the brim; a number of visitors came and the compositions demanded much time. It was natural that he wanted to be undisturbed. Thus it came about that he seldom had any conception as to what was going on within the family. Of course he let us take piano lessons [but] Father thought we just tickled the ivories poorly like dilletantes. We, in turn, played piano with a passion, and I dare say we were accomplished piano players. Of that he had no idea. Rehearsals for his concerts were held in the apartment and we boys listened to every note, we observed his verve and afterwards played four-handed what we had listened to, spirited and in his spirit. He was our idol. We were often invited to other families ... and there we played, to great applause, from memory the compositions of our father.

One day an acquaintance congratulated him on our successes. He was no little surprised. "Have the boys come over," he ordered sharply. Expecting trouble we slunk into the room of our father ... he demanded that we play for him ... we played up a storm, bringing out all orchestral voices. Smilingly our father listened and one could see the pleasure in his face ... Nevertheless my father did not want us to choose music as a profession; neither did my mother ... [but] in later years mother fostered our ambition due to a change of circumstances ... I learned violin on my own ... my father wanted no part of my plans. Only later, after I had achieved several successes ... did he reconcile himself to that fact, and the recognition which my artistic efforts received from my father I count among my most beautiful and joyful memories.

Now the father was gone. Whatever Johann may have thought of his father as a human being and family man, his respect for his father the artist never wavered:

My father was a musician by the grace of God ... he spread the fame of German dance music through the world and severe judges did not withhold acknowledgment ... that his sparkling rhythms stemmed from the pure spring of musical art. As a conductor he possessed that indefinable something which carried the players with him, implanted itself in the listeners, and made their hearts and pulses beat quicker. My father was a pure artist of the highest degree, but not for a moment was he presumptuous enough to put himself on the same pedestal with the heroes of great art. But his art made some sorrows vanish, smoothed furrows, raised life's courage, gave back the joys of life, comforted, rejoiced, elated ... and for this, humanity will preserve his memory.

From the way the son described the father's way of composing there could be no question of the spark of genius.

Musical composition in those days was clearly a simpler matter than it is today. In order to produce a polka ... it was only necessary for an idea to strike one ... and, oddly enough, an idea always did strike one. One had so much confidence in this happening that one would often announce a waltz for such and such an evening, while in the morning of the appointed day not a single note had been put on paper. In that case the orchestra generally assembled *en masse* in the composer's lodgings and as soon as he had produced a theme and a few pages ... everyone started practicing and copying. In the meantime the miracle of inspiration had repeated itself and the other half was composed. Thereupon there would be a rehearsal of the whole on the spot ... usually it received an enthusiastic reception upon presentation that night ... When Lanner on occasion fell ill ... but was committed to a composition for which not a single bar had yet been written, he would simply send my father a message: "Strauss, how about an idea?" That very evening the piece would be given ... to be received with a fresh ovation.

It was that respect bordering on reverence which prompted Johann to present a concert consisting only of his father's music, leading his father's orchestra, shortly after the older man's death. He did so because he had been approached by the musicians. However, this did not keep the Viennese from castigating him and accusing him of poor taste. Strauss was completely taken aback because he had hoped, or rather, had assumed that the Viennese would understand and appreciate the sentiments which had prompted that concert. Johann's reply to the criticism appeared in the *Wiener Zeitung* in December 1849. "Never will the son measure up, in the consciousness of his weakness, as compared with the proven strength of his father. God be my witness, no! But the nineteen-year-old man saw it as his duty not to remain a useless member in the lap of his family whose head and natural support a deplorable fate had removed from his activity ... the blessed spirit of my dear father was with me, he guided me to the joyful muse which now weeps at his grave and which hopefully will allow me to be worthy of my father."

Fickle Vienna soon forgot what it had considered Johann's lack of piety. The city was too busy growing, feasting, dancing. Changes had been brought about: the *Mondscheinsaal*, the famous dance establishment of Schubert's Vienna, had become a piano factory and the splendid *Sperl* a second-class establishment in which Vienna's ladies of the evening brazenly offered their charms and where good company no longer wished to be seen.

But Vienna had lost no time replacing these centers of entertainment. Franz Morawetz, who had immigrated from Russia, had built a steambath which soon became the rage of Vienna. But in winter, when nobody visited the bath for fear of catching cold on the way home, shrewd Morawetz, now blind, converted the building into a dance hall, and the famed *Sophiensaal* was born, a hall which was to be the dance meeting place of aristocracy, artists, and burghers alike. To dedicate the hall to the emperor's mother was in itself a shrewd move. And to this day the *Sophiensaal* remains one of Vienna's famous ballrooms.

Karl Schwender, who had come to Vienna from Germany, built the dance establishment *Neue Welt* (New World). He began as a waiter, and later used the knowledge gained to open a restaurant. Subsequently he added a coffeehouse, a ballroom, another three ballrooms, a theatre adjacent to the ballrooms, and, in summer, a splendid garden illuminated by hundreds of gas jets hidden among real flowers. Within ten years, after his modest beginnings in a stable, his magnificent edifice, able to accommodate five hundred people in the theatre and thousands more in his restaurants and ballrooms, was the talk of Europe, just as the *Apollo* had been in its heyday. But the item Schwender was most famous for, the item the Viennese sought out even if they did not go there for dancing, was pastry. An assembly of regimental size, all attired in white, complete with high chefs' hats, spent their time day and night preparing pastry for Vienna's sweet palate. *Mohnbeugel* and *Apfelstrudel, Nusstorten* and *Schokoladetorten, Topfenkuchen* and *Kaiserschmarrn*, the emperor's favorite dessert, were topped by a heaping helping of *Schlag*, an abbreviation of *Schlagobers* or whipped cream, and downed with a generous *Schale Gold*, a cup of coffee, mixed with cream to give it the appearance of a "cup of gold." To this day the Viennese have not learned the meaning of the word "diet," and it is to Schwender's dubious credit that he introduced them to the glories of Viennese pastries.

Of course the *Apollosaal* was still around, and although it had become somewhat shopworn and had lost its early glory, Vienna still flocked to its immense halls night after night. It was the new Dommayer's Casino in Hietzing, close to the emperor's pleasure palace Schönbrunn, the same Dommayer's where Johann had celebrated his first triumph, which had truly emerged as the dance establishment par excellence. True, Lanner had already composed his greatest waltz there, *Die Schönbrunner*, but it was not until the emergence of Johann Strauss Son that Dommayer's grew in stature and was recognized for its "class."

There was no place of renown in Vienna which did not vie for Johann's services. And there was no place, no situation that was not musically inspiring to him: the stillness of night, a walk in the garden, a drive through the Prater meadows at dawn on his way home from an engagement, or a pause between dances at a ball. The ideas were scribbled on theatre and ballroom programs, on any kind of available paper — on restaurant menus, on the starched cuffs of his dress shirt if need be. In solitude or in company, over coffee, wine, beer, or liqueur, at a leisurely or hurried pace, invention flowed. It seemed that the pressure of an impending occasion would heighten his inventive powers, and music was constantly demanded promptly by impresarios, committees, and the public. The birth of his *Accelerationen* waltz is a case in point. The ball had just ended. The last happily exhausted couples had danced their final *Schnellpolka* and laughingly vanished into the night. It was then, in the grayness of dawn, that Johann was deferentially approached by a committee member of the *Technikerball* (Technical Engineer's Ball), one of the most popular in Vienna, inquiring in a distraught voice whether the new waltz, composed especially for the occasion and allegedly ready, would be forthcoming. Strauss, exhausted, drenched in perspiration, hair disheveled, collar softened, and bow tie askew, listened to the anxious inquiry. Then, conquering fatigue, he retired to a corner of the deserted ballroom and sketched the impatient opening of the *Accelerationen* waltz, to be played the same night. The furiously driving crescendo of the opening immediately suggests drive, power, the increasing speed of a machine in motion. "Acceleration," the magic word of the machine age, had proved the seed for Johann's fertile imagination and a triumph for the ball of the Technical Academy.

The machine age, however, had its dark side. While Vienna danced madly, in the suburbs, where police were not readily at hand, bakeries were plundered by starving artisans now out of work for their skills were no longer needed. Taxpayers paid only under threat of military execution, and the newspapers cynically mocked ballroom habitués, then comprising one-fourth of all Vienna, who might pawn their pocketwatches or even their bedclothes to have enough money for an evening or two of dancing. Vienna swarmed with unemployed workers displaced by the machine, seamstresses were no longer needed, even at the starvation wages they had been paid, and many were left with prostitution as their only source of income. Vienna, hollow with hunger and decay, went on dancing nonetheless. Johann anticipated future events with his *Explosion* polka. And the explosion came inexorably in 1848. But the revolution did not capture his heart and his enthusiasm for it soon evaporated.

What had truly captured his heart and mind was the appearance in 1846 of Jenny Lind. The "Swedish Nightingale" had come to Vienna to appear in the opera *Ein Feldlager in Schlesien (A Military Camp in Silesia)* by Meyerbeer, and the composer did her the honor of conducting in person. Grillparzer wrote a poem to her and Johann, not to be outdone, composed his *Lind-Gesänge*. Anxious to hear her sing but unable to get a ticket for a performance, he bribed a violinist in the orchestra pit and joined a performance as a player.

Vienna was at a low ebb generally in its musical endeavors. Flotow, Lortzing, Herold, Meyerbeer, and Suppé, all second-rank masters, filled Vienna's musical appetite with shoddy wares. Lortzing, among the more promising composers with his operas *Zar und Zimmerman (Tsar and Carpenter)* and *Der Waffenschmied (The Armourer)*, unfortunately lacked what Meyerbeer had in such overabundance: public appeal. Lortzing, who together with Suppé shared the conductor's desk at the famed *Theater an der Wien*, was fully aware of Vienna's lowly musical state: "Here only Italian junk and dance music generally hold their own ... Beethoven is all but unknown ... the Italians and Strauss must take the blame ... my humble self is all but forgotten ... the trouble here is that anybody who steps before the public engages some fellow who writes for them, and in turn gets paid and dressed ... Since I have no truck with ghost writers ... it is natural that I am ignored ... to do so would mean to change my entire personality."[1]

Strauss needed no ghost writer or manager. He was besieged by every establishment to play at their dance hall, gala ball, house ball. He became a *must* at any major public or private ball. Together with the *Stefansturm*, the *Kärnthnerthor-theater*, and the *Prater*, Strauss became the main attraction for any visitor and foreigner, and a single concert at Daum's *Elysium* might be attended by as many as nine thousand enthusiastic, knowing listeners. But it was Dommayer who felt that he had first call, and it was there that Strauss performed most often.

By then elite Viennese balls had settled into a delightful routine. The evening opened with polonaise of marching pairs. After that the real ball music began with a waltz, a française, followed by a mazurka and two or three quadrilles. A cotillion was usually appended to the third quadrille which ushered in the intermission at which a sumptuous supper was served to recharge flagging energies. The second half opened with a waltz, featuring the ardently looked-for "Ladies' Choice." It then continued into the dawn with innumerable waltzes and polkas, to the total exclusion of any slow steps on the polished floors. With the opening of the second half the dandified but inevitable despairing dancing master who had held sway over the opening proceedings had long retired, and exuberant exultation took precedence over all restrictive mannerisms.

Soon demands forced Johann to travel beyond Vienna and cause equal delirium in Prague, Dresden, and Leipzig. On their travels the orchestra often dressed in gala uniforms of the *Bürgergarde* which much impressed their hosts, particularly in the Balkans where the uniform reigned supreme. The orchestra did not wish to fool anybody, only to represent Vienna elegantly, yet many reacted to the splendid uni-

---

1. Albert Lortzing (1801-1851) was a German opera composer whose *Zar und Zimmermann, Undine,* and *Der Waffenschmied* were well received in Germany during the middle of the nineteenth century. Financially distressed despite his successes, Lortzing in the end was reduced to conducting operettas and writing music for cheap farces. He lived and died in dire poverty.

forms in time-honored yet amusing manner. In Belgrade the local Pasha feted the "high Austrian dignitary." In Rumania Strauss was asked to dismiss the local Austrian consul. When Johann attempted to explain that his commission, position, and uniform were musical and not political, nobody believed him. An angry crowd gathered at his hotel and all but forced him "to do his duty." When the news of this episode reached Vienna, the authorities initiated a half-hearted investigation which was all but drowned in the laughter of all concerned. Once, on impulse, without prior plans, reservations, or passports, impetuous Johann attempted a journey to Warsaw because he felt that his presence would add to the festivities at an important affair of state. As was to be expected he and his company were stopped at the border and further passage forbidden. Johann expostulated in vain. "But I am Strauss; Johann Strauss from Vienna." "Yes, and I am the Tsar of Russia," was the mocking reply of the border guard. Eventually Johann convinced the officer on duty to call the local governor, but the governor was also unconvinced, and soon Strauss and company were herded into a room of the customs house until transportation for their return could be provided. Suddenly, in the best tradition of *deus ex machina*, there appeared on the scene the personal messenger from Her Imperial Highness, the Tsarina of Russia, commanding Johann to appear without delay before their majesties at Lashenski Castle. For a moment everybody in the comedy of errors—border officials, guard, Strauss and company froze into petrified silence—then smiles, bowings, scrapings, apologies, and explanations. (Strauss and his men had been suspected of being a band of highwaymen or insurgents in disguise.)

Upon his return to Vienna Johann's popularity was unbounded. Although he had divided his musical organization into four orchestras, it hardly resulted in an easier schedule since each promoter of each ball promised his audience a personal appearance by Johann Strauss. By then the finest dance events had concentrated on five establishments: *Sophiensaal, Volksgarten, Dianabad, Viktoria* Hotel and, of course, Dommayer's. Vienna and Strauss had become integral parts of each other's worlds, and life without the musician was unthinkable. Sometimes even death could not be without him. One Viennese dowager had a special clause in her last will calling for Strauss and his orchestra to play at her funeral. Thus it was that Johann and his ensemble played waltzes while walking in a funeral procession. Musically Johann proved himself as open minded as his father and Lanner by including classical and contemporary serious music in his program. While the father had included music by Mendelssohn, Cherubini, and Meyerbeer, Johann included such avant-garde composers as Liszt and Wagner. Although Bülow's music was then little known in Vienna, Johann performed excerpts from his *Julius Caesar* with great success. The audience was so taken with the music that a repeat of the overture and the march was demanded. Bülow was enchanted: "A charming magician ... who has given me one of the most refreshing musical delights ... he is one of my few colleagues for whom my respect is undiminished ... there is a conducting genius in his small genre as Wagner is in the sublime ... I am still filled with it, my heart and head still dance like intoxicated dervishes."

Wagner was no less captivated. "A single waltz by Strauss surpasses in grace, refinement, and truly musical content most of the labored foreign fabrications just as the spire of St. Stephan surpasses the dubious hollow columns of the Paris boulevards." Local historian Friedrich von Gaudy mused:

> The *Universum* was an amusement place at the farthest edge of the Leopoldstadt district. A stream of humanity floated in its direction and its open door. Light fell through into the outer darkness and the mass of people held back by police, who watched with envious eyes those who had been able to buy a ticket. Inside, unbounded joyfulness. Plates and bottles clinking on innumerable tables, between them hundreds of visitors, talking, laughing, walking up and down ... a ball of humanity beyond unraveling is massed around the podium in the middle of the gardens. There stood Johann Strauss. Now he lifts his bow and every Viennese heart beats higher; a look to the right, a look to the left along the orchestra, all hang on his eyes ... Not only with the bow but also with the foot does he mark time, moving his head pleasurably this way and that ... Now he throws the long-locked hair to one side with genial lightning eyes and grasps his violin to throw his own weight into the balance. Open-mouthed, the crowd stands as if in deep devotion. Suddenly the passionate enthusiasm breaks into roaring jubilation ...
>
> The clock strikes the tenth hour and the ball begins. Strauss now intones his footswinging sounds in the ballroom ... the crowd flows in like a wild sea ... the introduction sounds ... with sweetly dreamy eyes the Viennese girl eyes her partner and, on his arm, rocks in time to the reveling rhythm which lets you anticipate the waltz melody, but hesitates to bring it out in the open ... now the sound of the dominant chord —Strauss himself puts the violin to his chest and as the bow touches the string, an electric shock goes through the rows of dancers, and with speed reminiscent of Holbein's *Totentanz* [Dance of Death] they glide over the parquet, circling each other in double circles ...

Thus Johann played in the palaces of aristocracy, for the man and woman in the street who understood him intuitively, at the *Universum* in the Leopoldstadt, *Lindenbaum's Kasino* in Simmering, or *Zögernitz's Kasino* in Döbling, all of them in the suburbs.

Still, contemporaries withheld their final approval of the son. The father was dead but not forgotten, and many felt that it was still he who should bear the title of "Waltz King." Even the mighty music critic Hanslick knitted an artistic brow and took exception to heavy orchestration, trombones in waltzes, "Lisztian chords," "every corner contaminated by Wagnerian sounds." Hanslick, the influential music critic of the *Neue Freie Presse*, enjoyed Strauss's music as much as he did Offenbach's insouciant sounds. When he visited Offenbach in Paris, Hanslick, with an impish smile, played Strauss melodies for the composer. Despite criticism, the critic cherished Strauss's melodies: "Those wondrous sounds have the importance of a citation, a motto for everything that is beautiful and tender and gay in Vienna; they are to the Austrian not just beautiful words but a patriotic folk song without words."

In an extended sense Hanslick's withholding of initial approval was justified. It was to take many years and many waltzes before Johann was to grow beyond the ingrained format of the dance established by Lanner and his father. During the first twenty years of his artistic endeavors Johann, who was constantly experimenting, wrote over three hundred dances of all kinds. Among them we find close to one hundred fifty waltzes, a figure which in itself is witness to artistic diligence and staggering ingenuity. In that respect a bit of arithmetic will prove revealing. Each waltz, aside from introduction and coda, consisted of an average of five sections, each section of two parts. Each part of each section presented a new original melody, ten original melodies per waltz, fifteen hundred original melodies in Strauss's waltzes alone! Consider further that each melody was destined to appear only once, never to be developed or even used again, and a picture of inventive musical ingenuity appears which constitutes a feat unequaled by any composer in any field. Hanslick shook his critical head in the face of such wanton waste of melodic material. Steeped in the legacy of the Vienna classics, he felt that a melody was to be introduced, repeated, developed, and recapitulated:

> The narrowest framework and the most inexorable condition anywhere in the field of music prompt the waltz composer to offer full invention with the first downbeat and to discard it, freshly plucked, without fruitful use, only to win and waste anew ... the narrow tight form of the waltz does not permit the least development of a melody; once ended, it disappears without trace to make room for a second, third, etc., until all five waltzes have been rolled off like some unrelated picture series in a penny-arcade viewer. For a dance, five waltzes with at least five new themes are needed, often twice as many since usually they use a new theme for the second part of each waltz. This is inartistic waste which must exhaust even the most productive talent.

8

The Schubert of the Waltz

It was not musically but bodily that Johann became exhausted. One day, without warning, he simply collapsed at his mother's feet. Realizing that his father had stormed through life, raging to consume it before he became consumed by it, Johann observed the danger signal and decided to conserve his energies. A family council was called. It consisted of mother Anna and her three sons: Johann with his hair styled à la Emperor Franz Joseph, Josef with his shoulder length hair reminiscent of Liszt, and Eduard with his goatee and pointed moustache styled in the manner of Napoleon III. After serious discussion the family decided that Josef should continue where Johann had left off so that Johann could rest and recuperate while the family tradition of the Strauss orchestra was being perpetuated.

Josef was an enigma to many, constantly enveloped in a sense of tragedy and mournfulness. If Johann was all light and gaiety, Josef seemed possessed by a demon of darkness. Yet he was strong-willed, a trait inherited from his mother. When his father urged him to join the officer's corps, Josef replied decisively: "I do not wish to learn how to kill people, do not wish to be marked by hunting human lives ... better to seek death myself than to live with such a conscience—let me be where I am, let me be what I am." An architectural engineer, Josef joined the engineering department of a manufacturer of spinning machines, submitted to the city of Vienna an invention for a street cleaning device, supervised the construction of new buildings, and studied the construction of water mains. Despite his young years he had a promising future as an engineer and prepared to get his final diploma. Consequently he rejected the initial request of the family to take the helm of the orchestra. He pleaded insufficient knowledge of music, which was laughed down by the family, and ignorance of the violin, which was a fact. Finally his resistance gave way under concerted family pressure. Once decided, he approached his new profession with the thorough and persistent mind of the inventor and engineer. His aroused fervor prompted him to study music theory with famed Dolleschal, and violin with the family friend Amon, not so much to master the instrument but to understand it since it was the main instrument of Strauss music. Finally his reluctance, shyness, and reticence were subdued by determination.

On 23 July 1853 a new Strauss made his sensational debut at the *Sperl*. (Historians differ as to the locale of his premiere performance. Some maintain that the establishment was *Zum Grünen Zeisig*—The Green Siskin—but all agree on the date.) Josef was totally different in every aspect of appearance from Johann, and Vienna loved him for the difference. What raised eyebrows first was that there stood on the podium a Strauss without a violin. Josef had decided against it. To know the violin was one thing, to play it in public and before such a knowing public as the Viennese, was another. He followed the example of the conductors of military bands in using a baton. The other feature which fascinated the Viennese was that pale melancholy face with the burning eyes, again a vast contrast from his older brother. Although his very first waltz, even in his title, *The First and the Last*, still indicated the inward strain of resistance against his new function, it promptly established him in the hearts of his countrymen. The family breathed easier; success and continuity were assured. Slowly Josef's appetite was whetted, and soon another waltz, *The First after the Last*, appeared. And then the Strauss miracle of musical fertility happened all over again. Josef composed two hundred twenty-two waltzes. H. E. Jacob comments: "With the Father it was called forth by a strong will, in Johann it happened without his volition; in Josef it happened against his will."

Some of Vienna's best guessing games revolved around the question of which Strauss had written which waltz. The Strauss brothers were not above collaboration, and they laughingly started the guessing game by simply signing the name Strauss to their new musical collaborative inspiration. The guessing game still goes on because only on rare occasions did the brothers inform the public of their collaboration. We do know, however, that the famed *Pizzicato Polka* was composed by both Josef and Johann, and the *Trifolien Walzer* by the triumvirate of Johann, Josef, and Eduard.

Some of Josef's greatest waltzes match the creations of his older brother. *Dorfschwalben aus Oesterreich (Village Swallows from Austria)*, *Sphärenklänge (Music of the Spheres)*, and the third in his trio of famous waltzes, *Mein Lebenslauf ist Lieb' und Lust (My Life's Course Is Love and Joy)* mark him as the most Austrian. The last one reveals him as a true Viennese composer of charm and gentle grace, and it earned him the deserved title of "Schubert of the waltz." Another Strauss, Richard, transplanted Josef's little known *Dynamiden* waltz, opus 173 into one of his *Rosenkavalier* waltzes.

Yet despite that gentleness and charm, despite the adoration by the Viennese, despite an outwardly happy marriage, the morbid, melancholy streak continued.

Nonetheless he was in turn accepted, liked, then adored by public and professionals alike. Since at that time no organization existed to protect the creations of composers, Josef's lilting melodies were "borrowed" by minor musical lights as well as by publishers out to make a quick gulden, supplied with inane words, and hawked as genuine Viennese folk ditties. Josef was too busy to notice. It was he who was now conductor of court ball music, who led the Strauss orchestra at innumerable balls, at aristocratic palaces, and at the huge outdoor establishments so dear to the Viennese. But where Johann had been outgoing and worldly, Josef remained melancholy (the Viennese thought him romantic), more Spanish than Viennese, more hermit than gypsy. Hidden to all, Josef suffered from a latent emotional instability, but unlike his father he controlled it by his strong self-discipline. Neither the swagger of his polkas nor the tenderness of his waltzes could sway the deep depressions which racked his soul. Yet whenever the elegant man in black tails and white trousers, black hair, pale face and melancholy eyes stepped before his public, women swooned as fervently as they had before his dashing brother. The front always remained Straussian, but a deep-seated melancholia made him shun all close outside contacts, work feverishly, and smoke endlessly.

The end came suddenly and somehow matched the life of Josef. It started with an incident, trifling in itself. Josef, deeply depressed by the recent death of his beloved mother, had begun a tour of Russia, despite misgivings. Only his sense of correctness in fulfilling engagement contracts had prompted him to go with a makeshift orchestra. While on tour he was in constant dread of some catastrophe which might occur, and during a performance a missed cue by the first violinist threatened to disrupt the orchestra. The miscue suddenly loomed as a disaster as the orchestra became more dissonant with every bar despite the desperate ministrations of the conductor. The scandal, the failure suddenly assumed monstrous proportions in Josef's mind; terror rose within him. He collapsed on the platform, rolled down four steps, and landed in a coma at the feet of the first row of listeners. Johann rushed up from Vienna as did Karoline, Josef's wife. A brain concussion was the first prognosis of the Warsaw doctors. And during the first few weeks, while first Johann and later Fahrbach substituted as conductors, Josef's improvement seemed to bear out the doctors' opinion. When Josef suddenly took a turn for the worse, it was felt that Viennese doctors might be more competent and, on a journey resembling the elder Strauss's trip from Paris to Vienna, Josef's return was accomplished. Vienna medical competence came too late. Careful consultation by three specialists came to the unanimous conclusion that the worsening condition had come about through the bursting of a brain tumor. Some even felt that the tumor may have been with Josef for many a month and may have accounted for his melancholy. The tour he had begun with forebodings on 18 April 1870 ended on 22 July in death.

The Sons

Unfortunately, before one of his many orchestra tours into foreign lands Josef had made a promise with his brother Eduard that whoever outlived the other would completely destroy the musical creations of the other so that they would not fall into the hands of strangers. To the horror of the musical world Eduard felt bound by his promise to his brother. In 1907, after making the necessary arrangements, he hired a truck, had all the music of Josef loaded into it, had it brought to the factory of a Vienna furnace maker. Indifferent workmen, totally unaware of the treasures they were destroying, shoveled pile after pile of priceless manuscripts into the blazing furnace, as Eduard for five hours stoically watched the pages curl, catch fire, and turn to ashes in the roaring holocaust. Nobody will ever know what treasures by Josef (and perhaps by Johann) were lost to musical history in the blaze.

Josef Strauss (1827-1870).
The melancholy "Schubert of the Waltz."

9

The Frustrated Dandy

Johann's recuperative period after his collapse was of brief duration. But he was wise enough not to enter the fray too soon, and in 1853 he betook himself to Bad Neuhaus, a spa near Cilli, to enjoy its waters. But the orchestra had to go on, Vienna would have it no other way. The choice was not difficult because, long before Johann's sudden illness and Josef's death, brother Eduard, according to the will of the family council, had also been pressed into service. He was not without regrets. Eduard wrote in his memoirs, "I withdrew my application for acceptance into the Oriental Academy to which I had aspired for two years since my graduation from the *Gymnasium*. I did not do so with a light heart. Although the newly introduced course by Count Leo Thun was very pedantic, I had, according to my intentions, applied myself diligently, liked to read Cicero, and had improved my Latin and Greek without neglecting the other Romance languages such as Italian and Spanish."

Eduard had intended to pursue a diplomatic career with the same energy and zeal his brother Josef had intended to follow engineering. Two factors decided him otherwise. One was pressure from the family; the second was that, while Josef had forced himself to go into music, Eduard succumbed to its lure. Before taking charge, Eduard, like Josef before him, scrupulously attended to his musical studies; he learned musical theory with old Simon Sechter, the teacher of Schubert and Bruckner; violin with ancient Amon; and, upon Johann's advice, acquired a playing knowledge of the harp, which he studied with Zamara. Careful to acquaint himself with the intricacies of an orchestra in general and the Strauss style in particular, he first played with the orchestra under Johann and Josef before conducting his first concert. He was well prepared. Johann had personally taught him the waltz tempo and given the advice, "not too fast." Eduard, like Johann, cut an elegant and vibrant figure, and his handsome looks and immaculate elegance soon made him a favorite with the opposite sex and earned him the nickname *"Der schöne Edi"* ("Handsome Eddy"). But if his melancholy, brooding brother had been called a "Straussian Hamlet" Eduard was no less beset by morbid peculiarities. His memoirs, *Erinnerungen*, published in 1906, make oddly strident reading. His nature was easily bruised, and, often angered by being mistaken for his more famous brother Johann, Eduard was openly critical of some of his oldest brother's actions. Johann was well aware of Eduard's animosity and wrote him once: "You always look at the dark side ... are always thinking that I want to harm you. How old must you grow before you realize that your brother is not your enemy ...?" Eduard's predilections for pest holes, corpses, funerals, and the skeleton-filled catacombs beneath the cathedral of St. Stefan certainly give cause for thought. It is therefore not surprising that Josef approached Eduard, whose morbid kinship he recognized, and not Johann, with his odd request to burn their musical legacy.

Another totally non-Straussian trait was also hidden beneath the strutting gait, the smart front of the handsome man, elegant in his yellow overcoat, light gloves, and high hat: his inability to compose any dance music with life in it. His total of about two hundred fifty dances of various types show sound craftsmanship but musically are no more than pale clichés of his two older brothers' inspired work. Eduard was aware of his lack of creativity, and jealousy brought gnawing envy. Thus the schizophrenic trait of the Strauss family became even more pronounced within him. Brother Josef was a mournful soul, but that trait was clear to all who knew him. The difficulty with Eduard was compounded by the fact that his elegant exterior, smart conducting and easy social graces hid a morbidity and smouldering envy which in later years he had great difficulty concealing.

In Vienna Eduard actually had become more popular than his brother Johann. Whenever the elegant and handsome conductor appeared, in the streets, the salons, the concert halls, or the ballrooms, women would fight over his gloves whenever he deigned to remove them from his delicate hands. Johann, who in contrast to his brother, was totally devoid of professional envy, often jokingly referred to his younger brother's great popularity. When on occasion he found himself without money after having made a purchase he would laughingly request: "Please send them to my home, I am the brother of Edi Strauss."

As Johann went more and more in the direction of composition, Josef and Eduard were called upon to continue the Strauss tradition and to conduct the Strauss orchestras. Eduard had been introduced as the "newest" Strauss by his brothers at a "Monster Ball" at the Wintergarden of the Diana Baths on 5 February 1859. It was to be one of the unforgettable occasions in the musical annals of Vienna, because each of the brothers, Johann, Josef, and Eduard, brought his own orchestra! The ball's motto had been "Carnival's Perpetual Motion or Dance without End" but

Eduard Strauss (1835-1916) in court uniform.
The frustrated dandy—outward grace, inward envy.

those attending gasped when the three famous brothers and their ensembles appeared on three sides of the huge ballroom. Fourteen waltzes, ten quadrilles, nine polka francaises, eight polka mazurkas plus others, fifty dances in all, were played by the three brothers in rotation. Upon a signal from the oldest brother, the finale was played, to the spellbound attention of those who were fortunate enough to be present, by all three brothers and their massed orchestras in unison—a feat never again to be repeated.

After Josef's death, Eduard continued to uphold the family tradition of traveling. In London, Queen Victoria looked at him thoughtfully, happy reminiscences crowding her mind: "You remind me very much of your father ... It seems like yesterday when he played at my coronation ball. I still remember the pieces. Could you play some of them?"

In 1890 Eduard undertook with elan what Johann had done only reluctantly—a tour of the United States during which he visited seventy-three cities, an incredible feat reminiscent of his father's tour through England. But despite a charming exterior Eduard had become increasingly surly. What added to his growing distress was the realization that the Americans still applauded the Straussian creations but were no longer interested in dancing them. Even worse was the fact that he was constantly mistaken for his older brother Johann and addressed as such by public and press.

Undaunted by constant accidents which seemed to dog his tours—cholera, sun stroke, railway mishaps—Eduard continued to travel. He went to Germany and Russia to uphold the Straussian banner and glory. In 1900, one year after Johann's death, Eduard undertook one last tour of America. However, that time it was not musical ambition which fired him, but the desire to recoup a lost fortune, squandered by his wife and sons through unlucky stockmarket transactions. Not even the naive joy Americans took in his music could ease the painful sense of drudgery or dilute the toxin of materialism which had prompted the journey. Upon return to Vienna all that remained of Eduard Strauss was an elegant outer shell. He promptly disbanded the famous orchestra.

Death at the ripe old age of eighty-one finally closed his secret, never-healing wound—envy of his brother Johann. Straussian in appearance and performance but never in reality, Eduard wilted away because the lighthearted Viennese grace and humor which his brother had personified so prodigiously remained an elusive, painful, and agonizing enigma to him.

10

The Musical Crowd

It seems that Vienna had always resounded with music. As early as the thirteenth century Walther von der Vogelweide, the greatest of German Minnesingers, acknowledged that fact with his famous statement: *"Ze Ostarrîchi lernde ich singen unde sagen"* ("In Austria I learned to sing and poetize").

In 1548 the poet and musician Wolfgang Schmelzl, in his "Eulogy to the Praiseworthy Worldfamous Royal City, Wienne," lauds music:

> Ich lob diss Ort fuer alle Land
> Hier sein viel Singer, Saytenspiel
> Allerley gesellschaft Freuden viel
> Mehr Musikos und Instrument
> Findt man gewüsslich an keinem End.

> I praise this place above all lands
> Here are many singers, string'd play
> All sorts of partying, much joy
> More players and instruments
> Could surely nowhere else be found.

Full credit for the imaginative early development in Vienna's musical history, under the least promising conditions at the court of Emperor Leopold I[1] of Austria, must go, however, to Johann Heinrich Schmelzer.[2] A man of rare talent, he became Austria's first prominent violinist to be known beyond its borders. At a time when

1. Leopold I was one of the four "Dancing Emperors" of Vienna baroque (1657-1705). His interest in music was all-consuming. He was music patron, composer, and conductor of his court orchestra, one of the finest in Europe. Yet his most lasting monument to fame was the invention of the horse ballet. Vienna today perpetuates that tradition in its famous Spanish Riding School with its snow-white Lipizzaner stallions.
2. J. H. Schmelzer (1653-1701) was a prolific Viennese violinist and composer who wrote the ballet music for many of Draghi's operas, for which Emperor Leopold also wrote numerous airs.

the Vienna court was Italian-dominated in the field of music and Spanish-dominated in the field of power and influence, the Viennese Schmelzer, already known as a ballet composer of renown aside from his prowess on the violin, injected, in his own gay and inventive manner, the folk and dance melodies of Austria and Vienna into the music of the court. The court recognized and rewarded Schmelzer. At a time when, for all musical purposes, Vienna had become an Italian city where the names of Carissimi, Stradella, Cavalli, Draghi, Caldara, and Casti reigned supreme, Schmelzer was elevated to vice *Kapellmeister* and in 1679 to full imperial *Kapellmeister*, the equal of them all. Unfortunately, one year later, at the height of his career, he died of the plague.

But he had left behind the establishment of a style which was to be immortalized as the "Vienna" or "Danube" style of music and which was to invigorate and inspire a long line of musical giants. Haydn, Schubert, Johann Strauss, Bruckner, Brahms, Mahler, and Richard Strauss all found delight in its melodies of the Austrian Alps and the Vienna Woods, and they incorporated the dance and folk melodies into their own immortal masterpieces.

Inevitably Schmelzer's infectious rhythms and melodies had intruded into the stiff Spanish ceremonial of the baroque Habsburg court. Eventually arias, ballets, gavottes, and bourrés mirrored Austrian melodies at a time when parades, merry-go-rounds, *Wirtschaften* (a combination of stage play and social reception in which the entire Austrian Court, as well as visiting potentates, took part), and horse ballets made Vienna the musical, artistic, and social jewel of Europe. Imperial pomp added to the music: costumes with gold pieces and jewels, feather-bush helmets, headbands set with diamonds, and trumpet and timpani choirs. But the center of all entertainment in Vienna, for the court and the populace, always remained the dance in its various forms.

The unique artistic climate of the Habsburg Austrian court, where everyone from page to emperor either sang, danced, acted, played an instrument, or composed, has a fertile background. So much music was heard at the court of Emperor Ferdinand III (1637-1657) that it was said of his reign that *"Er stützte sein Szepter mit Leier und Schwert"* ("He rested his throne on lyre and sword"). His son Leopold I maintained one of the finest and largest orchestras anywhere. Four hundred operas were performed at his court and he personally composed a Requiem Mass upon the death of his first wife and a Lament after the deaths of his second and third wives. So aware was he of the musical attainments of his time that he personally collected the manuscripts of such musical greats as Stradella, Carissimi, and Tenaglia. The greatest opera production in the history of the Baroque, Cesti's *Il Pomo d'Oro (The Golden Apple)*, was produced under his reign in a theatre especially built for the occasion. Leopold was so charmed by the music of Draghi's opera *Il Re Gelidor* that he, the emperor, appeared as a dancer on the stage. As he felt death approaching, he commanded his court musicians to assemble in the adjoining antichamber and serenade him into the hereafter. Neither was there an artistic lull during the reign of Josef I (1705-1711), who followed his father to the throne. An eyewitness reported on Vienna's musical life, "The Viennese have absorbed music so completely, so perfect are their operas in poetic and musical composition, so magnificent their ballets and scenery, so lavish their costumes ... [they] now even outdo the lavishness of *Il Pomo d'Oro.*"

In the early eighteenth century, Apostolo Zeno, poet to the imperial court at Vienna, enthusiastically reported to his friends in Italy on the baroque court of Charles VI (1711-1740), "I could not begin to describe to you the applause with which my drama was received which was performed, to the marvel of all, only by the chevaliers and their ladies, who also danced, played, with the imperial Highness at the helm of the orchestra, with the greatest and most skilled mastery of a professor ... The ladies who sang the solos were simply magnificent, and if they were musicians by profession ... they could easily rank with the best even in Italy."

A musician of uncommon talent and understanding, Charles played Caldara's opera *Euristes* on the harpsichord and had his daughters Maria Theresia and Maria Anna sing solo parts in actual stage performances. Empress Maria Theresia in later years was heard to boast that she had been the youngest performer anywhere because her father had made her sing on stage at the age of five.

Emperor Josef II, Maria Theresia's son, was known to play chamber music with his personal valet Josef Stark, and Emperor Franz II, Josef's nephew, made it a habit not to let a day go by without chamber music being played. Those who took part in those sessions, aside from the family, might include Chancellor Metternich or Franz's personal valet. The artistic atmosphere was not restricted to the imperial court. It pervaded the palaces of aristocracy. Prince Lobkovitz would not allow any servant to wear the prized princely livery unless he played an instrument, preferably the French horn. Prince Rasumovsky, the Russian ambassador who married Austrian Countess Thun, played in large orchestras as well as with the most famous string quartet of his day, the Schuppanzigh, Beethoven's favorite chamber ensemble. So deep ran the musical grain of these long-suffering, forebearing Viennese princes such as Rasumovsky, Lichnowsky (who married Rasumovsky's sister), Lobkowitz, or Kinsky, that they patiently continued to champion and support Beethoven who reciprocated with verbal insults and immortal music.

What was it that brought Europe's artistic elite to Vienna? The rich royal and princely patronage? The favorable geographic location? The artistic climate of the court? The good wine? The relaxed atmosphere? It is a fair assumption that it was a mixture of all these virtues and advantages which brought to Vienna poets Metastasio and da Ponte from Italy and Hebbel from Hamburg, composers Gluck and Mahler from Bohemia, Beethoven from Bonn, and Brahms from Hamburg, and thus produced over the span of three centuries the most magnificent three waves of musical genius anywhere: Gluck, Mozart, Haydn, Beethoven, Schubert, and the elder Strauss; Brahms, Bruckner, Goldmark, Wolf, Mahler, Richard Strauss and the younger Johann Strauss; and, finally, the twentieth-century geniuses Schoenberg, Berg, and Webern.

There were also, of course, those who did not live permanently in Vienna but who passed through. Rossini was so enchanted with Vienna that he brought an entire troupe under his personal direction and captivated the city. Weber wrote the splendid music to *Euryanthe* there, only to be defeated by the clay-footed libretto of poetess Wilhelmina von Chezy. Liszt played in Vienna as a child and, by his own account, so impressed Beethoven that the diminutive giant publicly bestowed a kiss on him. Clara Schumann so loved the city that she enticed her husband Robert to come there. Schumann was enchanted: "Put together the pictures of the Danube, the tower of St. Stefan's and the distant mountain ranges, cover them with the faint perfume of Catholic incense, and you have a portrait of Vienna. And when the charming landscape comes wholly alive for us, strings may be heard which otherwise might never have sounded within us." But Vienna, then between historical musical waves, would partake only of the virtuosi: Paganini, Liszt, Thalberg, Tausig. Schumann's "new" romanticism fell on deaf ears. He did not succeed despite Clara's pianistic collaboration. Nor did Chopin. His music was not dashing or daring enough for the Viennese taste. Anton Rubinstein, who had received heady applause there as a child prodigy, was equally unsuccessful. Both had to leave Vienna to go on to fame, Chopin in Paris, Rubinstein back in his native Russia.

In 1862 Brahms came—and stayed. It was love at first sight between Vienna and the young man from Hamburg. So genuinely, so musically appreciative was his first Viennese audience that the retiring Brahms was able to report to his parents in unusually enthusiastic terms: "My concert went off splendidly ... the quartet was favorably received, I had an extraordinary success as a pianist. Every number was received with the greatest applause, I think there was total enthusiasm in the hall ... I played as freely as though I were sitting at home among friends ... this public is far more stimulating than our own. You should have seen how attentive they were, and heard the applause." Brahms, the gruff north German, musically became a Viennese, his *Liebesliederwalzer* a testament to his love of the city. It was inevitable that Brahms, in the process of Viennization, should become a close and admiring friend of Johann Strauss. When in later years Strauss's stepdaughter approached Brahms at a ball and requested him to write a *Widmung* on her fan, he graciously inscribed the opening bars of the *Blue Danube* waltz on it and beneath them the words *"Leider nicht von Brahms"* ("Alas, not by Brahms.")

Although Vienna had again reached a new zenith in musical history, it was far from a harmonious family. Brahms and Bruckner were cases in point. Anton Bruckner, the organist from St. Florian in Lower Austria, had come to Vienna upon the urging of conductor Herbeck to study and compose in what he had hoped would be congenial surroundings. But the same people of Vienna who had embraced Brahms were extremely critical of Bruckner's music, which transported Wagner's musical ideas into the symphonic realm. The Vienna Philharmonic Orchestra and its famous conductor Hans Richter, who so masterfully recreated Brahms's music, made Bruckner and his music the target of their cruel jokes and interpretations. Eduard Hanslick, Vienna's foremost music critic, while extolling Brahms's musical virtues, turned an acid-tipped pen on Bruckner as well as on Wagner. But not Johann Strauss. Strauss acknowledged the undisguised admiration of Brahms but found himself at pains to reciprocate. Brahms's musical idiom did not move him. He respected the friend and master but simply could not understand his art. Bruckner somehow struck a sympathetic chord in Strauss, and, one evening, when Bruckner returned to his simple abode after one of those devastating travesties to which his work had been subjected, he found a congratulatory telegram from Strauss on the table. Bruckner and Strauss had met only once, but a warm understanding had remained with both men. Over Bruckner's favorite dish, roast duck, the two men had exchanged Bayreuth reminiscences. "[There was] an unspoken kinship in music which [Strauss] never felt for his close friend Brahms ... Dance and Prayer spiritually shook hands" (Decsey, 1922).

If Vienna had only been able to leave the two composers alone to create in peace. But the gossipy city, which had always taken a paternal and proprietary interest in its great men and women, continued to relish the contrived conflict. Brahms's anti-Bruckner comments were avidly repeated in concert halls, coffee houses, and salons. Soon two hostile camps faced each other and, depending on who argued the case, Bruckner was that "mad Wagnerian" and Brahms "heir to the mantle of Beethoven," or Bruckner "the inspired composer in the great Germanic tradition" and Brahms the "dry formalist." Brahms, surprisingly in view of the world's acknowledgment of his creations, was never free from the barbs of his colleagues. Of course he could always count on certain defenders: pianist-composers Tausig and Cornelius, composers Goldmark and Brüll, and, of course, Hanslick. But he also was aware of his implacable adversaries. Hugo Wolf, who, despite his short life span and tragic ending, was to join the ranks of immortal *Lieder* composers, attacked Brahms to the point of viciousness. It was he, the admirer of Wagner and Bruckner, who vitriolically pinpointed Brahms's position in history: "A man who, upon returning to his home after a long absence, turned the rusted key with much effort to view the cobwebs in his home." As music critic of Vienna's fashionable *Salonblatt*, Wolf (on 31 January 1886) went even further:

> The retrograde progression of Brahms's [musical] production is striking. No doubt it could never rise above the level of the mediocre; but such noth-ingness, hollowness and hypocrisy as prevails in the E-minor Symphony has never so alarmingly seen the light of day in any other Brahms work. The art of composing without ideas has definitely found its worthiest repre-sentative in Brahms. Like the dear Lord Herr Brahms also understands the feat of making something out of nothing ... Enough of such gruesome sport! Let Herr Brahms be satisfied to have found ... the language which lends his mute despair its most eloquent expression: the language of the most intensive musical impotence."

Other blows came from unexpected sources and directions. Nietzsche, in a postscript to his *Der Fall Wagner (The Case of Wagner)* written in 1888 commented:

> The sympathy which Brahms undeniably inspires now and then has been an enigma to me for a long time, until I found out, almost by accident, that he affects a certain type of people. He possesses the melancholy of impotence; he creates not out of abundance, but thirsts after abundance.

Shaw, a prominent music critic before he became a playwright, found Brahms naive:

> To me it seems quite obvious that the real Brahms is nothing more than a sentimental voluptuary ... He is the most wanton of composers ... only his wantonness is not vicious; it is that of a great baby ... rather tire-somely addicted to dressing himself up as Handel or Beethoven and making prolonged and intolerable noises. *(The World,* 21 June 1893)

The hardest blow in the cacophony of adverse Brahms criticism, either true gems of incomprehension or manifestations of spite and venom, were struck by the American musical reviewers such as W. F. Athorp, Philip Hale, Edgar Stillman Kelley, and J. B. Runciman.

   Tchaikovsky and Brahms never appreciated each other's music because Tchai-kovsky mainly composed in musical images of program music while Brahms dwelt in the realm of absolute music. Yet one does not realize the depth of Tchaikovsky's dislike until one has a glimpse at his diary: "I played through the music of that scoundrel Brahms ... It annoys me that this self-inflated mediocrity is hailed as a genius. Why, by comparison with him Raff is a giant, not to mention Rubinstein ... while Brahms is chaotic and absolutely empty sere stuff."

It was to a great extent Brahms's acidulous sense of humor which made it difficult to be his friend. When young Bruch submitted a composition for Brahms's scrutiny, the older man remarked, not on the music, but on the beautiful music paper. In the presence of his friend, the Jewish composer Karl Goldmark, he pointedly posed the question: "Do you find it unusual that a Jew should compose a setting to Luther's text?" Surprisingly, Brahms admitted to his position in musical history as a neoclassicist, as well as to his bad temper and gruffness which in reality mantled many a warmhearted act to friends and family. When, in mock protest, he exclaimed "I have no friends! If anyone says he is my friend don't believe it," he uttered a tragi-comic exaggeration in a city which venerated him to his last day.

The music of Brahms's adversaries, Wolf and Bruckner, did not escape criticism either. As for Wolf, the Vienna press comments on his music were no less scathing than his about Brahms: "He once wrote musical critiques ... after hearing his songs we amicably advise him to return to writing critiques"; "[His music is] vulgar ... of shocking coarseness, the shrieking of wild animals"; "Childish, thin-sounding stuff in which emotions masquerade for spirit"; "Banal melodies and ridiculous harmonic cramps." Although Bruckner received three laurel wreaths (one of them from the emperor) and tremendous applause at the premiere of his Eighth Symphony, attended by Brahms, Siegfried Wagner, Wolf, and royalty, Hanslick was still vituperative:

> [A] characteristic of Bruckner's newest symphony is the immediate juxtaposition of dry schoolroom counterpoint with unbounded exaltation. Thus, tossed between intoxication and desolation, we arrive at no definite impression and enjoy no artistic pleasure. All flows with a lack of lucidity, lack of order, violently, into gruesome length ... It is not impossible that the future belongs to such nightmarish cacophonous style—a future which we therefore do not regard with envy.

Nor was Max Kalbeck, Brahms's friend and future biographer, any kinder in appraising Bruckner: "The enigma which Bruckner presents to us is dark ... the tonal ghosts are totally mad ... such stampings and rages, roars and neighs in wild profusion. It is our hope that the future is far distant which will enjoy such chaotic music" *(Wiener Allgemeine Zeitung*, 13 February 1883).

The Sons

It was not difficult to dislike Bruckner. In the flamboyantly romantic Vienna which the painter Makart so totally represented, Bruckner was the antithesis of Vienna's artistic image. His primitive speech bore in its lower Austrian dialect the stamp of the provinces. His close-cropped peasant head and smoothly shaven face stood in stark contrast to the Viennese fashionable mane and flowing beard, his floppy felt hat was oblivious of the chic high hat or bowler. While Vienna smoked the long thin "Virginia" cigar, Bruckner's ever-present snuff box and colored handkerchief dangling from his hip pocket labeled him, even from a distance, as the provincial peasant. His fears—of Brahms, of Hanslick, of Richter, of failure—never ceased, nor did his hunger, in his early years for sustenance, later for recognition, always for kindness. When the University of Vienna finally saw fit to bestow the honorary degree of Doctor of Philosophy upon Bruckner, his first comment was: "Hanslick will never forgive me." He was constantly wishing to please, thus allowed conductors to tamper with his symphonies. Any and every suggestion concerning "improvement" of his vast symphonic edifices promptly sent him back to his desk to "correct" or write another version altogether. There had always been a small group who shared Bruckner's views and championed his musical visions. They included Wolf, the future great conductors Schalk and Loewe, and Johann Strauss. Strauss's belief was vindicated when Franz Joseph honored Bruckner by underwriting the publication of his Eighth Symphony, which the grateful composer promptly dedicated to the emperor. When Richter and the Philharmonic, in a complete reversal of attitude, finally saw fit to do justice to Bruckner's music, Vienna, practically overnight, discovered "our" Bruckner.

Another musician who engendered dislike was a cantankerous little man acidulous of disposition, a master of conceit who was totally irresponsible, selfish, unscrupulous, faithless, and a genius of opera—Richard Wagner. From the very outset it had been a love-hate relationship between Wagner and Vienna, mainly because Hanslick, the fiercest and surely most literate Wagner critic, called the city his home. What he had to say was as devastating as it was readable. Out of sheer curiosity the public went to hear Wagner's operas after devouring Hanslick's comments:

> The Rhine Maidens [in *Das Reingold*], singing and swimming in the Rhine, encompassed in one hundred and thirty-six measures by no more than a diffused E-flat major chord, provide a tableau which achieves a predominantly visual effect ... From that point on the musical charm of the work declined rapidly ... the listener's sensibilities, taxed for almost three hours without interruption, wear thin, he leaves with the impression of utter monotony. I shall not waste words on the indigestible German stammer ... offered as poetry.

The second act [of *Die Walküre*] is an abyss of boredom ... Wotan appears, holds a long conversation with his wife and then, turning to Brünnhilde, gives an autobiographical lecture covering eight pages of text. This utterly tuneless, plodding narrative ... recalls the medieval torture of waking a sleep-crazed prisoner by stabbing him with a needle at every nod.

The two principal figures border on caricature, the dragon fight on comedy ... [Siegfried] is not a hero but a puppet ... a magic potion which restores to this fool the memory of all his stupidities he had committed ... is a theme better suited for comedy. In tragedy, where a moral will must dominate, it becomes an absurdity.

[The plot] which affected me so unpleasantly in prospect, proved even more repulsive and incomprehensible in performance ... the music ... is noticeably inferior ... *Götterdämmerung* ... is oppressed by a singular exhaustion and fatigue, something like the approaching affliction of middle age.

From tragedy[*Tristan und Isolde*] we demand ... that its characters act of their own free will ... the origin of their fate must lie with themselves ... [they] need no magic potion. The tragic fate of Tristan and Isolde had its original in a mistake for which neither is responsible. They are helpless victims—thus the very opposite of its tragic heroes.

Yet, to everyone's surprise, Wagner's early operas did find a home in Vienna's *Kärnthnerthortheater* when all of Europe had shown only closed ears, minds and doors to the composer. Strauss Son included Wagner excerpts into his repertoire before any theatre or orchestra in Vienna had performed them. *Lohengrin, Tannhäuser,* and *Der Fliegende Holländer (The Flying Dutchman)* were given first-class performances. Eventually, and even in the time of Bayreuth, the Wagner temple and mecca, Vienna was to prove itself indispensable to the composer. Wagner in 1861 finally witnessed his first actual performance of *Lohengrin* in Vienna, an overwhelming experience for him. He wrote in a letter to Minna Wagner, "I sat there, quite still, without moving [while] the tears ran down my face ... It is impossible to say what a deep, untroubled joy I experienced. Orchestra, singers, chorus—all of them excellent, incredibly beautiful ... The Opera here is heavenly; a mass of wonderful voices, each more beautiful than the next."

Fine performances were not always rewarded by Wagner with such praise. One of his most devoted Vienna disciples, Johann Herbeck, as director and conductor of the new magnificent opera edifice of Siccardsburg and Van der Nüll, was never able to satisfy Wagner who, often from a distance and upon hearing third-hand reports, shot missives at Herbeck, in which he heaped insults, reproaches and corrections upon the man who tried his utmost to acquaint Vienna with *Die Meistersinger*. However, upon attending the performance Wagner was forced to admit "how excellently the orchestra had performed." The difficulties did not end with *Die Meistersinger*. When Herbeck staged the older *Rienzi* the worst turn occurred. After the first solo trumpet note in the overture (one of the most difficult notes to play in the entire opera repertoire), Wagner left his box in disgust and returned later only to summon Herbeck and subject him and the performance to caustic castigation. Inexplicably it was one of the few operas Emperor Franz Joseph enjoyed despite his lack of musical appreciation for anything beyond Strauss. Whenever a foreign potentate expressed the wish to hear opera in Vienna, Franz Joseph usually requested that the magnificently staged *Rienzi* be performed.

The polarization of opinions on Wagner changed abruptly when Franz Jauner took over the reins of the Vienna Opera. This was no long-suffering idealist à la Herbeck but a hard-headed, successful businessman of the theatre who could point with pride to his brilliant and financially sound career as director of the renowned *Carltheater*. Although he espoused Wagner, he would allow no tantrums from the composer. Thus there began a unique period of artistic bargaining sessions. Such business hardheadedness Wagner understood and respected. Jauner had arranged for payment of royalties to Wagner, now he wanted something, or rather somebody, in return. He wanted the foremost Wagnerian conductor to reside and work in Vienna. Wagner agreed and thus Jauner and Richter entered the Vienna Opera on the same day as director and conductor, respectively. Wagner and Jauner continued to understand and appreciate each other, although Jauner, when the occasion warranted it and the artistic stakes were high enough, did not recoil from the use of blackmail. Wagner wanted the Vienna singer Amalie Materna to sing *Walküre* in Bayreuth. Jauner agreed on the condition that Wagner give Vienna the performing rights to the opera. Wagner acceded to Jauner's "request" with alacrity because by then the Vienna opera had attained such European preeminence in the quality of Wagnerian singers that Wagner was forced to depend on Vienna. By such devious dealings the entire *Ring* cycle was handed to Vienna. Wagner had no choice; he needed the foremost Wagnerian soprano, he needed the foremost Wagnerian conductor — both in Vienna. The surprisingly cordial relationship continued until 1876, when Wagner said goodbye to Vienna, never to return.

For over ten years after Wagner's departure Hans Richter remained the dominant force in the musical life of Vienna. In 1897, however, the new, magnetic personality of Gustav Mahler excited the Viennese musical minds. No greater contrast, in looks, background, or musical conception, could be imagined than that between the huge bearded Teutonic appearance of Richter and the burning, clean-shaven asceticism of Mahler's Semitic countenance. Vienna expectantly, hopefully looked forward to a clash of musical tastes and personalities between the two giants. It was sadly disappointed. Mahler and Richter respected each other's integrity. When Mahler was entrusted with the directorship of the Opera, Richter responded favorably to a London offer. Mahler was to lend to the Vienna Imperial Opera ten years of unsurpassed musical glory. As a young man he had been a disciple of Bruckner, who, in turn, saw fit to entrust to the aspiring genius the piano transcription of his Third Symphony. But as Mahler matured and developed his own romantic style, a style concomitant with his own time and temperament, he wanted no part of the Wagnerian transplants of Bruckner nor of the neoclassicism of Brahms. In his younger days the disciple had reported to Bruckner: "I conducted your splendid and powerful *Te Deum* ... Not only the entire audience but also the performers were deeply moved by the mighty architecture and truly noble ideas." Later disenchantment led him to report to his wife Alma: "Now that I have worked my way through Brahms I have fallen back on Bruckner again. An odd pair of second-raters. The one in the casting ladle too long, the other one not long enough. Now I stick with Beethoven. There are only he and Wagner."

With Mahler, the gigantic multi-faceted wave of nineteenth-century romanticism came to an end. When his voice soared in his *Symphony of a Thousand*, or when he jubilantly yet wistfully declaimed of life and eternity in *Das Lied von der Erde (The Song of the Earth)*, then, despite exaggerations, his voice had the ring of authenticity, authority, and genuine feeling. Side by side with him there labored the men who, although they created in the twentieth century, harked back to the nineteenth and those who attempted to break new ground only to emerge synthetic, coarse or showy, contrived or sugarcoated: Sibelius, Rachmaninoff, Respighi, Richard Strauss — a positive as well as negative phenomenon; original and creative in his operas, blatantly self-centered in his orchestral compositions. It is almost inconceivable that they created at the same time as such giants as Bartok, Schoenberg, Stravinsky, and Mahler.

Mahler's career as a composer may be compared to Promethean tragedy. Although he considered himself a composer first and a conductor second, his symphonic creations were dismissed as *Kapellmeistermusik* (conductor's music). But Mahler, undeterred, predicted that it would take fifty years to understand his message. Curiously enough his arithmetic was correct. It remained for the tortured, groping 1960s to comprehend Mahler's agonies and ecstasies. If Mahler considered conducting secondary to composing, his achievements in the former field were nonethless superlative. Nowhere, whether early in Budapest or late in New York, did he reach such artistic heights of interpretation as during the ten-year "Mahler era" in Vienna. His uncompromisingly high artistic standards turned antagonists into admirers. He fought and overcame the endemic indifference and incompetence of the musical bureaucracy in such a manner as to elicit a congratulatory and perhaps even envious comment from the emperor. Wagner and Mozart, Offenbach and Pfitzner, Gluck, Charpentier, and Beethoven all came under the fierce scrutiny of his superlative standards. It was Mahler who placed all of Beethoven's *Leonore* overtures between the acts of *Fidelio,* an innovation which has now become a tradition, a word he despised. When he was reproached for reorchestrating Beethoven, Mahler scornfully replied: "Your Beethoven is not my Beethoven." In support of his attitude, he could point to the historic precedent of Mozart's reorchestration of Handel's *Messiah.* When the music historian Max Graf reminded him that his faster tempi in Wagner's *Walküre* differed from those of Richter who had conducted the Bayreuth premiere, Mahler's terse reply was no less succinct: "He may have known them then. He has forgotten them since."

While Mahler considered Sibelius's music "hackneyed clichés served up with harmonization in the Nordic style," he was enchanted with the guileless gaiety of Strauss's *Die Fledermaus,* which he had performed while directing the Hamburg opera. He later introduced it at the Vienna Opera, the first time ever that an operetta had been performed there, thus raising the work into the realm of comic opera. It was he, together with Hanslick, who urged Strauss to compose music for the ballet, an idea enthusiastically pursued by Strauss but abruptly cut by death.

Vienna danced at what Hermann Broch has called Austria's "gay apocalypse." The macabre picture intensified when viewed from the vantage point of the emperor: the nightly dance whirl of Vienna's multilayered population; an aristocracy without meaning; a regime without direction; a middle class fighting for recognition; and a working class restricted and threatened by police measures on the one hand and an insecure future on the other. All congealed in a common nearsighted enjoyment of today, as the aristocrat, the minister, the general, and the politician thought only of short-term measures, the middle class of the night's dance, and the worker of tomorrow's bread. In such a state of affairs, Emperor Franz Joseph saw himself as the only stable center. Viewed through glasses of medieval rectitude,

Franz Lehár with Richard Tauber and Käthe Dorsch at the premiere of his operetta Friederike.

matters had to remain as unchanged and immovable as possible in an atmosphere where every new thought, urge, or quest for change was an implied call for destruction. Franz Joseph was completely oblivious of the legacy of Emperor Josef who had stormed the empire in quest of improvements, although under the aegis of monarchic divine right; nor did he even employ the grand sweep of absolutism which had made Maria Theresia the mighty empress of the realm. With a sense of duty, discipline, and dedication—yet without a monarch's vision—the glorified civil servant in an emperor's uniform labored to maintain the status quo.

Vienna danced and jubilated. Surprisingly, there was still much to celebrate. Barely six years after Strauss's death the young Hungarian Franz Lehár stood at the dimly lit conductor's stand of the *Theater an der Wien.* He was the son of a military conductor and had until recently conducted the orchestra of an infantry regiment.

His first two attempts at operetta had passed almost unnoticed. Thus it was with considerable trepidation that he raised the baton to the overture of *Die Lustige Witwe* (with a libretto by the same Victor Leon whose book for *Simplizius* had embarrassed Strauss), particularly since the sentiments of the entire company, even after the dress rehearsal, had been lukewarm about the entire work. But Vienna recognized it for what it was—the binding link between Strauss and the twentieth century—and rewarded Lehár with a thunderous ovation. Lehár had resurrected the Vienna operetta. Berlin followed Vienna's approval with six hundred performances of its own before *The Merry Widow* began its conquering course around the globe. It was to be Lehár's most enduring success. Despite a spate of lilting melodies in a great number of operettas only his *Der Graf von Luxemburg (The Count of Luxemburg)* came close to the *Witwe* in public acceptance. The success of a number of his later operettas was tailored to the magnificent voice of Richard Tauber, to whom they owed a large measure of their success, just as Strauss had tailored his works to the talents of Alexander Girardi.

Soon Lehár found himself in good company as the silver age of Vienna operetta dawned. There was Oscar Straus (no relationship to either Johann or Richard). Although a native of Vienna he saw no future in the field of operetta and removed himself to the more sophisticated atmosphere of the Berlin satiric revue theatre in which he tried his skills. After failing to become a Berlin Offenbach, Oscar Straus returned to Vienna and the romance of the Viennese operetta in which he achieved an auspicious success with his *Walzertraum (Waltz Dream)* in 1907. This was followed by another success, *The Chocolate Soldier*, based on Shaw's *Arms and the Man*. (Shaw hated it.)

Suddenly a spate of talented composers appeared. Emerich Kalman started his first efforts in 1909, but his success had to bide its time until 1915 and *Csardasfürstin*. A Hungarian like Lehár, he had a gift for lilting melody to which audiences gladly surrendered. But many years had to pass again until Kalman registered a world success with *Countess Maritza*. The reputation of Leo Fall was established in Vienna with two operettas, *Der Fidele Bauer (The Merry Peasant)* and *Die Dollar Prinzessin*. Another Viennese, Edmund Eysler, was an especially prodigious writer of operettas. In later years, however, his talent unfortunately disintegrated into production rather than creation. His first work, *Bruder Straubinger*, in 1903, harked back to Suppé rather than to Strauss.

A special place is reserved in the annals of the Vienna operetta for the amazing career and achievements of Robert Stolz, whose activities in the field of light music straddle two centuries. Having met Johann Strauss at the age of nineteen, the aspiring *Kapellmeister* received an impression that was to guide him for the rest of his rich life and that, in retrospect, proved to be the artistic turning point of his life. Seventy years later Robert Stolz, after an incredibly prodigious career which led him through operetta, songs, recordings, and film music, continues to conduct and record the works of the Vienna tradition and of his own labor and era, which he champions. In America he has won two Oscars, for his scores for the films *Spring Parade* and *It Happened Tomorrow*, yet he is securely anchored in the tradition and style of his beloved Vienna. Among innumerable major and minor stage, movie and song successes his most enduring is the film *Zwei Herzen im Dreivierteltakt (Two Hearts in Three-quarter Time)* of 1929. His American compositions include the musical *Mr. Strauss Goes to Boston*. Despite his advanced age (he was born in 1880), the amazing Robert Stolz continues to present to the world the great light music of his beloved city.

11

The Merry Apocalypse

The waning years of the nineteenth century foreshadowed in their diversity the calamities of the twentieth century. The peace and tranquillity which Martin Freud and Stefan Zweig cherished in retrospect was treacherously deceiving, because the conflict was already shaping. Vienna danced. Absolutism had given way to a deceptive pseudo liberalism, or, to quote the founder of the Austrian Social Democratic Party Dr. Victor Adler,[1] "Despotism mitigated by sloppiness" found itself eventually in a half-hearted and confused state between socialism and democracy.

The Ringstrasse had become the showplace of Vienna, while nearly sixty percent of Vienna's population, actually immigrants who filled the labor demand and market, lived in hovels and tenements in the suburbs. When financial disaster struck in 1873, the mass of laborers were the first to feel dreaded unemployment, and thus they constituted such a danger to law and order in the eyes of the authorities that deportation to their places of origin was contemplated. The finishing touches to the Ring and the building boom which followed were actually a result of the prevailing depression. Since no private capital could be made available in sufficient quantity for building purposes, it was the government which stepped in and supported the all-important building trades through the lavish buildings on the Ring. These were followed by apartment buildings of princely appearance (to blend in with the official buildings) such as the Heinrichshof, by architect Theophil Hansen, across the Ring from the Opera House.

Vienna danced. The new Opera House opened in 1869 with Mozart's *Don Giovanni* and the new *Burgtheater* with Schiller's *Wallenstein's Lager*. But in the sleekly neo-Grecian parliament building the minorities fought for supremacy of their nationalistic goals and the Social Democrats for universal suffrage. The

---

1. Dr. Victor Adler (1852-1918), journalist, politician, founder of the Austrian Social Democratic party. He died one day before Austria declared itself a republic.

disturbances in Parliament, which descended to a low of trumpet blowing and noise-makers and disintegrated into fist fights, erupted into similar disturbances and demonstrations in the Vienna streets.

With distrust and initial disapproval Vienna saw austere rectangular buildings rise among its Baroque palaces as Joseph Hoffmann, Adolf Loos, and Otto Wagner explored new avenues in architecture. Sigmund Freud, much to the dismay of the Viennese whose very lifestyle and actions shied away from his probings, delved relentlessly into the hidden recesses of the mind.

The liberalism which had almost imperceptibly risen to Vienna's surface, and glossed over deeper differences to erupt later, had fostered the blossoming of two of the greatest newspapers of its time, *Neues Wiener Tagblatt* and *Neue Freie Presse*. One of the foremost contributors to the feuilletons of the *Neue Freie Presse* was Theodor Herzl. Although of Jewish descent Theodor Herzl was a completely assimilated Austrian, aware of and concerned mainly with Austrian problems. But the Dreyfus trial, which he had been assigned to cover in Paris, starkly revealed to him the horrors and terrors of anti-Semitism abroad and at home. Dr. Karl Lueger, the handsome burgomeister of Vienna, had imperceptibly instilled the idea of anti-Semitism into the city, which saw a relentless influx of Jews who wished to escape from the unchecked exploitant feudalism of the provinces, and from the Russian tsar's pogroms. They brought to Vienna an "alien" element viewed with a hostile eye by the gentile populace and a fretful eye by the native *ansässige* Jews whose cultural attainments, life style, and fashionable mode of dress stood in dismayingly marked contrast to the kaftans, flowing beards, and sidelocks of the newly arrived. Lueger's anti-Semitism was soon to be reinforced by the rise of Georg von Schönerer, who made anti-Semitism a slogan while ostensibly fostering pro-German sentiments in Vienna's war of the flowers: at that time political parties at least had the grace to mark their identity by flowers rather than fearful symbols. The Social Democrats wore red carnations, the Christian Social party white carnations, while the German National party, Schönerer's group, wore the blue corn flower, the favorite of Bismarck.

Vienna danced. The 1870s saw the birth of future giants. Adolf Loos, the future architect of a new Vienna, born in 1870, was to describe the architecturally schizophrenic Vienna saw as *"Potemkimsche Stadt"* ("Potemkin City"), the city of the noble facade with misery lurking behind it. Four years later came another crop of giants. Hugo von Hofmannsthal illuminated Vienna's splendor in his writing and in his libretto to Richard Strauss's *Der Rosenkavalier*; Karl Kraus in his satiric writings directed the implacable beam of his penetrating wit on all that was decaying in Austria — particularly in Vienna; and Arnold Schoenberg began as the last romantic of Austria's musical era, a romanticism with which he imbued his disciple Alban Berg, then veered away into an unexplored musical land. It may be of passing interest that all three were of Jewish descent, a further indication of the proliferation of Jewish intellect and enterprise in the arts, commerce, and industry in an ever-growing Vienna. Thus, in the eddy of splendid and sinister developments at the opening of the twentieth century, two men, wittingly and unwittingly, set in motion fateful changes in the world and launched themselves into history. Herzl, with his book *Der Judenstaat (The Jewish State)*, laid the spiritual foundation for what was to be Israel, a prophecy to be fulfilled only decades after his death. Stefan Zweig, in his autobiography *The World of Yesterday*, emphasizes the impact that Herzl had, even on the day of his funeral.

> It was a singular day in July [1904] ... Suddenly, to all railroad stations of the city, by day and by night, from all realms and lands, every train brought new arrivals. Western, Eastern, Russian, Turkish Jews; from all the provinces and all the little towns they hurried excitedly, the shock of the news still written on their faces; ... it was a great movement whose leader had now fallen. The procession was endless. Vienna, startled, became aware that it was not just a writer ... who had passed away, but one of those creators of ideas who disclose themselves triumphantly ... to a single people at vast intervals ... It was a gigantic outpouring of grief from the depths of millions of souls that made me realize for the first time how much passion and hope this lone and lonesome man had borne into the world through the power of a single thought.

The other development, destined to change, frighten, and outrage the world in a brief moment in history, began with a slender young man with artistic ambitions but little artistic talent. Ignored and shunned, he was forced into the ignoble existence of sleeping in boarding houses for homeless men, damned to viewing Vienna as a cesspool rather than a melting pot and the Habsburgs and the Jews as degenerates. Following the rabble-rousing speeches of Schönerer, who was to become his idol, Adolf Hitler as early as 1906 became obsessed with a hatred of Jews, against whom he was to fulminate in *Mein Kampf*. Throughout his maturing years and throughout his early reign it was to be one of his deeply harbored obsessions to take revenge on the city which had so arrogantly ignored his early ambitions. Some historians feel that his triumphant return at the helm of his invading troops at the time of the *Anschluss* and the subsequent artistic, economic, and political rape of Vienna was the most cherished triumph of his life. The fates of Hitler, of Germany, and Austria might have been different had the Academy of Fine Arts in Vienna seen fit to accept him as a student and had channeled his energy into artistic pursuits.

The Merry Apocalypse

In typical fashion, Viennese life continued to be the café, where new ideas had always been born, debated, and realized. Students, journalists, philosophers, politicians, bureaucrats, spies, artists, writers, musicians, and composers would gather in their respective cafés to debate, plot, foment, create. But at the turn of the century no definite plans had evolved, either in the coffeehouse, in Parliament, or in the court. With their marked capacity to live from day to day, to implement one stop-gap with another—a method aptly nicknamed *fortwursteln* (muddling along)— the Viennese lived in their own glittering, fragile bubble, not heeding the consequences of minorities' aspirations, workers' and students' demands, social difficulties and inequities, and problems caused by a lack of housing, foresight, and direction. While scandals and protests rocked Parliament and spilled over into the streets in demonstrations and protests, Hofmannsthal continued to glorify Vienna and the Austrian tradition. Arthur Schnitzler and Hermann Bahr, both about a dozen years Hofmannsthal's senior, had been struck with his awesome writing. After having received an anonymous essay signed "Loris," Bahr imagined the author to be an old man who had filtered his magnificent thoughts and observations through the prism of poetry and philosophy to create a mature and sensual poetic comprehension. Great was his surprise when he invited "Loris" to the famous Café Griensteidl and there met Hofmannsthal, a beardless student in short trousers and a voice still too high to have fully matured. Schnitzler was no less affected for "having encountered a born genius for the first time in my life ... never again during my entire lifetime was I so overwhelmed." Stefan Zweig, seven years Hofmannsthal's junior, reminisced: "The emergence of young Hofmannsthal is and remains remarkable as one of the great wonders of early perfection ... at so early an age ... a flawless mastery of speech, such elevation of ideals, such saturation with the substance of poetry ... as this majestic genius who in his sixteenth and seventeenth year had inscribed himself upon the eternal rolls of the German language with verses that will not die and with a prose not yet excelled in our day."

While Hofmannsthal spoke of the glories that were Vienna, Schnitzler, although he lived and wrote in the same city, occupied a sophisticated dream world of doubt and laissez-faire, filled with the faint incense of decadence. Vaguely dissatisfied, wanly melancholy, and discomforted, he was nonetheless too smugly indifferent to effect change. Disillusioned and insecure, the characters in Schnitzler's plays are saved from becoming paper types by a superb grasp of the language and lassitude of Vienna at the turn of the century. A line from one of his plays reveals in cameo caption Vienna's prevailing twilight mood and drift: "With us indignation is as little genuine as enthusiasm; only pleasure at the misfortunes of others, and hatred of talent are genuinely felt here."

The Sons

Vienna danced as she grew. After London, Paris, and Berlin, Vienna had become the fourth largest city in Europe. Only one man had hardly changed during the last fifty years at the time of Johann Strauss's death—Emperor Franz Joseph. The humorless, pedantic, often narrow-minded monarch, solitary and nearly friendless, had become a symbol in Europe and in his empire. His abstract presence alone was a unifying factor. His bureaucratic attention to small detail rather than vast vista was taken as the epitomic expression of "the father of his country." As his empire shrank with every war and every peace, as the furies of misfortune dogged every step of his life, he remained the symbol of rectitude and integrity which inspired respect in the world, reverence and adulation in his subjects—a minor miracle given his solitary nature. The very loneliness of his office made him a symbol to the Viennese and they reciprocated with a warmth which found an echo in the song *Draussen in Schönbrunn* with words by Fritz Grünbaum and music by Ralph Benatzky. Its refrain mirrors Vienna's feelings:

> Draussen im Schönbrunnerpark
> Sitzt ein alter Herr, sorgenschwer
> Gibt in aller Herrgottsfrüh
> Schon für unser Wohl sich Müh'
> Gönnt sich nimmer Ruh' und Rast!
> Lieber, guter, alter Herr,
> Mach Dir doch das Herz nicht schwer
> Dass sie so an Kaiser hat
> Selig ist die Wienerstadt
> Was wir können woll'n wir tun
> Lass Dir bisserl Zeit zum Ruh'n
> Lieber, guter alter Herr von Schönbrunn.

> Out there in Schönbrunn Park
> Sits an old man laden with sorrow
> And in the Lord's early morrow
> He attends to our best
> Not allowing peace or rest.
> Dear good old man,
> Do not let your heart feel pain
> To have an emperor like you
> Blessed is Vienna city too
> All in our power we shall do,
> Have a minute's rest or two,
> Dear, good, old man of Schönbrunn.

Vienna danced in the splendor of its sunset achievements. Thus, in what represented a last flowering of all artistic endeavors which had their roots in the artistic background of centuries of Habsburg rule, in an atmosphere which Harry Zohn has captured in an anthology entitled *Der Farbenvolle Untergang (The Colorful Sunset, or Decline)*, Vienna exploded in myriad colors of artistic endeavors. Wherever one gazed, whatever field of artistic expression one beheld, it was studded with names destined to be immortal. During that fateful time, a century relinquished its intellectual and artistic treasure to the next. Bahr and his time and circle saw in this splendor "the morning glow of a new age," a tragically wrong assessment. Men of music — Schoenberg, Berg, Webern — intuitively sensed the proximity of the holocaust and expressed it in their work, while giants like Schnitzler, Zweig, and Hofmannsthal luxuriated in the splendor of their time and their city. Thus "Der farbenvolle Untergang" is more than an apt term for the times. It speaks of the Viennese achievements at the century's turn as "sunset," but its other meaning of "fall" or "destruction" also crowds the mind when applied to the Habsburg imperial edifice, whose century-old foundations were rotting while a bloody sun of approaching conflict and dismemberment illuminated Austria's horizon.

Vienna's dance was abruptly halted on 28 June 1914 by the gunshots of Sarajevo which murdered the heir to the throne of Austria and ushered in World War I. As the Viennese watched in benumbed bewilderment, an era which had lingered on for fifteen years became a relic, a way of life became a memory.

227

12

The King of Vienna

What sped Johann's recovery was a deputation to Bad Gastein where he was taking the cure in 1854. It came from the Russian railroad company of Sarsko-Selo with the request to appear in Russia for several seasons. Johann was hastily assured that the concerts were to be held in Pavlovsk, within easy reach from St. Petersburg by railroad and that a new concert hall, Vauxhall, was to be built to accommodate him. During intermission a fabulous buffet was to be served on a large promenade-balcony which would surround the entire building, and the hall would of course feature an imperial box for the pleasure of the Russian court and its aristocracy. The railroad company offered free transportation, sumptuous rooms, and board for Strauss and his entire retinue, and a fee to be surpassed only by the later American offer. The entire idea and offer was simply too intriguing, too attractive to be passed up. Little did Johann know that he was to go to Russia for twelve consecutive summers.

The Russian public was as ideal as it was naive. When Strauss appeared in Russia only Mihail Glinka had begun his first attempts at a truly Russian idiom in his opera *Ruslan and Ludmilla.* Tchaikovsky was only fourteen years old, Rimsky-Korsakov eleven, Borodin twenty-one, and Mussorgsky sixteen. Later Russia was to know its own musical heritage, but at the time Russian musical tastes were shaped by French and Italian operatic imports. Thus it came about that the Russians gained more from Strauss's presence than he from their musical repertoire. The father had been strongly influenced by his sojourn to Paris, but St. Petersburg had nothing to offer, in a musical sense, to the son. What the Russians lacked in music they made up in enthusiasm. Johann wrote to his friend and publisher Karl Haslinger on 1 September 1863: "One day the Tsar came with the Grand Duke to the concert. He requested his favorite selection, the *Bauern-Polka (Peasant Polka)* which evoked a storm of applause such as no Beethoven symphony ever received; even the orchestra members applauded wildly like the public and forgot that the composition is a miserable piece of trash. I doubt whether the polka would be as popular in Vienna as it is here. The public here literally devours this stuff." Johann, two to four times a week, in concerts which lasted up to five hours, literally played up a storm. He felt happy, and the Sarsko-Selo railroad was happy because traffic to Pavlovsk increased tenfold, not only because of Strauss but because people had discovered the beauty of the resort as the railroad had hoped they would. Johann was showered with requests for pictures and autographs, he was showered with flowers until additional rooms had to be rented — his entire hotel suite resembled a garden. One day a Russian aristocrat, angered because his wife had sent flowers to Strauss, challenged the composer to a duel. Strauss, in turn, sent a messenger to the nobleman inviting him to his suite. When the Russian arrived Johann opened the doors to his suite, overflowing with flowers, and asked that the nobleman point to the ones his wife had sent. The Russian promptly understood the graceful, subtle gesture in Strauss's invitation and the incident ended in apologies, embraces, and champagne.

The imperial family were among Strauss's most ardent admirers, always in the forefront with fervent applause, thus setting the tone for all present. Grand Duke Constantin, the tsar's brother and a fair cellist, even requested permission to play in the Strauss orchestra. A delirious public either carried Johann home on its shoulders at the end of the concert or demanded encore after encore until the train whistle announced the departure of the last train of the day to St. Petersburg. More than once the whistle was ignored in the heat of the concert and people spent the night sleeping on the grass, in private homes, in hotels, or simply sipping champagne until the departure of the early morning train.

Eventually, romantic involvement was bound to occur. The face that was to fascinate Johann was that of aristocratic Olga Smirnitzki. Despite a deep emotional involvement on both sides, nothing was to come of it. The aristocratic family did not see in the Viennese conductor, even a man as famous as Strauss, the suitor they had intended for their beautiful daughter. Johann did not always escape that easily. During another summer at Pavlovsk he again became romantically involved. But what he thought to be a secret love affair had been quite openly discussed within the damsel's family, who were not disagreeable to the idea. Before Johann knew it he was introduced to them as the bridegroom. While he looked on helplessly as if watching the affairs of someone else, a wedding day was set and sumptuous preparations made while Johann somnambulistically concertized as if he were a mere bystander watching the drama-comedy of his life. Only a last-minute kidnapping of Johann, from the carriage on its way to the church, and refuge in the Austrian embassy saved him from a seemingly inescapable marital fate.

Despite his twelve summers in Pavlovsk, neither his emotional involvements nor the beauty of Russia left any deep impressions on Johann. Compositions might carry such titles as *Grossfürstin Alexandra Walzer, Krönungslieder* (dedicated to Empress Maria Alexandrovna), *Abschied von St. Petersburg (Farewell to St. Petersburg), Olga Polka, Russische Marschfantasie,* or *Im Russischen Dorfe Fantasie (In A Russian Village),* and they might even contain an occasional Russian tune, but in spirit all these compositions were Viennese and their Russian motivation and emotional background soon forgotten once Strauss was back in Vienna. However, in one important sense Russia would always remain unforgotten. From there Johann returned literally laden with gold, the basis of his later wealth. The Russian railroad company had been pleased, and they were generous in reimbursing the young Viennese with monetary gifts far above their initial offer.

Vienna had changed in the years since the young emperor Franz Joseph had ascended the throne in stormy 1848. After the Christmas decree of 1857 demolished the ancient walls of the city, the Ringstrasse was built. The social change brought about in Austria and Vienna, so vividly demonstrated on the Ring, brought about an uneasy, cautious coexistence between the old aristocrats of the realm and the newly risen monied industrialists and banking aristocracy, many of them polishing a newly acquired baronic escutcheon. There was no doubt that artistic and musical patronage had slipped from the grasp of the aristocracy. The salons of Arnstein, Eskeles, Rothschild, Todesco, and Wertheimer were musical, literary, and artistic highpoints of Vienna's social life, rivaling the salons of the Esterhazys or Schwarzenbergs. Many among the new aristocracy, of course, lacked the necessary refinement and background to play major roles in Viennese high society or to distinguish between the artificial and the inspired, between artistic depth and blatant surface facility. Thus Vienna often displayed the splendor of the hereditary palace next to the vulgar or commonplace one of the nouveau riche, but at its best the new aristocracy could vie with the best Vienna had to offer. Bäuerle in 1848 wrote in the *Theaterzeitung:*

> There are talented Jewesses everywhere, but the greatest number is to be found in Vienna. It is astonishing how much knowledge they possess, how well they are able to engage in conversation, what superior judgment and views they offer, how felicitously they express themselves. Most of them speak three or four languages, sing Italian arias beautifully and support the arts conscientiously. One finds the most important artists at their soirées. They are true patrons of the theatre and concerts. They dress very simply but most tastefully. In conduct and appearance they are most charming and graceful ... They give their children the finest education. In all charitable undertakings, they set an excellent example.

Among the foremost literary salons of Vienna were those of the Todesco family, which had made its mark as early as the Congress of Vienna and was instrumental in reviving Vienna's social life in general and the literary salon in particular. The poet Hartman, who had been a guest of Sophie Todesco, wrote in 1864 to Paul Heyse, the later Nobel Prize winner: "You will become acquainted [in Vienna] with the kindliest woman and the finest character of this century and of our corner of the world. Acquaintance with her is to be treasured and will store beautiful memories for the future."

Shortly before that time another member of the family, Moritz Todesco, had made his personal mark on the financial market and aristocracy in Vienna. Refined by temperament and upbringing but Bohemian by nature, he had a palatial home that was always open as a meeting place for the literate and musical intelligentsia. If, in contrast to other branches of the family, his home was more often the meeting place of musicians and composers, it was to be attributed to the presence there of his mistress, Henrietta "Jetti" Treffz. Although she had borne him two children out of wedlock, her presence as lady of the house of millionaire Todesco was quite acceptable in the liberal climate of the Vienna of her time.

"She was as graceful as a reed," possessed of a voice which was often compared to that of Jenny Lind. Berlioz had been quite taken with her charms, and Mendelssohn had been so captivated by her voice and personality that he had dedicated songs to her. She was a daughter of the people. Her father had been a silversmith by the name of Challupetzky. After his death her mother married the attorney Treffz, whose name Jetti adopted. Her excellent figure and voice provided her with her first stage job at age fourteen. Thence she grew and matured under the protection of a number of "patrons," since talent and voice were not the only attributes which advanced her in her chosen profession of opera singer. Eventually she became an accepted and admired personality, a situation not uncommon in her time, a mistress of the world who, unencumbered by convention, chose her companions at her pleasure among the great of the world. As George Sand, Countess d'Agoult, and Henrietta Smithson had respectively chosen Chopin, Liszt, and Berlioz, so Jetti, who had shared the sumptous bed and wealth of Moritz Todesco, now chose Johann.

Johann, at age thirty-seven, had broken about a dozen engagements to be married. Wealthy, famous, startlingly handsome and unattached, he could freely choose from any stratum of society he cared to select. Jetti Treffz had invited him to discuss preparations for a ball in Todesco's palace. On the night of the ball the inexplicable happened. Jetti was as overwhelmed by Johann's natural charm as he was by her mature and spirited beauty. An innocent engagement for a house ball kindled a bonfire of instantaneous passion. There was no question concerning realities. Jetti, the charming, knowledgeable, sophisticated woman of the theatre and the world who stood far above Johann in experience and intellect, had done the chosing. Best of all, both kept their secret. On 26 August 1862 Karl Haslinger, Strauss's closest friend and publisher, opened a missive from his friend that made him gasp: "I will be expecting you to-morrow at my home at 7 o'clock in the morning to be my best man at my wedding which will take place one hour later. Answer immediately, you cheating music peddler."

When it became known that Johann Strauss had married Jetti Treffz in a simple ceremony at St. Stefan's Cathedral, attended by only a few of his closest friends, Vienna was aghast. Jetti Treffz? Why, she was forty-seven if she was a day (she admitted to forty-four) and Johann was thirty-seven. He could have married anybody he wanted. There was an emotional upheaval in the ranks of his admirers ranging from disappointment and disenchantment to furor and hysterics. Less expected but no less noticeable was the guarded reaction of Vienna nobility. They had accepted Jetti with the tacit, magnanimous tolerance of the times and had felt a vicarious pleasure discoursing with the mistress of Baron Todesco. But now that she had married, they were suddenly and sullenly disappointed because their studied forbearance had been wasted. And what of Moritz Todesco? Confronted with the *fait accompli* he proved himself the *grandseigneur* in the spirit of the Todesco tradition, speeding Jetti into marital bliss with avowals of his thanks for her love and his continuing friendship plus an undisclosed small fortune.

Jetti and Johann were oblivious of the furor they had caused. On the day after their wedding she addressed her husband's brother Josef: "I am so terribly happy and blessed to be able to belong to my Jean with all the power of my heart and soul that I am able to forget many a painful moment I had to suffer lately, and can look confidently into the future." Mahler once said: "To find the one-in-a-million woman one needs is as fortunate as the best idea which occurs to an artist." Johann and Jetti were such a pair, complementing each other fully and ideally. Johann's brother Eduard wrote to his wife some time later: "[Jetti] is irreplaceable. She writes all bills, copies all music for the orchestra, looks after the kitchen chores, and supervises everything with a care and kindness that evokes admiration."

Johann, as wordly as his background would permit, had not yet completely shaken off the occasional coarseness of the inn patrons with whom he had grown up. There Jetti became indispensable. She was as worldly as she was wise. Her talent for the society which had accepted her influenced the right people at the right time. The court, which had not forgiven Johann for his behavior in 1848 and had exhibited formal coolness toward its famous son, suddenly, miraculously, became mollified and the title of *Hofkapellmeister*, which had eluded him for so long, was bestowed upon Johann. With Jetti to look after her beloved Johann, life subtly but inevitably

The Opera Ball, one of the highlights of the Vienna Fasching season. From front door to stage door the opera house becomes one vast ballroom.

changed. Jetti became everything to him, private secretary, treasurer, confidante, adviser, director, manager, diplomat, wife, and mistress. Soon they moved into larger quarters in the Singerstrasse, thence to Praterstrasse, finally into the sumptuously appointed villa in Hietzing which was to remain Johann's winter home and which saw the birth of some of his greatest musical creations. More and more Jetti prevailed upon her husband to devote himself to composition and leave the conducting chores of the now world famous Strauss orchestras in the capable hands of his brothers. As usual, Johann followed her sound advice and, except for special occasions such as a court ball or an operetta premiere, completely retired from conducting activity.

Vienna had to accept Jetti Treffz as Johann's wife, but it did not always accept the music of their darling. Both Strauss and Offenbach were approached by the Vienna Press Association to write a waltz each for the *Presseball*, one of the more prestigious and inventive during Vienna's entire *Fasching* season. Offenbach, whose Viennese popularity was so great that he jokingly called Vienna his savings bank, promptly acceded to the request and submitted a waltz entitled *Abendblätter (Evening Papers)*. Johann, of course, also sent an untitled waltz on which the committee, on its own initiative, bestowed the contrasting title *Morgenblätter (Morning Papers)*. At the ball popular opinion gave the laurels to Offenbach. His waltz had to be repeated five times while dancing was continued after *Morgenblätter* had been played only once. Nobody realized then that this was one of the most significant advances in the waltz. Only history reserved the right places of the two creations, *Abendblätter* sinking into deserved oblivion while *Morgenblätter* remained one of Vienna's true waltz gems. Vienna, following Offenbach's sophisticated "made in Paris" label, momentarily ignored the Strauss creation. But over the years Vienna realized that it was the beginning of a new phase in Johann's artistic life, exuding poetry which had been absent from the genre until then.

Often it is not a musical line but a line of poetry, perhaps insignificant in itself, which opens to the inspired composer a previously unimagined artistic vista. Schumann experienced such inspiration through the final line of a poem by the obscure poet Adolf Böttger: *"Im Thale blüht der Frühling auf"* ("Spring blossoms in the valley"). The single line inspired the great romantic composer to write his First *(Spring)* Symphony. Johann was to be similarly inspired on reading the line *"An der Donau, der schönen blauen Donau"* by Karl Beck. The line fastened itself in Johann's mind and transformed itself into musical sentiments. A dream arose in his mind and gave rise to one of the loftiest melodic masterpieces of all times. Unfortunately for the birth of the waltz, Johann Herbeck had asked Johann for a long time for a choral waltz for the *Männergesangsverein*, Vienna's foremost male chorus.

Johann, eager to oblige, handed him the *Blue Danube* waltz and on 15 February 1867 the waltz was performed by the male choir and the Strauss orchestra, with Victor Keldorfer as the choir director. The reception was lukewarm, unenthusiastic. It should have come as no surprise, considering the innocuous words supplied by one Josef Weyl, house poet of the chorus and a policeman by profession. The timeless charm of the waltz was totally buried under the inane text:

Wiener seid froh	Viennese, be gay
Oho, wieso?	Oho, why, why?
Ein Schimmer des Lichts	A glimmer of light
Wir sehen noch nichts.	We see only night.

Such triviality, particularly amid the depressed mood after the 1866 defeat at the hands of the Prussians at Koeniggräetz, could only give rise to satirical comments and grim jokes. At the mention of the last two lines the Viennese would shield their eyes and scan the horizon in search of the promised but unseen silver lining at such time of disaster. Under the burden of meaningless text and grim mood, the immortal waltz was carelessly brushed aside. Eventually Franz von Germeth would change the opening to *"Donau so blau"* ("Danube so blue"), which remained whenever the waltz was sung, fortunately not too often. Only in the absence of words do the shimmering opening and the brilliant waltzes to follow speak for themselves, for Vienna, for Strauss. But for the moment, in Vienna *Blaue Donau* became a musical Cinderalla, waiting to be awakened by the kiss of Paris.

13

The One, The Only Johann

CERCLE INTERNATIONALE

CONCERT PROMENADE
À L'INSTAR DES CONCERTS PROMENADES DE LONDRES
ET DE VIENNE

DONNÉ PAR

JOHANN STRAUSS

Chef de musique des bals de la cour imperial et royal d'Autriche

ET

B. BILSE

Musikdirektor de sa Majesté le Roi de Prusse

PROGRAMME

Ouverture de Ruy Blas	Mendelssohn
Morgenblätter, Valses	Joh. Strauss
Potpourri de l'opéra Faust	Gounod
Bavarderie, Polka	Joh. Strauss
Ouverture d'Oberon	Weber
Künstlerleben (la vie d'artiste)	Strauss
Abendlied, executé par tous les instruments a cordes	Schumann
Kaiserstadt, Polka	Strauss

Huge placards announced Strauss's artistic presence to the citizens of Paris. Anywhere else they would have caused a sensation and a run on the box office, but not in Paris, because Paris was in the midst of its own sensation, the Paris World

Exhibition. Hans Christian Andersen reported upon his visit:

> [The Exhibition] is like a table spread for Christmas with magic parcels. There are parcels here of industry, wealth, art. Around them are exhibited sprinklings from all countries, playthings for adults. Here every nation remembers its home with a smile ... All portals bear the flag of France, around the world bazaar wave the flags of the nations ... From the towers the bells softly send their peals to earth. With the tones of church organs are mingled the hoarse nasal chants from the oriental cafés. It is the realm of Babel—a wonder of the world.

Austria's position vis-à-vis France at that particular moment was in delicate balance. Politically Austria was at a low ebb after two devastating defeats, one by France and Italy at Solferino, the other by Prussia at Koeniggräetz. But Austria was not the only country wary of the growing Prussian might. France was also keeping an eye on the German east and only a few years later, like Austria, was to feel the crushing fist of Prussian armor at Sedan. Thus an uneasy *modus vivendi* existed between Napoleon III and Prince Richard Metternich, the son of Chancellor Metternich, and Austrian ambassador to France. The situation was eased by the fact that Napoleon and Eugenie lived in a make-believe world of pleasure totally removed from reality, and Prince Metternich blended into the picture as the Austrian playboy. Nobody watching the splendid tableau Paris presented would have suspected that the mad splendor they were exhibiting was the last splurge of the waning power and glory of Napoleon's throne. Theatres did not seem to close, society did not seem to go to bed. Led by Empress Eugenie, Paris went on a mad orgy of glamor and joy. Eugenie led the dance in total negation of realities; Offenbach was the musical lion of the day, and immensely gifted Hortense Schneider played the title role in his latest operettic sensation, *La Grande Duchesse de Gerolstein*, in the evening, and held court in her boudoir at night surrounded by the titled heads of Europe from which circle she carefully culled her temporary favorite from time to time.

Despite the insecure political and diplomatic situation in which Austria found itself, the real power in the social whirl of Paris, titularly headed by the empress, was the charming, vivacious, shrewd wife of the Austrian ambassador, Princess Pauline Metternich Sandor. Eccentric Pauline smoked cigars and hunted in the Bois de Boulogne riding like a man instead of side saddle, to the shock of Parisian *haut monde*. Although her father had been a jockey, she quickly fitted herself into the demanding life as the wife of an ambassador. Soon her charm, her spirited caprices made her the most popular and best known Viennese in Paris.

Empress Eugenie, unsure of herself in the role which her rank and Paris society had thrust upon her, soon found Pauline Metternich of tremendous value to her.

Pauline became her confidential adviser, creator of new fashions, new games, new friends, new enemies. But in the process she also helped to raise bourgeois Paris to the rank of a great city of the world, a feat that neither Napoleon III nor Eugenie had been able to accomplish. It did not come as a surprise that Princess Pauline not only was among the chief advisors concerning the social splendor of the World Exhibition but that "her" ball at the Austrian embassy should be one of Paris's most splendid evenings.[1] A special ballroom opening onto the embassy gardens had been added to the embassy proper, its walls shimmering in white and gold. The ambassador of course favored an Austrian artist to play at the gala affair, and Strauss was chosen.

Surprisingly, however, it had not been the Austrian embassy but a Frenchman, Comte d'Osmond, a great admirer of Wagner and Strauss, who had prevailed upon Johann to come to Paris during the Exhibition. The Strauss orchestra had already been engaged for other festivities in Vienna, so Johann decided to come alone and secured the services of the Prussian orchestra of Bilse. But Paris was too much in love with itself to have some to spare, even for the darling of the dance world. The Paris correspondent of the *Daily Telegraph* reported:

> It is by no means easy to entertain ... two thousand persons, including an Emperor, an Empress, an Imperial Prince, a King, two Queens, two royal princes, Grand Duchesses, Highnesses, and all the diplomacy, wit, beauty and fashion of a great city; yet that was what was not only attempted but thoroughly effected ... The gate of the Grand Hotel wide open ... a court illuminated by great gas stars ... the stream of carriages began to flow at nine and went on till twelve ... the place was a fairyland ... in the centre a bed of flowers and a glittering fountain; on either side galleries lined with flowers; add to this a group of the best-looking and best-dressed people in Paris and you may have a faint idea of the beauty of a scene which astonished the eyes of those who have been ball-going ever since they could run alone.

Official Austria had recognized the importance of the occasion and, despite near-empty coffers, had allocated money for it. When Strauss arrived, the chandeliers of the ballroom resembled illuminated flower baskets, the background a rocky grotto complete with foaming cascade. Napoleon and Eugenie would not miss the ball given by the empress's friend, and their presence plus that of the king of Hannover and Prince Friedrich of Prussia (whom Pauline despised for obvious reasons)

1. It is a grim footnote to history that Princess Pauline died in Vienna in 1921 after World War I, having been forced to sell her precious gala coach to a local butcher to keep from starving, only to find the proceeds from the sale dissolving practically overnight due to rampant inflation.

made the Austrian ball one of the main events of the glittering World Exhibition. But it was not yet to be Johann's evening—he had not been told in advance that the Parisians liked their waltzes slower and their gallops faster. But nobody danced as Strauss made music. On that auspicious occasion an American visitor, Madame de Hergerman Lindencrone, reported:

> No one thought of dancing; everyone wanted to listen to his waltzes. And how Strauss played them!... With what fire and *entrain!* We had thought Waldteufel perfect but when you had heard Strauss you said to yourself you had never heard a waltz before ... The musicians were partly hidden by gigantic palmettos, plants, and pots of flowers arranged in the most attractive way. But he—Johann Strauss—stood well in front looking very handsome, very Austrian, and very pleased with himself ... The music was inspiring enough to have made an Egyptian mummy get out of its sarcophagus and caper ... the cotillion finished at half-past five in the morning.

The result of the ball, for Johann, was as curious as the occasion had been auspicious. As applauded as he had been at the ball, the news of his presence did not create a happy furor. If he was disappointed or concerned, he did not show distress but continued to concertize at the *Cercle Internationale.* One day there walked into one of his concerts the power of the Paris press in the person of Hyppolite Villemessant, wealthy, powerful owner of Paris's influential *Le Figaro.* The concert had already begun and Villemessant quietly took a seat to watch the spectacle and hear the music.

He was enthralled, not only by Strauss's bewitching music but by the sight on stage. It suddenly occurred to him that Strauss wielded his bow over a German orchestra, and the German musicians were hanging on his every move. The irony of the reversal immediately struck the fancy of the famous journalist. Germans doing the bidding of an Austrian; an Austrian victory over Germany—on French soil! Villemessant had also been aware of the tacit rapprochement, between France and Austria, one of the few political moves on which Villemessant agreed with Napoleon III. Returning to his office he devised, in concert with his staff, a series of articles on Strauss which indirectly would also serve the cause of Austro-French friendship. Strauss, delighted by the unexpected praise from France's foremost journalist, decided to pay him a personal visit. Villemessant spoke several languages fluently but, in his own chauvinist fashion, preferred to converse in his native tongue. Johann, trained through contact with Viennese and Russian aristocracy, spoke fluent French. The journalist was enchanted by the composer's implied compliment. Soon the favorable notices became a flood of praise. Strauss, not to be outdone, reciprocated with a soirée for the entire editorial staff of *Le Figaro* and also composed a polka for the occasion which Villemessant promptly published as a *Figaro* supplement. The inverse pyramid was beginning to build as Villemessant, in turn, gave a special soirée for Strauss. With Villemessant as host and Strauss as guest, everybody came: the composer Abroise Thomas, Dumas *fils*, Flaubert, Gautier, Turgeniev. The prince of Wales determinedly insisted that Johann come to London. Johann bowed and smilingly accepted—for a later date. Because now the demand for Strauss and the influx of admirers threatened to approach the flood stage. And in that wave the *Blue Danube* waltz swept to fame. Here the Parisians and the world heard it for the first time orchestrally, without words. Villemessant led all others in admiration: "I wish that the musicians of our lyric theatres would go and take lessons by listening to the admirable artists directed by Mr. Strauss, who has the devil in his body."

The French went so far as to supply their own words to the waltz, and they were, not surprisingly, superior to the hackneyed words originally attached.

Fleuve d'azur	Stream of blue
Sur ton flot pur	On your pure waves
Glissé la voile	Glides the Sail
Comme un étoile	Like a star.

Overnight Strauss was the undisputed toast of Paris, surpassing the success of Paris darling Jacques Offenbach. One newspaper reported, "His waltzes carry their sound to the utmost limits of civilization, in America and Australia as in China, where they evoke an echo at the Great Wall." Another newspaper avowed "Mr. Strauss is a gentleman who dances his own waltzes and quadrilles with violin, arms, neck, shoulders, and head. It is impossible for anyone to sit still; he would make the very pillars of the concert hall twirl and dance." And every concert, every ball, every midnight revelry demanded *Le Danube Bleu*.

In August of that year Johann finally was able to make good his promise to the prince of Wales, and he appeared in a number of concerts in London. On 15 August 1867 the following comment appeared in *The Times*:

> Covent Garden Concerts ... has secured the services of Herr Johann Strauss, a son of the Viennese Strauss of European celebrity. This gentleman, who strongly resembles his father in manner, seems also to possess a large share of those qualities which led to his father's renown. He conducts the orchestra like his father, fiddle in hand, and joins in the passages of some importance. This he does with wonderful animation, accompanied by a certain amount of characteristic gesticulation which also has something to do with the general impression created ... That the future success of the Covent Garden concerts depends materially on him we think unquestionable.

Like his father twenty years earlier, Johann made triumphant music. But there was one major difference. Where his father had covered uncertainty and restlessness with tyrannical dictation, the much surer son won everybody's admiration by his relaxed and urbane manner. If St. Petersburg had raved about the *Bauernpolka* and Paris had loved *Le Danube Bleu*, London chose as its favorites *Morgenblätter* and one of Johann's briefer but no less charming works, *Annenpolka*. Johann and Jetti, who accompanied him everywhere, felt promptly at home in London, and Johann reciprocated the wonderful Covent Garden reception by composing *Erinnerungen an Covent Garden (Remembrances of Covent Garden)*.

The *Blue Danube*, meanwhile, had become a river of the world. It might never be blue except in reflection of a cloudless sky, but Strauss had made it blue for all the world. And all the world wanted to play, dance, and sing it. Whereas the average waltz success would require three copper plates to satisfy the printing demand for it, *Blaue Donau* required one hundred plates amounting to about one million copies of that waltz alone. Hanslick one day counted eighty huge boxes in front of the publishing house preparing to ship thousands of copies to America. Why did *Blue Danube*, without words, become the world's greatest waltz success which far outpaced the popularity of even such great waltzes as *Morgenblätter* or *Geschichten aus dem Wienerwald*? The question is readily answered. The insipid text nearly forbade full appreciation of the music. Unshackled from stilted words, the music spoke for itself and, in turn, allowed the listener to form his own picture—the morning mist, the sundrenched stream flowing on to embrace new rivers and new inspiration. It is Strauss at his superlative, most Viennese, without darkness, storm, or stress. No demons distort the pleasure of melodic reflection in the stream, of sunbeams on gentle waves, a woman's smile, apricot blossoms in the *Wachau*, the romantic valley of German Nibelungen legend, with romantic ruins rimming its hilly borders. In *Blaue Donau* Johann had left behind the legacy of Lanner and Strauss, and in the symphonic setting of a waltz tone poem had immortalized his city's reflection in its river.

Equally descriptive in poetic terms is Strauss's *Geschichten aus dem Wienerwald (Tales from the Vienna Woods)*. There Johann does not attempt to imitate the romantic woods as Weber depicted them in his opera *Der Freischütz* or as Liszt did in his piano composition *Waldesrauschen (Forest Rustling)*. *Tales* is a love song in more than one sense. That it expresses Johann's love for his native city is of course an interpretation close at hand. But, as in his very first appearance at Dommayer's when he affirmed his filial devotion by playing his father's *Loreleyklänge* at the height of his triumph, so again in *Geschichten* he remembers and reminds us of his father by quoting in paraphrase the elder Strauss's opus 208. And the use of the zither in the relaxed *Ländler* theme, as instrumented by Strauss, lies the waltz even closer to its past and its locality because the zither, a typical alpine instrument, is often used at the *Heurigen*, those intimate gatherings of wine connoisseurs in the wooded vintner's foothills of Vienna. The premiere of *Tales from the Vienna Woods* took place in 1868 at a glamorous garden party of Prince Hohenlohe at the Augarten. Unlike the *Blue Danube*, *Geschichten* was immediately hailed as one of Strauss's masterpieces, and its popularity, second only to *Blue Danube*, has held throughout the century.

> Wer nicht liebt Wein, Weib und Gesang
> Der bleibt ein Narr sein Leben lang.

> He who doesn't love wine, woman and song
> Remains a fool his whole life long.

This famous saying was so much a part of Johann's life and motto that its waltz realization was preordained. Its vast introduction of ninety-one bars lifts the waltz back to the higher level to which Weber had briefly elevated it exactly half a century earlier. *Wein, Weib, und Gesang (Wine, Woman, and Song)* thus became another waltz milestone. The more it is played and examined the more the introduction becomes the important message in music, with the waltzes the expected charming appendices. Because in that waltz Johann asserts what his native language had made obvious: that Austria is part of the German-speaking world. The romanticism of the opening might easily have been a thought from the pen of Weber or Mendelssohn, and the final march theme, before the waltz is allowed to unfold, comes pictorially right out of *Meistersinger*. And Wagner, that complex genius, as well as Brahms, his musical antipode, reveled in that waltz by the master of relaxed musical enjoyment, worlds removed from complications, traumas, and frustrations.

Out of the wealth of Johann's famous waltz creations it is possible here to mention only a few. *Künstlerleben (Artist's Life)*, which preceded *Geschichten*, paints a carefree, gay picture of the Viennese artists' colony, particularly during *Fasching*. The polka *Leichtes Blut (Light Spirits)* raced through Viennese ballrooms, as did Johann's bow to neighboring Hungary in his *Eljen a Magyar*, which was first heard at a national festival in Pesth and idolized by the Hungarians. In a total variance of speed and substance Johann wrote his famed *Perpetuum Mobile.*

On 23 February 1870 Anna Strauss died. After presiding over family councils which raised Johann to fame and brought Josef and Eduard into the Strauss musical fold, and after finding that all her sons were men of their own destinies, the mother had gently faded into the background to live with her own thoughts and memories. Her love for her family remained undiminished although her sons had sought her counsel less and less. The only member of the family she had never addressed was Johann's wife because she had never been able to forget Jetti's previous role as the mistress of a nouveau-riche Jew, regardless of his title and position. An additional reason for Anna's bitterness against Jetti must have been loss of influence with her oldest son. When Jetti had entered his life, she brought to it a knowledge and practical wisdom of the world and stage which Anna Strauss could not match.

Strauss had just finished two splendid waltzes, *Freut Euch des Lebens (Enjoy Life)* and *Neues Wien (New Vienna)*, celebrating the rise of Greater Vienna, when his mother died. Death was a spectre which lamed Johann mentally and spiritually, and musical silence ensued. That silence had curious side effects. Just as in previous decades minor musical lights had put words to Strauss and Lanner melodies and had hawked them as genuine folk songs, so now Strauss's fellow composers made free use of his tunes to adorn their musical plagiarisms with Straussian feathers. Keldorfer "adapted" the *Accelerations* waltz for male choir and orchestra; Schulz Evler "prepared" the *Blue Danube* as a piano virtuoso piece; and Schütt "created" the *Emperor Waltz Capriccio*. Even the composers of the more rarified classic spheres were not averse to borrowing from Strauss. Robert Fuchs's Serenade No. 55 employed two Strauss melodies, and Felix Weingartner used *Fledermaus* themes in the finale of his Symphony in E-flat Major. This prompted Hanslick to remark sarcastically that such infusions hardly improved the music of those composers.

The decade from 1870 to 1880 unquestionably saw Johann at the apex of his career and at the nadir of his personal life. Vienna, to its immense satisfaction, saw Offenbach and Suppé supplanted by a Viennese in the field of operetta and *Indigo*, *Karneval in Rom*, *Die Fledermaus*, *Cagliostro in Wien*, and *Das Spitzentuch der Königin* were among the inspired results. *Indigo* had taken Vienna by storm in 1871, but the next operettic effort had to bide its time because Johann was invited to participate in the United States Anniversary Festival celebrating the independence of the first thirteen states. Although that momentous event had not taken place until 1776, Boston and Massachusetts had declared their independence from England in 1772 and were determined to celebrate exactly one hundred years later. Thus the Boston Peace Jubilee was slated to last from 17 June to 4 July 1872. Strauss viewed the offer with mixed feelings. It was surely an honor to be included in a festival of such magnitude. Giuseppe Verdi had been invited to participate and so had Hans von Bülow, who was to give the world premiere of Tchaikovsky's B-flat Minor Piano Concerto in Boston three years later; Wagner had composed a march for the occasion. Aside from the honor, however, Johann had been offered an honorarium of $100,000, an astronomic figure at that time, plus free transportation from Vienna to Boston for himself, Jetti, one valet, and a lady's maid, with the assurance that the money would be deposited in a Viennese bank before his departure. On the negative side was Johann's marked dislike of travel. The man who, when traveling by railroad, sat on the floor of his car sipping champagne, felt sick at the very thought of sea travel to the new world, a journey which then took fourteen days. In the end Jetti, the honor, the challenge, and, of course, the fee won out.

The small party set out from Bremerhaven on 1 June 1872. Their liner was a ship boasting a tonnage of five thousand, driven by steam but also outfitted with sails for use in favorable weather. No matter how calm the weather, however, a nutshell of five thousand tons was bound to roll, pitch, and yaw in the Atlantic. The diningroom was small, the cabins cramped, the bunks without springs. Even during quiet seas it was necessary to have racks on the tables with compartments for each dish and glass. There were no deck chairs and, during the night, after the dinner dance, lights were extinguished and the cabins remained in darkness. But fortunately there happened to be on board the regimental band of the First Prussian Guards, so there was dancing every evening—to Strauss waltzes, naturally. Johann did not partake of the dancing; he couldn't waltz. Despite the rigors of the journey and the inconvenience of accommodations, Johann surprised everybody by being the least seasick aboard.

New York, in those years, was a far cry from the famous skyline it now presents to the visitor. Then it simply was another flat harbor city. Johann hurried on to Boston where the city fathers had scheduled a public reception for the continental dignitaries of music. Verdi and Bülow were of course accorded the honors due such illustrious luminaries. But it was Strauss who was received with the most enthusiastic welcome. Huge placards in all major Boston thoroughfares displayed pictures of him on his throne on top of the globe with a fiddle bow for a scepter. The crowds went wild whenever the "waltz king" appeared in public. Although accustomed to such adulation, it grew so out of proportion that Johann could not decide whether to mingle with the ecstatic crowds or to retire to the safety of his hotel suite. Boston streets seemed unsafe for Johann as women rushed up to kiss his hand or the hem of his coat, men cheered whenever he appeared and, to satisfy the demand for a lock of his hair, a Newfoundland dog had to part with much of his coat. Eventually six burly specimens of Boston's police force were assigned to accompany him to all major functions.

The terms of the contract read that the committee was to build a wooden concert hall for an audience of one hundred thousand—an incredible figure. Had Johann Strauss taken the time to inform himself, had he read Longfellow, Thoreau, or Mark Twain, had he read at all, then he would have had an inkling of the vastness of the country whose guest he was. He was showered with affection born of that newly opened vastness; the young giant of a country, flexing its muscles and rejoicing in uproarious laughter, all but crushed its guest in lusty embrace. But Johann saw only the vexing and often ludicrous and exaggerated side of it and remained without a true understanding of the huge space and spirit of the country. But he had contracted to give fourteen concerts and was determined to give the best there was to give. When he entered the hall for the first time, he was appalled. To play for five thousand in Vienna had been a monster event, but one hundred thousand and

Concert at the Imperial Spanish Riding School in Vienna where one thousand sang while five thousand listened.

twenty thousand singers—this was no way to make music. Johann had consented to appear at two balls with three-hundred-piece orchestras in Boston and also at four concerts in the New York opera house. The first of the fourteen Boston concerts was to remain frightfully vivid in his memory. Days before the concert every seat, every bit of space had been sold out in the vast hall supported by slender pillars bedecked with bunting and innumerable flags. The day had been filled with more welcoming speeches and imposing celebrations of all sorts. But it was the night to

Strauss's concert at the Peace Jubilee Festival Hall in Boston.

which Bostonians looked forward, the crowning, in America, of the "waltz king." Johann's walk through the crowd had already been a terrifying experience. Although he was again surrounded by six husky constables, they had difficulty moving him through the innumerable outstretched hands wishing to touch him. They were closely followed by an equally frightened man, Strauss's valet, who carried his violin. As the crowd became aware of Strauss's presence there rose a roar of cheers beyond human description. Yet even then Strauss had no conception of size of the crowd until he stood on his specially built platform, one hundred feet above the audience, and looked down at the frightening sea of cheering, shouting, waving Americans. Strauss recalled the event:

> On the musician's platform there were twenty-thousand singers; in front of them the members of the orchestra—and these were the people I was to conduct. A hundred assistants had been placed at my disposal to control these gigantic masses, but I was only able to recognize those nearest to me, and although we had had rehearsals there was no possibility of giving an artistic performance, a proper production. But if I had declined to conduct, it would have been at the cost of my life.
>
> Now just imagine my position, face to face with a public of a hundred thousand Americans. There I stood at the raised platform, high above all the others. How would the business start, how would it end? Suddenly a cannon shot rang out; a gentle hint for us twenty-thousand to begin to perform the *Blue Danube*.
>
> I gave the signal, my one hundred assistant conductors followed me as quickly and as best they could and then there broke out an unholy row such as I shall never forget. As we had begun more or less together, I concentrated my entire attention on seeing that we should also finish together!— Thank Heaven, I managed even that. It was all that was humanly possible. The hundred thousand mouths in the audience roared their applause and I breathed a sigh of relief when I found myself in fresh air again and felt firm ground beneath my feet.
>
> The next day I had to take to flight before an army of impresarios who promised me the whole of California if I were to undertake an American tour.

The "magnetic, mercurial, irresistible, dazzling, brilliant, adorable" Strauss, despite fright, lack of understanding, and ensuing hardships, happily endured and did give Boston his lavish best. *Morgenblätter, Künstlerleben, Wein, Weib und Gesang, Pizzicato Polka, New Jubilee Waltz*, written especially for Boston—and, of course, the *Blaue Donau*—were demanded at every concert, over and over again. To all that Johann added a novelty of special significance for the occasion, *The Star-Spangled Banner* in waltz time. Wrote the *Boston Herald* of the opening performance: "The chief honors from a strictly musical point of view were carried

off by Herr Strauss whose activity, firmness and judgment made him a model conductor ... He has, apparently, not an idle muscle in his body while he is conducting."

Laden with treasure and American honors, Johann returned to the continent.
Then, hearing that cholera had broken out in Vienna, he immediately decided to
postpone his return there. The spa of Baden-Baden beckoned with splendid concert
fees, but Strauss demurred, pleading exhaustion. However, two thousand francs
per concert finally lured him to the world-famous rendezvous of royalty. There he
met with one of his greatest admirers, Emperor Wilhelm I of Prussia. Wilhelm had
mellowed since the disaster of Koeniggraetz and was delighted to see Strauss. Open-
mouthed Germans could see the Prussian king and the Viennese musician conversing
together on long walks. However, Johann's main occupation in Baden-Baden was
the "tables." There was no holding him back from the roulette wheels, and reports
have it that he left there all the fees he earned at the spa plus some precious American dollars. Before leaving, Wilhelm and Strauss exchanged presents. Wilhelm
honored Johann with the order of the Red Eagle and Johann reciprocated with
the *Kaiser Wilhelm Polonaise.*

When Johann finally saw fit to return to the *Kaiserstadt* he threw himself
feverishly into work on his second operetta, *Karneval in Rom,* a labor of love
which had been interrupted and postponed until after his return from America. Its
success prompted him almost immediately to write another operettic creation. *Die
Fledermaus (The Bat),* one of Strauss's most glorious creations and certainly the
most enduring of all operettas ever written, was removed from the Vienna boards
as a failure after only sixteen performances.

In 1872 there was another musical development in Vienna. Bösendorfer discovered that the riding stable of Prince Liechtenstein possessed excellent acous-
tics. It did not take much persuasion to convince the prince, one of Vienna's
great music patrons and art collectors, that the spacious expanse would make an
excellent concert hall. Ludwig Bösendorfer, part of Johann Strauss's intimate
circle, had inherited his father's pride, the world famous *Klavierfabrik* (a piano
manufacturing concern). Despite age, wealth, and industrial progress the son
continued in his father's prideful footsteps, imparting the finest manual workmanship to every individual piano which left the factory, often adjusting touch and
tone to the requirements of individual artists. Such adjustments were of course
nothing new to Vienna. Long before Bösendorfer, Beethoven had railed against
the yielding uniformity of tone on the *Hammerklavier* then manufactured in Vienna
and had demanded a stronger, sometimes even brittle tone, quite different from the
soft-voiced instruments then created. But now individual craftsmanship and attention to tone had truly arrived in Vienna. Bösendorfer, who had opened his piano

factory in 1828 and bequeathed it to his son, had made his one of the great piano names, which stood proudly side by side with Bechstein, Blüthner, Erard, Pleyel, and Steinway. From 1872 to 1913, when it was demolished to make way for an office building, the intimate Bösendorfer hall was the Viennese home of such great artists as Liszt, Rubinstein, and Bülow who relished the unequalled purity of tone emanating within its walls. After its demolition, allegiances were reluctantly shifted to Hansen's newly built, gilded *Musikvereinssaal,* to this day considered one of the world's acoustically superb concert halls.

Black Friday, 8 May 1873, blighted flag-bedecked Vienna only eight days after the World Exposition, which was to have surpassed all previous ones, had opened. Some of the reasons for Vienna's financial collapse were to be found outside its borders. France, after its unsuccessful war against Prussia, had been bled white by Bismarck. Since Bismarck, for reasons of his own, had not exacted monetary retribution from Austria after its 1866 defeat but had been satisfied to leave it demoralized and exhausted, Austria in general, and its capital in particular, had been able to recover fairly rapidly during the intervening years. Since the money markets of Paris were closed, whatever fortunes French finance could rescue after the military debacle had found a haven in Vienna. The French had been misled by rumors they accepted without checking their origin. Emperor Franz Joseph had grown into a monument of stability favoring the bourgeoisie and their banking and industry. Overenthusiastic Viennese, in a mixture of *braggadocio* and thoughtless optimism, had also seen fit to believe their own rumors and convinced others that their city was destined for an economic boom of grandiose proportions. Unscrupulous entrepreneurs spread rumors that Vienna's apartment buildings would triple to accommodate the expanded influx of workers to man the factories which were to be built. The World Exposition was to be visible proof of things to come. The ensuing boom was a colossus with feet of clay. *Die Neue Börsenzeitung (The New Stock Market Journal)* had warned in vain: "If somewhere ... there stands a deserted chimney it immediately becomes an engineering works; where the semiparalized arms of a debilitated windmill are seen to rotate, at once a milling concern is put on the market; someone stumbles on a boat lying on a river bank and proceeds to found an inland Lloyd whose steamships dart hither and yon ... inspiration transforms a carpenter sawing planks into a supply house for building material and invents a chemical concern while watching a boy shoot off a rocket."

Vienna would not listen. Stocks soared as late as March 1873, aided and abetted by the pomp and splendor of the coming exhibition. A passing slump in April was ignored. On 7 May the flight from the "market" began and one hundred firms ceased to exist. Black Friday the Vienna stock market collapsed to the crashing sound of one hundred seventy five bankrupt banks founded with little or no capital and over one thousand stock companies. The resulting disaster spread over most of Europe and prompted suicides on an unprecedented scale as paper fortunes were lost overnight. In Vienna where thousands had lost their life savings, the fury turned against a number of Jewish bankers and speculators. The stock market called for military and police protection. Vienna had invited Europe for a feast that had turned into a funeral. Even superficial investigation would have found that many, if not most of the bankers had been non-Jewish and that thousands of Jewish investors had also lost their unwisely invested savings. The Fahrbachs, father and son, added fuel by composing a couplet called *Krach Polka (Crash Polka)* whose anti-Semitic refrain was lustily joined by those who needed an outlet and scapegoat for their monetary losses.

Strauss, undismayed by the operettic failure of *Fledermaus* and unscathed by the Vienna financial collapse, decided to travel, this time to Italy, for another victory. Everyone, from organ grinders to counts, sang the melodies of Strauss, who, in turn, drank in the Italian musical spirit and melody which he was to store for future auspicious occasions. Just as he later would ameliorate hostility between Austria and Hungary, so Strauss now, through his music, ameliorated the Italian hatred of the Habsburgs and achieved, at least temporarily, a bond of love through music. Wherever he went and concertized he was triumphantly received. Great was his surprise when, upon returning from Italy, he heard about the memorable successes *Fledermaus* was enjoying in Berlin, Hamburg, and Paris.

Paris in 1877 again received Johann with an enthusiasm which bordered on frenzy. This time it was not only music which triumphed but also the Parisian entrepreneurs who had a field day with Strauss ties, Strauss gloves, Strauss hats, Strauss plaster busts, and thousands of pictures and copies of Strauss sheet music. Just as he had been persuaded to conduct twelve concerts of his music at the Berlin Kroll Opera House alone, so now he conducted, together with Olivier Metra, the opera balls in true Parisian splendor. Vigorous opposition and agitation by chauvinist French musicians was soon silenced by Strauss's generous gesture of donating one thousand francs to the Musician's Guild and by his request for membership in the Paris Musical Society. Finally the president of the republic conferred the Legion of Honor upon him as a palpable sign of French esteem.

Despite his Paris triumph, Johann remained totally unaffected by French music. His second love was Italian music. While Italy sang, danced, whistled, and hummed

Johann and Jetti Strauss.

The Sons

Strauss's tunes with its customary animation, Johann plucked some of his most ravishing melodies and waltz pearls from Italian inspiration. *Cagliostro in Wien*, *Das Spitzentuch der Königin (The Queen's Lace Handkerchief)*, *Der Lustige Krieg (The Merry War)*, and *Eine Nacht in Venedig (A Night in Venice)* all owe their creation to the visit to Italy, a marvelously reciprocal experience. Even if some of the works remained no more than seasonal successes, some of the waltzes, *Wo die Zitronen blüh'n (Where the Lemons Bloom)*, *Lagunen Walzer (Lagoon Waltz)*, and *Rosen aus dem Süden (Roses from the South)*, remain imperishable.

Flags lustily waving from Strauss's palatial home in 1878 belied the crumbling of relationships within. Realities had to be faced at long last which no longer could be ignored or wished away. Johann was fifty-three, Jetti sixty-two. While he was a public figure, receiving lures and avowals of love which hardly any man could or would ignore, Jetti had long passed the zenith of her life and been forced to retire into the shadows. She who had accompanied Johann to Russia and London and had partaken of his triumphs was no longer an asset or helpmate, but an albatross. There were few confrontations on the subject because they had too much respect for each other's intelligence to belabor the subject. The cultural discrepancy which had existed fifteen years ago and made Jetti the ideal helpmate had ceased to exist. While Johann had progressed and matured due to continued contact with writers and aristocracy in a multitude of European lands, Jetti had grown into a stout, motherly figure no longer a suitable partner, even in appearance, for the glowing figure of her husband. Slowly they drifted apart, with Jetti mostly confined to the home while Johann spent evenings and nights with friends. Her occasional visits to the Todesco home to visit her children did nothing to ease the creeping terror of advancing years, because the girls, grown to young womanhood, were living reminders of their mother's age. There was a silent terror of another kind which invaded Jetti's nights and days. In the glow of early passion she had never bothered to tell her young husband of another extra-marital issue, a son born at a time when she had not yet reached the plateau of acceptance as Todesco's mistress. Johann, equally enamored, had not bothered to inquire into Jetti's past. But the son, apparently driven by financial difficulties, had decided to break the fifteen-year-old silence and had approached his mother in his quest for money. Jetti, without financial resources of her own, presented the calamitous matter to Johann, who refused outright. The atmosphere became laden with dissent. What had been at one time a tacit drifting apart now became the scene of violent argument. Death ended the dilemma abruptly. One day, during Johann's absence, Jetti received a letter from her shadowy son which this time threatened rather than requested. Under the sudden cloud of looming catastrophe Jetti's heart gave way and she collapsed. Hastily summoned doctors diagnosed a stroke. She lingered, unconscious, broken in body and spirit, until 7 April 1878.

Johann was lost. He needed and craved attention. He sought it, had never been without it, and during the last two decades had had more than his share. Once he had written in a letter to Girardi: "Be good to me and praise me." Jetti had provided a goodly portion of that loving attention and inspiration so badly needed by her brilliant husband. He was shorn of it now. Nightly admiring glances, applause, and adulation helped but could not completely fill the sudden emptiness in his life. Johann hated and feared emptiness and voids just as much as death. The *palais* which Jetti and he had planned in the Igelgasse and which was now reaching completion stood untenanted. He groped for love but did not find it.

A few weeks after Jetti's death Vienna gasped in disbelief when the *Fremdenblatt* reported that Herr Strauss would shortly become engaged to Fräulein Ernestine Henriette Angelika Diettrich of Cologne. From there on opinions vary as to background details. Some maintained that it was love at first sight between Strauss and the charming young singer who had been recommended to the maestro for artistic advice concerning her career. Johann, lost and lonely, had simply fallen in love with the young creature on the spot, and she had become infatuated with the image of the figure of world renown rather than the man himself. Others, more realistic and perhaps better informed, described her, at age twenty, as being not outstandingly pretty, but very charming and exceptionally friendly. The banker Strauss (no relation), for years financial adviser to the entire Strauss family and particularly to Johann, commented: "The situation seems to be dating back some time and seems to have developed already during Jetti's lifetime. The lady is very rich and never was an actress." Ironically this passage was contained in a letter from the banker to his daughter-in-law Adele, destined to play a major role in Johann's life.

Angelika Diettrich, a picture out of Wedekind's world, breathing sensuality from every look, every spoken word, every gesture, was the antithesis of Jetti. Johann was dazzled. Here was the living image of eternal youth so ardenly pursued by Johann in his life and work, in the person of "Lili." The void of death, the stillness of his chamber, the emptiness of his life, all pushed and pulled him towards the young woman with the instinctive cunning of a creature who combined Eve and Jezebel in her slender body and her piquant face framed by Loreley strands of golden hair. A musical common bond could be held up to the world as an excuse of mutual interests, but actually it was not that which drew them together. To his suprise he found that once he had decided, it was only a short, if embarrassing, step from bier to bed. Angelika and Johann were married six weeks after the public announcement.

Angelika "Lili" Diettrich, Johann Strauss's second wife.

This time Vienna was openly exasperated. His sudden marriage to Jetti, admittedly considerably older than he, was excused by the undeniable fact that she was culturally and artistically the perfect match for a man of his talents. In Angelika, a woman some thirty years younger than he, such artistic points of interest could not even be pretended. It was so precipitous, ill-considered, inadvisable a step into what Johann hoped would again be marital bliss as to border on the ridiculous were it not so pitiable in retrospect. Alluding to Johann's notoriously poor selection of operetta librettos, Ada Teetgen aptly remarks: "Fräulein Angelika ... was certainly the most disastrous libretto to which the master could devote his energies." Johann was blind to the pitfalls of his new marital commitment. Angelika—Diabolika, as some came to call her—and her husband moved into the sumptuous house in the Igelgasse. But the disturbing drawbacks of an urban home soon became apparent; the visitors, collaborators, friends, and admirers saw no reason to change their habits of years past. Longing for solitude with his lovely bride, Johann bought a small estate in Schönau, a short railroad ride from Vienna. There, among sweeping terraces and in princely solitude Johann hoped to charm his bride and devote himself to music. In every aspect his hopes turned ashen. The best a Viennese newspaper could present in defense of Johann was a line from his own *Fledermaus*, alluding to his past suffering: *"Glücklich ist wer vergisst, was nicht mehr zu ändern ist"* ("Happy is he who forgets what cannot be changed"). The solitude of Schönau was not the atmosphere a creature of mercurial temperament like Lili craved. Soon she invented the image of the gilded cage, an impression of her husband's marital inadequacy, as an excuse to return in ever-increasing measure to Vienna and her former life and companions, the young artists' colony liberally sprinkled with handsome army officers. Angry confrontations followed and inevitably ended in Johann's hollow-eyed defeat. The weapon which Lili so skillfully used against her husband was one word thrust at him over and again like daggers: "old." What Johann had hopefully expected to be a new rosy spring dawn had turned into a storm-ridden winter night. Then, one day it was all over. The house was empty; Lili had vanished. And again the circumstances of her departure were a slap in Johann's face. None other than Franz Steiner, the son of Johann's friend and director of the *Theater an der Wien*, had made successful advances towards Lili until one day she simply exchanged Johann's estate for Steiner's quarters.

During the last months of Jetti's life and during his second marriage Strauss had attempted to work on several operettas. The first of three, *Blinde Kuh (Blind Man's Bluff)*, was the worst of Johann's defeats. No psychologist's insight is needed to explain the debacle which went far beyond the usual inferior libretto by one Rudolf Kneisel. Meanwhile, with Strauss in temporary hiatus, Suppé scored with

Boccaccio. Strauss's next opus, *Das Spitzentuch der Königin*, achieved only a brief success despite Johann's scintillating music, from which he could only salvage a set of waltzes which were published separately as *Rosen aus dem Süden*. The third operetta of that difficult period was successful only because it was the one work with lilting melodies on the Vienna boards when the catastrophe of the *Ringtheater* fire plunged Vienna into mournful silence. When Johann discovered Franz Steiner's dastardly deed he decided to withhold the next operetta, *Eine Nacht in Venedig*, from the Vienna stage and to give it to Berlin. Despite the still lingering Italian impulse, this one was a disaster also.

But Strauss discovered a way out of the operettic dilemma and his personal *cul-de-sac:* a return to the pure waltz, unincorporated and unadulterated. The result, *Frühlingsstimmen (Voices of Spring)*, is one of Johann's most fascinating compositions, because it is one of his least sensual yet most unusual. The fact that it is a piano waltz and not one for the violin (as one might expect from Strauss) makes it most versatile—it is suitable even for the beginner at his piano recital. It can be played or sung but always remains a creation of elfin grace, a vision of flowing gowns and bare feet whirling through the Vienna Woods. Its non-violinistic history is curious. It first emerged as a coloratura aria which Bianca Bianchi sang at an academy at the *Theater an der Wien*. Public reaction at first hearing was lukewarm: "Overloaded with coloratura, not enough melody." From that starting point the waltz took a well-known course and pattern. Russia took the waltz to heart and Italy relayed it jubilantly back to Vienna. Only upon its return did *Frühlingsstimmen* achieve popularity. Alfred Grünfeld, famous Viennese pianist and Johann's friend, popularized it in his concerts. From then on its acclaim rose to the point where Liszt asked whether he might also play it. It was especially dear to Johann because it was a spirit-lifting return to the clear spring of melodic purity from the murky, wordy waters of operetta.

At that point the controversial subject of instrumentation was raised again. Richard Specht averred that Strauss orchestrated all his music while Ernst Decsey asserts that he maintained a small army of orchestrators and adaptors to finish the work he had started. The first opinion seems more credible because Strauss was of course thoroughly familiar with all orchestral instruments from earliest youth in his father's house. In working out the orchestration (while leaving the copying to an army of copyists) he could neither be budged nor hurried. Manuscripts owned by Brahms and Reger show Strauss's handwriting, which testifies to his careful workmanship and delicacy in instrumentation.

Predictably Franz Steiner tired of his flighty mistress, Angelika Diettrich-Strauss, and discarded her. She then posed as the maligned wife, but nobody gave credence to her fabrications, and she finally died unmourned in 1919. Shortly after the Berlin fiasco of *Eine Nacht in Venedig* Strauss met a charming beauty, the widow of a true friend of the family. There still lived in the *Hirschenhaus* the family of Albert Strauss, who had advised all the Strausses, beginning with the father. Johann had often availed himself of the sound financial advice of the cultured man who could recite Grillparzer, Horace, or Raimund from memory. The banker's son, after three years of happy marriage to lovely Adele Deutsch, died suddenly. Adele all but retired from social life for a number of years. A passing encounter recalled to Johann the charming young woman. Although he had doffed his hat to the vaguely familiar face and had been rewarded by a friendly smile he had had no quick recall until he remembered that Jetti had commented on young Adele's lovely features. Despite the years of widowhood she was still winsome. Johann's interest was aroused. He began to visit his sisters—and their neighbors—in the *Hirschenhaus* more frequently. Soon the two lonely people, the celebrated composer and the quiet beauty, succumbed to their feelings for each other. When they announced their engagement, another *cause célèbre* whetted the Viennese appetite for gossip. First there was strong domestic resistance on both sides because Strauss was a (non-practicing) Catholic and Adele was Jewish. Second, the "affair Lili" was still very much in the news and in Johann's family considered unsolvable because to Johann's sisters divorce did not exist. Lili, in turn, did everything in her power to foil any peaceable solution, posing as the abandoned wife. But Strauss was not to be denied. With an energy seldom exhibited he went about matters with determination regardless of dire consequences which might ensue. First he decided to leave Catholic Vienna and settle in the German city of Coburg, capital of the duke of Sachsen-Coburg-Gotha, a Protestant. There Johann turned Protestant and applied for a divorce from Lili, which was promptly granted. Having accomplished those preliminary steps Johann called Adele to Coburg where they were officially married. Thereupon they returned to his home in the Igelgasse in Vienna.

Adele combined some of Jetti's home-making and administrative abilities with Lili's charm, superimposed on her Jewish beauty which later prompted the painter Lembach to paint her portrait. Johann was now fifty-eight years old, yet his letters to his bride, who made his marriage "the best of all," abound in youthful ardor and the flamboyant extravagance of a man forty years his junior. Yet maturity was evident in many ways. The happiness of his marriage to Adele became the foremost aim of his life. When traveling he dispatched midnight letters to her. That happiness also prompted him to divest himself of encumbering liaisons, suddenly turned unimportant, because to be true to his pearl of a wife became paramount to him. "The poetry of love, be it Catholic, Protestant or Jewish consists of ardent, soulful living

Adele Deutsch, Johann Strauss's third wife.

together ... amicably? ... I cannot imagine it because I am not in that disconsolate state in which I must bid farewell to earthly love. On this point I permit no reproach. Of course I mean you. Because ... I swear to you that to this very minute I have been faithful ... I am astounded myself but it is no miracle because you are close to my heart. Millions of embraces from your Jean."

Adele became the focal point of Johann's life and she in turn filled his life with all that was worthwhile to him. Her lids heavy with sleep she would share his nocturnal inspirations, his theatrical concerns, successes, and failures. She encouraged, supported, loved him, and looked after his needs and finances. "Cosima in three-quarter-time" was their friends' nickname for her (an allusion to the efficient dedication of Richard Wagner's wife). Needless to say Johann dedicated his *Adelenwalzer* to her. Adele, more than any of his previous wives, even more than Jetti, impressed upon Vienna and the world the imperishable image of the "waltz king." As a partner in marriage, in every sense of the word, she matched Jetti's efforts, although she lacked Jetti's knowledge and experience in theatrical matters. But even there her presence was clearly felt by all as she attended to correspondence and financial matters and, occasionally when Johann was under pressure, even decided who was to visit him. With Adele as the lady of the house, Strauss's palatial home saw itself restored to the relaxed splendor of earlier days, and the visitor to a grand soirée at the Strauss home could be sure that Strauss would receive with his beloved Adele by his side. Another happiness equally precious to Johann also returned again, the happiness of his small uninhibited circle of friends. Over *Gumpoldskirchner*, his favorite wine, or champagne, among witty, humorous, relaxed friends he would indulge in Domino, *Tarock*, billiards, *ecarté*, or a friendly game of penny-ante; nobody ever left the Strauss abode having lost or won any great amount of money. It was not unusual for Johann to leave the table unobtrusively when a sudden musical idea demanded immediate attention. However, if the present game was too heated and demanded his presence at the table, a stuffed shirt cuff would have to serve to receive inspiration. With domestic matters returned to happy stability, Johann again indulged in late morning sleep, breakfast in bed, and the study of the morning papers, his only reading matter except for an occasional libretto—and even in the papers it was the theatrical and musical news which had his foremost attention. Noon would find him in the study where he shared a habit with Brahms, working at a stand-up desk. He approached the piano only after the music had been conveyed to paper, then rang for Adele to listen to his new ideas. To the surprise of many first visitors he often used the tread organ *(Harmonium)* which, some felt, was his favorite keyboard instrument. He played it well and felt that its slightly nasal tone gave the music a special charm. Before dinner he liked a walk in his garden; he usually muffled up at the slightest intimation of windy or cloudy weather. Those walks brought him past a closed pavillion piled with dried laurel wreaths, bouquets, and other perishable mementos, then farther down to his stable where he delighted in having his splendid carriage horses paraded before him. He took an almost childish pleasure in his horses and the luxury carriage they drew and spent a small fortune on both. He was especially fond of two spirited black horses which he had brought back from one of his Russian tours and also proudly displayed a present from the publisher Cranz of Hamburg—a parrot who could whistle the *Blue Danube* waltz with unerring virtuosity. Dinner, whether he took it alone or with Adele, in a small circle of friends or with a large group, always remained the highlight of the day. When alone he preferred Viennese specialties, *Beuschl und Knödel* (lungs with dumplings), *Rostbraten und Kartoffelsalat* (well-done roast beef and potato salad), *Zwetchkenröster* (hot stewed plums), and *Kaiserschmarrn*, a favorite desert of Strauss and the emperor. (The Viennese identified all favorite foods of Emperor Franz Joseph by prefacing them with the word *Kaiser* [emperor]. Thus his favorite cut of bacon became *Kaiserfleisch*, his favorite desert *Kaiserschmarrn*, his favorite roll *Kaiser-semmel*, his favorite pear *Kaiserbirne.*)

To the surprise of all, Johann's "desertion" from Vienna and Catholicism, even if only temporary, was not taken amiss by the authorities. Although he had to relinquish his Austrian citizenship temporarily in order to take up residence in Coburg, he did not lose his coveted title and position as *Hofballmusikdirektor.* A bit of surprising bureaucratic sleight-of-hand and sophistry saved the day. The officials announced with a straight face, that, since he was not in the employ of the court, the title was only that and did not constitute a court position or a dereliction of duties and therefore need not be relinquished. Even more surprising, official Vienna also raised no barriers to Johann's theoretical emigration to Saxony or his leaving the (court-approved) Catholic faith to become a Protestant. With Adele near, Johann again energetically set to work. His first stage work after his marriage was also to be among his greatest, *Der Zigeunerbaron (The Gypsy Baron).* It was one of the rare occasions in his operettic career when he heeded the advice of his inspired librettist by fully paying attention to the text. Few later operettas equalled *Zigeunerbaron*, and his vain quest for suitable texts grimly led him astray in two still-born labors of love, *Simplizius* and *Ritter Pazmann.*

In 1888 Emperor Franz Joseph was to receive from his most loyal and devoted subject, on the occasion of forty years of reign, two of Johann's most inspired waltzes, *Kaiser-Jubiläum* and *Kaiser-Walzer (Emperor* waltz). By then Johann had had jubilee troubles of his own. The fifteenth of October 1884 was the fortieth anniversary of the Dommayer premiere, which had made the family of Strauss a musical dynasty. What had been a dance had become an expression of a spirit; the two Johanns, Josef, and Eduard had made the waltz the supreme expression of an age which was drawing to a close. Vienna was not to be deprived of an opportunity to celebrate, congratulate, and dance. Johann's city went all out to honor itself by honoring its native son. As pride, happiness, and exhaustion followed each other in predictable sequence, Johann had to receive, or rather endure, deputations from the city of Vienna, all Viennese theatres, the *Gesellschaft der Musikfreunde*, the *Männergesangsverein*, the German theatres, the Youth of Vienna, and the Vienna writers. He was deluged with innumerable poems, scrolls, laurel wreaths, and dedications as well as telegrams from Millöcker, Suppé, Bismarck, Billroth, Verdi, and Brahms. Nor could he avoid (even if he had wished to) the festival production at the historic *Theater an der Wien* with himself conducting the overture to *Indigo* and the opening bars of *Blaue Donau* before the frenzied joy of a happy city drowned out all efforts at music-making for minutes on end. When a semblance of order was finally restored there followed the second act from *Die Fledermaus* with Prince Orlovsky given the happy task of introducing all famous Strauss operettic figures. The evening culminated in a festival banquet at the Hotel *Lamm* with another inevitable round of dedications, speeches, honors, and medals. All this was followed in September 1885 by a three-day Strauss festival featured at the theatre at the *Friedrich Wilhelmstrasse* in Berlin. There Johann personally conducted the three hundredth performance of *Der Lustige Krieg*, the fiftieth performance of *Eine Nacht in Venedig*, and the four hundredth performance of *Die Fledermaus*.

All these festivities and honors were surpassed ten years later when Vienna celebrated *Fünfzig Jahre Künstlerisches Schaffen* (fifty years of artistic creativity) of the *Walzer-König*. Again the giants of music, Rubinstein, Leoncavallo, Nikisch, Schuch, and Goldmark, vied for the honor of praising Johann. Students of Vienna's famed conservatory, under the direction of Robert Fuchs, serenaded Johann with a concert of his own themes, and concerts were arranged in his honor by the Vienna Philharmonic and the *Gesellschaft der Musikfreunde*. The corps de ballet of the Imperial Opera performed a special ballet to Strauss melodies with the *Blue Danube* theme as its finale. Honors arrived from far-off Hawaii and a silver wreath, which traveled four thousand miles, came as a tribute from American artists. No other artist of his time was so beloved, so renowned, so honored.

One unique and extremely ingenious homage to Strauss was dreamed up by the Vienna newspaper *Neues Wiener Journal*. Its Paris correspondent collected words of praise from French and other artistic luminaries in many fields of artistic endeavor. The composer Ambroise Thomas recalled both Johann Strausses:

Cherubini applauded as if he had been a paid *claqueur* and chided me because I seemed less enthusiastic. But it was my delight with these truly classic waltz performances which silenced me. One night Cherubini was so charmed by Strauss [Father] that in his enthusiasm he threw a bouquet of violets towards his violin. The public took the cue and soon poor Strauss and his orchestra were bombarded with a regular hail of flowers. How much more would we have to bombard his great son with flowers today; Johann Strauss composes flowers.

Zola, while writing a congratulatory note to Johann Strauss, commented:

I have written twenty-two novels but I am at a loss for words as to how to pay homage to master Strauss. I am quite unmusical. My way of life left me little time for music ... Artists like Strauss enjoy the better part of life. We writers only show the world how miserable it is. He shows how beautiful it is and thus helps innumerable people with his music to make life more bearable. If I were to be born again I'd prefer to be an artist like Strauss rather than a writer.

Sardou expressed amazement:

What, already seventy years? I can't believe it. For me there is only an eternally young Strauss ... if there were no prejudices, I would demand that at my funeral a waltz by Strauss be played. With such music I would immediately find entrance into paradise. Nobody could possibly give me a better letter of introduction. You just watch, I'll have them put a Strauss waltz in my coffin so that I won't be bored in the next world.

Verdi happily commiserated with Strauss in his "ordeal":

I feel sorry for my friend Strauss for what is in store for him. His Viennese in their enthusiasm will eat him alive ... I honor him as one of my most congenial colleagues and the best I can wish for him on his jubilee is an iron constitution. Those Viennese are no joke. It is too bad that [Strauss] cannot substitute a double for those tough days which await him ... A double jubilee in Vienna and for Strauss yet ... well, may the Lord have mercy on him. [As a token of his esteem Verdi sent a *Falstaff* excerpt to Strauss.]

Sarah Bernhardt wrote:

I would prefer to be in Vienna during his jubilee, and even if I run the risk of making Frau Strauss jealous I would put my arms around the master and kiss and kiss him without end. This is the only way in which the women can pay homage to him.

October 14 became the most grandiose day in the life and history of the Strausses. An afternoon concert at the *Musikvereinssaal* under Eduard's baton, half music, half flood of adulation, was all but surpassed by an evening devoted to Strauss, first at the *Theater an der Wien* and then at the Imperial Opera.

As viewed through the eyes of the adored, however, it was not all joy. Love and honors can be as nerve-racking and exhausting as any premiere, and Strauss actually had to sneak out back doors, perspiring, pale, and near collapse in the face of such outbursts and offerings of love, otherwise he might have become the victim of adoration gone berserk. Amid the jubilation in which Strauss basked and suffered, he spoke only twice, modestly and deferentially as ever: "The honors bestowed upon me today I owe to my predecessors, my father and Lanner. They indicated the direction in which I was to progress. My achievements are but weak attempts to enlarge the form which I received from my father's hand. I am extremely happy but I feel that I have been distinguished too much by you. You do me too much honor ... it is enough already." And at the final banquet, "Could I express my feelings in music, I could do better because [music] has always come to my aid. If it is true that I have some talent, then I owe its blossoming to my beloved city of Vienna ... to her my toast: May Vienna blossom, grow, and prosper."

As years glided by in fleeting parade, Johann continued to create glowing music to mediocre libretti. In *Jabuka* he hoped to duplicate in a Croatian milieu what Smetana had masterfully accomplished for Bohemia in his *Bartered Bride*, Millöcker for Poland in *The Beggar Student*, and Strauss himself with an inspirational Hungarian libretto in *Zigeunerbaron*. It was not to be. Nor did *Waldmeister* in 1895 live up to the hopes of a comedy of errors so splendidly exploited in *Fledermaus* twenty-one years earlier. Nor did *Die Göttin der Vernunft (The Goddess of Reason)* prove more than a meager seasonal success.

Johann returned again to his first love, the waltz. Vienna was grateful and delighted when there appeared in brief succession such gems as *Kaiserwalzer*, Johann's bow to his emperor, *Adelenwalzer*, his musical embrace of his beloved wife, and *Gross Wien Walzer*, his greeting to his city which by then had expanded into Greater Vienna. *Seid Umschlungen, Millionen (Be Embraced, Ye Millions)* used words by Schiller which had been set to music by Beethoven, but the waltz was dedicated to Johann's friend Brahms who admired Strauss as much as he did Beethoven. *Geschichten aus dem Orient* was dedicated to Sultan Abdul Hamid, and *Töne aus der Raimund-Zeit* paid homage to those famous waltz men who shared the world of Raimund and Nestroy—Lanner, Drechsler, Kreutzer. Just as The Salzburg merchant Haffner would have been forgotten had not Mozart dedicated a symphony and a serenade to him, just as the music-loving nobles of Austria—the Lobkowitzes, Lichnovsky, Fries, and Kinskys—today are only recalled because Beethoven saw fit to dedicate his music to them; so Strauss rescued Abdul Hamid II of Turkey from oblivion.

Strauss did not have to prove himself any longer. Did the towering spire of St. Stefan have to prove its gothic splendor? Did the Belvedere or Schönbrunn have to prove their baroque magnificence? Surely Johann Strauss had entered into the history, the very fiber of all that was splendid and admirable about Vienna and the Viennese. But only seldom did Vienna now have the opportunity to see Johann as Karl Kobalt had seen him:

> The coal black curly hair ... a slight bow from his side, a thunderbolt of applause from ours. Silence. You wink with the bow, a half look shoots to the right, a half look to the left, from the corner of the eyes to the wings of the army which, forty men high, storms into the opus of its Lord and Master, playing it by heart ... and how they storm! Up and over the most dangerous waltz rhythms, over hill and dale, over the strings and over the bridge, irresistible. The point of your bow is always ahead of things. In a moment of elegy, the bow rises and falls in long waving motions, followed by the hand, the arm and finally the entire Johann sways from his hips. There follows a quicker tempo, the bow acquires a secret impulse ... jumps up and down, constantly quickening, the entire man takes up the motions ... You do not beat the tempo any longer, you flog it ... But the high point is yet to come. The true waltz ecstasy has not yet been reached. Suddenly the bow freezes in midair ... the conductor throws his head back, he tears the violin from his hip where he had propped it ... he tucks it under the chin and storms at the head of his brave men into the fortissimo. Now jumps and dances every fiber of this pale, dark man. His bow rages over the strings, his tone yells above the roar of the ensemble ... The front of his dress suit flies open, the tails fly ... truly this is three-quarter time personified in a black suit. A raging applause roars from the farthest corner of the electrified hall and drowns out the final chords. With a quick turn, half bow, half jump from the height, Johann Strauss suddenly disappears from the podium.

He was destined to disappear equally quickly from life. After a jubilee performance of *Die Fledermaus* at which he conducted the overture, a chill overtook him which soon deteriorated into double pneumonia. In his last hour he reached back into Vienna's history and, in a sense, into his own. The last melody to come from his lips was *Brüderlein fein, Brüderlein fein/Sollst mir garnicht böse sein*, Drechsler's melody from Raimund's *Das Mädchen aus der Feenwelt*. Drechsler had taught him how to compose a *gradual* which brought young Johann his license to perform in public. His life had come full turn.

They buried him on 6 June 1899. Wagner and Liszt, who had so delighted in listening to and playing Johann's tunes, had been dead sixteen and thirteen years respectively. Bülow, who had shared honors with him in Boston, had been dead five years, and friends Brahms and Bruckner had passed on two and three years before Johann. The funeral procession, winding as far as the eye could reach, the largest since those honoring Beethoven, Grillparzer, and Strauss Father, wended its way past all the places Johann had touched and illuminated with his charm, his spirit, his music: the home in the Igelgasse, the *Theater an der Wien*, the Imperial Opera, the *Musikvereinssaal:* "A hundred thousand people stood there with bared heads ... It was as if the gardens of Vienna were being carried to the Central Cemetery." Johann Strauss Father had been laid to rest next to his friend Lanner, Johann Son close to Schubert and Brahms.

Johann Strauss and Vienna—Hanslick once called them inseparable, as complementary to each other as *tonic* and *dominant*, two names deeply, eternally intertwined, the name of the artist and the earth that nurtured him. Thus Vienna mourned the loss of part of itself. A way of life, a century had been laid to rest.

Part III

The Spirit

14

Birth of the Spirit

It is significant that in the theatre of all lands, all ages, and all times the mask of comedy appears either side by side or intertwined with the mask of tragedy. Comedy, spoken or musical, indispensably important as an art in itself, became almost subconsciously even more important as an antidote to tragedy, inevitably, indispensably so, because without it life itself might become unbearable.

With the creation and rapid development of opera in Italy in the seventeenth century, there occurred a wedding of sorts as *opera seria* and *opera buffa* appeared side by side: a serious artistic creation, dramatic or even tragic, was followed and counterbalanced by a briefer, gayer creation. Those lighter insertions, sometimes even presented between the scenes of early serious opera, enjoyed more and more popularity as the centuries passed. Inevitably *opéra comique*,[1] in which spoken dialogue was used, became an art form in its own right, finding universal appeal in such works as *Komische Oper* or beggar's opera, *Singspiel*, and operetta. Soon specific theatres and singers became specialized and preeminent in these lighter musical presentations. In time those at first voluntary restrictions in role and repertoire became so strongly defined that poets, writers, and composers were commissioned by and even tied to that specific comic medium and even to specific theatres which featured it prominently. Composers, as well as artists, through such an arrangement, were able to specialize. Just as Shakespeare had before his mind's eye the actors of the Globe Theatre when creating his dramas and comedies, just as Goethe took into consideration the dramatic range of the actors of the Weimar Court Theatre and Schiller those of the Mannheim Theatre, so the *Theater an der Wien* and *Carltheater* in Vienna contributed to and achieved a level of lighthearted artistic creation and presentation eventually unmatched anywhere in its field. This came about by linking to their respective stages the genius and talent of such great

1. *Opéra comique* is not to be confused with comic opera. For the difference, see Percy A. Scholes, *The Oxford Companion to Music*, 9th ed., p. 725.

Austrian poets as Raimund, Nestroy, and Anzengruber and such inspired actors, singers, soubrettes, and comedians as Gallmeyer, Geistinger, Girardi, Blasel, and Schweighofer. This became, of course, a two-edged sword as those artists began to exact a certain price from the theatres for their availability, particularly since such binding contracts also tended to curb an actor's or actress's artistic growth. Just as the castrati of the sixteenth and seventeenth centuries had demanded of every opera composer music suitable to their peculiar talents, so these specialized artists of the Vienna comic musical stage demanded material which would present their vocal and comic talents to the best possible advantage. It was rumored that Alexander Girardi, the greatest of the Vienna comedian-singers, insisted upon a special song or couplet for nearly every new operetta in which he was to appear.

Viennese operetta! The words exude a lighthearted glow; yet until the commercialization of the form in the twentieth century, it eluded the historian because its charm, beauty, and gaiety, its beckoning and dreaming, its unsophisticated lightheartedness defied definition. The Viennese operetta, stemming from the burgher culture of Emperor Franz I, was more an outburst than a development. Among signs of depression, defeat, and decay on the one hand and among the fully enjoyed but jealously eyed French creations in the lighthearted field on the other, the demand for such an insouciant musical creation in Vienna became irrepressible. The spirit of Vienna demanded it, the lack of free speech and assembly spawned it as an outlet within a regime which silenced all stirrings of freedom, depended heavily on aristocracy and clergy, stifled the middle class, ignored the peasant, and persecuted the laborer.

The beginning efforts showed no signs of promise. Between the time of the Congress of Vienna and the Revolution of 1848 a type of culture reigned that was peculiar to Vienna and bore the symbolically satiric name of *Biedermeier*. Just as the German Meistersinger, a man of the people, wishing to emulate and revive the art of the inspired medieval Minnesinger, brought about a lowering of the poetic horizon, so the emphasis of Biedermeier expresses the lowered ideal of the Viennese burgher, his enjoyment of magic plays, coarse stage jokes, vulgar dialect dialogue, interspersed with *Possen* (farces) and commonplace couplets. It was to take a foreign impetus to make Vienna create an art form in the lighter vein.

Many events influenced the development of the Viennese operetta, including the technical revolution and the changes it brought about. The exhibit, in 1722 in the palace garden of Prince Schwarzenberg, of the *Feuermaschine*, an early type of steam engine to activate the prince's famous fountains, in itself ushered in the industrial age in Vienna. A new social stratum arose, altering, in the process, the social, political, and artistic status quo. The newly created feverish industrial and commercial activity, one aided by the other, was not totally a step towards advancement. It brought in its wake new, dubious, exploitive forces which brought about the disastrous financial disaster of 1873 and the rise of the working class, a fifth force within the realm. The working class, although suppressed in its early beginnings, was to make itself heard in all fields of endeavor with an increasingly louder voice, particularly since the burgher class was lamed into inactivity by the crash, the clergy were petrified in medieval images, and the staid aristocracy was more concerned with conservation of its privileges than with progress and development.

Yet, despite all those signs of negativism, reaching from the emperor down into all strata and phases of life, Vienna continued to grow explosively. While London and Paris between 1860 and 1880 grew approximately sixty percent in population, Vienna grew 250 percent. This city which had counted 350,000 souls in 1840 boasted nearly two million inhabitants in 1910. Surprisingly, of the roughly 1,700,000 citizens at the turn of the century, less than half were actually Vienna-born. Of the rest about fifteen percent had streamed in from the Austrian provinces, the others from all corners of the Austro-Hungarian empire. Some came to escape the feudalism of the empire, some to find better work, a better life for themselves and their families within the walls of the metropolis, some simply to turn a fast gulden. On nearly all of them Vienna exerted its incredible powers of assimilation. Thus, a surprising ninety-three percent of all inhabitants of Vienna spoke German. What was not surprising was that eighty-seven percent were professed Catholics, nine percent Jews, and three percent Protestants. Such an incredible influx necessitated expansion and increased building activity. Until the 1848 upheaval the overflow went into a circle of charming villages whose quiet greenery proved a delightful relief from the gray sea of cramped buildings in the medieval city. Finally Vienna's walls were razed as were the outer fortifications of the *Linienwall*. The added land was incorporated into the city and *Gross-Wien* thus gained two vital traffic arteries, the magnificent Ring boulevard and the outer *Gürtel* (belt). Yet even then dying Biedermeier's often tasteless ideas wrought their spell from which not even the emperor's pearl, the Ring, would be spared. A barely compatible mixture of neo-Gothic, neo-Grecian, Renaissance, and Baroque eventually emerged. Such lack of taste was beginning to be marked throughout the city as the well-to-do burgher began to ape the aristocrat with cheap busts, fake columns, and a bogus style, *Alt Deutsch* (Old German), an unsuccessful attempt at recreating something that never was. To all this was added a stream of people from the provinces and the empire states pouring into Vienna, while the Viennese, on foot, by railroad, or by horsedrawn carriage, sought respite in those outlying villages, Nussdorf, Heiligenstadt, and the Vienna Woods, with the inns of Grinzing and Sievering presenting an especially attractive lure.

The Spirit

All those influences—a lack of style, a conglomeration of immigrants, the flight of the Viennese into the suburbs—brought about a dearth of art which was particularly noticeable in the theatre. It was neither surprising nor new. Already Mozart's father had complained to his son about Vienna's poor theatrical taste. Slowly, however, through such giants as Haydn, Mozart, Schubert, and, in lighter musical fields, Offenbach, Suppé, and Strauss, the picture unfolded until the lowly German *Singspiel* and Vienna's coarse gaudy plays with music were elevated into the Viennese operetta which, at its very peak, was only a step removed from the world's great comic operas.

15

French Soufflé

The groundwork for operetta in Vienna had, of course, been laid by the German *Singspiel*, a rather crude form of comedy interspersed with musical interludes, solos, duets, and serenades, generally relegated to the sphere of less demanding suburban theatres. However, the impetus and inspiration for its unsurpassed blossoming did not come from German sources but from France, to be exact from Jacques Offenbach, the king of Paris operetta. Exported to Vienna, it enjoyed tremendous popularity. Suppé, although far from Viennese, took up the challenge for Vienna, and Strauss reached its triumphant pinnacle.

Except for its most glorious moments the Vienna operetta was a mixture of contradictions. One of its worst features, particularly in the hands of uninspired practitioners, was the insistence on local color. Such allusions to prevailing local situations or conditions were short-range reaches for knowing nods, and appreciative guffaws. The practice might provoke an extra round of applause, insuring a run throughout one winter season, but it also robbed the work of any lasting literary value. Worst of all, it often rendered impossible the transportation of the operetta to another locale where the jokes would certainly be lost. To avoid such a dilemma Vienna's literary hacks went to the other extreme and wrote intentionally bland texts in the hope of making them more saleable on the increasingly lucrative international market. This deliberate lack of color greatly contributed to an annoying sameness of what, in its inspired moments, was one of the world's most delightful art forms in the lighter vein.

There was, however, one more reason, perhaps the main reason, for the colorless libretti. That was the fact that the books were usually handled by hacks instead of writers or poets or men of the theatre. Offenbach, who could count on two experienced writers of the theatre, was more blessed in that respect than Johann Strauss, who only twice in his brilliant career had intelligent books to work with—*Die Fledermaus* and *Der Zigeunerbaron*. Suppé and Millöcker actually could boast only one world success each, *Boccacio* and *Der Bettelstudent* respectively. Thus, despite innumerable seasonal successes, the Vienna operetta of the nineteenth century could take full pride in only four masterpieces and even those, under close scrutiny, would be reduced to the two by Strauss which stand out among the four. It was left to another wave of twentieth-century operetta composers—Lehar, Kalman, Oscar Straus—to revive the art form. Generally speaking, the revival lasted until the advent of World War I. Soon thereafter the product became shabby through commercialization. It carried within itself the seeds of destruction which was hastened when, almost overnight, the saxophone supplanted the violin, and syncopation the three-quarter time.

Austria's trade with France had been strong in many fields, with a spirited exchange in both directions. But during the second half of the nineteenth century the most prominent Parisian export to Vienna went under the name of Jacques Offenbach. His father, Isaak Juda Eberst, cantor of the synagogue in Offenbach am Main, took the name of the city as his family name. Fourteen years later, in 1819, the family removed to Cologne. Cologne was a joyful place for the precentor and his ten children, of whom Jacob proved to be the most talented musically, particularly on the cello. Having freely imbibed of the joyful song-happy atmosphere of Cologne, little Jacob, at age fourteen, was sent to the famous Paris Conservatory for further study in cello and composition.

Paris was then mesmerized by the waltz. Johann Strauss Father was the social and musical lion and concertized in Paris for a full sixteen weeks. Offenbach could not escape the Viennese waltz fever. He, too, hesitantly tried his hand at a waltz which was heard for the first time in 1847. Despite his adopted French first name of Jacques, Offenbach had neither the enthusiasm nor the inclination to become involved in the revolution which disposed of Louis Philippe and eventually established the Second Republic. In 1848 he was back in Cologne where he bided his time by trying his hand at brief and insignificant *Singspiele*. In 1850 when the French situation was again calm, he returned to Paris as *Kapellmeister* at the *Théatre Français*, his first meaningful contact with the theatre. Soon the small-featured, lean man with the protruding Adam's apple, huge sideburns, and lively blue eyes behind a pince-nez on a black silk ribbon became a well known sight in Paris. His position left him sufficient time to compose. His aim was grand opera à la Meyerbeer, another German then at the pinnacle of operatic success in Paris with his works *Robert le Diable*, *Les Huguenots*, and *Le Prophète*. But Paris was a nearly impenetrable jungle, as the young Mozart had discovered nearly a hundred years earlier, and Offenbach's operatic attempts led nowhere. Seeing himself stymied in grand opera he decided to pursue little opera—*operette*—and two years later his first French production, *Le Mariage aux Lanternes*, brought him initial, modest acclaim. But Offenbach had full opportunity to learn in his capacity as theatrical conductor. A more experienced man on the Paris scene, Hervé (Florimond Ronger, 1825-1891), showed the way in frivolous operettic exercise. One of his ruses, roundly applauded by the Paris public, was to circumvent the censor's dictum allowing only two people on stage at the same time, by having dead people partake in his plays. Offenbach adjusted to Paris at a furious pace, and his next work, in a more parodistic vein, *Two Blind Men*, was a surprising success. Now there was no holding back. First he wrung from the censor permission to have three live actors on stage. Next he assembled a theatrical group for his own independent productions of operetta, and in the course of so doing discovered his future star Hortense Schneider as well as the perfectly matched librettists Halévy and Meilhac. Then he began a competition for operettic composers in which such future illustrious names as Bizet and Lecocq were prize winners. Soon he had to move to a larger theatre which could hold his swelling audiences. And, as a final triumph over initial adversity, he wrung from the censors concessions which allowed him as many as five people on stage, and eventually entire choruses.

In Vienna, operetta began crudely on the large plateau of burgherdom taste and *Vorstadt* (suburban) theatres because established theatres considered the genre beneath consideration. Thus the *Vorstadt* theatres had to make their own way under trying circumstances. While the imperial theatres, for example, could dip into imperial coffers to cover the deficits and failures of their artistic undertakings, the suburban theatres were dependent on private support only, and the supporters looked to their theatres primarily for escapist entertainment. To keep that patronage and thus survive, the repertoire had to be brought down to a low common denominator. Thus *Kasperl* and *Hanswurst*, the eternal comic figures of the German theatre, were alive and well in the suburbs but lived a life completely separate from the literary or musical efforts of the legitimate theatres. It was to take decades before a rapprochement between the legitimate theatre and the suburban theatre could be achieved, before operetta found a home in the *Theater an der Wien*.[1]

1. The *Theater an der Wien*, built in 1801 by peripatetic genius Emanuel Schikaneder, surely ranks among the foremost theatres in the world. There Mozart's *Zauberflöte* (libretto by Schikaneder) had its premiere as did Schubert's *Rosamunde*. There Beethoven personally conducted the premieres of *Fidelio* and his Fifth and Sixth symphonies. There his Violin Concerto and G-major Piano Concerto saw the light of the world. There Strauss, and Lehár after him, registered their greatest triumphs. After having condemned the building in 1955, the Vienna city administration fortunately experienced a change of heart. Instead the theatre was restored to its original splendor. It reopened with a gala performance on 28 May 1962. Appropriately the music of Mozart, Beethoven, and Schubert provided the program.

Vienna first heard Offenbach in 1856 when a troupe from the Parisian *Palais Royal* appeared in a number of guest performances. The work performed was his already well known *Two Blind Men*. Vienna promptly took to the insouciant parody and saucy music. Soon Offenbach's work appeared in German translation at the *Carltheater* under the direction of equally famous Nestroy, and audiences began to flock there. The *Theater an der Wien* attempted to follow suit only to find itself stymied by politics and a lack of voices, particularly the inevitable soubrette. For seven years the search went, until there appeared on the scene Marie Geistinger, a brilliant soubrette as well as a woman with a talent for the artistic and managerial facets of the theatre. She first appeared in a German version of Offenbach's *Beautiful Helena*, which overnight made her a star and Offenbach the uncontested rage of Vienna. Her performances were reinforced by Karl Treumann, then First Comic at the *Theater an der Wien*. When another comic talent, Karl Mathias Rott, joined the ensemble the competition became so vicious that Treumann decided to move to the rival *Carltheater*, which he also eventually managed after Nestroy's departure.

Treumann's acting career at the *Carltheater* started out with a surefire attraction. He had secretly sent to Paris for the text and score of *Die Hochzeit unter der Laterne*, the lightweight Offenbach opus, tailored to Viennese tastes; Vienna liked it. The *Theaterzeitung* reported: "Of the three pieces which Nestroy produced, the first one, *Die Hochzeit unter der Laterne*, is beyond any doubt the best ... the music makes up for the paucity of action. The music is by Offenbach whose work has been well received for years in the fashionable world. The music is light and graceful, avoiding all deep thoughts and tone painting but with lovely singable melodies ... we must praise the production which was of one piece ... the house was filled to capacity."

Offenbach protested against the unauthorized version and performance, which also had a new orchestration since only a piano score had been smuggled out of Paris. But he had no legal base for his argument and wisely avoided costly court action. The jubilant *Carltheater*, having beaten the *Theater an der Wien* to the draw, gave four more Offenbach creations in succession and also started the following season, 1859-1860, with Offenbach's *The Savoyards* and *The Husband at the Door*. Again the press loved it and commented on "that fresh and gay production ... the music, amusing, light and lively ... translation and change of locale well done."

On 17 March 1860 the hit of the season appeared in Vienna. The "musical-parodistic burlesque," *Orpheus in der Unterwelt (Orpheus in Hades)*, finally brought to the Austrian capital Offenbach's masterpiece of operettic art. The satire on Napoleon and France fell on understanding ears. What titillated the Viennese most was the reaction of aristocrats and censors alike. Sitting in their theatre boxes, watching the play amid the laughter of other patrons, but unsure of what they actually were witnessing, they could not decide whether to condemn or condone. Some decided to assure themselves and each other that this was a marvelous work of art, despite obvious sarcasm, satire, cynicism, vulgarity, and double-entendre, because nobody could decide where the line between straight theatre and vicious satire, between straightfaced allusion and immorality, lay. Nobody wished to risk voicing an opinion for fear of being laughed out of the theatre. Critics were surprisingly cool to the work. Some felt that the play was uneven, too highbrow for those who were unfamiliar with mythology and thus would miss the satiric thrust, and too vulgar and common for those who knew their mythology. The music also, the press contended, did not approach Offenbach's usual standards of invention, particularly since parody and satire were concentrated in the spoken word and not echoed in the music. Others complained that when Offenbach overstepped the limits of propriety he became caustic rather than cynical. As it turned out, nobody liked *Orpheus* but the public, which made it one of the most popular presentations in the *Carltheater* repertoire. The next offering, *Tschin-Tschin*, did not nearly match *Orpheus* in popularity, particularly since it had to compete with a Delibes opus in the *Theater an der Wien*. *Tschin-Tschin* was favored by public and press over its rival, which was hampered by a particularly platitudinous German translation.

Another theatre was then vying for recognition in the realm of operetta production, the *Kai-Theater* (Quay Theatre), so named because it was located near a Danube wharf. The press commented on the fine distinctions of the Viennese theatrical world: "While the old *Leopoldstädter Theater* was to be considered a true *Volkstheater* (people's theatre) the present *Kai-Theater* is more of a 'population' theatre where on any evening one can find high aristocracy, the financial *haute volée*, the bourgeoisie and even the lower population strata en masse. The *demimonde* which naturally must also be counted among the populace, is always represented in large numbers, in the audience as well as on stage."

In such a theatre and atmosphere Offenbach made his first personal appearance as a conductor in January 1861. His *Marriage under the Lantern* and *Magic Violin* immediately earned rave notices, flowers, poems, and laurel wreaths as "no Mozart or Beethoven before him." Theatrical reporters fell over themselves in praising the French master's accomplishments. "The importance of Offenbach's operetta is immediately obvious."—"The only *Singspiele* whose fine elements appeal to cultured senses."—"There can be no doubt that Offenbach's *Singspiele* belong among the outstanding innovations in the dramatic-musical field. His wealth of invention, graceful form and strict observance of style stand head and shoulders above the comic operas of most French composers."

What capped Offenbach's early triumphs in Vienna was the return of Nestroy to the city for a lengthy stay. No theatre could hold the thousands who thronged to see Vienna's idolized actor-poet in his old triumphs as well as in Offenbach's newest, *Daphnis and Chloe*. The 1860-1861 season ended with an acclaimed performance of "Offenbach's newest and most successful work," *Master Fortunio and His Love Song* which played nightly to packed houses. Just as Rossini had held the Viennese in his thrall in Beethoven's time, so Offenbach affected the Viennese now. They simply could not hear enough of his satire set to music. Offenbach reciprocated by bestowing a special honor on Vienna in 1861. He brought the star ensemble of his *Bouffes Parisiens* who performed under his personal direction. From then on, whether in French original or in translation, adjustment or ensemble, Offenbach's creations dominated the Viennese scene. Even the staid musk of Habsburg ceremonial could not keep the French perfume out—Offenbach presented a command performance before the imperial court. So delighted was the composer with his acceptance that he treated Vienna to another rare spectacle, a cello concert with his favorite cellist—Offenbach—as soloist.

On 9 June 1863 the *Kai-Theater* burned to the ground. It had been the first true operetta theatre in Vienna. From November 1860 to June 1863 nearly nine hundred performances had been given. Among them were no less than seventy-three French operettas. Eight hundred evenings had been reserved for the German repertoire with six hundred eighty evenings reserved for operetta. A total of twenty-five premieres were presented at the *Kai-Theater*, a formidable record anywhere.

Treumann, who had been active at the *Kai-Theater*, after its demolition moved into the then empty *Carltheater*, where he opened with Suppé's *Flotte Bursche (Gay Blades)*. After the Suppé opus, however, Treumann returned to the surefire Offenbach offerings. This did not keep shrewd and fickle Offenbach from deserting the *Carltheater* and Treumann for a more lucratively promising future with the *Theater an der Wien*. Despite all of Treumann's remonstrations, Offenbach concluded a three-year contract (1864-1867) with the larger theatre on condition that three each of his one-acters and three-acters be produced there each year. Thus it came about that *Beautiful Helena*, after its fabulous Paris success in December 1864, appeared at the *Theater an der Wien* as the first multi-act Offenbach production. It was destined to have an equal *éclat* in Vienna, thanks to Marie Geistinger, the most sparkling soubrette on German soil at the time. The opening of *Helena* on 17 March 1865, was the true beginning of operetta in Vienna, and the *Theater an der Wien* was its true home. The censor, as a matter of course, objected to several passages as "offensive to morality and decency" but, since the satire on Napoleon and his time was presented in the guise of Greek mythology, the blue-pencilers were nearly helpless amid roaring laughter sparked by allusions to the low-born manners of the high-born. Despite the four-hour-long performance which visibly tired the illustrious first-night audience, *Die Schöne Helena* was considered "considerably above *Tschin Tschin* but a cut below *Orpheus.*" From then on, until the advent of the Strauss era, Offenbach never disappeared from the boards of the *Theater an der Wien.* Soon there were to be no more one-acters as had been offered by the *Carltheater* but splendid, multi-act creations such as *Bluebeard* (1866), *The Grand Duchess of Gerolstein* (1867), *La Vie Parisienne* (1867), and the *Princess of Trapezunt* (1871).

Offenbach, in both Paris and Vienna, had reached the pinnacle of success. Vienna producers traveled to Paris, watched the local performances, then bought and adapted works for Vienna performances. Those, in turn, came to be regarded as the truest Offenbach productions anywhere in the German-speaking world, with Marie Geistinger, charming, glowing, fiery, coquettish, registering her own personal triumphs as Hortense Schneider did in her Paris appearances. Offenbach could do no wrong, although the press noticed that in *Bluebeard* "his music not only borrowed from his own but also 'requisitioned' in great measure from the compositions of one and all ... the master knows so shrewdly how to 'annex' and melts down so finely the pillaged raw material, that one cannot be angry with him but joins in with the jumping sounds."

Yet *Bluebeard* was far surpassed by Offenbach's third great triumph in Vienna, *The Grand Duchess of Gerolstein.* That satire and parody of the military and their blundering mentality, despite coarseness and martial airs, promptly took hold. The people appreciated the indictments that often made Offenbach's sparkling tunes take a back seat to the rapier edge of the spoken satire. And, while Geistinger again excelled, it was *Bumbum*, the classic military clown of limited mental horizon who carried the evening. Meanwhile a new soubrette had appeared on the Vienna scene. Josephine Gallmeyer, together with Marie Geistinger and Alexander Girardi, was destined to elevate Vienna operetta to a height never attained before or after.

The inevitable decline of Offenbach in Vienna began in 1872, after he had reigned supreme for nearly a decade. For a short while other Frenchmen, Hervé and Alexandre Charles Lecocq (1832-1918), attempted to fill the void created by Offenbach's popular demise. Offenbach of course continued to have his latest works presented in the Vienna theatres. But the spark had left them. There appeared a constant borrowing from previously acclaimed works, and only when he personally led the orchestra and ensemble could the public be observed to show enthusiasm. It was then that Charles Lecocq temporarily stepped into Offenbach's shoes. Despite repeated premieres between 1873 and 1882, only one of his operettas, *Mamselle Angot*, created anything resembling a stir in the general apathy which lately had greeted

The Spirit

French operetta. *The Bells of Corneville* by Robert Planquette (1848-1903) also had somewhat of a public success. But other works did not fare as well, even those by the splendid composer Leo Delibes, whose seventeen operettas were appreciated and even produced by Offenbach. (Today Delibes is remembered mainly for his opera *Lakme* and his charming ballets *Coppelia* and *Sylvia*.) After 1882 even Offenbach's works were unfortunately relegated to the Viennese suburban theatres.

16

Vienna Bonbons

As successful as Suppé and Millöcker may have considered themselves, there can be no question that Offenbach and his artistic product successfully resisted their attempts to wrest the operetta laurels from his grasp. It would take the entrance of a genius, Johann Strauss, to surpass Offenbach in his own field and to establish a genre which, at its best, was to surpass its French counterpart. Thus history records that, while Suppé and Millöcker opened the door to Viennese operetta and Strauss, their own greatest successes did not occur until Strauss had already successfully entered the field of operetta and had thus inspired what was to be known henceforth as Viennese operetta. The most interesting fact, again in historic retrospect, remains that unlike all others—Offenbach, Hervé, Lecocq, Suppé, and Millöcker—Strauss was not a man of the theatre. His artistic homes were the dance hall and the ballroom, which he was reluctant to leave for the unknown and vastly more involved music of the stage. A ruse brought him to that new level of musical endeavor he was to instill with new glory. When Strauss finally did venture into the operetta field, his great friend, the critic Hanslick, reminded him "to stick to his last" and continue to write waltzes. Vienna perversely listened to Hanslick rather than Strauss. Thus the greatest operetta ever written was shunted aside in shameful manner. Yet when Strauss ventured into serious opera, he was reminded that "operetta was his field." Appreciation from the Viennese often had to be achieved by either overwhelming them, as with *Indigo*, or by wringing it from their reluctant minds, as with *Fledermaus*. Strauss received hardly any advance encouragement, except from Jetti and Steiner. Always the Viennese could be counted on to be ready with vague disparagement or adverse criticism, like a mother constantly reprimanding her favorite child to bring him to or keep him near perfection. Eventually, paradoxically, it was left to Paris and Berlin to accept or reject this totally Viennese product, an open, honest stand which Vienna did not always take.

In defense of the Viennese and the Viennese critics it should be said that the Viennese operetta was not nearly as artistically definable as its satiric Parisian counterpart. It often limped along on an uneven string of trite dialogue, poor jokes, paper figures, and absurd plot, all hopefully held together by sparkling music.

In opera and operetta, comic or serious, music serves to complement the poetic and human and particularly the dramatic turns of the story, heightening or easing tension as the situation may demand. Strauss accomplished this with talent, as his music skipped lightly from frolic to farce to frivolity. Yet his music, more often than not, was condemned to be no more than a foil rather than a complement to the action. Only rarely was he permitted to detach himself from the shallow, the accidental, and the fortuitous and express in his music lasting values beyond situation comedy. Thus Strauss had been correct in expressing fear of the operetta and his desire to stay with the wordless waltz. Only a genius in his own right such as the librettist Schnitzer understood Strauss's reluctance to fit his music to words. He insisted that Strauss compose the music *before* the libretto was written. Like Beethoven, who needed to express symphonically in four overtures what he could impart only with great difficulty in the text of *Fidelio*, Strauss attempted to compensate for trite texts with overtures, dances, waltzes, gallops, and polkas which were the very lifeblood of his being.

Hanslick clearly noted that peculiar shortcoming when he, with unfailing instinct, pointed to the ballet of Strauss's opera *Ritter Pazmann* as the highlight of the work whose lame drama was otherwise totally alien to the waltz composer. While Offenbach trod a clearly marked musical path, Strauss vacillated. Nobody understood or bothered to point out, except perhaps Hanslick, that in opera the course of action lies in the text with only the dramatic highlights given over to the aria to intensify and heighten. In operettas musical interludes hardly ever contribute to the advancement of action; at their worst they are unrelated, even interchangeable. The musical interlude in comic opera (as in the American musical) evolves directly from the action, thus making it an integral part of the artistic fabric. Viennese operetta, on the other hand, waits for a cue to insert a song or dance in its nearly unvarying plot, much to the detriment of action and fluidity. (There are of course rare exceptions such as *"Ja, so singt man in der Stadt wo ich geboren bin"* in *Indigo*, or the insouciant *Natur-Walzer* in *The Merry War* which nightly brought audiences to their feet with shouts of joy.) Thus only few Strauss operettas would be remembered today were it not for their waltzes and wordless overtures. When Strauss was dancing in his operettas, all was well. His personal philosophy, *"Das Leben ein Tanz"* ("life is a ball"), made *Fledermaus* and *Zigeunerbaron* the immortal worldwide successes which even the Italians acknowledged by titling *Fledermaus "L'Orgia."* And the Viennese? They hardly cared about trite plots of intrigue, revenge, and mistaken identities. Johann Strauss's music was what they wanted.

Johann, who had the gift and inspiration to rise above abominable triteness, was one of the worst offenders in its use. Regardless of the public clamor for his music, he could have accomplished his avowed aim to raise the Viennese operetta to the higher plane of comic opera. Yet he made himself, through laissez-faire selection, a prisoner of hacks, formulas, and the public. Thus music did not heighten or enliven; instead, when dialogue threatened to become unbearable it became Strauss's mission to rescue the impasse liltingly. Public distaste allayed, the action would limp to the next rescue with Strauss making the best of a bad thing. Thus, through acceptance of inferior libretti he actually made himself a co-offender in a vicious cycle.

Unfortunately, few later operetta composers could even match Strauss's musical wit and genius. Subsequently the entire vehicle descended from genial charm into commercialism, to be exploited by an escapist Vienna and its melody-hungry public with a nearly total disregard for artistic values, style, and coherence. It was left to the American musical theatre to reach out for a new artistically high level of continuity: specific situations and actions *demanded* suitable music, which thus became an integral part of the work.

Franz von Suppé, "The Father of Viennese operetta."

17

The "Viennese" from Dalmatia

Vienna, in an anti-French mood after the 1870-1871 Franco-German war, and always secretly jealous of French successes in the "City of Music," now openly turned away from the French and to a musical figure closer to home, Franz von Suppé—to be exact, Francesco Ezechiele Ermenegildo Cavaliere Suppé-Demelli, born in Spalato on the Dalmatian coast in 1819.

Suppé knew the theatre thoroughly from the foremost vantage point, the conductor's desk. He had occupied that position for a number of years at the *Kai* and *Carl* theatres. Encouraged by what he saw and heard night after night, he decided to apply his acquired knowledge by writing music for *Possen* (farces) and incidental music for plays. It is an unkind turn of history that, despite later great seasonal successes, one of his earliest compositions, the overture to *Dichter und Bauer* (*Poet and Peasant*, 1846), should constitute his only lasting claim to salon orchestra fame. Suppé tried his skill at operettic music for the first time in a modest opus, *Das Pensionat* (*The Boarding School*) in 1860. His next attempt, *Die Kartenschlägerin* (*The Fortune Teller*), unfortunately was based on an even sillier book than most Offenbach libretti. The Vienna Press reported:

> Since it also lacked Offenbach's headlong madness and biting piquancy it turned into a mild fiasco ... and the music does not contribute anything to make it more palatable ... Herr Suppé must first learn that one must remain within the realm of pure operetta, a rule strictly observed by Offenbach ... Herr Suppé certainly should be born to the type as few others; talent and ability are present [yet] the operetta does not present a single number which is worth mentioning ... The performance was far from faultless ... and the music thankless. Despite honest labor it was love's labor lost.

Why should Suppé become the chosen one to save operetta from French captivity? The nephew of Italian composer Gaetano Donizetti, he was a martial-looking man with a huge moustache and beard who was often mistaken for a Russian general. Most un-Viennese in appearance, to the end of his days he never mastered the German language. Indeed, he was an unlikely candidate to succeed in the field of French or Viennese operetta. But all such drawbacks and initial failures left Suppé undaunted. Armed with his theatrical knowledge, he learned his lesson quickly and well. *Zehn Mädchen und kein Mann (Ten Girls and No Man)* in 1862 became a sensational success at the *Theater an der Wien* with splendid production, colossal nonsense, and pleasingly mediocre music. The same general conditions held true for *Flotte Bursche (Gay Blades)*, his next opus in 1863 which established the tradition of student romanticism (in Heidelberg, of course). As was to be observed innumerable times before and after, a weak book was held together by a string of uninspired but pleasing melodies. Thus, after Offenbach had ignited the spark in Vienna, Suppé set out on the road to operettic success. While Strauss still wallowed in waltzes, Suppé composed *Das Pensionat* sixteen years before Strauss's *Indigo*. When Strauss finally did emerge on the operettic scene, Suppé could point to thirty years of artistic activity.

If Offenbach was ensconced at the *Theater an der Wien*, Suppé now reigned at the *Carltheater*, where until 1872 no less than twelve of his operettas were performed, among them *Die Schöne Galathee (The Beautiful Galathea*, 1865), *Leichte Kavallerie (Light Cavalry)*, and *Banditenstreiche (Bandits' Capers)*. Despite his Italo-Dalmatian background and accent, Suppé came to be considered *Wienerisch*, Viennese. He promptly exploited his newly won local acceptance by creating *Franz Schubert*, a pastiche, the first of many to follow, a paste job of the delightful melodies of the great master for cheap operettic and monetary exploitation. But the knowing Vienna public did not accept all of Suppé without voicing its opinion pro and con. While the *Beautiful Galathea* had been granted its share of tunefulness despite "Wagnerian leanings in the overture," the cheap Schubert exploitation had to bear the full brunt of critical fury in newspaper reviews on 10 September 1864:

> It is a mistake to exploit the music under the guise of honoring a great master ... by showing him with a glass of beer and giving him pathos-filled speeches which would have never occurred to him ... or showing him, with pen and ink and notepaper, of course at the exact moment of creation ... It is a mistake to assume that a few anecdotes, with the help of famous melodies can be stretched into an original text ... thus the meager content of the *Müllerin Lieder* runs into farcical nonsense, coarse jokes about spinsters, a customary rowdy thrashing scene and a drunkard scene in which the hero plays a most deplorable role ... in the music also Herr Suppé commits a ... sin ... and in his orchestration he proves his talents as well as his shortcomings. Thus the rustling of the wind in dry

leaves [is] overlaid by an unnecessary trombone ... or he surprises us, in the midst of a Schubert melody, with a cymbal crash which Schubert apparently had forgotten to mark.

Unheeding, Suppé surged on, and in January 1876 he was to witness a first world success, *Fatinitza*, at the *Carltheater* which, within one year, ran up one hundred twenty five performances. Even Berlin had to admit that the music was "pleasant, fresh, and gay, bubbling with humor and with an originality which counts it among the best of its genre." If *Fatinitza* was a success (the libretto had been offered to Strauss first but had been rejected by him), *Boccaccio* (1879), the operetta to follow, was to overshadow it by far. Its timing, during a hiatus in the creations of Strauss, made its sucess even more complete. Those successes were aided by the shrewd pair of experienced librettists Zell and Genée. But the trio of Suppé, Zell, and Genee could not maintain such a level of success, and even the musically inventive Suppé could not avert or halt a decisive downward trend. *The Gascogne*, produced by the *Carltheater* in March 1881, folded after seventeen performances, and *Das Herzblättchen (The Sweetheart)*, which premiered at the *Carltheater* in February 1882, was a total loss which lasted only four performances.

Suppé refused to be responsible for these failures. Instead he blamed the fiascos on production and left the *Carltheater* to return to the *Theater an der Wien*. There *Boccaccio* had enjoyed a tremendously successful rerun, with Girardi in one of the two main roles. There Suppé's next opus, *Die Afrikareise (The African Journey)*, appeared in March 1883. But not even Girardi could prevent the inevitable. Suppé was drained of musical invention. *African Journey* did not last one month.

There can be no doubt that Suppé must be awarded the title of "Father of the Viennese Operetta." Despite his successes, however, it was his background which prevented artistic flight such as the Vienna-born Strauss was to exhibit. Born into Italian music, nurtured on Offenbach's French inflections, and settled in Vienna, he attempted, sometimes with relative success, to combine Italian melody, French insouciance, and Viennese *Gemütlichkeit*—"but his Italian is Donizetti *bel canto*, not Verdi drama, and his Viennese is not Strauss's heady Vienna wine, but Dalmation Suppe"[1] (Viennese Press comment).

1. The German word *Suppe* (without the accent) means "soup."

18

The Second Fiddle of the Trio

Both Suppé and Strauss, however, had to contend with a third man in the field of Viennese operetta—Karl Millöcker. Millöcker's background parallels that of Suppé. After starting as a flutist of great promise at the *Theater an der Wien* under none else but Suppé, he too, from 1869 to 1883, was *Kapellmeister* at the theatre. And, like Suppé, Millöcker came to the fore with his modest successes while Strauss was marking time between world triumphs. Aside from laboring in the shadow of Strauss, Millöcker had the added drawback of a total lack of flamboyancy, so necessary in the world of the theatre. His efforts, nonetheless, found unexpected support from the famous folk poet Ludwig Anzengruber. When Strauss went into temporary decline, Millöcker's talent for modestly lilting melodies and occasionally sprightly musical ideas assured him a place in Vienna's operettic sun.

Millöcker's first major effort, *Der Regimentstambour (The Regimental Drummer)* in October 1869 had the distinct disadvantage of being kept out of the two major theatres. It was produced at the modest *Theater in der Josefstadt* because the *Theater an der Wien* was then quite satisfied with the box office returns from Offenbach, Suppé, and Strauss. Since his first attempt was far from successful, Millöcker for another four years was relegated to the travails of theatre conductor. He was no more fortunate with his second effort, *Ein Abenteuer in Wien (An Adventure in Vienna)*, in January 1873. It lasted one month. His next effort, *Das verwunschene Schloss (The Enchanted Castle)*, to everyone's surprise proved an initial success, but that particular type of alpine folk operetta found no further supporters or longterm acceptance. What the Viennese wanted was a Viennese milieu or another smart locale such as Paris, Hungary, an oriental scene, or at least Russia. An operetta with peasant names such as Sepp, Andredl, Mirzel, and Traudel was not the dish the sophisticated Viennese wished to taste more than once. The Viennese press expressed this succinctly: "The closer the libretto comes to the description of the peasant and his life the less suitable these types appear for an operetta ... jokes about superstition, loutishness, and dullness make us laugh but such laughter does not

Karl Millöcker, who, with Strauss and Suppé, comprised the famous operetta trio of his time.

make us happy." Soon the dubious value of the novelty wore off and, despite lavish production and such top names as Girardi and Gallmeyer, the work lasted barely two weeks.

Millöcker's name, however, had caught on with the public—mainly because there was no one to overshadow his talents at the time. Yet, the public's fickle tastes are unpredictable. Millöcker's next production, *Gräfin Dubarry (Countess Dubarry)*, despite a better than average libretto, and a considerably higher level of sophistication, also lasted only twenty-two performances in 1879. (More than fifty years later Theo Mackeben, in 1931, drastically revised *Countess Dubarry* and staged it again at the Berlin Admiral Palace Theatre where it triumphed in three hundred performances.) But in December 1880 Vienna was treated to *Apajune*, and the press found it "witty, humorous, the music showing a fine talented hand with charming details ... several dances brought ecstasy to the house." Suddenly Millöcker was known beyond the confines of Vienna. Germany, Russia, and the United States (New York premiere, 8 May 1881) clamored for his music. Two years later in December

1882 came the long-awaited, long-delayed crowning success, *Der Bettelstudent (The Beggar Student)*.

Millöcker arrived at his greatest success by the back door, so to speak. Zell and Genée had concocted[1] two libretti. They were concerned about marketing them because they would have ready and interested parties in Millöcker and Strauss; the question was which to offer to whom. They first approached Strauss, who opted for *The Beggar Student* because its Polish milieu appealed to him. Everything about the story seemed right, the flamboyance of the Poles, the proverbial beauty of their women, the conflict between aristocracy and beggar student, patriot and foreign occupier. But now Zell and Genée had second thoughts. Strauss had descended from the artistic height of *Die Fledermaus*, Millöcker, on the other hand was apparently on the rise. They had to admit to themselves that Millöcker was no Strauss. Would his charming but limited talents suffice to make a success out of the other libretto, *Eine Nacht in Venedig*, when they knew full well that it was inferior? Knowing this and knowing Strauss, the two hacks set in motion a cheap ruse. They gave Strauss to understand that it was Millöcker's opinion that *Bettelstudent* was the inferior of the two books and that he wanted *Eine Nacht in Venedig*. Strauss fell into the trap. If Millöcker wanted it, Strauss had to have it. Without even taking time to read through the libretto, he let the title conjure up Venice, lagoons, gondolas, serenades, masked balls, and bought it.

Zell and Genée rubbed their hands in glee. Millöcker achieved the success which had thus far eluded him. Yet despite its world success, only one memorable melodic line is still remembered: *"Ach, ich hab' sie ja nur auf die Schulter geküsst"* (Her fair shoulder I kissed, 'pon my word, that was all"). The press was unanimous in its praise: "The best libretto Zell & Genée have ever written ... Herr Millöcker this time achieved a complete and uncontested success. His music ... is melodious, singable, light, and unpretentious ... The acting was excellent. Few stages could produce two comics like Schweighofer and Girardi ... Often he succeeded in expressing the national character of the music in heavy-lidded Slavic melodies and in a pretty mazurka."

Der Bettelstudent ran for two months and in less than two years had achieved one hundred fifty performances, a triumph for Millöcker, second to none, while Strauss at the same time floundered and faltered with *Eine Nacht in Venedig*. From Vienna *Bettelstudent* started its world triumph through Germany, Stokholm, Copenhagen, Basle, and St. Petersburg. Suddenly showered with wealth, Millöcker was

---

1. The word "concocted" is especially apt because *Der Bettelstudent* contains entire scenes from Sardou's *Fernande*, lifted literally by "poets" Zell and Genée.

finally able to relinquish the drudgery of conducting. For another of Vienna's idols, Alexander Girardi, *Bettelstudent* was also a special treat because he played the role of Symon Rymanovicz, the lover and hero, instead of the comic part which was his usual lot.

Compared to the Hungarian milieu later treated by Strauss in his *Zigeunerbaron*, with its wealth of Austrian and Hungarian melodies and its waltzes, arias, and csardas, the paucity of Millöcker's treatment of a similarly promising Polish theme is doubly glaring. While Strauss glorified the Hungarian and the gypsy in musical splendor, Millöcker only succeeded in exaggeration. But Millöcker could rest on his laurels. With the *Bettlestudent* his share of the profits reached ten percent, excelled only by the twelve percent which Strauss received. Over and above his regular share, his contract stipulated that every twentieth performance was to be an author's benefit, with all profits going to him after subtraction of daily expenses. Although he was never again to achieve the triumph of *Bettelstudent*, the name Millöcker carried enough respect to prompt splendid staging and performances for his catchy *Gasparone* in 1884, *Der Feldprediger* in 1886, *Der Arme Jonathan* in 1890, and *Das Nordlicht* in 1896. Typically, nothing survives of those operettas, many of which contain ingratiating tuneful passages. Strauss's honey was superior to the saccharine quality of Millöcker's tunes which were eventually relegated to the salon orchestra. The difference is hard to define; the melodies were there. What they lacked was the vibrancy, the *Schmiss und Schmalz* of Strauss to make them come to life and keep them alive. While Strauss spread his wings in renewed world successes, Millöcker grew senile amid his wealth.

Johann Strauss, in full dress uniform complete with decorations, leading his orchestra at the Imperial Court Ball.

19

Wienerkind

A city, an empire, and two generations who wished to forget were served by Johann Strauss with fiddle and bow. No pied piper could have engendered more gaiety and abandon which all eagerly accepted and frenetically embraced as Austria and its capital sank into the mire of genial laissez-faire and decay. So all-enveloping are Strauss's melodies in their carefree, ingratiating warmth that, upon hearing them, one can hardly think of text and continuity, but only of the lilt of the moment. The miracle was that the moment stretched into a lifetime of music, an inexhaustible wellspring of pleasure, a streaming and sounding of immortal youth rising from a soggy sea of poetic mediocrity.

Strauss's melodic invention was matched only by Schubert. Beyond that, however, similarity between the two composers is slight. Schubert fully understood the value of the word and respected it. Thus he was able to heighten its impact by integrating it with music. With Schubert the music was neither master of the word, as with Strauss, nor its handmaiden, as it had been before. That was why words and music became one in Schubert's *Lieder*. He meshed the two arts infallibly and raised them to immortal heights, while Straussian operettic gems remained shackled to unwieldy texts. While both masters spoke ever so eloquently of "their" Vienna, their intellectual and artistic intercourse speaks for itself. In his creations Schubert walked with Goethe and Heine, Strauss with Zell and Genée.

Another similarity between Schubert and Strauss is worthy of note. Schubert, the first great master of the German *Lied*, had never thought the art of songs which flowed from his quill to be important. Instead he beat his tousled head against the unyielding stone wall of opera. Similarly, the waltzes which flowed from Strauss's pen were so natural to him that he did not realize their value. While Bruckner delivered himself of *Ländlers* in his symphonies, Strauss, the man who grew up with the *Ländler*, aspired to nothing less than the "real" art of opera, disastrously attempting it first in *Simplizius* and then in *Ritter Pazmann*. Of course both geniuses moved on different levels. Music with Strauss was a quality of the soul, not an expression of human growth as was the case with Schubert. Strauss's waltzes were expressions of something inborn, a reflection of the whole man.

Musical development in some composers can be paralleled with personal growth, and certain of their compositions thus attain special significance. Strauss's music, however, contains few such markers because his music is "Strauss absolute." It is not merely an indication of the man, it is his total life. His biography can be summed up in one word that describes him, his time, a way of life: *Wienerkind*, a child of Vienna. Many of his friends and admirers took issue with such a way of life and its ensuing creative process. Others defended it with equal zeal and logic. Paul Bekker noted: "A waltz by Johann Strauss contains more melodies than a Beethoven symphony and the total number of Strauss melodies is much higher than that of Beethoven ... Yet the question arises: is the mark of musical creativity determined by the fecundity of melodic inventiveness? This is obviously not the case. Even if Johann Strauss had created 10,000 times the amount of melodies as compared to Beethoven, nobody would seriously compare Strauss's creative power to Beethoven's." Hermann Bahr added: "[Johann Strauss's] best talents were hampered by frivolity and indolence, pushed into lazy and disrespectful indifference or sulking withdrawal." Richard Specht differs totally in interpretation: "That carelessness, that relaxed ease, that armoring against all disturbances, is not all this the essential, the fertile ground for a genius like Johann Strauss?"

There can be no question that Strauss's very nature was partly the cause of the criticism directed against him. He never realized that to compose independently of the total text of an operetta was almost impossible, even futile. He never bothered to investigate whether a text fitted the music or vice versa. Although he grew out of the waltz, in itself basically a string of often unrelated melodies, Strauss continued to compose, even in the larger form of the operetta, in the fashion of the potpourri rather than a preconceived plan. He strung melodies together spontaneously rather than in a logical and methodical order, as Schnitzer eventually forced him to do. Most roles in Strauss's operettas remain figures in the poorest cardboard sense: bloodless, lifeless, spouting phrases. He poured his music indiscriminately over passionate outpourings, tender love scenes, sensuous double entendres or broad comic inferences, and mostly over inane stage patter. As operettic music progressed successfully, indolence regarding text dropped to ridiculous lows. There was not only a lack of pride on Strauss's part, but something approaching grinning masochism. One wonders whether Strauss was attracted to those low-brow texts, to that tavern humor which he had absorbed long before he rose into the rarefied sphere of poetry. Eventually, Strauss, and in a larger sense musical Vienna, relied on two saving graces in his operettas—his lilting waltzes and Alexander Girardi's stage artistry. Like no one else in his day Girardi was able to breathe a surprising degree of life into the comic characters he portrayed. Because of his genius, he, in later years, was able to inspire, and sometimes force, Strauss to create roles with a life of their own. Only on rare occasions, such as in *Die Fledermaus*, did he do justice to a good libretto. Those rare occasions clearly indicate that Strauss could have mastered a "style," either comic or dramatic, had he wished to combine his latent talent with self-discipline. This was again pointed up in *Zigeunerbaron*. Inevitably, however, the moot question arises whether Strauss, if bound into a straightjacket of style, could have continued to *"singen wie der Vogel singt,"* to "sing as carefree as a bird."

The Viennese did little to change Strauss's view of the matter. If the music was there, never mind the text; if Girardi was supreme and superb, to blazes with his ambitions for dramatic roles of which he was capable; back into the clown's suit of the funny man. That was so typical of Vienna's attitude in many fields; Viennese

Caricature of the masses of Strauss fans arriving in Vienna by the carload to hear their idol.

Strauss at his desk at the spa of Ischl. Strauss, as well as his friend Brahms, had the habit of working at a stand-up desk.

from the burgher to the emperor, resisted anything new. Much to the detriment of operetta and its success outside its birthplace, the Viennese paid attention to the music only. If they paid any attention at all to the plot continuity, then it was in the first act only. Following that, they gave themselves cheerfully to the sweeping grace and frivolity of the escapist music, tunes to be recalled with a fond smile after the plot and text had long been forgotten or discarded. Wagner's expression "Apotheosis of the Dance" certainly has an application to Strauss's *Fledermaus* or *Blue Danube*. The overture or a ballet interlude of any Strauss operetta often became the highlight of the evening. This was not a gradual development but a tidal wave which swept all, including Johann, before it, beginning with *Indigo*, his first work for the stage. Perhaps because it was first, it speaks of and to Vienna more than Strauss's later, superior works. It contains musical wealth: the spiritedness of his waltzes and the contrasting pictures of noisy medieval streets and quiet idyllic squares, are all woven into the action. Always gently melodious, sometimes melancholy, and even teary-eyed, it is never dramatic. That absence of drama, of tension, later repeatedly attempted with unvarying lack of success, provided the charm of *Indigo*. The music was truly a mirror of the man—charming, uncaring.

This, however, did not extend to his actual working habits. Once he had decided on a book, the easygoing, occasionally complacent man would work at fever pitch. Beneath the easy smile and jovial exterior lay slumbering a determination to be equal to both personal and professional demands. This quality in Strauss was not obvious, although it was evident from earliest youth. He was persistent in adversity or in the face of great obstacles, such as his father's refusal to grant a musical future. He had the courage to attempt his career, despite his father's artistic fame, and to withstand his father's attempts to entice him into an artistic reunion which might have assured an easy future. He aligned himself firmly on the side and position of his mother, but did not let his love for his father degenerate into bitterness. He did not buckle under wave after wave of adverse criticism, and eventually prevailed against Offenbach's preeminence in the field. These traits and reactions show a depth of character and a fortitude often obscured by lighter, more easily discernible qualities.

Naturally there were many sides to his personality. While he regretted any day on which he did not smile, his pathological reaction to hurt—retirement from company, brooding search for work—was swift and constantly recurring. He acted and reacted spontaneously—especially to music. The musical idea, the brainchild of the moment, was his constant companion, at the table, walking, in bed; it was his child, his master, mistress, servant. Sensuality bordering on ribaldry was second nature. His correspondence with publishers ranged from the jocular to the gaily obscene.

The Spirit

He was gregarious and loved crowds, but demanded absolute solitude when in musical labor. No unexpected visitors were admitted then; only the closest collaborators had access to his study. Although beloved by an entire city and everybody who came into contact with him, despite sumptuous soirées in his house, the circle of his friends remained small: the sculptor Victor Tilgner, Karl Goldmark, piano virtuoso and teacher Leschetitzky, piano maker Bösendorfer, pianist Grünfeld.

While conservative Vienna opinion manhandled Wagner, Wolf, and Bruckner, Johann reigned supreme, perhaps because his unspoken musical message, "You live only once—after you're dead life's no joy," appealed to the spirit of the Viennese. That attitude is doubly paradoxical and indicative. Death to Strauss had always been a traumatic spectre he could not face. Although he was for the greater part of his life a Catholic, he did not think of death as a transfiguration, a portal into another world, a happier life, but always as dissonance, horror, annihilation.

The lusty paradox thus expressed in the waltz in Catholic Vienna with its belief in a life hereafter seems more closely attuned in Strauss's, and Vienna's, mind to the Old Testament prayer "Let me live, O Lord, the dust cannot praise Thee." To be happy in whirling dance, to replenish the body with food and drink, was Vienna's idea of the good life, and it united all levels of society. And as Austria's horizons shrank in defeat and decay, *Beinfleisch* and *Apfelstrudel* (boiled meat and apple strudel), *Backhendl* (roast chicken) and beer, *Rostbraten* (roast meat) and wine, *Schnitzel* and *Kartoffelsalat* (breaded veal cutlet and potato salad) rimmed the narrow Viennese sights. While Austria suffered disastrous defeats at Solferino and Koeniggraetz and endured humiliating separation from the all-German body, the famous Vienna establishment *Weichselgarten* was filled to capacity night after night. Its patrons daily consumed three roast calves with its renowned brew. While trainloads brought the dead, injured, and maimed from the battlefield, the more sober-minded in Vienna were outraged to see eight thousand crowd into *Venedig in Wien*, a "Venetian Festival" in the Prater. Thus there were only two rallying and uniting personalities among the multiplicity of nations and races within the empire, the idolized Catholic emperor and the "waltz king," Johann Strauss. The circle of admirers of Johann, however, was not limited to Vienna or the empire; truly all of Europe was at his feet, and all the world knew of him. Perhaps Johann's greatest admirer, after Brahms, was another German from Hamburg. He was the conductor Oscar Fetras, who boasted that he knew all the works of all the Strausses (about fourteen hundred compositions) by heart. In an empire barely held together, Johann represented a truly Austrian spiritual element. The polka, the czardas, and the waltz mingled gracefully, jubilantly, even in his operettas. If Austria failed in diplomacy and in war, it triumphed in music.

An evening with Johann Strauss, surrounded by members of his family and close friends. Brahms is second from left, Adele Strauss stands behind the composer at the piano, Eduard Strauss is at extreme right.

One point remains yet to be explored in an assessment of Johann Strauss. What was the achievement of the son which, in retrospect, forced the talented father to hold onto the son's coattails for his own claim to immortality? Although Johann took credit only for having enlarged the form, his part in the development of the waltz is far greater because he accomplished what neither Lanner nor his father had been able to do: he freed the waltz from the tyranny of the dance rhythm and carried it beyond the empty, regulated beat. In doing so Johann had to overcome formidable obstacles placed in his path by friends, experts, foes, and the public itself. Therein lies the son's greatest waltz achievement. The expansion of the form had actually been accomplished on another level by Weber in his *Aufforderung zum Tanz*. Lanner and Strauss, had they been able to escape the public's voracious clamor for dance music, could have followed in Weber's path and developed the waltz along his lines on their own level. But both older masters decided to stay with the proven formula that was expected and demanded by their adoring customers—five short waltzes of the two eight-bar variety followed by a coda. The best they could accomplish was to open with a brief introduction before swinging into the breathlessly awaited waltzes.

Johann started where Weber had left off because Weber, after his brief excursion into *Invitation*, had lost interest in the form. First Johann lengthened the introduction as well as the waltzes, sometimes to as many as twenty bars until, in his *Morgenblätter*, the new waltz emerged. Then, three years later, when Johann was forty-two, opus 314 was born, the incomparable, unsurpassed masterpiece, *An der Schönen Blauen Donau*. At the peak of his career, the mature master wrote his most splendid waltz creation, a symphonic poem in waltz time. As that dreamy D major triad rises over whispering strings, it conjures up the image of that stream of ancient imagination, the stream of the *Nibelungen*, as morning mist rises from the Danube. It reveals church-spires looming up from villages climbing the hills of the Wachau Valley and, high above them, the splendid ruins of once mighty castles rimming the horizon, while dew drops glisten on apricot trees in the first rays of the morning sun. From that chord on there was no curbing the flow of genius as pearl after pearl crowded Johann's score.

A genius of such incredibly fertile musical imagination may be forgiven if periods filled with musical gems are interlaced with delightfully weightless interludes which show the skilled technician contriving a needed rhythm until the time when the bright gem of a theme inevitably reappears. When inspiration faltered, Johann slowed a waltz into an old-fashioned *Ländler* or speeded it into a gallop; he inverted an already established theme, introduced a variation of an earlier idea, or he recalled a native melody of Tyrol or Salzburg which in due course acquired the Straussian touch. Among the more than four hundred waltzes that Strauss composed, few routine compositions can be found. Even his quick-blooming and quick-wilting operettic creations contain few routine waltzes. Careful melodic contrasts and balance are always evident, as is skillful instrumentation. Often primitive in earlier years, his instrumentation improved, sometimes to symphonic quality and proportion, but it was never used to gloss over lapses of invention. Churning imagination and ever-increasing demands resulted in an occasional mediocrity caused by lapses in vision and discernment. But even though not every composition could be a *Wiener Blut, Blaue Donau*, or *Künstlerleben*, just the announcement, "A new waltz by Strauss" would suffice to ignite enthusiasm. And if the waltz invention of the evening was not his best, a Strauss waltz, sunny and singing, beckoning into a never-never land, overruled all judgment.

20

Wiener Schnitzel

"You should try your hand at operetta." None other than Offenbach spoke those complimentary words to Johann Strauss. Although Strauss initially rejected the idea, pleading ignorance of the stage, the seed had been planted and Offenbach was to rue the day.

Even if Johann wanted no part of the idea, Offenbach's suggestion had fallen upon Jetti's eager ears. A woman of the theatre and possessor of a splendid voice, she had resumed her concert career after marrying Johann and thus had become part of his triumphal tours to London and Russia. In advocating the idea of Strauss as an operetta composer, she was aided by two developments, the Franco-German conflict and the eagerness of Maximilian Steiner, manager of *the* operetta theatre in Vienna, the *Theater an der Wien*. The Franco-German war had finally brought to the surface what had long smoldered in Viennese hearts. Although they had flocked to hear Offenbach, now, under the guise of chauvinism they could safely turn against the Frenchman. Jetti's instinct told her that the time was ripe for a truly Viennese operetta composer. If the Viennese had enjoyed Suppé's efforts as "Viennese" they would jubilantly receive Johann. Steiner's more pragmatic mind translated Johann's lilting melodies into the jingling of the cash register. But Strauss was adamant. He was famous as the greatest composer of waltzes. Why leave a good thing? Why desert the waltz that flowed in his blood? Why leave the bursting ballroom to fill an empty, alien stage? In order to convince Johann of the soundness and adaptability of the basic idea Jetti finally resorted to a ruse. She secretly removed a number of her husband's compositions from the drawer of his desk in which he stuffed all his ideas for melodies and brought them to Steiner, who had words put to a number of them. And one day there appeared before the startled Johann a group of singers who proceeded to sing. Strauss's eyes lit up. He listened, smiled. "Not half bad." The point had been made.

Suddenly Strauss's mind was aflame. A libretto, *Die Lustigen Weiber von Wien* (*The Merry Wives of Vienna*), appealed to him, and he furiously set to work. En-

Marie Geistinger in the title role of Suppé's The Beautiful Galathea.

Josefine Gallmeyer in her role in Offenbach's The Princess of Trapezunt.

couraged by Jetti and abetted by Steiner, Johann's first operetta began to take shape. As had been the case with his father, melodies came easily. Strauss had given in to the entire idea of an operetta, but he had his own ideas as to who should sing it. Foremost on his list of performers was brilliant, exciting Josefine Gallmeyer. But Josefine had become too exciting once too often. A temperamental outburst, no rare thing with her, in an exchange of ideas with the director had ended in her slapping his face and stalking out of the *Theater an der Wien*, whereupon the *Carltheater* received her with open arms. Strauss had envisioned only Gallmeyer for the main role, a frivolous woman bordering on the erotic. Without Gallmeyer he wanted no performance of the work. He could not be budged. It was never performed.

But fate had decided in favor of the Vienna operetta, and Steiner saw himself as the instrument of that fate. He lost no time and in 1870 bound Strauss by contract to the *Theater an der Wien*, which he then managed in partnership with a soubrette of tremendous promise and later fame, Marie Geistinger. Steiner would not rest. Wishing to keep Johann in his operetta mood, he engaged a group of librettists who proceeded to collaborate on a book. The result was *Indigo und die 40 Räuber (Indigo and the Forty Thieves)* promptly renamed by mischievious Vienna tongues "Indigo and the Forty Librettists." It was boring, it was colorless, and it lasted four hours.

The date of 10 February 1871 was a momentous one for Vienna operetta. The occasion was reminiscent of Johann's debut, only this time he performed not in Dommayer's Casino but in the most prestigious operetta theatre in the world, the *Theater an der Wien*. Everybody who was anybody in musical Vienna was there in breathless anticipation. Viennese operetta by a Viennese! Geistinger in the role of Fantaska and Strauss conducting! The ticket supply had been exhausted weeks in advance, with scalpers getting as much as twenty times the original cost. Johann Herbeck, one of Vienna's foremost conductors, had to be content to watch the performance on a folding chair from the orchestra pit. Everything and everybody had been in happy confusion. Even the title had not been settled until a late date, and *Indigo, Fantaska, Ali Baba,* and *Forty Thieves* had been considered. But everybody was hush-hush concerning the sorest point, the libretto concocted by Steiner's "bookmakers."

When the houselights dimmed a hush fell over the audience only to be broken by a standing ovation when Strauss appeared at the conductor's stand. Steiner had spared no expense to provide Strauss and Vienna with as splendid a production as had ever been seen on any operettic stage. *Kapellmeister* Heinrich Ritter von Seyfried reminisced:

When Strauss stepped to the podium, there raged a welcoming jubilation through the overflowing house for ten minutes, ranging from the fully attended imperial court box to the last gallery seats ... after each act Strauss was recalled five or six times and registered a success as had never been seen in Vienna.

The critic for the magazine *Der Humorist* wrote:

France, not the noble conquered one [of the 1870-1871 war] but the cancanized France of Mister Offenbach was shot through the heart. Johann Strauss is Austria personified, all of Austria is in his camp and has chimed in with a resounding manifestation of Austria.

One imagined oneself at the *Volksgarten* or in a ballroom when the first waltz appeared in the overture ... At the gala number of the evening, the waltz song *Ja so singt man* the house broke into a shout ... one felt ... now, now Strauss must snatch the violin from the concertmaster and swing it under his chin ... to lead the dance.

Hanslick, as was to be expected of such an astute music critic, kept a cool pen.

It is an uncontestable fact that our Strauss has registered a furor with his operetta ... All this was accomplished by a sprightly ensemble accompanied by a puny orchestra consisting of four violins, a flute, an oboe, a bassoon and a harp. [The libretto] has the oriental charm of the Vienna suburbs; the dilletant hodgepodge cried to the heavens ... the action of those puppets on stage do not move even the most naive theatregoer ... Instead of a book of innate Viennese charm and humor we were handed a piece of patched hackwork.

The most enlightening comment came in a private letter to Johann from Anton Langer, a writer and former schoolmate:

Dear Friend: First of all my heartiest, sincerest congratulations on your splendid, well-earned success which pleases me doubly because it is a Viennese who with his first work came to the forefront ... You carry within you that heavenly well of melody through which Mozart, Haydn, Beethoven, and Schubert made our fatherland famous throughout the world ... Do not be misled. The libretto is no worse than *Tschin-Tschin* and numerous other Offenbach idiocies ... If an old friend may venture advice, refrain from the big production operetta ... an operetta from your pen needs but your music. You need not have half a hundred half-naked women on stage, or share your triumph with tailor, decorator, and light-effects man. Look for a good libretto and then "Good Luck" with your next work.

"Look for a good libretto"—sound advice, prophetic insight, totally ignored by Strauss.

Just as after the Dommayer debut, Strauss Father suddenly had a waltz rival in the person of his son, so Offenbach overnight had an operetta rival. It was a peculiar kind of competition. The French art of parody and satire, clad in olympian mythology, was never equalled in Strauss's operettas, which relied for their appeal mainly on music. Actually parody and sarcasm had not been alien to Vienna, even before Offenbach's entry on the scene. Kurz-Bernardon, who had produced young Haydn's first *Singspiel, Der Krumme Teufel (The Crooked Devil)*, also indulged in the production of a satire entitled *Innocence Protected by Minerva* or *The Gods of Love United* as well as *Amphytrion*, a parody of Wagner's *Tannhäuser*.

But times had changed. In a city which virtually idolized its emperor in song and deed, satire and sarcasm from an Austrian would have been ill received by the public. They accepted such stage treatment from Offenbach but they would not from Strauss, especially if the person of Emperor Franz Joseph had been the target. Censorship of course did its part to prevent parody and satire of any kind, which in Viennese libretti were unfortunately too often supplanted by idiocy posing as humor. Meilhac and Halévy knew Offenbach, Paris, and their time intimately and intuitively and deliberately employed these ingredients. Thus all three triumphed in Paris and in the world with an obviously Parisian product. Only in rare instances did such an intuitive understanding and cooperation exist between Strauss and the men who supplied his libretti.

Some musicologists feel that *Indigo* is Strauss's most melodious work, although not as charming as *Fledermaus* or as well organized as *Zigeunerbaron*. The main melody of the work and the main song which Vienna intuitively picked as its own and cherished, explains the work's success:

> *Ja so singt man in the Stadt wo ich geboren bin*
> *Ja so singt man ganz allein doch nur in Wien*

> Yes, that is how one sings in the city where I was born
> Yes, one sings that way only in Vienna

Vienna gladly suffered through the libretto to enjoy the exhilaration of Strauss's sparkling melody. It was left to the more sophisticated and less emotionally involved audiences in Berlin to rebel against the poorly written libretto. Librettists, soon aware of Strauss's lax attitude toward texts, continued to foist third-rate work on him. They either outlined the action only in the broadest romantic strokes without submitting the actual book in advance, or they gave him the text for the musical numbers only, without even bothering to outline the actual story. Thus in their operettas, Strauss's music had to stand alone.

While *Indigo*, after its triumph in Vienna, began its world tour and in April 1875 registered renewed acclaim in Paris, Strauss was already at work on his next operetta. Although the original libretto, *Piccolino*, by Sardou was French in origin, its Vienna adaptation by Josef Braun was a decided step away from Offenbach's style. The story of a painter's love and romance, extending from Switzerland to Italy, retitled *Karneval in Rom*, bypassed all satire in favor of a more lighthearted *Singspiel* style. There was a lyricism to both story and music which not only foreshadowed the future Viennese style of operetta but also was akin to lyrical opera, a genre never far from Strauss's mind. It was a lighthearted work along the lines of Donizetti's *Daughter of the Regiment* or Nicolai's *The Merry Wives of Windsor*. Work on *Karneval* was happily interrupted by Strauss's momentous journey to the United States, but when it was finally presented on 1 March 1873, Vienna loved every moment of it. With Strauss conducting and the ensemble again led by Vienna's favorite, Marie Geistinger, in the double role, it was an immediate success. No expense had been spared. A. Bredow, the painter of the Imperial Russian Court Theatre, had been brought to Vienna to design the Roman and alpine scenery, and the famous Franceschini was in charge of costume design. But bicycles on stage created the greatest sensation. The sport had just been introduced, so the wheeling on stage was a delightful and surprising touch which contributed to fifty performances of *Karneval* that very year. *Karneval*, surprisingly, proved more durable than *Indigo* and in 1921 was revived at the Vienna Volksoper by Felix Weingartner.

Strauss escaped financially unscathed from Black Friday, 8 May 1873. He was not careless with his money and he followed sound investment advice. Thus his fortunes gathered in Russia and the United States had not been risked in Vienna's giddy financial wave. Eager to create another operetta, he looked around for another libretto, as did Max Steiner. Actually, Steiner had a libretto of sorts, but he did not know what to do with it. It was a French script, *Reveillon (Dinner Time)* by Meilhac and Halévy, those two knowing collaborators of Offenbach. Whether they ever offered the script to Offenbach or whether he refused it will never be known. As a play it had been performed in Paris with considerable success. Knowing the reputation of the two collaborators, Steiner had bought the book sight unseen, only to find it totally unfit for the Viennese stage. But the Vienna publisher Gustav Levy suggested changing the locale, removing the objectionable parts and fashioning it into an operetta libretto.

Steiner summoned his two stalwarts, Karl Haffner and Richard Genée. Although they were no Meilhac and Halévy, Haffner and Genée (both Germans) were unquestionably the best pair of librettists Vienna could muster to do the task of "Viennizing" a French book. Karl Haffner, an East Prussian, hailed from Königsberg. It is ironic that such an introverted, lonely, melancholy man, then in his seventies, should have been called upon to collaborate on what was to be the epitome of sparkling Viennese gaiety. Artistically Haffner was a prisoner of the *Carltheater*, for which he was forced to write plays for a pittance. Despite the triumph of *Fledermaus* he was to die in abject poverty. Richard Genée, sparkling and vivacious as his ancestral French name might imply, was born in the port city of Danzig. Whatever theatrical qualities Haffner might have lacked and Strauss been unaware of, Genée possessed in profusion. He not only had been *Kapellmeister* in innumerable theatres from Riga to Prague but he had written a number of operettas which had made the European circuit, and some, as *Der Seekadet (The Sea Cadet)* and *Der Geiger aus Tirol (The Fiddler from Tyrol)*, had registered considerable successes with libretti either by him or by Zell under Genée's supervision. Thus the expert of the spoken theatre and the man of the musical theatre, both artists, combined to give Strauss one of the few fine books in his entire career.

There was rare understanding between the two men as Haffner and Genée scissored, adjusted, restructured, and altered. The French *souper* scene of the second act was enlarged to a huge ball which in itself offered added opportunities for virtuoso arias and ballets. Mistaken identities, flirtation, and intrigue were followed in turn by hangover, jail, pathos, near-drama, tears of mockery and of joy, and, of course, a happy ending. Thus, with Strauss's lilt superimposed, there appeared a masterpiece on the very threshold of comic opera, barely a step removed from Mozart's *Marriage of Figaro* and Richard Strauss's *Rosenkavalier*, the difference lying in the fact that da Ponte and Hofmannsthal had genius while Haffner and Genée had talent.

Through Strauss, and only Strauss, despite Suppé's and Millöcker's valiant and successful efforts, the operetta in Vienna became the Viennese operetta. It became operettic achievement without aping Offenbach's impudence and satire, it was sensuous without vulgarity because the high kick of the can-can, the swished skirt, the exposed thigh and derrière were a form of exhibitionism alien to Strauss. Offenbach, in turn, acquired some of Strauss's grace. The Vienna music critic Julius Korngold[1] related how Strauss, during an Offenbach performance, turned to Jetti and whispered "Fledermaus." A similar smiling comment by Strauss was overheard as he listened to the "Waltz of the Flower Maidens" in *Parsifal*.

Die Fledermaus was the perfect tonic for escapist Vienna. The refrain lingered and reverberated so that one found it difficult to return to reality. There was also

---

1. Julius Korngold succeeded Hanslick as the influential music critic of the *Neue Freie Presse*, which contained one of the most prestigious musical columns in Vienna. He also was the father of Erich Wolfgang Korngold (1897-1957) whose opera *Die Tote Stadt (The Dead City)*, composed at age twenty-three, was hailed as a masterpiece.

that rare event, a book worthy of Johann Strauss. Everybody was happy with it. It had enough *esprit de Français* left in it to bubble, but the music was wholly, unmistakably Viennese. Even the censors were unusually restrained, demanding the removal of only one line of dialogue and one stanza in Adele's song. The instrumentation was superior to anything Strauss had ever done. All Vienna eagerly awaited the premiere on 5 April 1874, with Geistinger singing the part of Rosalinde. Only Hanslick had reservations—the book was trite and Strauss's music too limited in scope. But another critic, Ludwig Speidel, described the reaction in the theatre: "[Strauss's music] invades the ear and streams through the blood into the legs and even the most lethargic man in the theatre unknowingly begins to nod his head, rock his body, tap his feet. Looking down from a box one could get seasick watching the audience weaving to the fascinating tones which Strauss elicits with his baton from the orchestra ... triumph, victory on all fronts. Oh, how the Viennese applauded Strauss. As was to be expected, the house shook with raging applause."

Laughter pervades the entire work, reaching one of the high points in the rippling, teasing laugh cascades of Adele the maid's aria: *"Mein Herr Marquis, ein Mann wie Sie ..."* (My dear Marquis, a man like you ..."). Hypocrisy, always a main ingredient in such a comedy of mistaken identities, is abundant, beginning with the quasi heartrending duet of Rosalinde and her husband while she eagerly awaits his departure so she can receive her lover: *"So muss allein ich bleiben, acht Tage ohne Dich! Wie soll ich Dir beschreiben mein Leid so fürchterlich"* ("Thus I must remain alone for these eight days in vain/How can I but describe to you how horrible my pain"). This duet in three-four time is surpassed by another in two-four rhythm, its staccato, pianissimo anticipation of extramarital joy barely suppressed in the pool of crocodile's tears; a high moment of musical comedy: *"O je, O je, wie rührt mich dies"* ("Oh my, Oh my, how I am touched"). When the governor of the prison appears to arrest the husband (and mistakenly arrests the chivalrous lover) he introduces his institution as "My beautiful large bird cage."

The musical champagne truly sparkles in the drinking song, which in its refrain contains one of the most memorable Viennese lines in all of Strauss's creative life— in waltz tempo, of course: *"Glücklich ist wer vergisst was nicht mehr zu ändern ist"* ("Happy is he who forgets that which can't be changed").

The second act with its spectacular reception and ball at the palace of Prince Orlofsky offers ballet, arias, even a csardas. As is proper on such an occasion, champagne flows freely, intoxicating all: *"Im Feuerstrom der Reben, Tra-la la la la la/ Sprüht ein himmlisch Leben, Tra-la la la la la"* ("The fiery stream of vineyards might,

Tra-la la la la la/ Throws sparks of heavenly delight, Tra-la la la la la"). Then comes the *Fledermaus* waltz, the highlight of the operetta. Of the nearly six hundred dances Johann had conjured up during his lifetime, perhaps only the *Blue Danube* is as clearly identifiable as the *Fledermaus* waltz. However, even the spell cast by this waltz cannot survive the unavoidable awakening to reality. The morning following the ball brings comic remorse, anger, and tears: *"Ja, ich bin's den Ihr betrogen/ Ja, ich bin's den Ihr belogen"* ("Yes, it's me, you have aggrieved me/ Yes, it's me, you have deceived me"). Thus thunders Rosalinde's husband Eisenstein, who is hardly in a position to pose as the personification of rectitude after the previous night's adventures. He is quickly cut down to size by Rosalinde, who, after trysting with her tenor lover, now decides to pose as the maligned, unforgiving wife:

> My husband is an evil man
> I won't forgive him, never can
> His faithless and disgraceful ways.
> He spent the whole of overnight
> With lovely ladies, young and bright
> Who did not have to force him
> But let the villain now beware—
> If he comes back again to me
> I'll scratch him till he cannot see
> And then I will divorce him.

What, in lesser hands, could have descended into crude low comedy, with Strauss becomes spirited, sparkling high comedy. A final vocal trio, worthy of Mozart or Richard Strauss, reveals the playful innocence of all parties, and a mock refrain, blaming that bubbly evil, champagne, brings the comedy of errors to its brilliant finale. Yet *Die Fledermaus*, that crowning glory of Viennese operetta, lasted for only sixteen performances. Comments are divided as to why the operetta suddenly became a disaster, especially after its initial success. Some point to Hanslick's negative review, others attribute the fiasco to sickness in the ensemble which depleted the cast to such an extent that continuation became impossible. But most chroniclers overlook another important factor: the lack of spirit and money in Vienna. Regardless of the beckoning champagne of Strauss's *Fledermaus*, the public, drained of resources by the crash, had its mind on tomorrow's meal rather than tonight's theatre visit. There was a limited number of well-heeled people remaining among Vienna's music lovers, only enough left to fill the *Theater an der Wien* for sixteen performances.

No one took defeat more lightly than Johann. While Steiner, Geistinger, Haffner, Genée, and Vienna gasped in disbelief at the unexpectedly short run of Strauss's masterpiece, he went on his extended and successful journey to Italy. While Triest, Rome, Naples, Verona, Livorno, Milan, and Genoa danced, sang, and whistled Strauss tunes in the streets, the courtyards, and at innumerable gala concerts, Strauss, in turn, turned Italian.

Meanwhile, Berlin—the city most unlikely to appreciate Viennese operetta—received *Fledermaus* with open arms and cheered it in one hundred consecutive performances. The Berlin press commented: "With *Die Fledermaus* Strauss has become sovereign ... in his operetta pulses noble fiery blood, the same sunny joy of life as in his dance rhythms. Strauss has given the libretto a seductive sparkling musical garment." No one was more surprised than Strauss to find upon his return that *Die Fledermaus* had scored so successfully in Berlin, Hamburg—and Paris. Overnight Strauss again had become the toast of the French capital.

One of the most admirable traits of the Viennese is their amazing recuperative spirit. Eighteen seventy-four and 1875 became vintage years for the arts in Vienna. Richard Wagner came to the city to raise money for his Bayreuth venture. In the hope of having an opera produced at the prestigious Imperial Opera House, he personally conducted concerts of his own music at the *Musikvereinssaal*. This brought him less money than he had expected but produced the greatest outpouring of Wagner enthusiasm he had ever received in Vienna or anywhere else. Karl Goldmark premiered his sensuous oriental opera *Die Königin von Saba (The Queen of Sheba)*, which Johann Herbeck produced. It caused as much of a sensation in Vienna as the luscious profusion of color on canvas which made Hans Makart one of the social lions and artistic leaders of his day in Vienna. Hanslick's friend and protegé, Adelina Patti, appeared in *Lucia di Lammermoor* and, with Strauss in hiatus, Vienna took a fleeting look at and liking to another Frenchman, Lecocq, and his concocted operettic soufflé, *Mamselle Angot*, performed at the *Carltheater*.

All but forgotten was Offenbach, once king of operetta. Old, chained to a chair by gout, his strength ebbing, he could not stem the Strauss tide nor did he intend to. Because now, finally, at the end of his life and career, he hoped to achieve what he had set out to do as a young man. Grand opera à la Meyerbeer had been his youthful aim. Only now, at the end of an incredibly fruitful career which had given Paris and the world ninety-seven operettas, was he to return to his first, last, and greatest love. *Les Contes d'Hoffmann (The Tales of Hoffmann)*, his only opera, was to be his last work. The libretto by Jules Barbier and Michael Carré was founded on stories by E. T. A. Hoffmann, a German romantic novelist and master of grotesquerie, horror, and madness. In it Offenbach was to play his last trump card over Strauss; he succeeded where Strauss was to fail. With *Contes* he hoped to atone to the world for all the frivolous insouciance and lacerating sarcasm dispensed in a lifetime of operettic music. The opera, his main concern for a number of years, in the end became an obsession. As he felt death approaching he urged Leon Carvalho, the manager of the *Théatre-Lyrique:* "Make haste, make haste to mount my piece; I am in a hurry and have only one wish in the world—that of witnessing the premiere of this work." He was to be deprived of that last satisfaction. Four months before the premiere he died while Paris danced to *Fledermaus* and *Danube Bleu.*

Fledermaus finally broke through into the realm of comic opera. Following the example of Gustav Mahler, who had performed it in Hamburg where he headed the Opera, the Vienna Imperial Opera belatedly scheduled *Fledermaus* for its first *evening* performance on 28 October 1894. Since the Strauss work previously had been performed only in the afternoon, the change to evening performance raised it into the realm of Mozart, Rossini, Donizetti, and Nicolai. Strauss had reached the pinnacle of fame. At age forty-eight, musically, artistically, and socially he surpassed his father's fame and fortune, boasting a villa at the spa of Ischl where the emperor also had a summer villa, a palace in the Igelgasse in Vienna, and a country estate in Leobersdorf near Vienna. He had more Strauss jubilees than he cared to attend and the Cross of Honor of the French Legion. His tour of Paris was a Viennese triumph. Paris had sparkled with a festival performance of *Indigo* on 13 January 1877, using the *Blue Danube* as the last-act finale. In more than one sense the tables were turned. Now Paris fabricated a French translation of the Viennese text after the French original of *Die Fledermaus.* The triumph was complete. Wrote Strauss to the director of the Paris performance: "I do not have to wait for a second performance to tell you how happy I am about the immense success which your excellent artists and your splendid production have achieved."

21

Asti Spumante alla Vienna

It was not Paris but Italy that pulsed in Johann's blood. The first fruit of the Strauss-Italy romance was *Cagliostro in Wien*[1] that charming Italian fraud glamorized by the Viennese composer. The timing for the production was well chosen. Vienna celebrated its two-hundredth anniversary of the successful defense against the Turks, and everybody streamed out to *Türkenschanzpark* (Turkish Entrenchment Park) to ogle the remnants of the Turkish ramparts. *Cagliostro* was just the right jewel for the occasion. Its premiere on 27 February 1875 coincided with the famous Wagner concert, one of the momentous occasions in Viennese musical history. While Wagner was covered with laurels, adulation, scorn, cheers, and catcalls, many were noticed to steal away to hear at least the final act of *Cagliostro*. The libretto again was by that dependable duo, Zell and Genée; unfortunately it detracted from rather than added to the glamor of the evening. But the occasion was equally significant in the theatrical history of Vienna because the music of Strauss was balanced by the art of Marie Geistinger and by the first appearance of another future star of the first order, Alexander Girardi in the droll role of Blasoni.

Marie Geistinger was now Vienna's idol, vivacious, charming, enticing. It had not always been that way. For many years she had to share the limelight with Josephine Gallmeyer who had shone in the earlier Offenbach creations. However, Geistinger was now Vienna's foremost comedienne and soubrette supreme, the sex symbol of her generation. Her stage portrayals were realistic, charming, and persuasive, but her personal outlook on life was unstable and irrational. Without seeking advice she squandered her fortune, her career, and her life. She raced through

---

1. Count Alessandro Cagliostro, alias Giuseppe Balsamo (1743-1795), was a Roman adventurer, alchemist, magician, mesmerist, and necromancer. Although prominent at the court of Louis XVI, he returned to Rome in 1789 where he was accused of heresy and condemned to death. The sentence was commuted to life imprisonment. He died in a Roman dungeon.

Alexander Girardi, Vienna's greatest folk actor-singer-comedian, and a close friend of Johann Strauss.

Vienna's theatrical skies with meteoric brilliance only to sink swiftly, ending in dire poverty with the auctioning off of her belongings.

Not so with Alexander Girardi. At the time of his first great success in *Cagliostro* he had already come a long way from his initial profession as a black-smith in the Styrian capital of Graz. There his mimicry and theatrical talent had caught the attention of a female admirer whose support enabled him to leave Graz for employment at the Vienna *Tuchlaubentheater* and eventually work up to the prestigious *Theater an der Wien* to become the idol of Vienna. Despite his distant Italian ancestry, Alexander Girardi was the substance of all the lovable char-acteristics as well as exasperating traits of the Viennese: "the Golden Viennese heart," a ready wit and fast retort, a funny voice which at a moment's notice could switch from jubilant praise to quaking complaint. The only sounds resembling music he had ever heard in his youth were the metallic rings of a blacksmith's hammer on iron; he lacked any kind of musical training, but a photographic musical memory and an infallible ear more than overcame the initial handicap. All those talents and characteristics combined with a most important ingredient, as far as the Viennese were concerned: he was funny—funny through mimicry, through voice, in joy and in sorrow. Inevitably he was propelled to a pre-eminence in theatrical life which not even Gallmeyer or Geistinger could match. Johann wrote to Girardi: "On your shoulders rests not only every play, but the very existence of the *Theater an der Wien* ... You can imagine how every author who writes for the stage clings to you as closely as possible ... for it is you alone who decides whether he is to be or not to be." That statement was reinforced by the observations of the Viennese writer Hermann Bahr. Bahr was not only an eminent writer in his own right and in touch with all facets of Vienna's artistic life but, as the husband of famous Vienna-born opera soprano Anna Bahr-Mildenburg, he was at the center of all Viennese musical activities. Bahr's first-hand observation was, "For the last twenty years every actor, down to the last provincial town, when he attempts to be irresistible, copies the vulgar yet mysterious, quiveringly agitated voice of Girardi ... assumes his innocently cynical glances ... there is not a young man among us, who, when approaching a girl, does not involuntarily mimic him."

Two such Viennese artistic products as Strauss and Girardi were bound to become close friends. In fact Strauss considered his friend almost as a mascot and good-luck charm: "Tell me how you want this," he once wrote to Alexander. "I shall not go on with my orchestration until you give me your views."

Cagliostro began that long line of seasonal successes in which the audience was happily mesmerized by the beguiling Strauss tunes upon which the book placed the kiss of death. The opening evening was to be repeated many times. The *Neues Wiener Tagblatt* recorded that "The audience demanded three repetitions of the waltz and the entire house linked arms and swayed in waltz time. It seemed as if old and young, rich and poor wanted to embrace and turn in waltz time and the scene on stage was almost vividly duplicated in the hall."

But Strauss was not satisfied to be fully successful in the Viennese milieu and only more or less successful in the Italian genre. Remembering his Paris triumph he decided to attempt a bit of Offenbachian sarcasm.

The book *Prince Methusalem* by Wilder and Delacour was sarcastic, but the question remained whether Strauss was the man to write sarcastic Viennese music about Frenchmen in Italy. "Methusalem, a prince of less than blue blood" sparkled briefly only through Strauss's gaiety and whimsy. Franz Jauner had provided a splendid production, hoping for a duplication of the *Fledermaus* success. On 3 January 1877, the court presided in the imperial box and landed and monied aristocracy and their brilliantly beautiful women in lavish "Makart" finery adorned the dress circle. Most enthusiastic and knowledgeable were Vienna's youth who inhabited the gallery. The conductor's desk was adorned with a laurel wreath befitting the man who had musically triumphed in Paris. Temporarily, music carried the desolate libretto, devoid of charm and even sense, to success. Actually the languid *cavatina* *O Schöner Mai* ("Oh Beautiful May") had to be repeated, and it soon resounded in Vienna's streets and homes. On the whole, however, *Prince Methusalem* proved a definite regression from *Fledermaus*. The story line, dethroned monarch becomes Minnesinger, could have been mastered by the tongue-in-cheek style of Offenbach but not by the straightforward naivete of Strauss. Thus only puppets emerged without real identification, and the much applauded music could triumph only briefly over the barren text. "It is regrettable that the bouncy melodies of our Strauss have to be content with such a boring text. Operettas today are only satires set to music, against which tonsure, saber, scepter, or even immortality are equally unprotected, and priests, generals, monarchs, and gods are equally lashed with bow and fiddle. But naivety fortunately has not deserted our otherwise so sophisticated time. Thus we still find husbands laughing at *Beautiful Helena*, staff officers at the *Grand Duchess of Gerolstein* and a duped public at *Prince Methusalem*," wrote Daniel Spitzer in *Wiener Spaziergänge (Vienna Strolls)*. In order to do "a piece in the French manner" Johann had, again, waded into a morass of idiocy. It is difficult to comprehend Strauss's thinking when he actually had advance knowledge of the book's low caliber. When the authors suggested that they should return to the original French format of one-act operetta Strauss countered: "Why one act? The public is accustomed to yawning through three acts, we shouldn't let them off so easily."

On 9 April 1878 Jetti died. Before her sudden death and during the early months of his hasty marriage to Angelika Johann had worked on an opus entitled *Blinde Kuh (Blind Man's Buff)*. Aside from an inferior libretto, this time approaching disaster, Johann found himself at a disadvantage from the outset. The disintegrating status of his marriage had an additional debilitating effect on him and his work. *Blinde Kuh* was fated to be Strauss's first total artistic defeat. Born of dissension, sorrow, anger, humiliation, and frustration, the music never took flight; only the overture and the waltz were applauded. After the premiere the theatre yawned emptily. Even in Strauss-happy Vienna *Blinde Kuh* did not survive thirty days.

On 1 February 1879, Franz von Suppé enjoyed the greatest triumph of his operettic career. Despite his "obviously generous use of Verdi, Offenbach, Meyerbeer and Strauss," *Boccaccio* became an uncontested success. It was Suppé who had been offered the book for a new operetta entitled *Das Spitzentuch der Königin (The Queen's Lace Handkerchief)*. But being busy with Zell and Genée's *Donna Juanita*, he was unable to avail himself of it. Only then did the librettists peddle it to Strauss. For once somebody else's loss was a fair (not total) gain for Strauss, and the premiere of *Spitzentuch* in October 1880 was a resounding success. The audience demanded

The Ringtheater in flames, one of the worst disasters in theatre history.

the repetition of five numbers and the box office was the largest in six years. The libretto was, as usual, mediocre, but Strauss had again found his *Schmiss und Schmalz* and that was all the Viennese had come to hear. The press, however, did not overlook the threadbare fabric: "Take the frankness of *Boccaccio,* the fate of *Othello,* take the dances of *Le Roi l'a dit* and the politics of *King Bobeche,* take Mozart's faithful women and you have the *Spitzentuch* in all its meandering and twisting and its transparently lightweight workmanship." Strauss, realizing the truth of the above observation as well as the fate of the operetta, gathered its most ravishing melodies, its waltzes, into one bouquet and called it appropriately *Rosen aus dem Süden (Roses from the South).*

On 8 December 1881 Vienna witnessed one of the greatest disasters in the history of the theatre. A festive crowd had assembled at the *Ringtheater* to watch Offenbach's *Tales of Hoffmann.* There was the usual anticipatory murmur and greetings of friends in the dimly lit house. Someone in the audience remarked: "I smell smoke." The sentence had barely been uttered when the stage curtain, billowing into the audience, revealed a stage already ablaze. FIRE!

Panic gripped the full house as the audience turned en masse in a rush to the doors. But the terrified knot of humanity threw itself against doors which opened into the theatre. Pressure increased and people were crushed at the doors as the flames lashed out into the gracefully curved theatre. It took firemen with axes hours before they could force the doors, only to find mounds of charred corpses; soon ambulances and hundreds of coffins were brought before the theatre where morticians worked without let-up amid the almost unbearable stench of burned flesh. It took weeks before most of the victims of the *Ringtheater* fire could be identified. The fire is credited with having brought about two major theatre safety features throughout the world: the asbestos curtain, separating stage from audience, and doors opening outward in theatres and other public places.

Only two weeks before the *Ringtheater* fire Johann had presented Vienna with a new operetta, *Der Lustige Krieg (The Merry War).* It was to give Vienna its stamp at a time when, after the fire, nobody went to a dance or a theatre, when Offenbach's opera was kept off Vienna's stages for years, when Vienna's amusements were at a standstill, except for *The Merry War.* Only Johann could rouse Vienna from its mournful mood at that terrible moment in its musical history; but Strauss magic prevailed. While officials mournfully bowed under the weight of public indignation over what was considered carelessness regarding public safety, while the mayor of Vienna resigned and the grizzly identification of corpses went on, only two men dispelled the gloom, Strauss and Girardi. Otherwise, predictably, the fate of *Der Lustige Krieg* was preordained by previous instances and predicaments. The *Neues Wiener Tagblatt* of 26 November 1881 said:

> It will always remain a mystery why a composer of the caliber of Johann Strauss does not act with more sureness in judging matters concerning his inventiveness ... One should think that the man from whose pen came *Die Fledermaus* and *Karneval* ... and other equally splendid productions, which delighted not only Vienna but every place where the word operetta has meaning, would receive ... hundreds of texts ... one among them should be just right in the eyes of those with keen judgment. But that does not seem the case ... Is Johann Strauss perhaps so careless in his choice of material ... because he feels it in his power that the magic formula of his music will make the barren staff bloom? ... The composer of the *Fledermaus* has won so many victories over adverse conditions that it must seem so by now.

Yet, during its brief reign *Der Lustige Krieg* imprinted its own stamp on mourning Vienna. It was again an Italian rococo piece in the fashion of *Cagliostro*, *Karneval*, or *Nacht in Venedig*, once more evidencing the staying power of the Italian influence on Strauss. The premiere, however, marked an extraordinary event. *Der Lustige Krieg* excelled in lavish production and was marked by an especially rich orchestration. But above all it had Girardi and the *Natur-Walzer*. Girardi, by then, was a star of the first order. But there were some who felt that an up-and-coming comic, Schweighofer, was soon to rival him. When the rumors reached Girardi he went to his friend Strauss and demanded a special song in that new operetta he was readying. Strauss demurred, "This is a fine time to ask me for a new couplet. This operetta is finished, it is well rounded; you have a beautiful role in it. It doesn't need another song." Girardi replied, "It does so—Sure I do a lot of mugging in it but where is my great song, our great song that will bring down the house?" "Sorry my friend, but this operetta, in my opinion, doesn't need another song"—this was Strauss's rejoinder. "Then find yourself another comic." Since there was no alternative, Strauss relented. The result was the *Nature* waltz. And Girardi's unfailing theatre sense carried the performance for seventy consecutive evenings. Never before had one couplet carried an entire evening. When Girardi had finished *"Nur für Natur,"* Vienna was his. Only Gustav Pick's *Fiakerlied*, as sung by Girardi four years later, was to top the triumph of *Nature* waltz. Night after night audiences demanded repeat after repeat of the waltz ditty, then joined in as if intoxicated, particularly when upon repetition of the refrain, Girardi, with a twinkle, a ritard, a gesture, a pathetic smile all his own injected heavy Viennese accent into the couplet thus making it a Viennese jewel, a marvel of innuendo and double entendre:

Nur für Natur	But for Nature
Hegte sie	Harbored she

Sympathie	Sympathy
Unter Bäumen	Under Greens
Süsses Träumen	Sweetest Dreams
Liebte Gräfin Melanie	Thus loved Countess Melanie

Nobody actually knows who brought the text for the couplet to Strauss's attention. The book had been hammered together by the ubiquitous pair of Zell and Genée, but the verse might have come from Franz Wagner, Vienna's music man of all trades, folk singer, music dealer, and librettist. Girardi, however, insisted that he had found the couplet text and suggested it to Strauss, who supplied the perfect waltz.

Girardi's triumph proved decisive for Vienna operetta because from then on Strauss operettas became even more tailored to Girardi's talents and requests. Girardi possessed the Austrian knack for parody, the Italian penchant for improvisation and lust for singing, the Viennese inclination for all that was relaxed and easygoing. He was that rare combination of the jester with the ingratiating voice, the comedian who walked the edge of tragedy.

If *Der Lustige Krieg*, despite Strauss, Girardi, and the *Nature* waltz, was to enjoy only a limited existence, fate had chosen Strauss for one more immortal triumph. Through intrigue Strauss had been robbed of a good book with Polish milieu and through poor judgment he was to fail with a "Slavic" book, but he was not to be denied his triumph with a Hungarian story. Strauss, however, would have to run the dreary gamut once more before fortune beckoned. In all fairness Strauss can only be half-blamed for the next miserable libretto for *Eine Nacht in Venedig (One Night in Venice)*, because Zell and Genée had deceived Strauss in favor of Millöcker. But aside from the cheap ruse Strauss opted for the Italian libretto because, after the French fiasco of *Methusalem*, he yearned to return to the Italian scene which he dearly loved. The disaster was compounded by the fact that the operetta was given in Berlin. Strauss chose the German city over Vienna for purely personal reasons. Rumor in Vienna had it that Lili, Strauss's estranged wife, had become the mistress of Franz Steiner who had succeeded his father Maximilian as director of the *Theater an der Wien*. Actually tongues wagged so loosely that, according to some, Lili was the companion of Steiner the father—according to others, the mistress of Steiner the son. When the gossip reached Strauss, he thought it a fitting revenge to take his latest operetta away from Steiner and the *Theater an der Wien*. Nobody was to cuckold Strauss and get away with it. Half of Europe would love the honor of opening the new production. Berlin bid for it and, having been promised a gala production in the brand-new *Friedrich Wilhelm Städtisches Theater*, Strauss chose the German city.

For once Johann was mildly disturbed about the libretto, and about its reception by the smart Berlin public. Rumor concerning the general opinion reached him even before the premiere; the text, the tongues wagged again, was unadulterated trash; compared to it, *Der Lustige Krieg* sounded like a Shakespearian masterpiece. Uneasy, Strauss at first decided not to conduct the premiere. Only at the last moment did he change his mind in the hope that the proverbial Strauss magic would save the day. For once it did not. Newspaper critic Ferdinand Gross on 3 October 1883 wrote:

> The premiere of *Eine Nacht in Venedig* took an unpleasant turn which, in Viennese terms, could be called a theatre scandal. The first and second acts were greeted with friendly applause, the dull libretto preventing stormy acknowledgement as certain musical numbers would have deserved ... [but] during the rendition of the Lagoon Waltz there developed unrest which later on deteriorated into a caterwauling maliciously started in the galleries. From the beginning the mood of part of the public struck one as peculiar since Johann Strauss ... was received rather coolly. Even the most beautiful numbers did not catch on and met with public apathy ... The part of the tenor which read "At night all cats are grey and gently cry meow" became the signal for a regular cats' serenade from the gallery. The noise abated only when the greater, more intelligent part of the public through "Bravo" calls forced a repetition of the waltz. But ... the sorry spectacle was repeated ... the waltz could not be finished ... Strauss sat at the conductor's desk, pale and trembling ... The operetta was rejected in Berlin. In a few days Vienna will have its say.

The opening reception actually had been friendly; after all, it was Strauss bowing on the podium. The first act came off in fairly entertaining fashion. At first even the dissenting voices were drowned out by friendly applause. It was the constantly compounded silliness of the script which prompted audience disapproval in ever increasing volume. The disapproval eventually became so strong that the leading tenor, upon whispered instructions from off-stage, continued to sing without words. This only tended to increase the catcalls from the audience which sentenced all belated on-the-spot efforts to inevitable failure.

> One cannot understand how Strauss could bring himself to set to music so confused a mess of silliness and nonsense. Not those who wrote the libretto but he who brought it on stage bears the responsibility and therefore Herr Strauss should not complain if the success was not complete. It was he who from the outset made it impossible. *(Kreuz Zeitung)*

> It is to be regretted that the musical ideas of Strauss ... which did not deserve such fate, lost their impact in such a manner ... the finale of the second act left the most favorable impression ... from there on the musical value of the work decreased as the text became obnoxious. Strauss is too fine and

delicate [a composer] to compound such blockhead nonsense; but alas, every time he attempts to contend with the coarse jokes of his collaborators he comes out second best. *(National Zeitung)*

Vienna was determined to make up for the Berlin debacle, and anxiously awaited 9 October. Strauss's personal feelings had to give way to artistic needs, and the Vienna premiere was again at the *Theater an der Wien*. The house was packed to the bursting point and scalpers had reaped small fortunes. When Johann appeared, he received a standing ovation. Although the Vienna public also made no bones about its feelings concerning the book, the evening was a splendid success. There was, however, no question that compared to Berlin the quality of the Vienna ensemble was superior. The spirit of the Vienna public also added to the charm and success of the hour. The *Lagunen Walzer*, fitted with new words and sung incomparably by Girardi, was received enthusiastically enough for three repetitions. But it was the sensual *Gondellied (Gondola Song)* which conjured up the lazy lagoons, and Girardi's mimicry which saved the day for *Eine Nacht in Venedig*. However, despite innumerable curtain calls for Strauss there was no doubt that his music had foundered on the boring libretto.

The most exasperating element of the fiasco was Strauss's own view. He wrote to a friend:

> The nature of the book is such that with the best intention I could not find inspiration in it ... It is scatterbrained and bombastic without a trace of action ...
>
> I never saw the libretto dialogue, only the words of the songs. There I put too much nobility into some parts which were unfit for the whole. There is nothing in this book to which a noble interpretation would apply.
>
> At the dress rehearsal I discovered the whole story! I was simply horrified ... nothing but nonsense. The music has nothing in common with such crazy inartistic material ...
>
> Only one thing gives me satisfaction—that it was found impossible to prevent failure in Berlin. I should rejoice still more if the entire thing was soon to be shelved. Anybody who wants it can steal it; I shall shed no tears.

Difficulties of all sorts were to befall Johann in particular and Vienna operetta in general. "Working with two librettists always makes for double work for the composer," he complained to his brother Eduard. But other, more serious difficulties arose, such as the depletion of the ranks of the Vienna ensembles. Knowingly or intuitively Strauss had written roles and arias for specific favorites of the Vienna stage. He made no secret of asking Girardi's advice and tailoring songs to his style. With such emphasis on one star, even if a great talent, the famous ensemble work which had been one of the proud hallmarks of Viennese operetta for many years was bound to suffer. Besides, many artists had either retired or passed away and new talent had to be discovered. Thus, imperceptibly, the style descended to a level of coarseness which had been tolerated only in the earliest infant days of the genre. "Continuity of story line, if we can speak of story line at all, seems inevitably to culminate in a face slapping scene," said a Vienna press report. The Vienna theatrical scene also underwent changes. Some of the more prominent suburban operetta stages encountered unbearable financial difficulties and disappeared and it was eventually left to the *Theater an der Wien* to be the sole support of the operettic repertoire of Vienna. Although the end of the century saw the building of three new theatres in Vienna between 1889 and 1898, they restricted their repertoire to spoken plays; worse, whatever operetta began to lack in textual and musical content, was glossed over in splendid productions.

Strauss's activity by then was greatly hampered by Vienna's celebration of his forty years of musical activity. And Vienna led the way by conferring upon its "child" honorary citizenship and celebrating with a monster theatrical concert at the *Theater an der Wien*. The program included the Overture to *Indigo;* the *Blue Danube* waltz (by popular demand); the first act of *A Night in Venice;* the waltz from *Blind Man's Buff;* and the entire second act from *Fledermaus.* The grand ballroom scene from *Fledermaus* was, of course, the ideal occasion to introduce Vienna's favorite actors, singers, and melodies. Girardi sang the *Nature* waltz, and even the first strains of the yet unfinished *Zigeunerbaron* were heard for the first time.

22

Hungarian Goulash

While attending a performance of *The Merry War* in Budapest, Adele Strauss had suggested to Johann that they visit the Hungarian author Maurus Jokai, one of the shining lights on the literary horizon of Hungary, and former protégé of Petöfi.[1] Upon his return to Vienna, Strauss brought with him Jokai's romantic novel *Saffi*, which he handed to the Viennese journalist and writer Ignatz Schnitzer with the request to examine its possibilities for an operettic libretto. Even before he had met the writer, Johann had known about Schnitzer's enthusiasm for Hungarian literature. The choice of Schnitzer was especially logical because he had translated Petöfi into German. In Schnitzer, who was knowledgeable about Hungary and its literature as well as about artistic and musical matters, Strauss finally found a worthy counterpart. Hopes ran high that Strauss, at that late hour, had finally awakened to the realization that, as he wrote Max Kalbeck, "a composer must sleep in the same bed with his librettist." Due to Schnitzer's insistence on immaculate workmanship, continuity, and unhurried development, work on *Der Zigeunerbaron (The Gypsy Baron)* proceeded unusually slowly and required two years from inception to premiere. The results proved the effort worthwhile. *Zigeunerbaron* was fated to be the last blaze of operettic fireworks to illumine the nineteenth-century Vienna sky.

Work on *Zigeunerbaron* began in November 1883. Schnitzer, in a conversation with a fellow journalist, gives a glimpse of the phenomenon that was Strauss.

> The development of the action and the dramatic division into acts from the original book happened practically before Strauss's eyes ... we casually discussed song texts and their fitting into the development of the action, with me doing all I could to satisfy the difficult composer ... Under these circumstances the operetta developed like a mosaic quickly assembled from tiny stones ... The inspiration [of Strauss] is truly instantaneous and occasionally he found the melody after one look at the text, such as the entrance couplet

1. Sandor Petöfi (1822-1849) was a Hungarian poet and patriot who inspired the lyrical and intensely patriotic sensibilities of his country. He lost his life during the Hungarian revolutionary war.

[of Zsupan], *"Das Schreiben und das Lesen"* ("Writing and Reading") ... Strauss is as harsh on his own compositions as he is with his librettists ... In *Zigeunerbaron* he recomposed certain numbers as often as four or five times.

Strauss plays the piano mostly when guests are present, after supper. This is not done to make himself heard but simply because he feels the urge to make music. If one does not want him to play one has only to ask him not to do so ... When playing he becomes too heated and involved in the music that one has to ask him to stop lest he become sick from nervous tension ... He mostly improvises on the piano and plays serious music such as fugues; seldom dance music. If an original idea comes to mind he notates it immediately in a handy note book ... one comment [by Strauss] concerning the scoring of *Zigeunerbaron* is typical: "Look, all this I scored from memory; that's the way I prefer to compose. Others get into the habit of composing at the piano; but then they do what the piano wants them to do, not what they want to do. He who doesn't have it here—and he pointed to the heart—won't be able to squeeze it out of the piano either."

Der Zigeunerbaron depicts gypsies, buried treasure, romance, drama, and of course, high comedy. An abandoned gypsy girl turns up as a pasha's daughter; a humble but brave man is ennobled for his deeds by his sovereign and declared "baron" by the gypsies. The music is that of gypsy tunes, czardas, and the Viennese waltz.

Franz Liszt had brought the gypsy music of Hungary from the stable and the village green into the concert hall. In the process the singing, sobbing gypsy fiddles had lost some of their genuine originality but, in turn, had become known and loved by all the world.

Strauss had been immediately captivated by the story and its possibilities. To emphasize the milieu he had wanted Barinkay, the hero, to make his entrance to czardas strains. But Schnitzer, patiently, wisely, convincingly, argued that this would be a mistake, that Barinkay was a man of the world only now returning to Hungary. Strauss agreed and the result was an entrance in the universal waltz tempo with the blazing refrain: *"Ja! das Alles auf Ehr'/Das kann ich und noch mehr!"* ("Yes! All that, 'pon my honor!/All that I can do, and more!"). Egged on by Schnitzer and the director of the *Theater an der Wien*, Strauss worked as never before, and this time even paid attention to scenario and stage arrangement. One scene—the entrance march—was particularly on his mind as he described his idea of it in a note to Schnitzer: "eighty to one hundred soldiers (on foot and on horseback), camp followers in Spanish, Hungarian, and Viennese costumes, people, children with armfuls of flowers which they will strew into the path of the returning soldiers, etc., must appear, with the stage deepened right to the back wall; it must be a grandiose picture because this time we wish to present Austrian military splendor and the people in a joyful mood over the victory." Later, in Saffi's aria *"Habet acht vor den Kindern der Nacht"* ("Beware of the Children of the Night"), Strauss touched on the elusive splendor that was to lead him on throughout his life—the operatic aria. Again, with Schnitzer's inspired collaboration, he rose to operatic heights in the love duet: *"Und mild sang die Nachtigall ihr Liedchen in die Nacht/Die Liebe, die Liebe, ist eine Himmelsmacht."* ("And gently the nightingale sang her song into the night/Love, oh love is truly heaven's might.")

But what would Viennese operetta be without its comic moments, without a comic role for Girardi. The role of Zsupan, the Swine King, was made to order.

> *Das Schreiben und das Lesen*
> *Sind nie mein Fach gewesen*
> *Denn schon von Kindesbeinen*
> *Befasst ich mich mit Schweinen.*
>
> *Ja, mein idealer Lebenszweck*
> *Ist Borstenvieh, ist Schweinespeck.*
>
> The art of writing and reading
> With me always took a beating
> Because since childhood's time
> I handled only swine.
>
> Yes, my ideal aim in Life's surcease
> Is bristle beasts and bacon grease.

Girardi the artist breathed life into the figure of the boastful crafty swine breeder until he expanded the role into a mixture of what had been Falstaff and was to be Ochs von Lerchenau in Richard Strauss's *Rosenkavalier*. Beyond the clumsy crude exterior, the crafty mind, the greedy trader and soldier (of sorts), Girardi's knowing wink held up a mirror to his time.

Minor objections by the censors had to be overcome. *Die Geheime Sittenkommission* (The Secret Morals Commission) had to be mentioned without the word "imperial," and its orders could not be carried out by the "gracious order of his majesty," nor could gypsies live in "wild" marriage. But all this was easily overcome and the premiere was finally set for 24 October 1885 at the *Theater an der Wien*. The director, Franz von Jauner, had spared no effort to provide a production true to its subject in every detail. He had even traveled to Raab in Hungary to observe Hungarian life in general and the authenticity of the gypsies in particular. He returned, enriched with original costumes and customs. The Vienna press reported:

The entire evening grew into a great triumph for the composer ... the stormy applause with which Herr Strauss was received and which erupted after every theme of the overture, repeated itself with every song ... The evening was one of the historic operettic highlights in Vienna's history. Karl Streitmann sang the gypsy baron Barinkay with the power and splendor of youth and strength and the ensemble which had been assembled represented the most splendid roster in the Vienna of the time, with the comic figure of Zsupan the swine breeder, as depicted by Girardi, the comic highpoint of the evening.

Strauss wrote to Girardi: "It is in your power to decide what is to be and what is not to be ... the popularity which you enjoy is a natural consequence of your performance ... all your triumphs in popularity and recognition were dearly bought with the sweat of your brow and artistic devotion. Lady Luck surely smiled on you, there can be no question about that!!" There were, at that time, three names in Vienna which were spoken with various degrees of reverence: Franz Joseph, Johann Strauss, and Alexander Girardi. Dramatist Karl Schönherr wrote: "In the long line of Vienna's genuine folk actors who rose from the people and devoted their art to the people, a line which includes such illustrious names as Kurz-Bernardon, Raimund and Nestroy, Girardi was the last and glorious finale of an art which died with him ... Girardi was not a folk actor, but the people personified, strengthened, deepened, and refined." A fellow actor, Alexander Moissi, praised Girardi: "The most important and strongest feature of Girardi was his kindness, pure human kindness of the heart in all its shadings ... a great genial artist, completely in control of all technical detail, whose performances showed not only the great actor but the human being as well ... I have seen him in all his famous roles ... he touched me most when he was called upon to portray kindness and humanity ... It was not important which role he played, I did not even consult the program. He was there and that sufficed."

As for Strauss, the evening of the *Gypsy Baron* premiere was to be an event unmatched in the history of operetta. The packed house demanded so many repetitions of so many numbers that the entire operetta was sung almost three times that very evening, and the operetta itself repeated eighty-five times that one season alone. Johann—finally—had another unqualified, enduring success, his first since *Fledermaus*, and his second most popular work in Europe as well as in New York, Philadelphia, Pittsburgh, Chicago, and Detroit.

Gypsy Baron, unexpectedly, also proved as important politically as in the field of operetta. It fulfilled a mission, provided understanding between Austria and Hungary when efforts at diplomacy, politicking, intrigue, and saber-rattling had been to no avail. The waltz and the csardas thus fulfilled more than musical unity, and the finale became a triumph for both nations.

Alexander Girardi, in one of his most cherished roles, as Zsupan the Swine King in Strauss's The Gypsy Baron.

Strauss was sixty years old. The list of recent years was impressive: *Indigo,* 1871; *Karneval,* 1873; *Fledermaus,* 1874; *Cagliostro,* 1875; *Methusalem,* 1877; *Blinde Kuh,* 1878; *Das Spitzentuch der Königin,* 1880; *Der Lustige Krieg,* 1881; *Eine Nacht in Venedig,* 1883; *Zigeunerbaron,* 1885. From the exuberant *Indigo* to the splendid *Zigeunerbaron* the Vienna operetta, through Strauss's genius, had established itself firmly, supremely throughout the world.

23

Burnt Toast

The work to follow *Zigeunerbaron*, again in collaboration with Schnitzer, was to have been an adaptation of *Der Schelm von Bergen (The Rogue of Bergen)*. The two men were already in intense consultation with Girardi, when Strauss, through the comment of an acquaintance, found out that a similar figure, a kind, reluctant executioner, was also the central figure in Gilbert and Sullivan's *Mikado*. The subject was dropped.

In 1885, a fortunately shortlived phenomenon made its appearance in the German music theatres of Europe. Victor Nessler's Old German opera *Der Trompeter von Säckingen*, with its sentimental story line accompanied by Nessler's tawdry music, created a style and time that never existed except in the fantasy of Nessler and his ilk. It was unrealistic, misshapen, and sentimentally fraudulent. But the time for such sentimental trumpery was ripe, and *Trompeter* became an overnight success. What prompted such mistaken appeal? It appears that Nessler's opera had become the poor man's answer to Wagner's Siegfried, Wotan, and Valhalla, appealing to the most banal artistic instincts and visions—bogus Germanism rampant.

Again Strauss took the bait. For a long time now he had been caught in opera fever, his not-so-secret passion for "serious" music. Still naively ignorant of the theatre, he fell prey to most of its intrigue and ruses, was broken-hearted when a seemingly promising libretto escaped him, heedlessly searched for another one, a good one, a bad one, any libretto, stubbing his artistic toe over and over again in the process. Max Kalbeck keenly observed the scene:

> Whether [Strauss] could not judge, did not have the independence or energy to stick to judgment, the fact remains that everybody's opinion was correct, particularly the one of the last person asked. He lent an ear to a great number of uncalled advisers who often knew less on the subject than he and thus threw him into the most terrible confusion. Before he decided on a subject, veritable palace revolutions took place in the Igelgasse and the intrigues ... were often more amusing to the innocent bystander than the libretti

Theodor Reichmann in his role in Nessler's The Trumpeter of Säckingen. The opera was as ridiculous as the costume.

Studio of the painter Hans Makart in Vienna. Aquarell by Rudolf Alt, 1885.

eventually selected. The deciding factor in the selection was the prevailing taste of the public. It was the starting point in the search for a scenario and vocal numbers.

Strauss's collaborator, Zell, strongly warned him against those false friends and incompetent advisors, but his words went unheeded. The prevailing taste of the public hungered for the "Old German" never-never land. Firm in his decision and desire to reach a "higher plateau," Strauss promptly selected the most unlikely German hero possible, Grimmelshausen's *Simplizius Simplizissimus*.[1] "I am no longer the good-natured, indulgent Johann in the matter of books submitted to me ... [*Simplizius*] generally and in musical consideration will be treated much more gaily by me than *Zigeunerbaron*. Whereas in *Zigeunerbaron* Hungarian rhythm had to be taken into consideration, this time some Viennese will appear in my work, particularly in the overture, and in some situations I can strike a more serious note." Things seemed to fall into place. Jauner was now managing the *Carltheater* and eagerly sought the next Strauss premiere. Of course production, orchestra, and ensemble would be of the very best. Whatever the *Theater an der Wien* could do the *Carltheater* could do better. Everybody wanted to start afresh; something better, something bigger, something new. But closer examination showed that it was the same shoddy old theatre. Despite Jauner's efforts, the premiere went to the *Theater an der Wien*.

Johann had arrived at the *Simplizius* libretto via a circuitous route. Rumor had it that Victor Leon, Lehár's later librettist, had written a successful scenario, *The Double*, for the famous Spanish harpist and composer Alfred Zamara. The work was pronounced a novelty and proved a success in Munich. Young Leon belonged to that new wing of the theatre which cried out for new story lines, realism, naturalism. *The Double* was then considered a milestone on that road. Johann invited Leon for dinner. The young newcomer responded to the honor with delight and alacrity. They discussed stories and in the course of conversation Victor mentioned that he was working on another libretto for Zamara, *Simplizius*, a story of the Thirty Years' War. Johann should have been on guard immediately since that grim event was hardly to yield a likely story background for even a "serious" operetta. But the casual remark ignited his interest. If Zamara wanted it, Strauss must have it. Thus, during the course of the evening and the courses of the champagne

---

1. Hans Jakob Christoffel von Grimmelshausen (1625-1676) was kidnapped at age ten by Hessian soldiers and pressed into service in the Thirty Years' War. He was self-taught in letters and the law. His major work, a picaresque novel entitled *The Adventuresome Simplizius Simplizissimus* (1669), was an immediate success. Some consider it the first biographical novel and among the greatest novels of the seventeenth century.

Johann Strauss's billiard room.

dinner Victor Leon switched allegiances. Strauss waxed enthusiastic. Here was the "real German stuff," no more simple, trite, cut-and-dried plots for him. He was totally blinded to its unsuitability—a hermit, barely able to speak, a pure naive fool, released to manhood by woman's love—and to the fact that somebody else had already written a magnificent work on the subject, Wagner in *Parsifal*. Leon was to go on to notable successes (his most spectacular, the libretto to Lehár's *Merry Widow*) but *Simplizius* turned out to be his weakest work. *Simplizius*, which was to have been gayer than *Gypsy Baron*, only became longer and had to undergo drastic cuts. Actually the work was doomed to failure from the outset because Strauss was forced to work at cross purposes—to combine the innate Straussian lightheartedness which the public expected with his avowed intention to deviate from the traditional forms and characters of the operettic past. Yet Johann felt inspired. He worked without rest, passed up a Strauss cycle in Berlin, and handed his score over amid soaring hopes and enthusiam. Leon was so confident of success that he refused a flat fee in favor of a percentage agreement.

The premiere on 12 December 1887 had everything. The vivid picture of the Thirty Years' War, complete with glinting armor and Wallenstein's camp, disguises, plots, and counterplots—everything except Johann Strauss. The public yawned and sat on its hands. Despite Johann's supposed magic, the aim remained as unattainable as was to be expected from the beginning. Waltz themes constantly collided with serious action and lilt ran afoul of symbolism. Like Parsifal, Strauss searched in vain for a common denominator for grim war and carefree peace. Opera (and Strauss clearly intended *Simplizius* as a forerunner to a later opera) is not easily composed, as Beethoven, Schubert, Schumann, Wolf, and Humperdinck could sadly attest. While individual numbers charmed the audience, the work itself was a failure. To make things worse, a fire alarm during the second act brought people to their feet, ready to flee the theatre. After they were calmed by advice from the stage, a second alarm sounded from the gallery. Surprisingly, the only man to remain calm during the double hubbub was Johann Strauss. He simply repeated the lilting waltz romance and thus saved what little there remained to be saved of the evening. The splendid production could not conceal the weaknesses and contradictions. Surprisingly, Hanslick praised the music: "*Simplizius* has today a rare advantage over all previous works of Strauss; the music is unforced, unaffected throughout, naive in the best sense of the word ... the instrumentation is dainty and alive ... obviously not from the pen of a man striving for mere effect but from a pure musician who is anointed with a drop of Mozart's oil." But Hanslick continued in scathing terms when he discussed the action and stage direction: "[*Simplizius*] does not move but is artificially stretched by artificially filling empty holes and by pushing it ... Mr. Leon has done little with the people which surround the main figure ... their sentimentalities are served in large steins, their wit and humor in tiny liqueur glasses. The two main humorous figures ... are completely out of style and have little to do with the basic theme." Ernst Decsey, the music critic of the *Neues Wiener Tagblatt*, assessed the failure even more realistically: "Like a stream dreaming of beauties left behind and beyond recall, so the music of *Simplizius* is touching, because its gaiety is forced and no longer artistically naive."

Groping for a new style of musical theatre Strauss had abandoned that "artistically naive" plateau without creating a new or artistically superior one. Gaiety had departed, leaving a void. Yet Strauss went on because he could not help but compose, going with open eyes into literary quicksand from which often even his music could not extricate him. Pressures from publishers, competitors, his own ambition, theatre directors, all played a considerable part in his failures. Another problem was that Johann preferred men of the world of art and music, to men of the theatre. Watching the ill manners of those who guzzled wine at the dinner table or attended one of his soirées in business suits, annoyed him and turned him against theatre men in general. Thus he never truly established lasting and valuable theatrical or literary connections, so necessary in his field, but depended mostly on the house-hacks of his publishers.

"For an excellent book I'd be willing to make great sacrifices," the disgusted but not discouraged Strauss sighed as he kept up an uncaring search. In reality he had learned little from the experience of his collaboration with Schnitzer in producing *Gypsy Baron*, an experience of true artistic understanding that resulted in an artistic libretto. He seemed to have remembered only that Jokai had been a Hungarian and that Schnitzer, although Viennese, had been deeply interested in Hungarian literature. Thus when Strauss learned that another Hungarian writer, Ludwig Doczi, was enjoying a moderate success at the *Burgtheater* with his play *The Kiss*, he sought the writer out. Doczi had excellent credentials. If Schnitzer had translated Petöfi into German, Doczi had an even more monumental feat to his credit; he had translated Goethe's *Faust* into Hungarian, as well as Hungarian drama into German. Strauss, impressed, entrusted Doczi with the writing of a book for Strauss's ambitious dream of an opera. What he received in turn was *Ritter Pazmann* — undramatic, unfunny, senseless.

Consider the opening gambit. Old Count Pazmann feels his honor has been besmirched by the king, who kissed Pazmann's wife on the forehead. Thereupon the queen allows Pazmann to kiss her — on the forehead, of course. Thereupon the king is offended. Such dreary, witless inanity became the basis of the plot, a comic opera without comedy, with "action" that hinders rather than stirs or advances. The main consideration was not human drama or human comedy, but fitting a role to the talents of a Girardi, a Blasel, a Schweighofer, or a Pallenberg. To tickle the Viennese funny bone with a role tailored to a comedian's talents was to insure half its success; the other half was the music of Strauss on which one could always depend and would not have to worry about. So intent was Johann on opera that he again closed his mind and wasted his sparkling gems in bookish wasteland. Thus it is not surprising that the ballet music of *Ritter Pazmann* is the highlight of the opera. Hanslick went so far as to call it "an opera built around a ballet." The *Pazmann* waltzes and polkas promptly became famous and popular as independent concert pieces, but otherwise, despite revampings, *Pazmann* became another corpse in the graveyard of operettas.

Vienna had been eager for the Strauss opera. It was to be another "first" for the musical city, a Strauss opera at the Imperial Opera House. (Strauss's *Fledermaus* had of course been heard within those hallowed halls, but that was operetta or comic opera, at best.) The premiere on 1 January 1892 saw the entire artistic apparatus of the famed Opera House at Strauss's disposal in a splendid production. There were gems throughout the work; the drinking song, the romance of Ritter Pazmann, and, of course, the ballet were received with stormy applause, as if the public felt that Strauss, in those musical interludes, delivered from bookish nonsense, had spread his wings. But after it was all over, *Ritter Pazmann* had failure written all over it and the end came after nine performances.

With *Fürstin Ninetta (Countess Ninetta)*, Strauss was back to operetta, this time with two librettists, journalists Hugo Wittmann and Julius Bauer (if one journalist could do such a splendid job with *Gypsy Baron* how much better would two journalists be). Undaunted as ever, Strauss was in a hurry. The contract with the journalist-librettists specified "prompt delivery" of a new operetta libretto. Again all the outward ingredients were there, a splendid *Theater an der Wien* production; one of Strauss's most glittering gems, the *Pizzicato Polka*; Girardi in the role of Kassim Pasha; an eagerly awaiting public; and a packed house including Emperor Franz Joseph. *Fürstin Ninetta* remained, however, in operettic twilight, neither failure nor wild success; despite seventy-five performances it never moved beyond the Vienna boards.

Soon thereafter Strauss heard Smetana's *Bartered Bride* in German translation and production and was enchanted by the charm of the melodious opera by the Bohemian master. It stirred memories in Johann; he had missed out on a Polish milieu when Millöcker was handed the book for *Bettelstudent*, but his entry into the Hungarian world of music in *Zigeunerbaron* had had the blessing of the gods. Thus, when Gustav Davis and Max Kalbeck submitted to Strauss a book entitled *Jabuka*, a story with Croatian background, his eyes lit up. His enthusiasm ran even higher when he discovered in the book that the comic figure, Joschko, was a direct descendant of Frosch, the jailer in *Fledermaus*. The operetta simply would have to be a success because there was the perfect role for Girardi.

But Strauss by then had more enthusiasm than time to do his work in solitude because of the fiftieth anniversary celebrations in his honor. Vienna and the world did not permit him solitude. Since the premiere of *Jabuka* coincided with the celebrations, anticipatory excitement was high. The house was of course sold out, and the animated spirit of the glittering audience interrupted the actual performance innumerable times. Surprisingly, nobody minded, least of all Girardi. The highlight of the evening was reserved for the third act. Girardi had not been overly busy in the

*Official portrait of Johann Strauss at the time
of his Jubilee.*

entire operetta but for the third act Strauss had written the inevitable couplet for his comic friend. Girardi had secretly written and added another verse to the couplet, which related to the anniversary. When he, in his masterly comic fashion, sang the verse it transformed the house into a happy orgy of shouting, weeping, and waving of handkerchiefs. And all of it was crowned by the appearance of the composer on stage, following Girardi's rendition of the couplet. Several minutes later the jubilant storm abated and the audience, in sudden total silence, expectantly looked at the two men on stage, Girardi and Strauss. Neither of them spoke. Girardi slowly bowed to Strauss in his inimitable fashion; Strauss bowed to Girardi, imitating him smilingly. No more, no less, but the house understood and again a happy hurricane engulfed Vienna's great son.

The *Theater an der Wien* was by no means alone in its celebration. The Imperial Opera added a new ballet-tableau, "Vienna Dance Music," in homage to Johann, and the *Carltheater* produced a festive play on the entire Strauss family. At the highlight of all festivities was the Grand Concert. The Vienna Press reported that as Strauss appeared on stage

> all rose from their seats and exploded into shouts of jubilation, a raging, roaring delirium ... What passed before us was half a century of tone creation, more than half a century of Viennese local history. In the eloquent language of tones one was reminded what treasures in pleasant sound Johann Strauss had strewn during the course of his life. Whenever one of the favorite waltzes was intoned, a sort of joyous intoxication ran through the audience, and ... naturally with the *Blue Danube* waltz the public broke in with applause and almost started to sing and dance. The older generation proved itself renewed to the present generation and the majority of those present heard many a splendid work for the first time. One could not help observing that many beautiful women and young girls who listened entranced barely could sit still in their seats, but sent glowing looks of thanks to the master, who himself had forgotten some of those pearls from his treasury.

Jabuka, despite Girardi, did not fulfill Strauss's hopes for another *Zigeuner-baron*. A little over a year later, on 4 December 1895, another Strauss operetta, *Waldmeister (Woodruff)*, with a text by Gustav Davis, bowed at the *Theater an der Wien*. Strauss, who had at first hesitated, for a change decided to read the libretto and was soon attracted to what seemed a bright comedy of errors and mistaken identity (which had worked so well in *Fledermaus*). But the relaxed tempo and wit of the Old German comedy had outlived its usefulness. Besides, the locale of this "Viennese" operetta was laid in—of all places—Saxony, and Girardi, as Viennese as *Schnitzel*, played a professor with a Saxonian accent. The libretto itself had been fashioned by a comedy writer who turned it into a "gag" book totally unsuited to stage. The result was provincial *Fledermaus*—"tea compared to champagne." In now time-honored repetition, the overture and the waltzes again became the highlights of the evening, for the rest—oblivion. Significantly, nobody disputed the beauty of music which featured an interesting novelty, a sort of *Tonmalerei*, a musical background to the spoken dialogue, which proved more interesting than the inane text itself. Yet again, the severest critic of them all, Hanslick, tipped his hat to Strauss:

> It is no *lèse majesté* to say that Mozart's golden sound reigned in the orchestra. *Waldmeister* is filled with gaiety from beginning to end ... the locale of the action is not specified but the music expresses it beyond any doubt. It is an Austrian, a good Viennese work. The libretto belongs among the better operettic texts ... there are less comic characters as there are comic situations ... Strauss, to the joy of all, returned to the spirit of *Fledermaus* ... If *Waldmeister*, despite its ingratiating sweetness, does not sound as new and exuber-

ant as the older incomparable operettas, it will surprise nobody. Suffice it
to say that the seventy-year-old Strauss still excels and surpasses all living
operetta composers.

Even Hanslick was not infallible. According to its creator *Waldmeister's* appeal
ranged somewhere between "fiasco to half success."

Nobody felt less undaunted than Strauss. Two years later the news made the
rounds that there would be another operetta by Strauss: *Die Göttin der Vernunft.*
But the *Goddess of Reason*, destined to be Strauss's last operettic work, was poisoned
for Strauss by other than musical matters. Willner and Buchbinder had prepared
a book for Strauss which he, after surveying the preliminary scenario, praised as
having wit and humor. However, after having had opportunity to read the finished
libretto he changed his mind and was so negatively impressed that he asked to be
released from his contract to compose the music. However, the librettists would not
hear of it and insisted that Strauss honor his contract with them. In a letter liberally
sprinkled with "honored master," Willner, who also happened to be an attorney,
made no secret of the fact that Strauss would be unsuccessful in any attempt to take
the case to court because they, his collaborators, had kept their end of the contract
and had delivered the libretto. Strauss, disgusted and embittered, demurred; he
wanted no part of it. Adele Strauss, deft and shrewd as ever, suggested a way out
of legal difficulties: find a publisher who would buy the operetta before it was composed. This came to pass when the publishing house of Berté eagerly bid for it and
thus became "owners and publishers of a new operetta by Johann Strauss with a
book by Dr. A. M. Willner and Bernhard Buchbinder." Berté, wishing to protect
himself on all sides, also contracted with the *Theater an der Wien* for the performance rights.

The artistic spirit must be unfettered, but circumstances underlying the *Göttin
der Vernunft* had no such conducive elements. Needless to say, the half-hearted efforts of a Strauss still ranked above anything his contemporaries could have created.
Yet Strauss was so disgruntled that, for the first time, he boycotted a premiere performance. Thus the best efforts of the *Theater an der Wien* came to naught and
Göttin played to half-empty houses soon after the premiere. It gained temporary
momentum when the poet Felix Salten revamped the book with an enlarged and
more effective role for Girardi. But he could not prevent its joining the line of
previous operettas which had opened with brilliant premieres, lasted through the
winter snow and had disappeared with the spring thaw.

A posthumous attempt was made to write a Strauss operetta from already exist-
ing material. The libretto, *Wiener Blut*, named after Strauss's famous waltz, was
again by Victor Leon and Leo Stein, assisted by Adolf Miller, the able knowledge-

able Viennese conductor of the *Theater an der Wien*. Strauss's drawer yielded a plethora of melodies. Jauner put all his resources at the work's disposal, with first-class singers and production. The result, a total failure, crushed Jauner into a nervous breakdown. "I cannot understand these people anymore," he repeated over and over again. Three years later *Wiener Blut* became a roaring success.

24

Schlagobers

The experience with *Göttin der Vernunft* and with it the stark realities of an outside world which had become alien to the sheltered Strauss had brought about the realization that not necessarily was *Das Leben ein Tanz* (life was not a continuous ball), that not everybody was possessed of a *Goldenes Wiener Herz* (golden Viennese heart). People could be cruel, demanding, rude—even to Johann Strauss. He came to a decision. He would write ballet music.

He could not overlook the possibilities nor resist the charms of ballet, particularly in the light of recent experiences in the world of operetta. Ballet had never been as finely developed an art in Vienna as it was in Paris or later in Russia. Seldom was an entire evening at the opera given over to ballet. For the greater part it remained part of an opera performance, the *Schlagobers* (whipped cream) atop Vienna's delicious operatic fare. To write a ballet, which surely would be given the distinction of a performance at the Vienna opera house, was a logical conclusion in the creative life of Strauss. He would not have to compose for a given text, and, more encouraging, even in his less successful operetta productions, it had been the dance sequences, the ballets, which had been praised as the highlights. His friend Hanslick had clearly said so. Creative fever again possessed Strauss. His choice of subject, *Aschenbrödel* (*Cinderella*), was most felicitous. He went into seclusion and started work.

One of Strauss's sometime librettists, Buchbinder, has given us a remarkable picture of Strauss in his late years.

> He was Viennese as was his music. An arch-Viennese of the most delightful sort, that gaiety of spirit paired with superficiality which once was known as *Gemütlichkeit*. He never cared what the next day would bring and clung to the present hour with pleasurable well-being. To us younger people who had the pleasure of coming in contact with him he seemed like a big child. He did not belong to the present with its hateful wrangling ... He had remained young, without understanding of the times, because he had retired from the world. He never went anywhere. Whoever wanted to see him had to come to him ... I can still see him. In the billiard room of the main floor

Johann Strauss in his later years.

all discussions took place ... He did not sit still for long. There was always ... an electric vibration in the man ... When questions of daily affairs were talked about he sat quietly, listened, smiled, seldom participated, while smoking his old-fashioned, browned Meerschaum pipe. But once one began to talk about work, the picture changed. He came alive, twitched in his chair, gesticulated ... constantly moved his legs, changed places, while his eyes sparkled. There was something special about his eyes. Sometimes they smiled guilelessly, then suddenly they flashed demonically. One became hypnotized by them. The musical magician of Vienna was a sorcerer ... He appeared always in sartorial splendor and the latest fashion ... the thick bushy hair was always pitch black and he looked like a man in his fifties ... One must have worked with him to really know him. Everything in him was alive ... the fingers, the nostrils, the lips, the lids, a youthful redness rose in his cheeks, he looked ten years younger. Suddenly he took in the large vista of the theatre and started to write with the writers, improvised scenes, new thoughts, new twists of action ... "Let's have something new. I have the melody already. It came to me last night" ... While he was talking everything in his face smiled ... [while others talked] he fell silent. One noticed after a while that he was not listening. He composed in his mind ... [suddenly] he left the room and did not return ... How fantastically facile Strauss worked nobody can imagine. He was beyond compare ... we would arrive ... to discuss a number. We asked whether he had composed to the text we had furnished ... "Of course, I have already started with the instrumentation but I don't know whether you'll like it." We went to the piano ... he began to play ... slowly he forgot about his listeners and, gently waving his head, weaving his body into the rhythm he played, obviously enjoying it, for himself only. When he was finished ... we awakened as if from a dream. Before we could speak he spoke lively. "Actually I composed the number twice" and he began the second version. His wife asked in astonishment: "When did you do that? Until two o'clock you played cards? "Oh, at about three o'clock. Then I lay down but it still bothered me. Then I decided that it wasn't good enough, so I got up and composed it over again."

Worries in the general sense of the word he never knew ... He was satisfied to let his spouse think and act for him. But he gave much thought to the anxieties of his personal well being. Between autumn and spring he did not leave his room for months. Anything but a cold ...

An invitation, however, overrode all his fears of sickness. The occasion was another milestone in Vienna's musical history, the twenty-fifth anniversary of the *Fledermaus* premiere. He was requested to personally conduct the most famous operetta overture of them all at the festival performance on 22 May 1899. He was not feeling well because, despite all precautions, he was suffering from an attack of bronchitis. But the occasion overrode all other considerations. He received a standing ovation when he appeared at the wreath-draped conductor's stand, and con-

ducted with his proverbial vigor. Upon bowing to the storm of applause at the conclusion of the overture he was drenched and felt himself shiver in the cross drafts.
Despite attacks of dizziness he continued work on *Cinderella* and on 26 May even
received a distinguished visitor who had traveled four thousand miles to meet him.
Less than two weeks later Adele Strauss was to receive a heart-felt note from the
distraught visitor:

> When I talked and smoked with him in your house only twelve days ago he
> seemed in all ways his old natural self; alert, quick, brilliant in speech, and
> wearing all the graces of his indestructable youth; and now, why, it seems
> impossible that he is gone! I am grateful that I was privileged to have that
> pleasant meeting with him and it will remain a gracious memory with me.
>
> Mark Twain

Sources Consulted

Nineteenth century sources were often found wanting because the present-day method of detailed documentation was then either unknown or ignored. Thus the author was obliged to approach opinions and quotations with circumspection. If quotations were undocumented but appeared in a number of sources, their accuracy was assumed for lack of definitive evidence. If statements or opinions pertaining to the same event differed, the author, after careful consideration, either selected the most convincing interpretation or presented a dissenting opinion of his own. Autobiographical sources were sometimes found to be biased, distorted, or totally incorrect, mainly because of the lapse of time between event and recollection. Bibliographic sources have been listed according to subject matter, and primary sources have been identified by an asterisk. However, the author found himself unable to list in any way the countless European reviews, critiques, and articles—many without source, date, or even author's name—which had been consulted.

General

Adler, Guido. *Handbuch der Musikgeschichte.* Berlin, 1930.
Ferguson, Donald N. *A History of Musical Thought.* New York: Appleton-Century-Crofts, 1959.
*Gal, Hans, ed. *The Musician's World. Great Composers in their Letters.* New York: Arco Publishing Co., 1965.
Graf, Max. *From Beethoven to Shostakovich.* New York: Philosophical Library, 1947.
Grove, George. *Dictionary of Music and Musicians.* New York: St. Martin's Press, 1966.
*Nettl, Paul. *The Book of Musical Documents.* New York: Philosophical Library, 1948.
Riemann, Hugo. *Musiklexikon.* Leipzig, 1929.
*Slonimsky, Nicolas. *Lexicon of Musical Invective.* New York: Coleman Ross Co., 1965.
Stein, Werner. *Kulturfahrplan.* Berlin Grünewald: Verlag Herbig, 1946.

Literature

Alker, Ernst. *Franz Grillparzer; Ein Kampf um Leben und Kunst.* Marburg a. L.: N. G. Elwert, 1930.

Baumann, Gerhart. *Franz Grillparzer, sein Werk und das Österreichische Wesen.* Freiburg: Herder, 1954.

_____. *Arthur Schnitzler. Die Welt von gestern eines Dichters von morgen.* Frankfurt a. M.: Athenaum Verlag, 1965.

Bergstrasser, Arnold. *Hofmannsthal und der europäische Gedanke.* Kiel: Lepsius & Tischer, 1951.

Brill, Siegfried. *Die Komödie der Sprache. Untersuchungen zum Werke Johann Nestroys.* Nürnberg: H. Carl, 1967.

Coenen, F. E. *Franz Grillparzer's Portraiture of Men.* Chapel Hill: University of North Carolina Press, 1951.

Hammelmann, Hanns A. *Hugo von Hofmannsthal.* New Haven: Yale University Press, 1957.

Liptzin, Solomon. *Arthur Schnitzler.* New York: Prentice Hall, 1932..

Michalski, John. *Ferdinand Raimund.* New York: Twayne Publishers, 1968.

Preisner, Rio. *Johann Nepomuk Nestroy: Der Schöpfer der tragischen Posse.* Munich: Hanser, 1968.

Schaeder, Grete, and Hans Heinrich. *Hugo von Hofmannsthal und die geistige Welt.* Hameln: F. Seifert, 1947.

Schmid, Martin Erich. *Symbol und Funktion der Musik im Werk Hugo von Hofmannsthals.* Heidelberg: C. Winter, 1968.

Schreyvogl, Friedrich, ed. *Franz Grillparzer: Dichter der Letzten Dinge.* Graz: Stiasny Verlag, 1958.

_____. *Arthur Schnitzler: der Dichter und sein Werk.* Berlin: S. Fischer, 1922.

Vancsa, Kurt. *Ferdinand Raimund, ein Dichter des "Biedermeier."* Innsbruck: Tyrolia, 1936.

*Zohn, Harry, ed. *Der Farbenvolle Untergang: Österreichisches Lesebuch.* Englewood Cliffs, N.J.: Prentice-Hall, 1971.

*Zweig, Stefan. *The World of Yesterday.* Lincoln: University of Nebraska Press, 1964.

Music

Abert, Hermann. *W. A. Mozart.* Leipzig, 1955. A revised and enlarged edition of Otto Jahn's *Mozart.*

Abraham, Gerald, ed. *The Music of Schubert.* New York: W. W. Norton, 1947

Adler, Guido. *Gustav Mahler.* Vienna: Universal Edition, 1916.

*Anderson, Emily. *Letters of Mozart to His Family.* New York: McMillan, 1938.

Auer, Max. *Anton Bruckner: sein Leben und Wert.* Musikwissenschaftlicher Verlag, 1934.

Bates, Ralph. *Franz Schubert.* New York: Appleton-Century, 1934.

Beyes, Ruth. "The Tragic Star of Hugo Wolf." *Musical Courier,* March 1960.

Blom, Eric. *Richard Strauss: Der Rosenkavalier.* London: Oxford University Press, 1930.

Decsey, Ernst von. *Johann Strauss.* Stuttgart: Deutsche Verlags-Anstalt, 1922.

_____. *Franz Lehar*. Munich: Drei Masken Verlag, 1930.

_____. *Hugo Wolf*. Berlin: Schuster & Löffler, 1919.

Engel, Gabriel. *The Life of Bruckner*. New York: Roerich Museum, 1931.

Furtwängler, Wilhelm. *Johannes Brahms, Anton Bruckner*. Leipzig: Reclams Universal Bibliothek, 1942.

Geiringer, Karl. *Brahms: His Life and Work*. Boston: Houghton Mifflin, 1936.

_____. *Haydn: A Creative Life in Music*. New York: W. W. Norton & Co., 1946.

Graf, Max. "Strauss-Hofmannsthal Letters." *Musical America*, Feb. 1953

Grun, Bernard. *Die Leichte Muse. Kulturgeschichte der Operette*. Munich, Langer Muller, 1961.

Gutmann, Albert. *Aus dem Wiener Musikleben*. Vienna: A. G. Gutmann, 1914.

*Hanslick, Eduard. *Aus dem Concertsaal*. Vienna: W. Braumüller, 1870.

* _____. *Concerte, Componisten und Virtuosen, 1870-1885* Vienna: W. Braumüller, 1885.

* _____. *Aus meinem Leben*. Berlin: Allgemeiner Verein für deutsche Literatur, 1894.

_____. *Geschichte des Concertwesens in Wien*. Vienna: W. Braumüller, 1869-1970. 2 volumes.

Hughes, Gervase. *Composers of Operetta*. New York: St. Martin's Press, 1962.

Jacob, H. W. *Johann Strauss, Father and Son*. New York: The Greystone Press. 1939.

Kalbeck, Max. *Johannes Brahms*. Berlin: Deutsche Brahms Gesellschaft, 1908.

Kobald, Karl. *Alt-Wiener Musikstätten*. Zurich: Amaltheaverlag, 1919.

_____. *Johann Strauss: Das Bild seines Lebens und seiner Zeit*. Vienna: H. Epstein, 1932.

Kralik, Heinrich. *The Vienna Opera House*. Vienna: Verlag Brüder Rosenbaum, 1955.

_____. *Das Grosse Orchester. Die Wiener Philharmoniker*. Vienna: Wilhelm Frick Verlag, 1952.

Lang, Oskar. *Anton Bruckner: Wesen und Bedeutung*. Munich: Beiderstein, 1947.

Lange, Fritz. *Joseph Lanner und Johann Strauss*. Leipzig: Breitkopf & Härtel, 1919.

Liess, Andreas. *Wiener Barockmusik*. Vienna: Ludwig Doblinger, 1946.

Maecklenburg, A. "Hugo Wolf and Anton Bruckner." *Musical Quarterly*, July 1938.

*Mahler, Alma. *Gustav Mahler: Memories and Letters*. New York: The Viking Press, 1946.

Mendel, A. "Anton Bruckner." *The Nation*, 18 November 1931.

Mitchell, Donald. *Gustav Mahler: The Early Years*. London: Rockliff, 1958.

Mittag, Erwin. *Aus der Geschichte der Wiener Philharmoniker*. Vienna: Gerlach & Wiedling, 1950.

Newlin, Dika. *Bruckner, Mahler, Schönberg*. New York: King Crown Press, 1947.

Niemann, Walter. *Brahms*. New York: Alfred A. Knopf, 1929.

*Pleasants, Henry, ed. *Vienna's Golden Years of Music*. New York: Simon & Schuster, 1950.

Prawy, Marcel. *The Vienna Opera*. New York: Praeger Publishers, 1970.

Redlich, Hans F. *Bruckner and Mahler*. New York: Farrar, Strauss & Cudahy, 1955.

Specht, Richard. *Johann Strauss*. Berlin: Marquardt & Co. 1909.

_____. *Gustav Mahler*. Berlin Schuster & Loeffler, 1913.

_____. *Das Wiener Operntheater*. Vienna: P. Knepler, 1919.

Stefan, Paul. *Neue Musik und Wien*. Leipzig: E. P. Tal & Co., 1921.

_____. *Die Wiener Oper*. Vienna: Wila Verlag, 1932.

_____. *Gustav Mahler*. New York: G. Schirmer, 1913.

_____. *Bruno Walter*. Vienna: H. Reichner, 1936.

Sources Consulted

*Strauss, Eduard. *Erinnerungen*. Vienna: F. Deuticke, 1906.
*Strauss, Adele. *Johann Strauss schreibt Briefe*. Berlin: Verlag für Kulturpolitik, 1926.
Teetgen, Ada B. *The Waltz Kings of Old Vienna*. London: Jenkins, 1939.
Trojan, Felix. *Das Theater an der Wien*. Vienna: Wila Verlag, 1923.
*Walter, Bruno. *Theme and Variations*. New York: Alfred A. Knopf, 1946.
_____. *Gustav Mahler*. New York: The Greystone Press, 1941.
Weigl, Bruno. *Die Geschichte des Walzers*. Langensalza: H. Beyer & Söhne, 1925.
Wellesz, Egon. "Anton Bruckner and the Process of Musical Creation." *Musical Quarterly*, July 1938.

Habsburg

Benedict, Ernst. *Kaiser Josef II*. Vienna, 1936.
*Bourgoing, Jean de. *The Incredible Friendship. The Letters of Emperor Franz Joseph to Frau Katharina Schratt*. Albany: State University of New York, 1966.
Goldsmith, Margaret. *Maria Theresia of Austria*. London: A. Barker, 1936.
Janetschek, Ottokar. *Emperor Franz Joseph*. London: T. Werner Laurie Ltd., 1953.
McGuigan, Dorothy G. *The Habsburgs*. New York: Doubleday & Co., 1966.
Redlich, Joseph. *Emperor Franz Joseph of Austria*. New York: Macmillan, 1929.
Tschuppik, Karl. *Maria Theresia*. Amsterdam: A. de Lange, 1934.
Zeman, Z.A.B. *Twilight of the Hapsburgs*. New York: McGraw-Hill, 1970.

Vienna and Austria

Barea, Ilsa, *Vienna*. New York: Alfred Knopf, 1966.
Ewen, David and Frederic. *Musical Vienna*. New York: McGraw-Hill, 1939.
Friedländer, Otto. *Letzter Glanz der Märchenstadt*. Vienna: Ring Verlag, 1942.
_____. *Wolken drohen über Wien*. Vienna: Ring Verlag, 1949.
Gartenberg, Egon. *Vienna, Its Musical Heritage*. University Park: The Pennsylvania State University Press, 1968.
Graf, Max. *Legend of a Musical City. The Story of Vienna*. New York: Philosophical Library, 1945.
Groner, Richard. *Wien wie es war*. Vienna: Verlag Fritz Molden,
Johnston, William M. *The Austrian Mind*. Berkeley: University of California Press, 1972.
Kann, Robert A. *A Study in Austrian Intellectual History*. New York: Frederick A. Praeger, 1960.
Lansdale, Maria H. *Vienna and the Viennese*. Philadelphia: John C. Winston Co., 1902.
Leitich, Anna Tizia. *Verklungenes Wien*. Vienna: Wilhelm Andermann Verlag, 1942.
Levetus, A. S. *Imperial Vienna*. New York: John Love Co., 1905.
Lhotsky, Alphons. *Geschichte Österreichs*. Graz: Hermann Bohlaus Nachf.
Sedgwick, Henry D. *Vienna*. Indianapolis and New York: The Bobbs Merrill Co., 1939.

Srbik, Henrich, and Lorenz, Reinhold. *Die geschichtliche Stellung Wiens.* Verein für Geschichte der Stadt Wien, 1962.

Trollope, Frances. *Vienna and the Austrians.* London: P. Bentley, 1838.

Uhlvitz, Karl and Mathilda. *Handbuch der Geschichte Osterreichs.* Vienna: Lenschner & Lubursky, 1941.

Wechsberg, Joseph. *Vienna, My Vienna.* New York: The Macmillan Co., 1968.

Index

Index

Index

354

Index

Index

Index